THE WALL STREET JOURNAL

LIFETIME
GUIDE TO
MONEY

By *The*

Wall Street

Journal's Personal

Finance Staff

$

LYNN ASINOF

JONATHAN CLEMENTS

KAREN DAMATO

TOM HERMAN

GEORGETTE JASEN

DEBORAH LOHSE

ELLEN E. SCHULTZ

THE WALL STREET JOURNAL

LIFETIME
GUIDE TO
MONEY

EVERYTHING YOU NEED TO KNOW
ABOUT MANAGING YOUR FINANCES
—FOR EVERY STAGE OF LIFE

EDITED BY

C. FREDERIC WIEGOLD

Personal Finance Editor

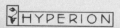

NEW YORK

Library of Congress Cataloging-in-Publication Data
The Wall Street Journal lifetime guide to money : everything you need to know about
managing your finances—for every stage of life / by The Wall Street Journal's
personal finance staff; edited by C. Frederic Wiegold.
p.   cm.
ISBN 0-7868-6132-0
I. Finance, Personal.   I. Wiegold, C. Frederic, 1947–   .
II. Wall Street Journal (Firm)   III. Wall Street Journal (Firm).
Personal-Finance Staff.
HG179.W316   1997
332.024—dc20   95-45519
CIP

Book design by Margaret M. Wagner

FIRST EDITION

2 4 6 8 10 9 7 5 3 1

CONTENTS

2

MASTERING THE SECRETS OF SUCCESSFUL INVESTING

52

8

CUTTING YOUR TAXES AND SAVING YOUR SANITY
360

9

Steering Clear of Mistakes and Scams

408

TWENTY WAYS TO SHOOT YOURSELF IN
   THE FOOT   *441*

10
PUTTING THE PIECES TOGETHER WHEN YOU DO NOT FIT THE MOLD
445

SINGLE PEOPLE, MULTIPLE PROBLEMS   *448*
Coping with the Conflicts of Single Parents   *450*
Money Matters for Unmarried Couples   *452*

OLDER PARENTS OF YOUNG CHILDREN   *454*

SEAMLESS SOLUTIONS FOR BLENDED
   FAMILIES   *457*

DEALING WITH THE FINANCIAL PAINS
   OF DIVORCE   *459*

ESTATE PLANNING AND NONCITIZEN
   SPOUSES   *465*

AFTER THE DEATH OF A SPOUSE   *467*

PROVIDING FOR A DISABLED CHILD   *470*

FINANCES FOR THE TERMINALLY ILL   *473*

IN LINE FOR A BIG INHERITANCE?   *477*

SURVIVAL GUIDE FOR THE NEWLY
   UNEMPLOYED   *480*

REALITY CHECK FOR THE SELF-EMPLOYED   *482*

GLOSSARY: WATCHWORDS OF WEALTH
485

ACKNOWLEDGMENTS

$

This book represents a collaborative effort by a number of talented people, beginning with the reporters on *The Wall Street Journal* Personal Finance Staff who wrote the individual chapters:

- Lynn Asinof *(Chapters 5 and 10)*
- Jonathan Clements *(Chapter 2)*
- Karen Damato *(Chapters 1 and 3)*
- Tom Herman *(Chapters 8 and 9)*
- Georgette Jasen *(Chapters 6 and 7)*
- Deborah Lohse *(Chapters 4 and 8)*
- Ellen E. Schultz *(Chapter 4)*

John R. Dorfman, Nancy Ann Jeffrey, Vanessa O'Connell, Andrea Petersen, and Eileen Kinsella provided valuable assistance. Thanks also to former colleagues Earl C. Gottschalk Jr., Barbara Granito, and Scott R. Schmedel.

The *Journal*'s Daniel Hertzberg was an energizing force in this project from the beginning. Richard J. Tofel brought us together with Hyperion and gave us enthusiastic support. F. James Pensiero helped us the final distance. Glynn Mapes offered good advice and was generous in allowing us the time we needed. Special thanks to Paul E. Steiger and John A. Prestbo for their guidance and patient counsel over the years.

Many financial professionals, government officials, consumer advocates, and individuals have shared their knowledge and experience with us as we have sought to report the news of personal finance for *Wall Street Journal* readers. What they have taught us is reflected throughout this book, and we are grateful for their help. Thanks to Price Waterhouse LLP for reading our tax chapter. Any errors, of course, are our own responsibility.

Leslie Wells and her colleagues at Hyperion were great to work with. Thanks for making us look good.

Finally, to our families and friends, our heartfelt appreciation for your support, encouragement, and understanding. Without you, this would not have been possible.

C. Frederic Wiegold
New York

PREFACE

$

Your money matters. You work hard for it. You need it for the necessities of life. You want to be able to use it to get more out of life. But you do not have a lot of time to worry about it.

That is the guiding idea behind *The Wall Street Journal*'s Your Money Matters column, a regular feature that for two decades has been helping readers make the most of their personal finances. That is also the idea behind this book, which is intended for *Journal* readers and nonreaders alike.

Written and edited by the same people who produce the *Journal* column, the information in the pages that follow will help guide you around life's financial pitfalls and show you how to make the fullest possible use of your opportunities. You will find a wealth of information about saving and investing, financial planning, insurance, company and government benefits, credit, and real estate. You will learn about stocks, bonds, and mutual funds. You will find out how to keep more of what you earn, how to save for your child's college education, and what to do to plan for a comfortable retirement.

No one can tell you what to do in each and every circumstance, and laws and regulations are constantly changing. Indeed, lawmakers and regulators may be making significant changes even as you read this. But *The Wall Street Journal Lifetime Guide to Money* should be a useful tool to help you think through financial problems for your-self and set meaningful priorities in our ever-changing financial environment. It will show you that there is much you can do for yourself in managing your own finances. And it will arm you with the knowledge you need to get the most out of stockbrokers, insurance agents, accountants, and other financial professionals—and to protect yourself from incompetents and crooks.

This book is an outgrowth of the *Journal*'s popular Your Lifetime Guide to Money series. Each of the first nine chapters looks at the major topics in personal finance from the perspectives of people in three broad age groups: 20s and 30s; 40s and 50s; and 60s and beyond. This structure reflects the fact that the financial problems and opportunities people face—and the strategies needed to deal with those problems and opportunities—tend to be closely related to age. People in their 20s and 30s, for instance, are grappling with the problem of how to save money for a home, or for college for the kids, or for retirement. People in their 60s are trying to figure out how to take money out of savings in a way that will make their nest eggs last as long as possible.

To be sure, some people do things earlier or later in their lives than others. For example, it is not uncommon these days for people in their 40s or 50s to be starting families and facing many of the same problems as 20-year-olds who are just setting out. Similarly, a 50-something executive who deals with corporate downsizing by taking early retirement is likely to face many of the same concerns as much older retirees. Still, breaking down the major issues in personal finance by age will help you find the information you want and need quickly and efficiently.

If you want to jump-start your personal finances, read Chapter 1, which gives an overview of the entire book, then zero in on the appropriate Through the Ages section in each of the following eight chapters. Those looking for a more detailed reference to dip into as questions arise, now and in months and years to come, will find it in the pages following the Through the Ages sections.

The tenth chapter deals with the special situations of many people who simply do not fit the conventional mold. Among them are singles, including single parents and unmarried couples; older parents of young children; and people dealing with divorce, the death of a spouse, and unemployment.

The final pages of this book include an extensive glossary of personal finance terms and a directory of organizations that can assist you when you want additional information or help. You will also find a model financial inventory to organize your records, a handy Buyer's Guide to Life Insurance, and a useful—and accessible—Guide to Retirement Planning. The life insurance and retirement-planning guides include worksheets that should greatly simplify the tasks of figuring out how much life insurance you really need and how much you ought to be saving for retirement.

THE WALL STREET JOURNAL

LIFETIME
GUIDE TO
MONEY

1

TAKING CONTROL OF YOUR FINANCES

eel like your finances are a mess?

It is time to banish that thought and take control.

Almost everyone feels uneasy about money, at least sometimes. And no wonder. It is so much easier to spend than to save. The choices in investing, insurance, and the like can seem mind-numbingly complex. Stories about the rare person who is able to retire at age 50 or the investor who doubled his or her money in just two years only add to our feelings of inadequacy.

But take heart. Much of the worrying is unnecessary. Many people are in better financial shape than they think they are. Even if your finances do leave much to be desired, worrying is not the answer. Taking action is. With a little guidance, you can do much on your own to diagnose your financial health, make specific plans to improve it, and then feel the relief that comes with being more in control.

At its core, financial planning is about just that: taking control. Instead of letting money matters run your life, you can organize your finances so that you can use money to get more out of life, now and in years to come. You do not have to become a full-time financial planner or investment specialist, either. Once you have developed your plan and put it to work, it should take only a little time each week to keep your finances on track. Sure, some people truly enjoy looking after their money; for them, it is almost a hobby. But the rest of us have other things to do with our time.

What we want to do is figure out how to use our resources better so that we can reach our important life goals, whether that means buying a house, sending our children to college, or paying for our own well-deserved retirement. The challenge is to catch a few more of the dollars that flow through our hands, and then save and invest those dollars appropriately.

We also need to make sure we have a strong safety net to help ourselves and our families if something untoward happens tomorrow. That means asking some unpleasant "what if" questions—questions such as, "What if I am hit by a bus?" "What if my home is damaged by fire?" "What if I have to replace the refrigerator, or the furnace, or the car?" The next step is to take the appropriate action—perhaps by buying a life insurance policy or beefing up existing coverage, starting an emergency rainy-day fund or adding to one, revising a will or drafting a new one.

The trick to getting these jobs done is to stay focused on the objective and to avoid complicated financial strategies and products when simpler ones will do. Most people can accomplish a great deal for themselves and their families—with only limited time and effort—if they just remember to keep it simple.

KEEP IT SIMPLE, GET IT DONE

Stockbrokers, insurance agents, and other financial specialists can make personal finance sound unbearably complicated. The jargon alone—terms like "zero-coupon" bonds, "level-premium" insurance, and "asset allocation"—can make your head spin.

It does not have to be that way, though. Just take things a step at a time and do not allow all the "experts" to make organizing your finances more difficult than it has to be.

Are you struggling to put more dollars into savings? Have money deducted automatically from your paycheck or transferred from your checking account each month. Need more life insurance fast? Buy low-cost "term" insurance, which simply promises to pay a death benefit if you die while the policy is in force. Need more variety in your investments? Use mutual funds, which let you pick an investment approach and leave the job of selecting individual securities to the pros. If you work for a big company, you may be able to get most of the insurance you need and do most of your retirement saving without looking any further than your employee-benefit plan.

One of the simplest ways to feel more in control of your finances is to organize your personal files and get a better grasp of what you have. Also look for opportunities to trim the number of financial products and providers in your life. Keeping track of five brokerage accounts, three Individual Retirement Accounts, and eight insurance policies is simply too much work. Clean up the clutter, and you will have more time for other, more enjoyable activities.

THINK BIG, THINK CHANGE

As you give your finances a makeover, strive to keep an eye on the big picture and to prepare yourself for change. In managing money, as in other aspects of life, many of us lose sight of the forest because we focus too closely on the trees. A person who enjoys picking investments, for instance, might spend hours mulling over whether to move $5,000 from one mutual fund to another.

But there can be a real benefit in looking at everything more broadly. That avid mutual fund investor, for instance, might snag a surefire, no-risk return of 18% or more by using that $5,000 to pay off a high-interest credit card balance. Or, if he feels stuck in a dead-end job that is making him miserable, the smartest "investment" might be the time and money it takes to earn an advanced degree or to start a sideline business that could grow into a second career. Indeed, because most of us earn the vast majority of our money from work, it is important to keep in mind that decisions about our personal finances are intertwined with those about our careers.

Also consider how you and your family are affected by bigger trends. For example, many people believe that future retirees will receive stingier benefits from an overburdened Social Security system. Corporate employers, which have been downplaying traditional pension plans, are not going to pick up the slack. For today's younger workers, that means much of the burden of financing a comfortable retirement rests squarely on their shoulders.

It may also mean a change in the whole concept of retirement. As life expectancies continue to lengthen, many people may not have the financial means to leave the workforce at age 60 or 65 and spend the rest of their days at leisure. Some experts believe that many of us will be working, possibly on a part-time basis, well into our "retirement" years.

On a more personal level, it is essential to remember that change is part of life. The numbers that shape our financial lives—figures such as our earnings and the value of our investments—are always in flux. In the years ahead, something you have no way of predicting now could turn your life upside down and shake up your finances. It might be something like a divorce or an extended period of unemployment. Or it could be some joyous event, such as a big promotion or the birth of a child.

The inevitability of change is an important reason to build a safety net of savings, insurance, and essential legal documents, such as a will. It also means that financial planning is not something you do once and then wash your hands of. Planning is a process you should repeat periodically throughout your life.

It is never too soon to start. It is also never too late.

FINANCIAL PLANNING THROUGH THE AGES

As with physical exercise, the hardest part of putting your finances in shape is getting started. Whether your personal finances need some fine-tuning or a major overhaul, the key is to pick a single, relatively narrow task and start on it now.

The following sections highlight the most pressing financial issues for people in different age brackets. As you read the relevant section, jot down things you need to work on and identify the one project you will tackle first.

Your 20s and 30s

Most of us could happily spend every dollar we take home—and then some. Spending certainly is more fun than putting money aside for an emergency or some longer-term goal, such as our retirement, the children's education, or the down payment on a house.

There is no getting around it, though. If you are going to be able to afford what you need and want later on, you must set some dollars aside today. When it comes to retirement in particular, there is more pressure than ever on people in their 20s and 30s. With changes in company retirement plans and possible cutbacks in Social Security, younger people now bear more responsibility for financing their own retirement.

FACING THE CHALLENGE

Whatever your goals, the sooner you start saving, the less painful it will be. Once you have made a start, you will find that there is a special satisfaction in facing up to the challenge. Honest.

The easiest way to build up substantial sums with limited discomfort is to save automatically. The top choice is having dollars deducted from each paycheck and funneled directly into savings and investments. That way, the money does not pass through your hands. You cannot forget to save it—and you will not get a chance to spend it.

If you are building up your emergency fund, you can usually have a portion of your pay invested in U.S. savings bonds. If you are working on a retirement nest egg, tax-advantaged savings plans at work are a great idea. A close second choice for long-term investments is having money automatically deducted from your checking account each month and invested in mutual funds. Mutual funds collect dollars from many individuals to buy a mix of stocks or other securities. Many fund companies make it easy to invest automatically as little as $50 or $100 a month. (For more information about mutual funds and other investments, see Chapter 2.)

How much should you be saving? As a rule of thumb, aim for 10% of your gross pay. But do not give up in disgust if that target seems way too steep. Start with some number—any number—and plan to increase it over time.

Do not set your savings target so high that you feel you are starved for spending money. You probably will not stick with the saving plan if the pain is too great. But do not go too easy on yourself, either. If you start out small, make concrete plans to increase the dollars you save. Plan to set more aside beginning six months from now. Or promise yourself you will save most of your next salary increase.

Here is another idea to help you save more: If you received a big tax refund last year, ask your company payroll department to withhold less tax from your paycheck and then have that money automatically invested.

IT PAYS TO START SAVING EARLY

A person who saves $50 a month beginning at age 25 will have far more at retirement than a person who waits to age 30 or 35 to begin saving the same monthly amount.

AGE YOU BEGIN SAVING	ACCUMULATED VALUE AT AGE 65
25	$174,550
30	$114,694
35	$74,518

NOTE: Assumes 8% investment return. No adjustment for taxes.
SOURCE: The Ayco Company L.P., Albany, N.Y.

You will accumulate money a lot faster if you let Uncle Sam or your employer lend a hand. People who are not covered by retirement plans at work can usually make tax-deductible contributions of up to $2,000 a year to Individual Retirement Accounts (IRAs). Married couples can kick in up to $4,000—and starting in 1997 that is true even if one spouse has no paying job. People who are covered by employer plans may still be able to make some deductible IRA contributions if their income is under certain amounts. (See Chapter 8 for more information on this and other deductions.)

Making a tax-deductible IRA contribution is a great idea. To begin with, it is like having the government subsidize your retirement savings. If you are in the 28% tax bracket and you make a

$2,000 deductible IRA contribution, you will lower your federal income tax bill by $560. As a result, that $2,000 contribution really costs you only $1,440.

Moreover, the money you put in an IRA grows tax-deferred until you withdraw it in retirement. Because you do not have to pay tax on the earnings each year as you go along, you can accumulate more money faster in an IRA than in an ordinary taxable account—even if the IRA and the non-IRA investments earn the same rate of return.

Even better than an IRA are the 401(k) retirement-savings plans offered by many large corporations. Not only do employees who participate receive attractive tax advantages, but they also often earn a bonus in the form of a matching contribution from their employers. These contributions might amount to 50 cents for every dollar the employee puts in up to a set limit. Too many employees do not participate in their 401(k) plans or do not contribute the maximum amount eligible for matching by their employers. In essence, they are saying no to "free money"—clearly a mistake. (See Chapter 4 for more details on how to make the most of this and other employee benefits.)

TAKE STOCK

How should you invest the money you set aside? Put emergency funds and sums you expect to spend over the next few years in supersafe "cash equivalents," such as bank accounts and money market mutual funds. But invest at least 60% of the money in IRAs, 401(k) plans, or other retirement accounts in a broad mix of common stocks—securities that make holders part owners of business corporations.

Many investors are afraid of stocks because they worry about market "crashes." Anyone who had money in stocks in 1987 is not likely to forget October 19 of that year, when the Dow Jones Industrial Average of 30 big stocks tumbled a heart-stopping 508 points, or nearly 23%. Over long periods, however, stocks have gone up much more than they have gone down. Money invested in stocks has grown an average of about 10% a year over the past seven decades. That is far more than people made by investing in such alternatives as bonds and bank accounts. The heftier returns from stocks can be the difference between having enough money for retirement and coming up short.

Here is one rule of thumb for how much of your long-term investments to put in stocks: Subtract your age from 100 and add a percentage sign. At your age, though, you might even want to be more aggressive than that. If you can tolerate the ups and downs, it actually can make good sense to put 80%, 90%, even 100% of your retirement money in stocks and stock mutual funds.

JUST SAY NO TO DEBT

Some people in their 20s and 30s make a mess of their finances practically before they begin. From early in their working years, they form the habit of spending more than they bring home. They accumulate big debts on credit cards or with other loans and then struggle to pay the interest each month.

You obviously do not want to dig a hole like that for yourself. Although you may already be saddled with certain types of debt, such as student loans, try to avoid taking on new debt other than a home mortgage. It is fine to use credit cards for convenience, but pay the balance each month. If you find you cannot get by without ever-increasing debt, you need to take a hard look at where your money goes. It is time for a spending diet.

Meanwhile, if you have accumulated savings or investments, consider using some of those dollars to reduce your debt burden. While it is painful to take money out of bank or brokerage accounts, paying off a loan can actually be one of the best investments you make. (Chapter 6 has many more ideas about dealing with debt.)

ESTABLISH A SAFETY NET

You are young, you are healthy, and you may think you do not need to worry about grim matters like insurance. If that is your attitude, think again. Although the odds of calamities—such as serious illness, home fires, and death—are slight, the financial and personal hardships can be huge. While you work at accumulating money for the future, make sure your basic safety net is in place now.

Review your health benefits at work to make sure you have the coverage you need. If you do not have any health insurance, buy an individual policy. Even if you are just renting an apartment, be sure to have insurance on the contents. Rental policies can cost as little as $100 to $300 a year.

You do not need life insurance if you have no dependents. Once you have children, though, you will probably need more than at any later time in life. No-frills term insurance is usually the simplest and lowest-cost option. For a 35-year-old man, a $250,000 policy might cost just $200 to $300 for the first year.

Do not overlook life insurance for individuals—typically women—who do not work outside the home but care for young children. If that person died, the surviving spouse would face hefty new expenses for child care. (Chapter 3 helps you find the insurance you need at a price you can afford.)

If you have kids, also commit to the rather unpleasant—but relatively simple—task of writing a will. If you die without a will, state laws could divvy up your money very differently from the way you would wish. More important, in the event both you and your spouse died, a court would pick a guardian for the children without your having a say. No one wants to think about such dire developments, of course. Just hire a lawyer, do the will, and be done with it.

HOME, HOME ON THE BLOCK

You do not have to buy a house in your 20s or 30s. Some economists believe renting could be as good a financial deal or even better. Still, if you are like most people, owning a home is probably near the top of your list of personal, lifestyle goals.

Fortunately, buying residential real estate has usually been a winning financial bet over time. Although real estate prices sometimes slump sharply, they have generally risen nicely in the long run. Owning a house also forces you to save money: You build substantial equity over the years as you pay down the mortgage.

If you are looking to join the homeowners' ranks, keep in mind that the transaction costs involved in buying and selling real estate are steep. So do not buy a house if you will outgrow it or need to relocate in just a couple of years. Also think twice before stretching

20s–30s

- Start automatic savings plan.

- Pay down credit cards.

- Invest in stocks and stock funds.

- Make a will.

- Check insurance.

to buy the biggest home you can. Many people underestimate their housing expenses by not adding in such costs as home repairs, improvements, and lawn care. You do not want to be so strapped for cash that you do not enjoy your life. (Chapter 7 gives you the lowdown on real estate.)

Your 40s and 50s

These years can be a real juggling act, particularly for people who had their children in their 30s. With retirement beginning to loom large on the horizon, these are the years when most people become serious about setting money aside. Ideally, these are high-earning years in which you have plenty of income to sock away.

But at the same time that you are focusing more on your retirement, your children may also be at their most expensive. You may be using much of your discretionary income—and dipping deep into savings—to pay college bills. Bills for children's weddings or the care of aging parents may also be sopping up dollars that would otherwise go into retirement savings.

Take a hard look at what you can really afford, making sure you are providing enough for your future needs. To boost savings, use tax-advantaged retirement plans, such as 401(k) plans. Structure your investment portfolio for strong performance while working to keep it simple. Then check your safety net for holes. Because your assets and earnings have increased over the years, and your responsibilities have probably changed, more insurance or a revised will may be in order.

BE REALISTIC ABOUT RETIREMENT

At age 30, retirement was so far off that it was almost unimaginable. By now, though, you have probably given some thought to when you would like to retire and how you would like to live. The next step is a hard-nosed evaluation of whether your current savings and the additional amounts you set aside will be sufficient to pay for the retirement lifestyle you want. If you do not start saving until your 40s, you will probably need to put aside at least 20% of your pay. The retirement-savings worksheet in the Guide to Retirement Planning, Appendix D, can give you an idea of where you stand.

Planning for retirement goes hand in hand with planning the rest of your career. People in their 40s and 50s can face tough decisions about whether to leave a longtime employer for a seemingly more promising job elsewhere. One factor to consider is the impact of a job change on the pension and other retirement benefits you will collect later on.

Recognize that many people will not be able to afford to retire as soon as they would like. For financial reasons or personal satisfaction, many of us may end up working as consultants or part-timers once we leave the full-time workforce. That is glum news, obviously, if you hate what you are doing. Consider getting additional academic training or starting a sideline business that might grow into a new career.

Even if your finances seem to be in great shape, be extra cautious about trying to retire completely while still in your 50s. Your retirement could last 25 years or more, and you do not want to come up short on funds down the road. A few more years on the job, even at a reduced schedule, could have a big impact on the size of your retirement nest egg.

Some parents find they simply cannot afford the twin goals of building a decent retirement fund and paying steep college bills. As they work through the numbers, husbands and wives need to discuss with each other—and with their children—their views on how much of the college-cost burden parents should bear. Some people feel they owe their kids an Ivy League education, whereas others feel that children should take part-time jobs and borrow money to pay most of the bills themselves. It is strictly a personal decision; there is no right and wrong. Many parents borrow against the equity in their homes to pay part of the college bills.

SUPERCHARGE YOUR SAVINGS

To get the most bang for your savings bucks, contribute as much as possible to tax-advantaged retirement plans. Depending on the type of plan, you may be able to contribute money you earn before it is taxed or deduct contributions on your tax returns. The money invested in retirement-savings plans grows with no tax until you pull it out. If your company has a 401(k) savings plan, your employer will probably kick in money to match up to half of your contribution, up to a certain limit. Be sure to contribute enough of your pay to get the largest possible match; that is free money savvy savers cannot afford to turn down. If you work in the education field, ask your employer about a 403(b) retirement plan.

If you (and your spouse, if you are married) are not covered by a retirement plan at work, you can make tax-deductible contributions to an Individual Retirement Account. For single people, the maximum is $2,000 of compensation a year. Married couples can contribute and deduct up to $4,000; beginning in 1997, that is the case even if one spouse has no paying job. If either you or a spouse is covered by an employer retirement plan, you still may be able to deduct some IRA contributions if your income is under certain amounts. (Chapter 8 has details on this and other deductions.)

If you are self-employed or have a sideline business in addition to your regular job, you can contribute some of your self-employment income to a Keogh plan or a Simplified Employee Pension-IRA, two types of tax-advantaged retirement plans especially for people like you.

Putting hefty sums away could become a lot easier in a few years. By then, you may be finished paying college bills for your kids. Meanwhile, avoid tapping long-term savings for short-term needs. That means resisting the temptation to borrow from your 401(k) plan to pay for a vacation or to buy a new car. If you leave one job for another, do not take money accumulated in your former employer's retirement plan and spend it. Either leave the money in the old plan or have it transferred directly into your new employer's retirement plan or into an IRA. (Chapter 4 can help you make the most of your employee benefits.)

There is one piece of (sort of) good news: Over the years, as your income has grown, you may have seen your spending climb apace. At this stage of life, you probably have more flexibility to trim some discretionary spending and set more money aside than do people in their early 20s who are struggling to pay the rent. Think twice be-

SAVE MORE WITH A 401(K)

When you save through a 401(k) plan at work, both Uncle Sam and your employer lend a hand.

Look at the numbers for three employees: One contributes $100 each month for 25 years to a 401(k). Another does the same thing but also gets a 50% matching contribution from his employer. The third ignores the 401(k), takes the $100 and pays 28% income tax, then invests the remaining $72 in a taxable investment account. All three earn an 8% annual return.

MONTHLY INVESTMENT	BALANCE AFTER 25 YEARS ($)
Employee A Pretax dollars in 401(k)	68,474
Employee B Pretax dollars in 401(k) with 50% employer match	102,711
Employee C After-tax dollars in taxable account	48,092

NOTE: Assumes earnings on investment outside the 401(k) are taxed at 28% each year. Money in the 401(k) is assumed to be withdrawn and fully taxed at 28% after 25 years. SOURCE: The Ayco Company L.P., Albany, N.Y.

fore moving up to a bigger, more expensive home that could seem way too large when the kids move out.

As your assets have grown, you may have accumulated an impressive collection of investment accounts and products. It is time to sort through the clutter to figure out what you have and whether you are putting your investment dollars to the best use. Make mutual funds, rather than individual stocks and bonds, the mainstay of your portfolio. Funds pool investors' dollars to buy a mix of securities of a particular type—say, growth-oriented stocks or 7- to 15-year bonds. They make it easy to spread your money around while not losing track of what you have.

The largest portion of your long-term holdings should be in stocks and stock funds. Stocks, which represent ownership interests in the issuing companies, have historically performed far better over the long run than such alternatives as bonds and bank accounts. Avoid overly complicated financial products. Among the investments you can live without are limited partnerships, futures, and options. (Chapter 2 helps you make sure your investments are working as hard as you are.)

BEEF UP THE SAFETY NET

You are counting on the salary you will earn over the next 10 to 20 years to fund your retirement and take care of your family. Check whether you have enough life insurance to replace those earnings and to provide for your dependents in the event of your early death.

Also think about how your family would fare if you were disabled and unable to bring home a paycheck. If you do not have any disability insurance at work—or have only very limited coverage—consider buying an individual disability policy. Unfortunately, premiums are steep, typically 2% to 3% of income, or more.

One of the cheapest and smartest insurance buys is an "umbrella liability" policy that increases the amount your insurer will pay if you are sued. The cost is just $100 to $300 a year for $1 million of coverage. Check with your home insurance agent. (See Chapter 3 for help with your insurance needs.)

Finally, resolve to devote some time to the task of getting your will in shape. There is simply no excuse not to have one. If you do have a will, but it dates back five or more years, it may be time for an update. For instance, the person you named ten years ago to be guardian for your newborn baby might be almost a stranger by now.

Even if you do not feel wealthy, you may be rich according to estate-tax rules. Check the rules if your assets, including the death benefits of your life insurance policies, add up to more than $600,000. You can ease the potential estate-tax bite by incorporating tax-cutting trusts in your will and by more evenly dividing up assets between husband and wife. (Read the estate-planning section in Chapter 5, then call a good lawyer.)

40s–50s

- Boost savings.

- Contribute to 401(k).

- Give portfolio a checkup.

- Buy additional insurance?

- Update will.

YOUR 60S AND BEYOND

Over the years, you have worked hard to build a nest egg for your retirement years. Now that time is almost upon you, or already here. The period of life that begins around age 60 is characterized by sweeping lifestyle changes—and by some momentous financial decisions that can affect you and your family for many years to come. Here are some of the important challenges for people in this age bracket:

• Have a vibrant, active retirement, but do not rush into retirement before you can really afford it.

• Tend your resources carefully by investing prudently, but not too conservatively.

• Arrange your affairs so that a surviving spouse will be provided for and assets divvied up appropriately at your death.

TIME TO RETIRE?

The primary goal for many people in their early 60s is to retire as soon as possible. They want to leave the pressures of the job behind and have more time for travel and leisure activities that are hard to cram into the Monday-through-Friday working routine.

But think carefully and double-check your numbers before you jump ship. With people living longer, today's 60-year-olds may be around for another 25 years. Do not take the leap unless you are sure you will be able to afford the lifestyle you want over an extended time. (For assistance with this decision, read the Guide to Retirement Planning, Appendix D.)

THINK OF THE LONG TERM			
You may have more years ahead of you than you think.			
AT AGE	THE AVERAGE PERSON IS EXPECTED TO LIVE THIS MANY MORE YEARS		
	TOTAL POPULATION	MEN	WOMEN
0 (newborn)	75.5	72.1	78.8
15	61.4	58.1	64.6
25	52.0	48.9	54.9
35	42.6	39.8	45.3
45	33.6	31.0	35.9
55	24.9	22.6	26.9
65	17.2	15.3	18.8
75	10.9	9.4	11.9
85	5.9	5.1	6.3

SOURCE: Reprinted courtesy of Metropolitan Life Insurance, *Statistical Bulletin*.

Keep in mind that working an additional two or three years, at what are probably the highest earnings of your career, could have a big impact on your retirement nest egg. You could squirrel away substantial sums in tax-advantaged retirement plans and qualify for a bigger company pension and a more generous Social Security check. Take a look at the numbers before making a decision.

Also consider options other than leaving work cold turkey. Many people in their 60s and later years derive considerable personal satisfaction and spendable income from continuing their careers on a part-time or consulting basis.

Review your medical coverage in deciding when to leave work.

Many employers are requiring retirees to pay a bigger share of their medical insurance costs. If you leave before your company's minimum early-retirement age, you probably will not be entitled to any health coverage at all—a very costly proposition.

YOU BUILT A NEST EGG—NOW WHAT?

Many of today's retirees are big-time money managers. They have to be. Gone are the days when retirees received almost all their income from a monthly pension check and Social Security. Today, more and more retirement income is coming from 401(k) savings plans, Individual Retirement Accounts, and other retirement programs in which the individual participants call the investment shots.

If you receive a lump-sum payment from a company savings plan when you retire, that could be the single largest sum you will ever be handed in your life. A $50,000-a-year middle manager who spends 25 years with a single company can walk away with a staggering sum of $300,000 or more. With so much at stake, make sure you educate yourself about investing and about the rules that govern withdrawals from different types of retirement plans. (Chapter 2 can help you become the savvy investor you will have to be.)

In picking investments, you need to be equally wary of taking on too much risk and too little. Too many retired investors have been led astray by commission-hungry salespeople, including some who present themselves as "financial planners." In the 1980s, for instance, many folks were persuaded to put the majority of their retirement money into high-risk, hard-to-sell limited partnerships, which invested in everything from office buildings to shopping centers to oil wells to cable television. Many of those partnerships ultimately went belly-up. To protect yourself, spread your money around and stick to time-tested vehicles, such as mutual funds and bank accounts.

But you can also play it too safe. While some retirees have lost big money in overly risky investments, probably a greater number have been pummeled by being too cautious. They put all their money into fixed-income holdings, such as bank accounts and bonds, which do not deliver returns that are high enough to keep the money growing faster than the rate of inflation.

Invest some money in stocks and stock mutual funds because they are likely to provide higher returns and help you stay ahead of rising prices over what could be many more years of life. How much should you put in stocks? One rule of thumb is to subtract your age from 100 and add a percentage sign. By that measure, 65-year-olds might put 35% of their investment portfolios in stocks or stock funds. But many advisers believe that retirees should be more aggressive and put at least half of their investment dollars in stocks.

The good news is that you probably have a long retirement ahead of you. The bad news, from a financial standpoint at least, is that you have to make your money last. Besides picking the right investments, you have to watch how fast you draw down the accumulated savings. In the early years of retirement, unless your wealth is immense, you should try to use only a portion of your investment earnings to pay living expenses. The rest should be reinvested. If you keep adding to your nest egg, it should produce higher earnings in future years.

You also need to pay attention to which accounts you tap first. Except in a few cases, it usually makes sense to use the annual earnings and the accumulated value of taxable investments and bank accounts before dipping into tax-advantaged retirement plans.

PROVIDING FOR YOUR LOVED ONES

No one likes to think about death. But it is there on the horizon. Make sure a surviving spouse will be provided for, through accumulated assets or life insurance. Be sure your will is up-to-date and reflects how you want your holdings parceled out when you (or the two of you) are no longer around. Estate planning is particularly crucial—and often most thorny—for people who own a family business or who want to provide for both a current spouse and the children from a previous marriage.

If you have not done so already, it is time to think about the federal estate tax and how big a bite that levy might take from what you leave behind. The estate tax is separate from income tax. Federal estate tax is due whenever someone dies and leaves more than $600,000, usually including life insurance proceeds, to someone other than a surviving spouse. The top rate is a steep 55%. Many states also levy estate taxes on their own.

If you are a candidate for estate tax, leaving all your money to your spouse is not the answer. That just means a huge tax bill at the second death. You can provide for a surviving spouse and also trim the estate-tax bill by arranging your will to have some dollars flow into a simple kind of family trust. Another way to cut the potential estate-tax bill is to pull insurance proceeds out of your estate by transferring policies to a special life insurance trust.

If you have more money than you will ever need—and you are absolutely positive about that—consider making substantial gifts to family members and charities. In addition to the emotional satisfaction of making gifts while you are alive, such moves trim the estate tax.

Other creative estate-planning strategies, often involving life insurance, can make sense for multimillion-dollar estates. Just be sure the strategy makes as much sense for you and your family as it does for the commission-paid insurance agents who love to sell the big-dollar policies used in estate planning.

But before you become totally carried away, here is a very important reminder: You worked hard to build that nest egg, so make sure you enjoy it. Do not feel obliged to preserve all your wealth for others. (Chapter 5 has many useful tips on estate planning, including the strong recommendation that you get professional help.)

60s +

- Check nest egg.
- Review medical coverage.
- Keep buying stocks.
- Work part-time?
- Update estate plan.

BOOSTING YOUR SAVINGS

"Where does the money go?" That is a question many people ask at the end of each month. And it is one of the crucial questions for anyone who is trying to get a better handle on personal finances.

A central part of managing your money is figuring out how to afford important life goals. But you cannot do that without knowing your current resources and how much money you are adding to savings and investments each year. If you have been coming up short on savings—or even spending more than you earn—you will need to take a tough look at where all the dollars you bring home disappear. It is time to dig out the calculator, pull open the filing cabinet, and delve into some numbers.

BIG $ QUESTION NUMBER 1: HOW MUCH ARE YOU WORTH TODAY?

A road map can help you reach a destination in your car, but it is of little help if you cannot find where you are on the map. So, too, in personal finance. As you work at building a nest egg for the future—or conserving that nest egg through your retirement years—it makes sense to add up the numbers and see what you have today. Most people have no idea what they are worth. You might jot down a top-of-your-head guess before you proceed.

Then use the following worksheet to calculate your financial starting point more precisely. It may take a little time to gather all the bits and pieces of information, but the exercise itself is simple. First, you add up the value of your real estate, your investments, and other assets. Then you tally your liabilities—the amounts you owe to others on mortgages and other loans. You find the bottom-line number on what you are worth—what professionals call your *net worth*—by subtracting the liabilities from the assets.

For some people, adding up the equity in a home and the dollars patiently salted away in retirement plans and U.S. savings bonds might produce a much larger number than they had thought. But other people may receive a rude shock. If you have built a nice investment portfolio, for instance, but also racked up a lot of debt on a home-equity credit line and other loans, the bottom line might be much less impressive than you had thought. A listing like this of your assets, liabilities, and net worth is called a *balance sheet.* It is a good idea to repeat this exercise every few years to see how you are doing.

YOUR PERSONAL BALANCE SHEET

Add up the *assets*—your investments and the property you own. Subtract the *liabilities,* or amounts you owe. The balance is your *net worth.*

DATE _____

ASSETS
Enter recent account balances or estimated market values.

Bank accounts and certificates of deposit _____

Brokerage accounts _____

Mutual fund accounts (including money funds) _____

Stocks and bonds held directly _____

U.S. savings bonds _____

IRAs, Keoghs, 401(k)s, 403(b)s, and other self-directed
  retirement plans _____

Deferred annuities _____

Other investments _____

Cash value of life insurance policies _____

Lump-sum value of pension _____

Principal residence _____

Other real estate _____

Collectibles, antiques _____

Automobiles _____

Personal property _____

Other _____

Total Assets _____

LIABILITIES
Enter outstanding loan balances (not monthly payments or maximum credit available).

Mortgage on principal residence _____

Home-equity loans or credit lines _____

Other mortgage debt _____

Credit card balances _____

Auto loans _____

Student loans _____

Other debt _____

Total Liabilities _____

NET WORTH
Subtract total liabilities from total assets.

Total assets _____

Total liabilities − _____

Net Worth _____

Big $ Question Number 2:
How Much Are You Setting Aside?

People who earn $25,000 a year and those who earn ten times as much often find themselves in the same boat where managing money is concerned. They have no trouble spending all the dollars they bring home, yet they have precious little idea where the money goes.

In truth, you do not necessarily need to know where every $100 goes. But you do need to pin down the single most important part of the money-flow equation—the amount you are setting aside each year in savings and investments. In your working years, one rule of thumb is to save at least 10% of your gross pay—that is, your pay before taxes and other deductions. Surveys suggest that many people think they are saving a larger percentage of their pay than they are. So take a few minutes to look at your numbers and get the facts.

Worksheet 1.2 on page 24 can guide you in adding up the money you pumped into savings and investment accounts last year. The worksheet looks at amounts that are automatically deducted from your pay—such as contributions to 401(k) accounts at work—as well as money you invest directly or through automatic transfers from your checking account.

Big $ Question Number 3:
Where Does the Rest of the Money Go?

If you have been saving tons of money, you do not have to poke into your spending habits any further. The rare souls who regularly sock away one-third of their pay obviously do not need to lose sleep over how they spend the rest. Most of us, though, should probably be saving more than we are. Taking a look at our spending patterns can help us to do that.

No, you do not have to lock yourself into a fixed budget. Just paying careful attention to how much you spend for various things can nudge you to take specific steps to increase the amount you set aside.

The first step is to make a quick calculation of how much you spent on living expenses and everything else last year. Using Work-

WORKSHEET 1.2
YOUR PERSONAL SAVINGS CALCULATOR

Estimate amounts invested, minus any money withdrawn, from each investment category. (Some items—such as investment earnings that are reinvested—have been omitted for the sake of simplicity.)

FOR YEAR ENDED _____

PAYROLL DEDUCTIONS

401(k) or other retirement plans   _____
U.S. savings bonds   _____
Other   _____
Subtotal A   _____

DIRECT PAYMENTS OR AUTOMATIC TRANSFERS

Bank accounts, certificates of deposit   _____
Brokerage accounts   _____
Mutual fund accounts (including money funds)   _____
Stocks and bonds held directly   _____
U.S. savings bonds   _____
Individual Retirement Accounts, Keogh plans   _____
Deferred annuities   _____
Other   _____
Subtotal B   _____
Total Savings (Subtotal A plus Subtotal B)   _____

sheet 1.3, add up your total income and subtract the amounts you paid in taxes and set aside in savings. The rest you obviously spent somewhere, even if you have no idea where.

Next, using Worksheet 1.4 on page 26, piece together your spending by major categories. Reviewing last year's canceled checks and credit card statements can help you estimate how much money you spent on housing, clothing, entertainment, insurance, and other things. (If you use a personal finance computer program, you probably have already assembled this information.)

If you are like many people, a surprisingly large sum of money disappears in miscellaneous spending. Consider carrying around a small notebook for one month and jotting down each and every expenditure to get a better handle on where that money goes.

Worksheet 1.3
HOW MUCH DO YOU SPEND?

Total your income for last year and then subtract money you paid in income taxes or stashed away in savings. The rest you spent—somewhere.

FOR YEAR ENDED _____

INCOME
Some numbers can be taken from your latest tax return. Omit interest and other investment income, such as dividends and capital gains, if you are reinvesting that money and not using it for living expenses.

Wages (before taxes, other deductions) _____

Interest income (optional) _____

Other investment income (optional) _____

Pension _____

Social Security benefits _____

Alimony and child support _____

Other _____

(A) Total Income _____

SPENDING ON CREDIT
If your credit card balances went up because you were borrowing to finance vacations or everyday spending, enter the year-over-year increase in your credit card balances.

(B) Total Spending on Credit _____

TAXES AND SOCIAL SECURITY
Take numbers from your latest tax return, year-end pay stubs, or W-2 forms.

Federal taxes withheld from pay _____

State and local taxes withheld _____

Additional taxes paid with returns _____

Social Security and Medicare tax withheld _____

Subtotal _____

(Subtract any income tax refunds) − _____

(C) Total Taxes and Social Security _____

ADDITIONS TO SAVINGS AND INVESTMENT ACCOUNTS
Enter amount from previous worksheet (Your Personal Savings Calculator).

(D) Total Savings _____

NET SPENDING
Add up your total income plus any spending on credit, then subtract your total taxes and Social Security and any additions you made to savings and investment accounts.

How Much You Spend (Line A plus Line B, minus Line
C and Line D) _____

WORKSHEET 1.4

🐦 WHERE DO YOU SPEND IT?

Examine your checkbook, credit card statements, and personal files and estimate annual expenditures in each category. The total should approximate the "net spending" number from the previous worksheet (How Much Do You Spend?).

FOR YEAR ENDED _____

HOUSING

Rent or mortgage
Real estate taxes
Utilities (including phone)
Home insurance
Repairs, maintenance, improvements
Other
Total Housing

FOOD

Groceries
Work/school lunches
Dining out
Total Food

CHILDREN

Education/child care
Camps, lessons, etc.
Total Children

WORK-RELATED EXPENSES

Union dues, professional associations, etc.
Other
Total Work-Related Expenses

VACATIONS/TRAVEL

ALIMONY/CHILD-SUPPORT PAYMENTS

MEDICAL/INSURANCE

Medical/dental insurance premiums
Unreimbursed medical/dental expenses
Life/disability insurance premiums
Total Medical/Insurance

ENTERTAINMENT

Movies, sports, family activities _____

Hobbies _____

Pet care _____

Other _____

Total Entertainment _____

CLOTHING

_____

TRANSPORTATION

Auto loan or lease payments _____

Repairs and maintenance _____

Auto insurance _____

Gas, tolls, parking _____

Mass transit _____

Total Transportation _____

GIFTS

To charity _____

To family and friends _____

Total Gifts _____

PROFESSIONAL SERVICES

Lawyer _____

Accountant _____

Other _____

Total Professional Services _____

LOAN PAYMENTS

(Other than mortgage and car) _____

MISCELLANEOUS/PERSONAL

Haircuts, other personal care _____

Newspapers and magazines _____

Other _____

Total Miscellaneous _____

Total _____

ACHIEVING YOUR GOALS

Now that you have a clearer picture of your finances, the time has come to see how they measure up in light of the goals you want to achieve. Although the basic guideline is that most people should try to save at least 10% of their pretax pay, that is only a guideline and not the right number for every working individual. How much you should be saving depends on your goals, how far away they are, how much you have already put aside, and what other resources you will be able to tap.

For most people, the two biggest financial goals are funding a comfortable retirement and financing a college education for their children. The retirement-savings worksheet in the Guide to Retirement Planning, Appendix D, will help you figure out how much you need to set aside for your later years; for more information about setting money aside for children's college education, see Chapter 5. The accompanying savings calculator can help you figure how much to set aside for a specific, short-term goal, such as a new car two years from now or the down payment on a first home you hope to buy in five years.

Whatever your goals, it is important that you not set a savings target that is so high you cannot stick with it. Do not be too easy on yourself, though. If you start small, make plans to increase the amount you save.

SAVING FOR A SHORT-TERM GOAL

How much do you need to set aside each month to afford a $2,000 vacation next year? Or a $20,000 car five years from now?

These are the monthly figures required to end up with $1,000 after various time periods, assuming your money earns 3% after tax. If you are trying to accumulate $7,000 in four years, for example, multiply 7 times $19.63 to get the required monthly savings of $137.41.

TIME PERIOD IN YEARS	MONTHLY SAVINGS TO ACCUMULATE $1,000
1	$82.19
2	$40.48
3	$26.58
4	$19.63
5	$15.47

SOURCE: The Ayco Company L.P., Albany, N.Y.

Retired? You are not off the hook where saving is concerned. Indeed, setting money aside for the future is as important for you as it is for younger folks. Even with a relatively modest level of inflation, bills for food and medical care and other living expenses will be considerably higher ten years from now than they are today. If you can reinvest at least part of your annual investment earnings—income from interest, dividends, and capital gains—then your nest egg will continue to grow and potentially produce higher income in future years.

TOUGH AND NOT-SO-TOUGH CHOICES

If running through the numbers shows that your spending is way out of whack with your earnings and what you need to be saving, it is time for some tough decisions about where you live, what you drive, and how you spend your free time. People who go crazy every time they hit the mall with credit cards in hand may need to discipline themselves by cutting up the plastic and living on a strict cash diet.

Consider giving yourself a fresh start by using some accumulated savings to pay off high-cost credit card balances. (If you cannot climb out of the hole you have dug for yourself, see Chapter 6 for information about debt counseling and bankruptcy.)

What about all the folks who are not in such dire straits but who know they should be saving more? You may be looking for someone to tell you what percentage of your income you should be spending in various categories, such as housing, food, and the like. Do not look for that here. It simply is not realistic.

A MATTER OF CIRCUMSTANCE

An affluent couple living in the same house for many years might spend less than 20% of their income on housing. A couple just out of college and starting their careers in a big city, however, might find mediocre accommodations eating up twice that share of their pay. It is a matter of circumstance.

Everyone also has his or her own spending priorities. Some people feel it is imperative to drive a new Cadillac every year. Others drive their cars until they fall apart, but they would not do without a European vacation. This is the bottom line: There is no particular budget within which you need to live. Rather, you should look at your personal spending habits—whatever they are—and make some decisions about where you can grab additional dollars for long-term savings.

You might, for example, decide to give yourself a monthly dollar limit on spending for restaurant meals, movies, and other entertainment. You might scale back your vacation plans for next year or decide to skip the house-cleaning service and scrub the toilets yourself.

Deciding where to trim your spending is just the first half of the

THE MORE YOU EARN, THE MORE YOU SPEND

Here is how households in various income brackets spend their money.

	ALL HOUSEHOLDS	HOUSEHOLDS WITH INCOME OF $50,000 TO $69,999	HOUSEHOLDS WITH INCOME OF $70,000 OR MORE
Average income before taxes	$33,854	$58,449	$108,124
Average number of people per household	2.5	3.1	3.1
Average annual spending ($) for			
Food	4,359	6,273	7,685
Housing	9,528	13,768	20,558
Clothing	1,733	2,780	4,098
Transportation	5,232	8,114	11,441
Health insurance/ health care	1,654	2,027	2,533
Entertainment	1,526	2,679	3,511
Insurance/pensions/ Social Security	3,083	6,152	10,431
Contributions	1,021	1,421	3,769
Gifts	978	1,540	2,647
Other	1,413	1,981	2,534
TOTAL	30,527	46,735	69,207

SOURCE: Bureau of Labor Statistics 1992 data, cited in *The Official Guide to the American Marketplace*, New Strategist Publications Inc., Ithaca, N.Y.

job. Next, take immediate action to put those dollars into savings. Have more money deducted from your paycheck and channeled into a retirement plan. Or sign up to have money automatically transferred each month from your checking account to a mutual fund.

Cutting back on current spending is tough. So also go after income you have not yet gotten in the habit of spending. Scheduled for a salary increase soon? Before you figure out how to spend those additional dollars, make arrangements to have them put into a retirement plan or investment account.

PUTTING TOGETHER YOUR FINANCIAL SAFETY NET

Those daredevil circus aerialists who fly through the air with such apparent ease cannot be obsessed with the risk of falling down. Still, they usually do not leap for the swinging bar without having a safety net firmly in place.

It should not be any different when it comes to looking after the financial well-being of ourselves and our families. Yes, it is important to have a positive outlook. Yes, we ought to plan for long and healthy lives. Yes, we need to provide for long-term goals, like sending the kids to college and being able to retire in at least a reasonable degree of comfort. And yes, it is always possible that we will win the lottery or make a killing in the stock market.

But it is also possible that the car will be stolen, that the furnace will have to be replaced, that little Lucie will need braces, or that we could lose our jobs in a corporate "downsizing." And while it is not pleasant to admit it, death will someday come to us all. We invite unnecessary trouble for ourselves and our loved ones if we do not have a financial safety net of savings, insurance, and essential documents, such as a will. Without them, a temporary financial setback can be magnified way out of proportion, and a personal trauma can turn into a financial disaster. Fortunately, putting together that safety net is not as difficult as you might fear.

BUILDING A FINANCIAL CUSHION

The idea of saving money for a rainy day may seem terribly old-fashioned. It certainly is not exciting. But there is probably nothing more important than having a financial cushion to smooth the way if you lose your job, or the roof has to be replaced, or the car suddenly dies.

Having an adequate emergency fund will allow you to deal with inevitable, if unexpected, expenses with minimal disruption and without having to go into debt. It will also make it possible to take greater risks with the rest of your assets. Once you know you have money that you can use in a hurry if you need it, you will have more freedom to invest for the longer term without worrying so much about what will happen if the stock or bond market takes a dive. You will also be able to survive a temporary setback without depleting your retirement fund or selling the house.

Financial experts generally recommend that people have an emergency fund equal to between three and six months' spending money. A generous emergency fund is critical for families that are relying on a single wage earner to support a couple of kids. Accumulating rainy-day money is also particularly important when you are just starting out and do not have many other assets you could tap in a crunch.

The less you have, of course, the harder it can seem to set something aside. But it is essential to make accumulating an emergency fund one of your financial priorities. One of the least painful ways to build up an emergency fund is to have a little deducted from each paycheck or transferred from your checking account each month.

As a general rule, you want to park your emergency money where you can get at it easily and where it is not subject to big investment risks. Money market mutual funds are a popular choice, and for good reason: They offer higher interest rates than bank savings accounts, and they give you easier access to your money than some other alternatives. But many people spread their emergency reserves among a couple of options, such as certificates of deposit, U.S. savings bonds, and U.S. Treasury bills. That makes it possible for them to tap a portion of their reserve fund immediately, but it locks in somewhat higher returns for the part that may not be needed for three to six months.

Some people, particularly high earners, may balk at parking tens of thousands of dollars in such low-risk, low-return holdings. Some of them might indeed maintain a relatively small rainy-day fund— as long as they have a plan for how to generate a lot of cash in a hurry. For instance, you may have substantial holdings of stock and bond mutual funds, as well as large sums accumulated in home equity, a company savings plan, and a cash-value life insurance policy. In the event of emergency, you might plan to sell some fund holdings. Your backup plan, in case investment prices are in a slump, might be to borrow temporarily against your savings-plan balance or your insurance policy or your home. Some people sign up for a home-equity credit line solely to use in an emergency.

SELECTIONS FOR SAFETY AND SECURITY

Your emergency fund is not the place to try to make a killing. You want to be able to get at it quickly, and you want it to be secure. Stocks and bonds usually do not make sense here, because they tend to fluctuate too much in value over short periods of time. You should look to more conservative investments with which you can count on getting out what you put in, plus some reasonable interest.

Still, you should not be oblivious to the level of interest you are earning. You may be able to boost the earnings on your rainy-day dollars by shifting from a savings account to a money market mutual fund—or by moving your certificate-of-deposit money from your current bank to another one across town.

Here's a closer look at the principal options.

• **Savings accounts.** Savings accounts at banks and thrift institutions, such as savings and loan associations, used to be about the only place for hardworking people to accumulate savings. Today, there are many other choices, and they usually pay more interest than you can earn on a savings account. Moreover, banks often discourage small savings accounts by charging fees that eat away at the interest. Still, these deposit accounts are generally insured by the federal government up to $100,000, and they are handy. You may be able to reduce or eliminate the service charge by finding a bank or thrift offering special deals, perhaps for young savers, for those over 50, or for depositors who agree to keep some minimum amount in a combination of accounts.

• **Certificates of deposit (CDs).** CDs issued by banks and savings institutions are a better choice than savings accounts once you have built up enough savings that you can afford to leave some of your money alone for a few months. Like other deposit accounts, CDs are generally insured up to $100,000. The way they work is simple: Holders usually earn a set yield over a CD's term. There are penalties for withdrawing money early.

Many people should pay more attention to their CD holdings than they do. It is very easy, when a CD matures, to let the bank automatically "roll over" the proceeds by simply putting the money into another CD. But there can be a payoff in higher interest earnings for people who do a little shopping. Compare yields and penalties at a couple of local institutions. Also check with your broker, if you have a brokerage account. Many securities firms offer bank CDs, with no commission charges to buyers, and the yields may top those from local banks. Some people also buy CDs direct from out-of-town banks. *The Wall Street Journal* publishes a weekly report on CD yields, listing some of the highest yields available nationwide.

If you tend to keep far more money in your checking account than you need to pay bills, you might shift some of those dollars into CDs. Consider the other banking services you use when you shop for CDs. Some banks offer "free" checking, for instance, if you keep a certain minimum amount in CDs and other savings accounts.

• **Money market funds.** Money market mutual funds have replaced savings accounts as the basic savings vehicle for millions of families. They are convenient, and their yields generally beat the average yields available on savings accounts, three-month CDs, and, sometimes, even longer-term CDs. Like other mutual funds, money funds pool your money with that of other investors to buy a portfolio of securities. Money funds buy commercial paper (which is essentially an IOU issued by a company), U.S. Treasury bills, and other short-term, generally low-risk investments.

While money funds are not federally insured, fund companies have almost always managed to keep money fund prices at an unchanging $1 per share. Yields float up and down with prevailing interest rates. There are no early-withdrawal penalties, and you tap your money fund balance simply by writing a check. *The Wall Street Journal* publishes a weekly report on money fund yields and an extensive list of individual fund yields.

If you have other mutual fund accounts, it is probably most convenient to use a money fund from one of the same fund companies. But money funds are not all alike. Some funds have noticeably higher yields than others, either because they have lower expenses or because they buy somewhat more risky securities.

Check a fund's prospectus (that is, the official offering document) for information on expenses and the types of securities the fund buys. The least risky—although generally the lowest yielding—money funds buy only Treasury securities.

The interest from most money funds, like that of bank CDs, is subject to income tax. People in the highest tax brackets may do better in tax-free money funds—those that buy the tax-exempt obligations of states and cities. Some tax-free money funds buy securities from only one state and its municipalities because those obligations are free of that state's income tax as well. Take a close look at yields to figure what type of money fund is likely to deliver the highest after-tax return.

• **U.S. savings bonds.** Series EE savings bonds are a classic gift for the birth of a baby or other family event. They are also a solid choice for your cash reserves and are easily ordered through a local bank or purchased by payroll deduction at many employers. These government obligations offer top-notch security, of course. Redemption values can be counted on to rise every six months, in line with current interest rates.

In the first five years you own a bond, the rate is set at 85% of average recent yields on six-month Treasury bills. After that, the return is 85% of average recent yields on five-year Treasury securities. You are guaranteed a minimum return of slightly over 4% if you hold a bond for 17 years. Somewhat different interest rules apply to savings bonds purchased before May 1995. All of this, however, means that it is not always obvious what your savings bonds are worth at any given time. To find out, you might have to take them down to your local bank and check on their value.

Savings bonds have tax appeal: Federal income tax can be deferred until the bonds are redeemed. (The bonds grow in value for 30 years.) The interest on Series EE bonds, like that of other U.S. obligations, is also free from state and local income tax.

The minimum investment is $25, for a $50 savings bond that can be redeemed for that face amount in 17 years or less. The maximum investment is $15,000 (purchase price) per person per calendar year. One caveat: Except in cases of emergency, savings bonds cannot be redeemed before six months have elapsed.

• **Treasury bills.** Issued by the U.S. government and backed by the government's ability to tax, Treasury bills, or "T-bills" as the pros call them, are as safe an investment as you can buy. You can select Treasury bills that mature in three months, six months, or one year. Their yields usually beat the average yields on bank CDs of the same maturity, and they sometimes yield more than money funds. An additional plus is that income from Treasury bills is exempt from state and local taxes.

For the small saver, the drawback is that the minimum investment is $10,000. Beyond the minimum, Treasury bills are sold in $1,000 increments; for instance, you could buy an $11,000 T-bill. But if your emergency fund is large enough, Treasury bills are ideal for the portion of the money you will not need for, say, three to six months.

Three-month and six-month Treasury bills are sold at weekly auctions, usually on Mondays. One-year T-bills are usually sold every four weeks. All can be bought at no charge directly from the government through what is known as the Treasury Direct system. But you will need a cashier's check or a certified check from your bank, which will probably cost about $10 or so, and there is a $25 maintenance fee for accounts above $100,000. Selling before maturity can be a headache with the Treasury Direct system because the securities first have to be transferred to a broker or bank. (Phone 202-874-4000 for additional information.) You can also buy Treasury bills through a bank or broker; fees typically range from $50 to $75, although sometimes there may be additional fees to maintain an account.

One feature that can be tricky to understand is that Treasury bills are sold at a discount to their face value. The difference between the price and the face value translates into the yield. It works like this: Say you bought a six-month bill directly from the government at a time when six-month T-bills were yielding 5%. You would submit cash or a bank check or certified check for $10,000 and get back a check for $243.20. When the bill matured, you would receive the full $10,000. The $243.20 six-month return on an investment of $9,756.80 is equivalent to a 5% annual yield.

• **Short-term bond funds.** Funds that buy short-term bonds take a little more risk than money funds, but their yields are sometimes higher by as much as a percentage point or two. That is an extra $100 or $200 a year on a $10,000 investment. For many people, the higher yield makes them a reasonable place to park a portion of their emergency reserves. These funds are essentially lending money to corporations and other borrowers by buying debt instruments with maturities of one to five years. There are also tax-exempt varieties, which buy tax-exempt municipal obligations of comparable maturities.

But buyers have to understand that the shares of short-term bond funds fluctuate in price. They rise when interest rates fall and fall when interest rates rise. That means short-term bond funds are particularly attractive when interest rates are stable or falling. But they underperform money funds in some periods of rising rates.

In fact, if interest rates rise quickly enough, you can lose money, as investors did in 1994, which was an especially devastating year for all kinds of bonds. On average, that year's "total return," which includes interest payments plus price changes, on mutual funds that buy short-term corporate bonds was a negative 0.45%. Funds that invest in short-term Treasury securities had a negative total return of 0.91%.

Watch out for short-term bond funds with yields that are significantly higher than those of their peers. In recent years, some funds have bought very risky securities that boosted their returns tremendously in some periods but produced steep price declines in others.

One popular provider of straightforward, low-expense bond funds is the Vanguard Group in Valley Forge, Pennsylvania.

Insuring Your Family's Future

Many of us have gripes about insurance—about a pushy agent who keeps calling or about the medical claims our health insurance company turns down. Still, insurance is fundamentally a very powerful instrument. It is the mainstay of the financial safety net for most families.

Insurance is about sharing risks and minimizing the financial cost of events we would rather not even think about. For instance, it is not very likely that your house will burn down this year. But it could happen, and the cost of rebuilding the structure and replacing your possessions would be immense. That is where insurance comes in: If a large number of families pay a few hundred dollars a year each, the resulting pool of money should be sufficient to pick up the tab for the few who suffer a devastating fire.

Most people get some of their insurance coverage through work and buy the rest directly. (You can find information about employer-provided coverage in Chapter 4, and details on most types of insurance you purchase for yourself in Chapter 3 and in the Buyer's Guide to Life Insurance, Appendix C.) In general, most people should have the following:

- A policy to cover damage to your home and contents—or only contents for a rented dwelling.
- A policy to cover your vehicles.
- Liability coverage, usually included in both auto and homeowners' policies, that pays if you cause an accident or are sued.
- Health insurance, or a managed-care program such as a health maintenance organization, to pay medical bills.
- Life insurance, if you have dependents who would be financially harmed by your death.
- Disability insurance that provides income if a current breadwinner becomes disabled and is unable to bring home a paycheck.

Documents You Should Not Be Without

You know you are supposed to have a will. (Whether you really have one is another matter.) But you may not know that a will is just one of a handful of important documents that most individuals should have—and that too many do not.

Like a will, these other documents deal with subjects we would all like to ignore: death, disease, family disaster. But they are all necessary to provide for your family and yourself. They may also be easier to obtain than you think. What are these must-have papers? A will, a durable power of attorney, a living will, a health care power of attorney, and a personal financial inventory.

• **Will.** Although many people think of a will as a tool to parcel out assets, its central role is to provide for people. If you have young children, the most important provision is the selection of a guardian who would raise the kids if both parents died. For business owners with adult offspring, the key challenge is to allocate the business and other assets so that the parents' death does not trigger a nasty fight.

Even people of modest means need wills to make sure their money goes where they want. Die without a will, and there is no money for your favorite charity or someone you are involved with in a long-term but nonmarital relationship. State law might divide your money equally among a surviving spouse and children, even though many people would rather it all go to the spouse. Review your will at least every five years and whenever there is a birth or other major family change.

• **Durable power of attorney.** Who would tend to your banking and other financial affairs if a serious illness or other crisis left you unable? Your family could go to court to have a guardian appointed. Or, in advance, you could authorize a spouse or other trusted individual to make financial decisions for you.

Most financial planners and attorneys recommend that clients sign a durable power of attorney naming such an agent. A "durable" power of attorney is worded so that it remains in effect even if the person granting it becomes incompetent. But they note that this simple and handy document is also a potent one. You have to have complete confidence in the person to whom you give such broad financial power. You can revoke a power of attorney at any time by tearing it up. Some people tell the selected agent about the power of attorney, but then they leave the document with the attorney who prepares it.

• **Living will and health care power of attorney.** Advances in medical technology have raised some painful new questions: Would you want to be sustained on mechanical life support at the end of your life? Would you want "extraordinary" measures taken to prolong your life if there were no chance of recovering from pervasive cancer or another dread disease?

However you feel about such issues, you should prepare a living will to give guidance to your loved ones. Couple that living will with a health care power of attorney (also called a health care proxy) that names an agent to carry out those wishes if you are no longer able to make your own medical decisions.

These two documents are sometimes combined in a single form, and many attorneys prepare the medical forms when they do a regular will. You can also obtain the proper forms for your state at no charge by calling Choice in Dying, a national not-for-profit group (800-989-9455).

• **Personal financial inventory.** This is the easiest of the essential documents—a simple listing of your professional advisers and the location of key documents that your survivors might otherwise have to scramble for in the event of your disability or death.

Among the items to include:

• Names and phone numbers of your attorney and accountant.

• Location of wills and other important documents.

• A listing of all insurance policies, bank accounts, investment accounts, credit card accounts, and loans. Be sure to include account numbers and specify where related documents can be found.

• The location of safe-deposit boxes and of the box keys and a complete list of contents.

For husband and wife, the inventory can pull together basic information on the separate financial matters that each one routinely handles. (To make life a little easier, you can use the Personal Financial Inventory in Appendix B.)

ORGANIZING YOUR RECORDS

You know it is there somewhere. Your passport, that is. Or the year-end brokerage statement your accountant has been requesting for several weeks. But if 15 minutes of scratching your head and rifling through an overstuffed file cabinet does not help locate such documents, your personal files, like those of most folks, are crying out for a makeover.

There are pressing financial reasons to get a better handle on all the papers swirling around: Tax preparers charge less when they do not have to sort through a mess. Good records can also substantially cut the taxes you will pay years from now when you withdraw money from an Individual Retirement Account or sell a security or a home.

Perhaps more important, organizing your files can make it easier for a spouse or other family member to pick up the pieces if you are suddenly not around. It is also a crucial step in understanding what you have and where your money goes.

How do you get your act together? One way is with the aid of a kit that suggests specific files and what to put in them. (A good one is sold by Maryland financial planners Michael and Mary Martin for about $20, 800-695-3453.) But you can battle the paper tiger on your own if you arm yourself with a few simple office supplies, such as hanging files and

GOING FROM PILES TO FILES

If you are starting a home filing system from scratch, aim for between 12 and 24 major categories for your hanging files. Here are some major headings to consider:

Banking
Mutual funds
Brokerage accounts
Retirement plans

Insurance—home and auto
Insurance—life and disability
Medical insurance and expenses
Estate planning

Work
House purchase and capital improvements
Mortgage
Autos

Taxes
Product warranties and manuals
Schools and child care
Personal financial inventory

manila folders to slip inside. If you are short on drawer space, look for inexpensive plastic filing crates that hold hanging files and can be stored in a closet.

Another important tool is a big garbage can. That "circular file" is just the place for many of the papers crowding your desk drawers and closet shelves. If you have always kept your important papers in piles, not files, between one dozen and two dozen file categories should be enough to put things in order.

As you weed through your existing papers, look for valuable, hard-to-replace items that would be better kept in a safe-deposit box. (Make photocopies and keep the copies at home with a list of safe-deposit contents.) Also look for papers that you need but rarely consult; some of those can be moved to "deep storage" in your attic or elsewhere.

What to Toss, What to Keep, Where to Put It

• **Banking.** You do not need every canceled check for posterity. Many financial planners say bank statements and routine checks for groceries and the like can be thrown out after a year. (If you are not ready to part with them that soon, store them in the attic for a few years.) But take pains with canceled checks that substantiate tax deductions, that verify major purchases, or that are particularly significant in other ways. Pull out those checks when you get your bank statement each month. File tax-related checks under "taxes" or specific subject files, such as "charitable giving" or "medical expenses." Later on, they will go with a copy of your completed tax return. File big-purchase checks with related product warranties or in a safe-deposit box with an inventory of household possessions.

• **Home.** Keep the deed to your home in a safe-deposit box. With it, keep materials that would document the condition of your home and its contents in the event of fire or other disaster. That could include a written inventory, receipts, appraisals, photographs, or a home-video tour. Tax law generally lets you defer tax on home-sale profits if you roll the money into a new principal residence. Until you eventually do pay tax on the gains, keep a file with purchase and sale documents, including copies of federal tax Form 2119, on every home you have owned.

Have a separate file folder or a spiral notebook with pockets in which you jot down capital improvements and save receipts, blueprints, and the like. Those expenditures increase the home's cost for tax purposes and decrease any taxable gain later on. Repairs and routine maintenance, such as fixing leaks or repainting the living room, do not count. Capital improvements, which add value to a home, prolong its useful life, or adapt it to new uses, include big-ticket items such as a new roof or bath. But even small improvements, such as planting a few new bushes or wallpapering a dowdy old bathroom, can add up.

• **Individual Retirement Accounts.** Keep careful records of all contributions to nondeductible IRAs. When you pull money out of these retirement plans, the after-tax contributions will not be subject to tax. In any year you make a nondeductible contribution, the Internal Revenue Service says you should stow away copies of the Form 8606 you file with your return, the first page of the tax return, and the annual statement you receive from the IRA trustee.

• **Insurance.** Pitch the expired policies for the Buick you traded in last year and the house you sold back in 1992. Documents for current policies can be kept at home.

• **Investments**. Have a separate manila folder for each mutual fund or brokerage account, and ruthlessly weed out the mess of old annual reports, proxy statements, and promotional brochures. Keep careful records of what you paid for securities to ease tax reporting and avoid overpaying tax when you sell. Mutual fund investors, in particular, sometimes overstate their taxable profit by not including reinvested distributions in figuring the cost of the shares they sell.

If your year-end mutual fund statements are cumulative—showing the full year's transactions—you can save just that one statement for each year. Keep all the confirmation notices for individual security purchases in your brokerage account; keep all your brokerage statements if the year-end one is not cumulative. Be sure to keep track of stock splits. When you sell securities, keep the purchase and sale records with a copy of the tax return.

• **Personal financial inventory.** Remember that central list of professional advisers and key documents? If you have not done it already, organizing your files will make the task of preparing that list easier. You can prepare your own list, or use the one in Appendix B. You might put the inventory in the very first file in your cabinet and also store a photocopy in your safe-deposit box. In the same file, you can store photocopies of the documents in your safe-deposit box. Be sure both spouses, and possibly other family members or advisers, know the location.

CLEANING UP YOUR ACT

As you weed through existing files (or piles) of financial papers, here are some things to pluck out.

DISCARD

- Most non-tax-related checks that are more than a year old
- Expired insurance policies with no possibility of claims
- Records from cars and boats you no longer own
- All but the most recent cumulative pay stub for this year
- Clearly expired product warranties
- Utility bills more than one year old
- Old mutual fund annual reports and proxy statements
- Most credit card bills and receipts more than one year old

MOVE TO LONG-TERM STORAGE

- Records of nondeductible IRA contributions
- Death certificates, after estate is settled
- Military records for possible veterans' benefits
- Tax returns and supporting documents (more than a year old)
- Information on possible pensions from former employers

SAFE-DEPOSIT BOX

- Birth and marriage certificates
- Deeds and other records of ownership
- Contracts
- Passports
- Stock and bond certificates
- Copy of financial inventory
- Home inventory, big-purchase receipts, appraisals

• **Taxes.** Have one folder to capture materials you will need in preparing your next return. At the end of tax season, put copies of your federal and state returns and all supporting documents in a single folder. Some pieces of your federal return, such as Form 2119 on a home sale and Form 8606 on nondeductible IRA contributions, should also be copied and filed elsewhere.

What about that mountain of old tax returns? Many individuals, including some accountants and planners, keep them for decades. But that is probably unnecessary, these professionals concede. Only the most recent year's materials need to be in your active file. Put another six years' worth in the attic and consider chucking the rest. The IRS generally has three years to examine your return, but it has six if there is substantial underreporting of income. There is no time limit for fraud.

• **Wills.** Putting your will in your safe-deposit box is not the right way to keep it secure. The reason is that many states limit access to a person's safe-deposit box after he or she dies. Consider keeping a copy of the will at home and leaving the original with your attorney. Destroy old wills and drafts of the document because they can lead to confusion and disputes among heirs.

GETTING PROFESSIONAL HELP

You do not have to do it all yourself. In fact, you probably cannot do everything alone. Although it is important to take responsibility for understanding your own financial situation and planning for the future, you will probably need a team of professional advisers and product purveyors to help with certain personal finance tasks.

When it comes to drafting a will and estate planning, for instance, you simply owe it to yourself to get help from a lawyer who specializes in handling such matters. For certain other jobs, such as buying life insurance and picking investments, you will have to decide whether to proceed on your own, to use the help of a commission-paid sales agent, or to hire a fee-paid adviser.

Whenever you hire someone to help, the challenge is to find the right person and to educate yourself enough to ask intelligent questions and make the big decisions. Remember, you are hiring people for help only; you are still part of the process.

PICKING PROFESSIONALS AND PRODUCT PROVIDERS

Selecting the right person to work with can take you halfway to having a particular task done. Pick a capable estate-planning attorney and show up for the initial conference, for instance, and you can sit back and wait for the drafts of your will and other documents. But it can be tough to find people whose expertise and manner are right for you. And in the case of product sellers, such as insurance agents, stockbrokers, and many financial planners, you have to be concerned about whether that person is acting in his or her best interests rather than yours.

SEVEN SMART STEPS

• **Start with referrals, but do not stop there.** Ask friends, family, and existing advisers for names of people to consider, but do not take those suggestions as gospel. Your Uncle Harry may not know enough about investments to really gauge his broker's skill. Your accountant may be giving you the name of a lawyer he knows from the golf course, not extensive professional dealings. Many specialists simply do not know enough about each other's fields to evaluate ability.

• **With names in hand, pick up the phone.** Ask potential advisers a handful of questions about their training, areas of expertise, philosophy, and pay. You are looking for people who might be a reasonable match for your needs. If you invest heavily in tax-free municipal bonds, for instance, you want a broker who is active in that area. You probably want a lawyer who specializes in estate planning to prepare your will; if your family circumstances are relatively simple, however, you probably do not need the most expensive estate-planning specialist in town.

• **Make the time to meet.** See at least two candidates, in person, even if it means paying for their time. Personal chemistry is important in any advisory relationship, and a face-to-face meeting is the best way to judge. It can be tough to decide about one person after an initial meeting. If you see a few, you will have a basis for comparison.

• **Ask for references and really call.** No one is going to give the name of a disgruntled client, of course. But it still makes sense to ask your top candidates for names of existing clients in circumstances similar to yours and to take the time to call. Ask about the adviser's strengths and weaknesses; we all have some of both. Try to gain a clearer sense of the person's philosophy and working style and what he or she might be able to do for you.

• **Watch out for conflicts of interest.** In accepting recommendations from stockbrokers, insurance agents, and other commission-paid sellers, just remember that those folks do not work for you. They are paid by their firms to sell you products, and they may have a financial incentive to push something that is not in your best interest. Many financial planners are also in the product-selling camp. Be prepared to do some additional research and to think for yourself. Even fee-paid advisers can have conflicts of interest. If a local insurance agent refers many clients to an estate-planning attorney, for instance, that attorney might be loath to criticize the insurance-related strategies the agent suggests. If you are seeking an unbiased second opinion on a transaction, hire someone with no such relationship.

• **Consider the cost of "free" advice.** You do not pay a life insurance agent directly, but the money still comes out of your pocket. When an agent sells a policy, the insurance company pays commissions and other compensation to that person and recovers those dollars in charges against your policy. Similarly, stockbrokers sell many mutual funds without an up-front commission, or *load.* But the mutual fund companies typically still pay brokers a commission. The companies recover that money from you in the form of higher annual fees or other charges against the funds. Individuals who buy investments and insurance direct from the issuing companies typically get products with lower expenses. Another option, if you are not prepared to do it yourself, is to pay fees to a fee-only adviser who will help you buy low-cost products.

• **Do not let the "experts" push you around.** A lot of personal finance advice is subjective. There is no one investment portfolio that is right for you. Two knowledgeable accountants can differ about whether a particular tax strategy makes sense. Do a little research on your own. If you are uncomfortable with an adviser's suggestion, say so and ask for other options. Also listen to yourself if you have some reservations about a particular adviser or product provider. You are paying the bills, one way or another. If you have doubts about a person's ability or do not feel comfortable with that person as a counselor, it is probably time to go somewhere else.

Should You See a Financial Planner?

Why not take a load off your shoulders and simply dump your muddled finances into the lap of a financial planner? It is a tempting fantasy for most of us, but the reality is somewhat different. Before you can even sit down with a planner, for example, you will need to do a fair amount of paperwork, pulling together a basic financial inventory that includes such things as a list of investments and their purchase prices. Then there is the fact that many financial decisions are simply too personal to expect someone else to make them for you.

A wise and knowledgeable planner may provide valuable assistance and encouragement, but for a fee that could add up to thousands of dollars. And you will still have to make fundamental decisions about such matters as how much investment risk you can comfortably stand and how you might want your family to carry on in the event of your death. Meanwhile, some other planners may be only too happy to have you sit back and rely on them. There are some outright con artists in this crowd, as well as many insurance agents and securities sellers who use the cloak of planning to push their usual products.

The sad truth is that the very thing that can make hiring a planner so attractive—the opportunity to turn your problems over to someone else—also poses great risks. Moreover, sorting the good planners from the bad can be tough. By the time you finish reading this book, you will probably decide you can handle much of your personal finance work yourself. If you do decide to hire a planner for certain tasks, you will be better equipped to select someone and get the most from that person's help. The national planner organizations listed in Appendix A can help you find members in your area.

CHECKING OUT PLANNERS: QUALIFICATIONS

Just who are these folks who call themselves planners? They are a very diverse bunch. For one thing, there is no single educational program that people must complete or a single designation they must earn to do business as financial planners. Indeed, anyone can have "Financial Planning" painted on an office door.

Decent training does not ensure that a planner will dish out good advice, of course, but it is a good place to start in gauging a planner's competence. Some planners are accountants or lawyers by training or have advanced degrees in finance. There are also a handful of special designations that planners can earn by taking required courses and passing exams.

The best-known financial planner designation is the Certified Financial Planner (CFP) mark from the CFP Board of Standards in Denver. Certified public accountants (CPAs) who provide planning services can earn the Personal Financial Specialist mark from the American Institute of CPAs. The American College in Bryn Mawr, Pennsylvania, grants the Chartered Financial Consultant (ChFC) designation, often to life insurance agents who have already earned the school's Chartered Life Underwriter (CLU) mark.

Look for planners with a broad mix of educational and professional credentials—for instance, a lawyer by training who previously worked in product evaluation at a brokerage house and holds the CFP designation. Equally important, you want an adviser who has several years of experience providing comprehensive planning; that is, someone who is not primarily selling insurance or giving tax advice. You want a planner who has been at it long enough to have acquired not just knowledge but also a rarer quality—wisdom.

CHECKING OUT PLANNERS: COMPENSATION

A minority of planners are "fee-only" advisers, meaning they are paid only by their clients and do not sell any products. Most planners, though, have a disturbing conflict of interest in the way that they do business: They present themselves as informed and impartial advisers and charge hefty fees of $1,000 or more. But they make much more money by selling investments, insurance, or other products to their clients and pocketing sales commissions.

These "fee-and-commission" planners essentially wear two hats: Planner John Doe, operating as John Doe Advisory Services, will charge fees for a written plan or verbal advice. Then, operating as a licensed insurance agent or as a broker for a securities firm with an unfamiliar name, Mr. Doe will offer to sell various products to implement a client's financial plan. Planners who operate this way typ-

---

THE QUESTIONS TO ASK

An essential part of finding a good financial planner is asking the right questions. Start with these, and follow up with questions of your own about anything you do not understand and any special concerns you may have.

- What is your background, education, and experience? How do you stay current?

- How do you get paid? Are there conflicts between your interests and mine?

- My most urgent concern is _____. How might you tackle that?

- How much experience do you have working with clients whose income and circumstances are similar to mine? Are there a few I could speak with?

- Are there other people in your office who would be working on my plan? Are there other people or resources you might tap in complex areas, such as tax planning, individual stock selection, insurance policy evaluation, and estate planning?

- May I see a sample of a written financial plan?

- If you sell insurance and investments, from what companies? Will you tell me your commission on each product you recommend?

- If you do not sell financial products, can you recommend specific investments and insurance policies and help me obtain them at a good price?

ically charge lower fees than fee-only planners because they earn most of their compensation from sales commissions. But the products these planners sell typically have higher expenses built into them than the products recommended by fee-only planners.

Fee-and-commission planners can be torn between lower-commission products that are better for the client and higher-commission choices that are more remunerative for them. They may be more inclined to address clients' problems with products than with tax strategies or other approaches that do not generate a sales commission. Certainly, some fee-and-commission planners will put your interests first. But to bypass that built-in conflict of interest, consider leaning toward the fee-only folks.

2

MASTERING
THE SECRETS OF
SUCCESSFUL
INVESTING

$

Successful investing can be remarkably simple.

That may sound surprising, even unbelievable, if you are befuddled by Wall Street and its bizarre world of options, futures, penny stocks, and limited partnerships. But the fact is, there is much about Wall Street that you can safely ignore. Indeed, most people fare far better if they bypass arcane investment strategies and exotic financial instruments. The first secret of successful investing is to focus on a few crucial but relatively straightforward decisions and to stick with investments that you understand.

Any money you set aside and do not spend is technically an "investment," even if you stash it in the mattress or bury it in tin cans out in the backyard. But organizing your finances and reaching your goals will be much easier if you make a distinction between "saving" and "investing."

Think of saving as what you do with the money you set aside to take care of emergencies or to buy things you may need or want in the next few years—a new refrigerator, perhaps, or a vacation, or the down payment on your first home. High returns are not the top priority; security is what you want most. As discussed in Chapter 1, this is money you are counting on being able to get at easily and quickly. You should keep it in conservative investments, such as certificates of deposit, money market mutual funds, and Treasury bills.

Investing, on the other hand, is best thought of as a longer-term activity. That means years, not months. Investing is the effort to make your money grow over time, ahead of taxes and inflation, so that you can accumulate enough to pay for long-range goals, such as a college education for your children or a comfortable retirement for yourself. You should not begin investing until you have built up adequate emergency savings. But you should start investing as early as you can.

TIME IS YOUR FRIEND

Time is important because the investments with the best overall performance also tend to bounce around in price over the short term. The further off your goals are, the better positioned you will be to ride out the inevitable reversals—and the more aggressive you can be in seeking high returns. Those high returns will then make it easier to reach your objectives.

Where do you find those generous long-term returns? In the stock markets of the world, where the shares of companies of all types and sizes are bought and sold. So-called common stock, which gives an investor an ownership interest in the company that issued the shares, is the hands-down winner when it comes to generating healthy inflation-beating gains over the long run.

True, the new inflation-indexed Treasury bonds that the U.S. government was planning to introduce in late 1996 were being designed specifically to offer returns protecting investors from the ravages of inflation. That is something no other domestic investment can guarantee. As a result, inflation-indexed Treasury bonds would be a valuable addition to many people's investment portfolios. But your long-term goal should be to do much better than just keep ahead of inflation, and stocks are still your best bet to achieve that goal.

Since the end of 1925, the Standard & Poor's 500—an index of larger-company stocks—has produced an average annual "total return" of 10.5%, according to Chicago's Ibbotson Associates, an investment-research firm that has calculated the long-term results for various types of investments. (Total return includes both securities price changes and earnings from stock dividends or bond interest pay-

THE GOOD, THE BAD, AND THE AVERAGE

Investment returns can vary enormously from year to year, especially for stocks and longer-term bonds. As a result, to ensure that you achieve returns that approach the historical averages, plan on sticking with your investments for at least five years, and preferably longer.

	1926–1995			1946–1995		
	AVERAGE (%)	HIGHEST (%)	LOWEST (%)	AVERAGE (%)	HIGHEST (%)	LOWEST (%)
Standard & Poor's 500	10.5	54.0	−43.3	11.9	52.6	−26.5
Small-company stocks	12.5	142.9	−58.0	13.8	83.6	−30.9
Long-term corporate bonds	5.7	42.6	−8.1	5.8	42.6	−8.1
Long-term government bonds	5.2	40.4	−9.2	5.3	40.4	−9.2
Intermediate-term government bonds	5.3	29.1	−5.1	5.9	29.1	−5.1
30-day Treasury bills	3.7	14.7	0.0	4.8	14.7	0.4
Inflation	3.1	18.2	−10.3	4.4	18.2	−1.8

SOURCE: © *Stocks, Bonds, Bills, and Inflation 1996 Yearbook*™, Ibbotson Associates, Chicago (annually updates work by Roger G. Ibbotson and Rex A. Sinquefield). Used with permission. All rights reserved.

ments.) Over the same time period, intermediate-term government bonds gained 5.3% annually, and 30-day Treasury bills delivered 3.7%. Meanwhile, inflation climbed at a 3.1% average annual rate.

Unfortunately, in the short run, stocks are also subject to large, sometimes sudden price swings. Since World War II, stocks have gained as much as 52.6% in a single calendar year—1954. But they have also lost as much as 26.5%, in 1974.

Time plays an important part in making the risk of such gyrations bearable. But to achieve decent performance and still be able to sleep at night, you may also want to mix stocks with more conservative choices, such as bonds and cash. That is what investment professionals mean when they talk about such concepts as "diversification" and "asset allocation."

It is also important to make a long-term plan and stay with it. If you try jumping in and out of the stock market in an effort to catch the times when prices rally and to sidestep the downturns, the lesson of history is that you are almost certain to fail. More often than not, you are apt to end up chasing last year's hot investment while the real money is being made elsewhere.

This chapter guides you in devising an investment strategy and building an investment portfolio you can live with through thick and thin—with only limited modifications and without big demands on your time. You will learn about the importance of keeping investment expenses under control and about making the tax laws work for you in building your nest egg. You will also learn how to get the most out of a stockbroker—and why you may be better off without one.

AS SIMPLE AS ONE, TWO, THREE

Whether you are building an investment portfolio from scratch or giving an existing portfolio a checkup, three basic decisions are especially important to your success.

First, you have to decide on your asset allocation. That means figuring out how you want to divvy up your portfolio among three main investment categories: stocks, bonds, and supersafe "cash" investments, such as certificates of deposit and money market funds. You may also want to add a fourth category, "hard assets," which include gold, energy stocks, basic-materials companies, and real estate.

Once you have decided on your asset allocation, the second step is to consider how you want to diversify within each investment category. When you diversify, you spread your bets across an array of individual securities and market sectors, in an effort to reduce the risk that your portfolio will be badly hurt because a particular company gets into trouble or the market as a whole takes a dive.

Finally, having settled on your asset allocation and your diversification strategy, the third step is to pick the best possible investments. In the past, investors have relied heavily on individual stocks and bonds. But increasingly, savvy investors—as well as people who simply have better things to do with their time than worry about picking individual stocks and bonds—have turned to mutual funds.

Mutual funds, which pool your money with money from many

> **THE FOUR LITMUS TESTS**
>
> It is a simple test: Dip a piece of litmus paper in a liquid, and if it turns red, the liquid contains acid. When selecting an investment, you should apply four equally simple tests before parting with your money:
>
> - The investment should be easy to understand.
>
> - There should be a good chance of making money.
>
> - There ought to be a ready market should you need to sell in a hurry.
>
> - The investment should be relatively inexpensive to buy, hold, and sell.

other investors to buy a portfolio of securities, let you choose an investment approach and leave the job of selecting individual securities to professional money managers. Mutual funds make it possible to achieve instant diversification, and they are an easy way for individuals to start on a regular investment program: Many fund companies can arrange to have as little as $50 or $100 a month deducted from your bank account and invested in any of a variety of stock and bond funds. Funds are also an easy route into some of the riskier areas of the securities markets, such as high-yield "junk" bonds and the emerging stock markets of developing nations.

INVESTING THROUGH THE AGES

As you make choices about allocating your assets, diversifying, and picking individual investments, your financial sophistication and your stomach for risk clearly will be important. But your goals and how long you have to achieve them will be even more critical.

What are your goals? Everybody has different priorities. But people of a similar age tend to face similar financial demands. That is where we turn next. The following sections highlight a number of the most important investment challenges and opportunities for people in various age brackets.

YOUR 20s AND 30s

If you are in your 20s and 30s, you probably have plenty of dreams but only a little cash. You want to send your newborn to a good college. There is that house you want to buy. You would like to retire early. It all can seem overwhelming. How do you even know where to start?

The first thing to do is to check your safety net. Putting together an emergency reserve can seem pretty dull, especially if you know someone with the annoying habit of boasting about that great high-technology fund he invested in. But before you can become serious about investing, you must have some emergency money, just in case you are hit with a large medical bill or you lose your job. If you do not have three to six months of spending money tucked safely away, go back and read Chapter 1.

Your emergency reserve should be in conservative investments, such as certificates of deposit, money market mutual funds, Treasury bills, and short-term bond funds. Indeed, these investments are a good parking place for any money you might need within the next three years. If you are within a few years of buying your own home, for instance, you may also want to keep your down payment money in a supersafe investment vehicle.

CAPITALIZE ON YOUR ADVANTAGE

To meet longer-term goals, such as your child's college education and your own retirement, you are going to have to accumulate substantial wealth. Your best chance of doing that is to invest regularly in the stock market. And although you may not have much spare cash when you are young, you do have an equally valuable asset: time. If you start socking away money for retirement in your 20s and early 30s, you have a huge advantage over those who wait until their 40s.

For instance, T. Rowe Price Associates, one of the biggest mutual fund companies, figures that if you invest $100 a month starting at age 30, you will have over $177,000 by the time you retire at age 65, assuming your money grows at 7% a year. But if you do not get around to saving for retirement until you turn 45, amassing that $177,000 becomes much tougher. T. Rowe Price calculates that you will have to squirrel away $335 a month to accumulate $177,000 by age 65.

How much should you be saving for retirement at this age? If you want to take early retirement—quitting the workforce at, say, age 55—it is crucial that you start a campaign of heavy-duty savings by the time you reach your mid-30s. That means stashing away 20% of your "gross," or pretax, income each year. Those who are willing to wait until age 65 before retiring can settle for a more sedate savings rate of 10%.

If you cannot afford that much, then start with 5%, or even 1%. The really important thing is that you make a start. Then increase your savings rate whenever you can.

LEAN TOWARD STOCKS

When picking investments, lean toward stocks. Consider an "index" fund, which simply buys all the stocks in a particular market index such as the Standard & Poor's 500 or the Wilshire 5000, in an effort to match the index's performance. Index funds will give you broad stock market exposure in a single fund, and they do not eat up too much of your investment gains with management and administrative expenses.

Alternatively, you may want to invest in one of the broadly diversified mutual funds that include a smattering of all stock market

ONE-STOP SHOPPING WITH LIFE-CYCLE FUNDS

The mutual fund companies listed here offer a variety of well-diversified funds, each earmarked for investors of different ages and different tolerances for risk. The idea is to provide shareholders with a broad collection of securities in a single portfolio. The Stagecoach LifePath funds differ from the others in that those funds become progressively more conservative as they approach their designated maturity dates.

Dreyfus Group
One Exchange Place
Boston, MA 02109
800-645-6561
- LifeTime Income Portfolio
- LifeTime Growth and Income Portfolio
- LifeTime Growth Portfolio

Federated Investors
Federated Investors Tower
Pittsburgh, PA 15222-3779
800-245-5040
- Managed Income Fund
- Managed Growth and Income Fund
- Managed Growth Fund
- Managed Aggressive Growth Fund

Fidelity Investments
82 Devonshire Street
Boston, MA 02109
800-544-8888
- Asset Manager: Income
- Asset Manager
- Asset Manager: Growth

Oppenheimer Funds
P.O. Box 5270
Denver, CO 80217-5270
800-525-7048

- LifeSpan Diversified Income Fund
- LifeSpan Balanced Fund
- LifeSpan Growth Fund

T. Rowe Price Associates
100 E. Pratt Street
Baltimore, MD 21202
800-638-5660

- Personal Strategy Income Fund
- Personal Strategy Balanced Fund
- Personal Strategy Growth Fund

Putnam Investments
One Post Office Square
Boston, MA 02109
800-225-1581

- Asset Allocation Funds—Conservative Portfolio
- Asset Allocation Funds—Balanced Portfolio
- Asset Allocation Funds—Growth Portfolio

Stagecoach Funds
111 Center Street
Little Rock, AR 72201
800-222-8222

- LifePath 2000 Fund
- LifePath 2010 Fund
- LifePath 2020 Fund
- LifePath 2030 Fund
- LifePath 2040 Fund

Vanguard Group
P.O. Box 2600
Valley Forge, PA 19482
800-662-7447

- LifeStrategy Funds—Income Portfolio
- LifeStrategy Funds—Conservative Growth Portfolio
- LifeStrategy Funds—Moderate Growth Portfolio
- LifeStrategy Funds—Growth Portfolio

sectors and a helping of bonds in a single portfolio. For instance, many fund companies now offer "life-cycle" funds, which combine stock market and bond market investments in portfolios that are designed for particular age groups.

Because of the benefits that come from years of stock market compounding, you should get into the habit of saving some money every month when you are in your 20s and 30s, even if the sum is relatively small. While many mutual funds demand investment minimums or $1,000 or $3,000, funds will often waive these minimums if you agree to an automatic investment plan. Such plans automatically deduct $50 or $100 from your paycheck or bank account every month and plop it straight into the fund. It can be a great way to pay yourself before you are tempted to blow the money on something of little or no lasting value.

An automatic investment plan can be a terrific way to start accumulating money for retirement or your children's college education. At this age, you are probably at least 25 years from retirement, and your kids may be more than a decade away from college. That is plenty of time to ride through some rocky spells and make decent long-run gains.

USE "DOLLAR-COST AVERAGING"

When you start young and save regularly, you take much of the risk out of stock market investing because you are using the time-tested buying technique of "dollar-cost averaging." Dollar-cost averaging involves investing a fixed amount every month, no matter what is going on in the stock market. When stock prices are higher, your monthly investment buys fewer shares. But when prices are lower, your monthly purchase will garner more shares. Because share prices rise over time, you should eventually end up with shares that are worth far more than the price you paid.

One of the best ways for people to give their investments a boost when they first start out is to open an Individual Retirement Account. You can contribute up to $2,000 a year to these accounts, and you will not have to pay tax on the income until you take the

20s–30s

- Aim to save 10%.
- Set up automatic investment plan.
- Consider index or life-cycle fund.
- Dollar-cost average.
- Contribute to 401(k) and IRA.

money out. As a result, your dollars will build up much faster than if you invest in an ordinary taxable account.

But the best part is that if you are not covered by a retirement plan at work, or you make less than $35,000 a year ($50,000 a year for married couples), you can deduct some or all of the contribution from the income you have to pay tax on. For someone in the 28% tax bracket, a $2,000 deductible IRA contribution will lower the federal income tax bill by $560. That $2,000 contribution actually costs you only $1,440.

GET THE BOSS AND UNCLE SAM TO HELP

The tax laws can make the office an even better place to start investing. Many companies now offer 401(k) retirement-savings plans, which allow employees to have money deducted from their pretax pay and invested in a variety of investment options. This has all the advantages of automatic investing, plus the benefit of lowering your

A PORTFOLIO FOR YOUR 20S AND 30S

If you are trying to decide how to spread your investment money, use this pie chart as a starting point. You may want to put more or less of your money into bonds, depending on your stomach for risk. When investing your foreign-stock money, consider putting a small portion into an emerging-markets fund.

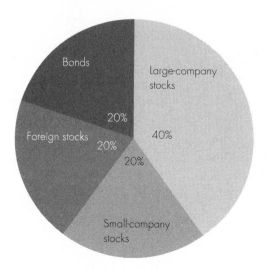

tax bill. Not only that, but many employers kick in as much as 50 cents for every dollar the employee puts in up to a set limit. Even without the tax benefits, that is like earning 50% on your investment. And if you change jobs, you can take the money with you.

The bad part is that an employer-sponsored 401(k) plan may be the only company retirement plan you will have to depend on in your old age. If you do not contribute, you will get nothing. So aim to make the maximum contribution allowed. At the very least, make some contribution. If you just don't have the spare cash, consider asking your parents if they will reimburse you for your 401(k) contributions. (For more details on how to make the most of this and other employee benefits, see Chapter 4.)

SURVIVING THE BUMPS

If you are investing for retirement or for your toddler's college education, your best chance of reaching your goal is to buy a broad collection of stocks and bonds or a few well-chosen mutual funds and hang on for the long haul. But how do you handle a market drop? Here are some tips:

- **Remember you are investing for the long term.** Over a ten-year period, stocks almost always outperform bonds and "cash" investments like money market funds and bank certificates of deposit.

- **Look at your whole nest egg.** If one of your mutual funds plunges 20%, take a look at what has happened to the value of your entire portfolio. If that abysmal fund was just 10% of your nest egg, your portfolio's overall value would be down only 2%.

- **Think in percentages.** Suppose your $35,000 portfolio suddenly shrinks by $1,400. That can seem scary, but put it in perspective. Recognize that your portfolio has dipped just 4%.

- **Invest regularly.** Use dollar-cost averaging, which involves putting, say, $100 into the market every month. This allows you to take advantage of falling prices to buy more shares at lower cost. Over the long run, you should come out ahead.

- **Rebalance your portfolio.** Shift some money from investments that have done well to those that have declined in value. That way you will maintain your target percentages for how much of your portfolio is in key market sectors, such as U.S. stocks, foreign stocks, bonds, and cash.

YOUR 40S AND 50S

If you failed to save much when you were in your 20s and 30s, this can be your chance to make up for lost time. After all, you are likely to be making more money than you did a decade ago. The problem is, you also are probably faced with a slew of financial distractions. Your children need a college education. Your aging parents want financial help. You still have that mortgage to pay off.

But whatever the other financial demands, it is important at this age that you do not shortchange your retirement savings. If you have not started accumulating a healthy sum of money by now, you really owe it to yourself to begin. Otherwise, you may never be able to afford the comfortable retirement you want. Those who have delayed saving for retirement until their 40s should look to stash away 20% of their pretax income each year. If you have been saving regularly since your early 30s, try to squirrel away 10% to 15% annually.

Aim to make smart use of tax-advantaged investment plans, including Individual Retirement Accounts and employer-sponsored 401(k) retirement savings programs. If you are self-employed or have a sideline job, you can contribute some of your income from self-employment to tax-favored Keogh and Simplified Employee Pension plans.

Employer-sponsored 401(k) plans, which allow you to have money deducted from your pretax pay and put into a variety of investment options, are especially attractive—providing you use them wisely. The money deducted from your pay lowers your tax bill, and many employers add as much as 50 cents of their own money for every dollar an employee contributes, up to a certain limit. The money grows tax-deferred until you take it out. If you change jobs, you can transfer your 401(k) balance to an Individual Retirement Account or your new employer's retirement plan.

STICK WITH STOCKS

Much of your investment money should continue to be shoveled into stocks and stock mutual funds. Although you will want to boost your bond holdings as retirement approaches, do not go overboard on fixed-income investments. One rule of thumb suggests you should subtract your age from 100 and then put that percentage of your portfolio into stocks. Using this rule, a 45-year-old should have 55% of his or her portfolio in stocks. That might seem like a lot. But in truth, the rule tends to generate rather conservative portfolios, and many middle-age investors would be well advised to put a higher percentage into stocks and stock funds.

Still, you have to take into account your own risk tolerance. Adding a small position in bonds can help to dampen the price gyrations of a stock portfolio, without sacrificing too much in performance.

Supersafe U.S. Treasury securities are a good choice. They are easy to buy and sell, they are backed by the full taxing authority of the federal government, and the interest they pay is exempt from state and local income taxes. The new inflation-indexed bonds that the Treasury was planning to introduce in late 1996 also promised to offer returns protecting investors from rising prices. But people in their 40s and 50s are often in the high tax brackets that make them prime candidates for tax-exempt municipal bonds. "Munis" are issued by state and local governments. The interest they pay is generally exempt from federal income tax, and it is exempt from state and local taxes as well, for in-state investors. Because of the tax advantage, municipal bonds generally have lower yields than Treasury or corporate bonds. Yet once you consider the federal income tax on interest payments from Treasury securities and the federal and state income taxes on interest paid on corporate bonds, municipals are often an attractive investment for people in higher tax brackets. This is especially so for people who live in such high-tax states as California, Massachusetts, and New York.

If you have been investing regularly over the years, you may already have accumulated a sizable portfolio. Once a year, take the time to review what you have to make sure you are getting the most out of your investment dollars. Make a list of all your holdings, including those in 401(k) accounts and other retirement plans. Tally how much of your money is in stocks, bonds, and money market investments. Consider whether that asset allocation makes sense for you.

THE TAX MAN COMETH

Taxable bonds typically offer far higher yields than tax-free municipal bonds. But once you figure in taxes, you may be better off opting for municipals. The following table shows after-tax returns for five different federal income tax brackets. State and local taxes would further erode your pretax gains.

RETURN BEFORE TAXES (%)	RETURN AFTER TAXES IN FIVE FEDERAL TAX BRACKETS (%)				
	15%	28%	31%	36%	39.6%
5	4.25	3.6	3.45	3.2	3.02
6	5.1	4.32	4.14	3.84	3.62
7	5.95	5.04	4.83	4.48	4.23
8	6.8	5.76	5.52	5.12	4.83
9	7.65	6.48	6.21	5.76	5.44
10	8.5	7.2	6.9	6.4	6.04

WEED OUT THE LAGGARDS

Every year, you should also review each individual security and fund to see how it has performed over the past three years compared with similar stocks and funds. Weed out the laggards, aiming to reduce the overall number of holdings. Most investors buy funds on an ad hoc basis, so that they end up with a host of different funds, many of which pursue the same investment objectives. If you own more than a dozen funds, you probably own too many. Avoid overly complicated financial products. Among the investments you can live without are limited partnerships, futures, and options.

Making mutual funds the backbone of your portfolio is probably the easiest way to reach your investment objectives. If you enjoy picking stocks and you have the time and skill it takes to be good at it, you may also want to cherry pick some individual issues in an effort to enhance your portfolio's performance. Keep in mind, though, that according to some studies, over 90% of a portfolio's return is determined not by which investments you own but by your asset allocation: how much of the portfolio is in

40s–50s

- Review asset allocation.
- Cut number of funds.
- Dump losers.
- Go easy on employer's stock.
- Consider municipal bonds.

stocks, how much is in bonds, and how much is in supersafe investments.

Be particularly leery of betting too much money on any one stock, especially if it is your employer's stock. You may think the prospects for your company are wonderful. But what happens if your employer gets into regulatory trouble, or its accounting turns out to be phony, or the company's product becomes uncompetitive? You could end up both unemployed and owning a fistful of worthless shares.

In selecting mutual funds, look for funds that tap into a particular stock market or bond market sector. For instance, consider buying funds that specialize in larger-company stocks, smaller-company stocks, and foreign stocks. Within these categories, you could diversify even further, by investing with fund managers who have a distinctive investment style. Some investment managers focus on "value," looking for bargains among the stocks of companies that appear cheap compared with their earnings or assets; other managers follow a "growth" investment style, buying stocks that may have little or nothing in the way of current earnings but have the potential for rapid earnings growth. Among foreign-stock funds, you might want to own one fund that invests in developed markets like Germany, Japan, and the United Kingdom, and another that specializes in emerging markets like Malaysia, Thailand, and Turkey.

BE TAX SMART

You want to reserve investments that generate big tax bills for tax-sheltered retirement accounts and save tax-efficient investments for your taxable account. For instance, consider putting stocks with rich dividend yields in your retirement account, where you will not have to pay taxes on the dividends until you withdraw the money. Reserve low-yield growth stocks for your taxable money. Similarly, put corporate bonds in your retirement account and Treasury bonds in your taxable account. Why? The interest on government bonds is not subject to state and local taxes.

A PORTFOLIO FOR YOUR 40S AND 50S

As you grow older, consider reducing your stock holdings. But do not go overboard. Plan on owning a healthy amount of stock throughout your 40s and 50s, and even into retirement.

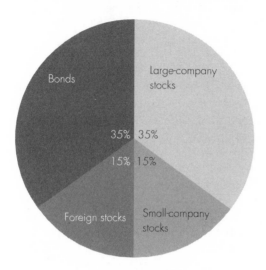

Never put investments that are already tax-advantaged—such as an annuity or a tax-free municipal bond—in a tax-favored retirement plan like an Individual Retirement Account: You will not gain any additional tax savings and you could end up having to pay unnecessary taxes on the income generated by the investment when you finally withdraw the money from the retirement plan.

What if you have been virtuous and are now thinking about early retirement? Before saying good-bye to your boss, make sure you have sufficient funds to carry you through a retirement that might last 30 or 35 years. One rough guideline suggests that—providing you hold a balanced portfolio of 50% stocks and 50% bonds—you can spend 4% or 5% of your money each year and still have enough growth to keep up with inflation. That means that you will need at least $1 million in savings if you want $50,000 in pretax annual retirement income from your portfolio. This money would be on top of Social Security and any pension you might receive.

ANNUITIES SHOULD NOT BE YOUR FIRST CHOICE

Thanks to the understandable desire to avoid paying more taxes than you have to, tax-deferred annuities—especially variable annuities—have exploded in popularity. With an annuity, you can contribute as much as you want each year, and you are not constrained by how much earned income you have. The money grows tax-deferred until you withdraw it.

But annuities also come with some hefty disadvantages. These include sizable annual fees and surrender charges for withdrawals during the first seven years or so. With variable annuities, which allow you to decide how to invest your money among an assortment of investment funds, or "subaccounts," you also have to pay the annual expenses of the investment funds. When you finally take the money out, investment earnings are subject to tax at ordinary income tax rates—even if those earnings reflect gains that would be taxed at lower capital-gains rates if your investment were in an ordinary, taxable account.

Because of these drawbacks, you may be better off keeping the money in a taxable account and using it to buy and hold a collection of stocks or stock mutual funds. The longer you hang onto the stocks, the longer you delay paying taxes on the capital gains that you have earned. And when you do sell, those gains will be taxed at preferential capital-gains rates.

In any event, you should not consider buying an annuity until after you have taken advantage of other opportunities for tax-deferred investment growth, such as a 401(k) plan at work. These employer-sponsored retirement-savings plans not only make possible tax-deferred growth, but they also are funded with pre-tax dollars; in effect, Uncle Sam picks up part of the tab. Moreover, many employers match at least part of their employees' contributions.

What if you have made the maximum possible contribution to your company and Individual Retirement Accounts, and you still have additional retirement money to sock away? At that point, a variable annuity could make sense. But when you pick an annuity, lean toward those with modest annual expenses and no surrender charges, and make sure that most of the subaccounts in the annuity have good performance records. Also plan on putting all or most of your money into one or two of the subaccounts that invest in stocks. Why? To overcome the high expenses of a variable annuity, you need the high returns that typically come only from stock market investing.

YOUR 60S AND BEYOND

By the time you reach your 60s, you may have learned quite a bit about investing. That is good, because once you retire, you will need everything you know—and then some. After you leave the workforce, your standard of living depends on Social Security, your company pension, and your retirement savings.

Sound scary? Think of it as an opportunity rather than a burden. If you manage your money well, your retirement could turn out to be anything but frugal. But to achieve investment success in retirement, it is imperative that you continue to invest for growth and not allow yourself to be driven by your understandable concerns about the need for current income. If you retire at age 65, you could well live another 20 years. Very few people reach retirement with a big enough nest egg that they can afford to sit back and simply live off the interest for two decades.

YOU STILL NEED STOCKS

At your age, you still need to keep a healthy chunk of your money in the stock market. One rule of thumb suggests that you subtract your age from 100, then put that percentage of your portfolio into stocks and stock funds. A 65-year-old, for instance, might keep 35% of his or her investment portfolio in stocks. But many retirees may want to keep as much as 50% of their portfolios in stocks. Even the most skittish individuals probably should not let their stock positions drop below 30%.

Does that surprise you? After all, retirees do need income from their portfolios. And most of us have been led to believe that investing for income means forsaking growth and focusing on yield. We have also been taught that stocks are dangerous and bonds are safe. Why else do they call bonds "fixed-income" investments?

But investing for "yield" is a dangerous mistake. So is simply writing off stocks as risky and counting on bonds to be secure. Too many retirees make both of those errors.

To begin with, if you buy investments only if they generate a high level of current income, you will end up with most of your money in certificates of deposit, bonds, and "fixed annuities," which are a type of insurance contract that pays a fixed rate of return. Although these investments do generate a fair amount of income, they usually produce little or nothing in the way of capital gains. As a result, the real, after-inflation value of your investment and the income it generates will gradually decline as the cost of living rises.

At a modest 3% inflation rate, for instance, your retirement lifestyle will become increasingly grim as the purchasing power of your money is cut in half in just 23 years. To fend off that threat, you must ensure that your portfolio's value continues to grow along with inflation.

BEWARE OF HIDDEN RISKS

There is also another problem with simply shopping for investments with the highest yields: That approach can—and often does—lead investors to take risks that they are not prepared for and, in many cases, do not even realize they are taking.

Consider high-yield "junk" bond funds. These are mutual funds that specialize in buying bonds that are rated below investment grade by the major credit-rating agencies or that have no rating at all. They can be very appealing to someone looking for current income because they typically kick off more immediate income than any other type of mutual fund. But companies that issue junk bonds occasionally default, which causes their bonds to fall in price and, thus, drags down the share price of any junk-bond fund that owns those issues. In effect, the fat dividend checks that you receive from a junk-bond fund will often come at the expense of a decline in the fund's share price. For unsuspecting investors, that can be a nasty surprise.

You say you would never be so foolish as to put your retirement money in junk of any kind? Maybe. But in the early part of the 1990s, many investors bought U.S. government bond funds thinking their holdings would be as safe as Fort Knox. What they did not realize was that many of the U.S. government bonds in those funds were really so-called derivative securities—bonds that had been taken apart and reassembled by Wall Street wizards to create hybrid securities with customized performance characteristics. Unfortunately, many of those souped-up derivative securities did not work as expected, and investors lost a lot of money.

The truth is that even plain-vanilla U.S. Treasury securities can lose money. And the risk is especially great for people who buy bond funds rather than individual bonds. In 1994, a devastating year for bond market investments of all kinds, mutual funds that invest in long-term U.S. Treasury bonds lost an average of 6.31%—even after taking interest payments into account.

Yes, the government does guarantee that you will get your interest payments, even if it has to raise taxes. If you buy a Treasury note or bond and hold it until maturity, you will definitely get back exactly what you are promised, plus those interest payments. But the prices of all bonds—including Treasury securities—rise when interest rates fall and fall when interest rates rise. If you have to sell before the bond's maturity date, you can indeed lose money.

With bond funds, you can lose money even more easily because the funds never mature. Instead, they carry on forever, with their share prices changing daily to reflect the changes in the value of the bonds they hold. Many retirees have come to recognize this only belatedly: After collecting years of generous interest payments, they are horrified to find that the value of their bond fund is substantially less than the sums they invested.

PAY ATTENTION TO "TOTAL RETURN"

So what should you do? Invest for "total return." Total return consists of the income generated by an investment and any rise or fall in the investment's value. Getting some growth from your portfolio, rather than just income, is especially important if the bulk of your retirement income is from a company pension that is fixed and, thus, not adjusted upward with the increase in the cost of living.

The best way to obtain a decent total return is to invest a healthy portion of your portfolio in stocks and stock mutual funds. That advice is anathema to many retirees, who fear their wealth will be devoured in a stock market crash. But adding a small position in stocks will not necessarily boost your portfolio's risk level. Indeed, history suggests that, over time, a portfolio that is 25% in stocks and 75% in bonds is no more risky—but much more rewarding— than an all-bond portfolio. That is because stocks and bonds do not always rise and fall in tandem. When bond prices are hit, stock prices may provide offsetting gains that smooth out your portfolio's performance.

With a portfolio that is 50% in stocks and 50% in bonds, you may be able to cash in up to 5% of your investment portfolio each year, to meet spending needs and pay taxes, and still receive sufficient capital gains to allay the threat from inflation.

Here is how the math works. Although year-to-year results can vary sharply, on average, stocks have historically delivered over 10% a year, bonds have returned between 5% and 6%, and inflation has run at 3%. Based on those historical results, if you split your money equally between stocks and bonds, your overall portfolio's return would be around 8%. With that sort of gain, if you withdrew 5% of your money each year and left the other 3% in your portfolio, your portfolio's growth would match the 3% inflation rate. In the real world, your results would vary from year to year, and you would surely have years when your portfolio actually lost value. But over time, history is on your side.

Moreover, you do not have to buy the most aggressive stocks. Dividend-paying "blue-chip" stocks and stock mutual funds that focus on more established, dividend-paying companies (often called "equity-income" or "growth-and-income" funds) can be smart choices. That is because high-yielding stocks tend to be more sedate and less prone to dramatic short-term losses than other stock market investments. But do not entirely ignore more aggressive areas of the stock market, such as foreign stocks and small companies.

THREE INCOME-GENERATING STRATEGIES

What about getting income from your portfolio? Here are three investment strategies for generating income from a portfolio while still getting enough growth to offset the corrosive effect of inflation.

The first strategy is the simplest. All you have to do is buy one or two "balanced" funds. A balanced fund is a mutual fund that owns a mix of stocks and bonds. Some balanced funds actively vary the mix, but most settle for a fixed allocation of 60% stocks and 40% bonds. With a balanced fund, you should be able to cash in around 5% of your fund holdings each year and still have enough growth to keep up with inflation. This presumes that you reinvest your income and capital-gains distributions in additional fund shares. Alternatively, you could take those distributions in cash and then sell a few shares each year to hit your 5% target.

But balanced funds have some drawbacks. The stock portion tends to be invested exclusively in blue-chip U.S. stocks, so you do not get the benefits that come from diversifying into smaller companies and foreign stocks. Meanwhile, the bond portion is usually spread across a mix of government and corporate bonds. People in a high tax bracket may be better off with some of their money in municipal bonds, which usually pay interest that is exempt from federal income tax and, for in-state investors, from state and local taxes, as well.

If you want tax-free income or you wish to be more adventurous with your stock portfolio, consider a second strategy: Build your own balanced portfolio. You can replicate the asset allocation of a balanced fund by dividing your money between stocks and bonds. But with the second strategy, you can pick the stock and bond investments yourself, thereby fine-tuning your portfolio. You might, for instance, try to select the best stock mutual funds from a variety of market sectors, including blue-chip, small-company, and foreign stocks. Meanwhile, for the bond portion of your customized balanced portfolio, you may want to combine municipal-bond, government-bond, and foreign-bond funds. Or if you want to make your customized balanced portfolio even safer, you might consider adding a healthy helping of the inflation-indexed Treasury bonds that the government planned to introduce in 1996.

With this second strategy, you can obtain income from your portfolio by taking your dividends and interest payments in cash and by occasionally selling investments. When selling, you may want to trim the stock and bond investments that have recently performed best. You can leave alone investments that are struggling, so they have a chance to bounce back.

The first and second strategies share one major drawback. Although they rely on a mix of stocks and bonds, stocks and bonds are occasionally hit hard in the same year. As a result, you could be forced to sell investments when they are at depressed prices.

The third strategy avoids that problem. With this strategy, you take three years of spending money and pop it into a money market mutual fund, certificates of deposit, or short-term Treasury securities. If you are aiming to spend 5% of your portfolio each year, you would wind up with 15% of your money in some sort of supersafe investment. By tucking this money away, you create a cushion. No matter what happens to the stock and bond markets over the next few years, you know that you have three years of spending money that is easily available.

What do you do with the rest of your money, the other 85% that is not in supersafe investments? Be as aggressive as you want. As an extreme example, imagine that you put most of the 85% in stocks, with a small amount in bonds. Every year, you would cash in a portion of your stocks to replenish your three-year supply of spending money. What happens if the stock market crashes? Do not sell any stocks that year. Instead, wait for stock prices to recover. Because you have three years of spending money in supersafe investments, you can sit on your hands until the market recovers.

Is three years really going to be long enough? Since World War II, there has been only one market crash—1973–74—when it took longer than three years for the market to return to its previous peak level, as measured by the total return of Standard & Poor's 500-stock index. But even then, the recovery did not take too long. Investors who sat tight through the 1973–74 market drop had to wait fewer than four years for stock prices to touch bottom and then return to their precrash high.

TAP TAXABLE ACCOUNTS FIRST

As you enter retirement, and in the years that follow, it is important to pay attention to which investment accounts you draw on first. Unless you are among the most affluent or those in a few special circumstances, it is usually wise to use the annual earnings and the accumulated value of your taxable investments and bank accounts before dipping into tax-advantaged retirement plans, such as employer-sponsored 401(k) plans and Individual Retirement Accounts. (You can learn more about withdrawing money from retirement-savings plans by reading the section on Tapping Retirement Assets in the Guide to Retirement Planning, Appendix D.)

60s +

- Invest for total return.

- Be mindful of inflation.

- Watch fixed-income risks.

- Build a balanced portfolio.

- Tap taxable accounts first.

Indeed, with so much at stake, it pays to proceed cautiously in evaluating your retirement investments and mapping out your retirement-investment strategy. Because the transition from work

TWO PORTFOLIOS FOR YOUR 60S AND BEYOND

A classic balanced portfolio—with equal amounts of stocks and bonds—is a good choice for many retirees. But if you like the idea of holding a cushion of cash, plan on holding more stocks to compensate for the low returns you will earn on your cash holdings.

A BALANCED PORTFOLIO

Bonds 50%

Large-company stocks

30%

10%

10%

Small-company stocks

Foreign stocks

STOCKS AND BONDS
CUSHIONED WITH CASH

Cash

Large-company stocks

15%

35%

Bonds 25%

13% 12%

Foreign stocks

Small-company stocks

to retirement is one of the stages of life at which it can make sense to get professional advice, some people will want to seek help from a financial planner to get retirement off to a good start. If you think that is what you would like to do, be cautious: There have been too many horror stories of retired investors led astray by commission-hungry salespeople, including some who presented themselves as "financial planners." Before calling a planner, at least spend enough time with the other sections in this book devoted to Your 60s and Beyond to familiarize yourself with the important issues. (Also review the information on financial planners in Chapter 1.)

WHAT ABOUT AN IMMEDIATE ANNUITY?

Immediate annuities are old-fashioned insurance products that have a great deal of appeal for some investors because they deliver a check a month for life, and a portion of that check is tax-free. But immediate annuities also have several drawbacks, not the least of which is that the purchase is usually irrevocable.

The monthly checks investors receive from immediate annuities are typically larger, sometimes several times larger, than the interest payments they receive on certificates of deposit. But the main reason is that a portion of the monthly payout is the return of a part of your original investment. That is also the reason there is no income tax on part of the monthly payments; such a "return of principal" is always tax-free.

Another drawback to consider is that the payments of most immediate annuities do not rise with inflation. There are some contracts that offer rising payouts, but the initial checks are smaller than those from annuities with fixed payments. (There are also a few variable immediate annuities where the payouts vary with the performance of the underlying investment funds.)

Because of the various drawbacks of immediate annuities, even some insurance-industry executives recommend that retirees put no more than a quarter of their money in such contracts. And if you do decide to put part of your money in an immediate annuity, it is wise to check the offerings of several insurers before handing over your money. There can be many differences from company to company.

Comparison shopping is especially critical for those who are about to quit the workforce. Often, a company will allow an insurer to offer annuities to its employees. The employer, however, may not have checked out either the annuities offered or competing products. As a result, employees would be well advised to do some comparison shopping on their own.

BUILDING A PORTFOLIO YOU CAN LIVE WITH

Every investment is risky. The question is, what sort of risk should you be taking?

Supersafe "cash" investments, such as certificates of deposit, Treasury bills, money market mutual funds, and savings accounts, are often called "risk-free." If risk is defined as the chance of losing principal, then this label is well deserved. You are highly unlikely to lose the money you put in a money fund or a CD.

That is why these investments are smart places to squirrel away money you might need soon, like your down payment on a new house or your emergency money. When it comes time to buy your new home or tap into your emergency reserve, you want to be absolutely sure that the full amount is still there.

But even though you cannot lose money with a savings account or a Treasury bill, such investments are not truly 100% risk-free. In fact, these conservative investments leave you wide open to one devastating risk—the risk that the value of your money will be eroded by inflation.

Figure in inflation and taxes, and you will probably make little or no money owning CDs, Treasury bills, and their ilk. That is not a big problem if you are just parking some cash for a brief period while you wait to buy a house or pay for next semester's tuition. But the corrosive effect of inflation is a major problem for long-term investors, who are looking to pay for retirement or their newborn's college education.

For long-term investors, these supersafe investments are totally inadequate, because they do not generate healthy inflation-beating gains. Instead, people who are investing for the long haul need to own securities with a proven track record of outperforming inflation. Bonds have managed that feat to a modest extent. And the new inflation-indexed bonds that the Treasury was planning to introduce in late 1996 promise returns that keep investors ahead of inflation. But in the pantheon of inflation-beating investments, stocks are the true heroes.

FINDING THE RIGHT MIX

Many investors think the secret to success on Wall Street is finding the next superstock or guessing which way the market is headed. Not so. Over 90% of a portfolio's return is determined by one simple decision—how much of the money is in stocks, how much is in bonds, and how much is in supersafe cash investments. This is your so-called asset allocation.

It should be no great surprise that asset allocation is so important. History shows that stocks generally outperform bonds and bonds typically beat cash. Even if you have the good fortune to pick some stellar stocks, you will find it hard to beat the stock market averages if you have half your portfolio in bonds. Similarly, even if you buy a bond fund that is run by a superb money manager, that fund is still unlikely to outperform even a mediocre stock fund.

What does this mean for your investments? If you want to boost your portfolio's long-run results, the simplest, most surefire strategy is to cut back on bonds and cash and increase your holdings of stocks.

YOUR TIME HORIZON IS CRUCIAL

That advice does not mean you should bet heavily on stocks at all times, nor does it mean that you can settle on an asset allocation and then call it quits. Your asset allocation will depend partly on your tolerance for market price swings. But a much more important consideration is your time horizon. Even the most aggressive investors should own conservative investments if they will need to get their hands on the money in just one or two years. Conversely, even the most risk-adverse investors should consider a healthy dose of stocks if they are investing for a retirement that is 20 or more years away.

As you draw closer to your investment goal, you should gradually change your investment mix. If you are investing your daughter's college savings, for instance, you should be far more aggressive with the asset allocation when she is 5 than when she is 15. Similarly, the closer you get to retirement, the more conservative you should be with your retirement savings.

In addition to varying your asset allocation as you approach your investment goal, you should also look to rebalance your portfolio regularly. Left unchecked, your portfolio will become increasingly aggressive. How so? Because your stocks will tend to generate the highest returns, they will grow to take up an ever larger share of your portfolio, and your portfolio will, thus, become increasingly risky.

To combat that threat, you should aim to rebalance your portfolio once or twice a year by adding to the sectors that have done poorly and trimming back those that have done well. Sometimes you will be adding to the stock portion, if stocks have recently done poorly. Most of the time, though, you will be moving the money to other areas.

One way to do that is to take some of the profits from your stock market investments and reinvest that money in bonds and cash. But when you sell an investment that has appreciated in value, you will realize a capital gain on which you may have to pay taxes. You can minimize this problem by regularly adding money to your portfolio

AVOID "MARKET TIMING"

Establishing an asset allocation and then occasionally rebalancing should not be confused with "market timing." Market timing is a controversial strategy that involves shifting in and out of stocks in an effort to catch bull markets but sidestep market crashes. Market timing is an appealing concept, but unfortunately successful practitioners are rare indeed. One problem is that market gains tend to happen relatively quickly, so it is easy for market timers to miss out on those gains. Many investment experts believe it is better to settle on a mix of stocks, bonds, and cash and then stick tenaciously with this mix through good times and bad.

RISK REWARDED

Picking a winning stock or a topflight bond fund will certainly help your portfolio's return. But the driving force behind your long-run investment performance is your asset allocation—how you divvy up your money among stocks, bonds, and cash.

PORTFOLIO	ANNUALIZED RETURN 1926–1995 (%)
Aggressive (90% stocks, 10% bonds)	10.2
Growth (75% stocks, 25% bonds)	9.6
Balanced (60% stocks, 30% bonds, 10% cash)	8.7
Conservative (40% stocks, 30% bonds, 30% cash)	7.4
Income (20% stocks, 40% bonds, 40% cash)	6.0

NOTE: Stocks are represented by the Standard & Poor's 500-stock index, bonds by intermediate-term government bonds, and cash by 30-day Treasury bills.
SOURCE: © *Stocks, Bonds, Bills, and Inflation 1996 Yearbook*™, Ibbotson Associates, Chicago (annually updates work by Roger G. Ibbotson and Rex A. Sinquefield). Used with permission. All rights reserved.

and using it to help bring your portfolio back into balance. You simply use this new money to buy investments in "underweighted" areas.

SPREADING YOUR RISKS

Do not put all your eggs in one basket. You have probably heard that so often that it has become a cliché. But it is sound advice when it comes to building an all-weather investment portfolio.

A properly diversified portfolio should produce reasonable returns in most market environments, thus giving you a smoother ride over the market's bumps. Diversification works because not all investments do well at the same time; nor do they all do poorly at the same time. When bonds are struggling, stocks may provide offsetting gains. When auto stocks are stalled, computer stocks may be sizzling. When U.S. stocks are in the dumps, foreign stocks may take up the slack. When everything else fails, gold, real estate, and other hard assets may rescue your portfolio.

Diversification not only will make your portfolio more tranquil, it also may lead to better investment results. The reason is that a well-diversified portfolio will tend to cushion you from rude market shocks, making you more willing to take on greater risk by putting more of your portfolio into stocks. That, in turn, should raise your long-run returns.

PERFORMANCE VERSUS TRANQUILITY

You will achieve some diversification when you decide on your asset allocation and spread your money among the three major asset categories: stocks, bonds, and supersafe cash investments. When picking among these categories, you make a trade-off between performance and tranquility. The more you put in stocks, the higher your returns but the greater your portfolio's price gyrations. The more you sink into bonds and supersafe investments, the greater your portfolio's tranquility but the lower your portfolio's return.

Owning hard assets can also help to dampen the swings in your portfolio's value. The impact on performance will depend on which hard assets you own. Real estate, energy stocks, and basic-materials companies, such as paper and chemical makers, will tend to help your portfolio's performance while also making it more tranquil. Gold is more effective in calming a portfolio's price swings, but its contribution to your long-run return will be negligible. Keep in mind that if you own your own home, you already have a big investment in real estate. Unless you have a very large portfolio, it may not make sense to take on even more exposure to hard assets.

But deciding how to allocate money among the broad asset categories is just the beginning. To have a well-diversified portfolio, you also need to make sure you own securities within each asset category that are spread across a number of market sectors. This is especially important when investing in stocks. If you buy individual stocks, consider investing in at least 15 or 20 different companies. By owning a broad array of companies, you reduce the chance that your portfolio will be badly hurt if a single stock gets pummeled.

An easy way to achieve that sort of diversification is to buy a stock mutual fund, which might own anywhere from 20 to 300 stocks. But even if you buy a mutual fund, you may find that you are still making a fairly concentrated bet. Most stock funds invest in just one segment of the market. They may, for instance, specialize in blue-chip stocks, smaller-company stocks, or foreign stocks.

AIM FOR BROAD MARKET EXPOSURE

You may want to own a variety of stock funds to ensure that you achieve broad stock market exposure. Similarly, if you prefer to pick your own stocks, try to own companies from a variety of industries and consider using funds to tap into market sectors where you have no exposure.

Bond investors can also end up making fairly concentrated bets. Just as stock investors tend to have a disproportionate amount of their portfolio in American blue-chip stocks, so bond investors tend to have much of their money in U.S. government and municipal bonds. These top-quality bonds are considered extremely safe. Indeed, Treasury securities are backed by the full taxing authority of the U.S. government, so investors are guaranteed to receive the promised interest payments.

But these bonds tend to be hit hard when interest rates rise. One way to reduce your vulnerability to interest-rate changes is to hold bonds of various maturities. When interest rates rise, the prices of all bonds fall. But a one-percentage-point increase in interest rates has a bigger impact on long-term bonds, which typically mature in 20 or 30 years, than on intermediate-term bonds, which generally mature in 10 years or less. Least affected are short-term bonds, which mature within 2 or 3 years.

Investors in U.S. government and municipal bonds may also want to move some of their bond money—only a small part of it—into foreign bonds and junk bonds, which are less affected by U.S. interest-rate changes. For U.S. investors, the performance of foreign bonds is driven primarily by events overseas and changes in the dollar's value in world currency markets. The performance of junk bonds, which are issued by companies whose financial condition is considered sufficiently precarious that they might default on their interest payments, tends to be driven by the overall performance of the economy and by the health of individual issuers. For taking on the added risk that comes with junk bonds, investors earn higher yields than those who stick with safer bonds.

DIFFERENT MATURITIES, DIFFERENT REACTIONS

Prices of longer-term bonds are more vulnerable to interest-rate changes than are prices of shorter-term bonds.

MATURITY OF BOND	PRICE CHANGE WITH VARYING INTEREST-RATE MOVES (%)			
	–2 POINTS	–1 POINT	+1 POINT	+2 POINTS
2 years	+3.8	+1.9	–1.8	–3.6
5 years	+8.8	+4.3	–4.1	–7.9
10 years	+15.6	+7.4	–6.8	–13.0
20 years	+25.1	+11.6	–9.9	–18.4
30 years	+30.9	+13.8	–11.3	–20.6

NOTE: This table assumes that each bond initially trades at its par, or face, value and yields 7%. Your actual gain or loss may be somewhat different, depending on how much interest you collect during the course of the interest-rate change.
SOURCE: The Vanguard Group of Investment Companies.

Get Help or Go It Alone?

To use a broker or not to use a broker, that is the question. How should you decide? Contrary to what you might believe, the decisive factor should not be laziness or ignorance.

A good broker can provide a number of valuable services, beyond buying and selling stocks, bonds, and other investments. He or she can help you establish an investment plan and pick investments, encourage you to become more financially disciplined, and push you to take action. A broker can also prod you to take greater risk and then—when the market dives and you start to panic—stand there as a buffer, making sure you do not dump your investments at a bad time.

But do not think that you can select a broker, hand over your cash, and then forget about it. That would be extremely unwise. A broker is there to help you make investment decisions, not to make them for you.

KEEP FULLY INFORMED

In order to give you good advice, a broker has to understand fully what your investment goals are, what sort of investments you are comfortable with, and what else is happening in your financial life. You, in turn, need to keep yourself fully informed about what is going on in your account and why particular investment decisions are being made.

If you fail to take those precautions, you leave yourself wide open to three sorts of problems. To begin with, your broker could make investments that—while perfectly sensible—are not right for you. Or you could find yourself at the mercy of one of the many brokers who are inexperienced or not particularly knowledgeable. Finally, as anybody who has ever read the financial pages knows, there are unfortunately a number of unscrupulous brokers out there. Brokers typically are paid based on the amount you trade, so some brokers encourage their clients to trade excessively or buy high-commission investments in an effort to generate fat commissions for themselves. Even if your broker seems like a nice person, it pays to be vigilant.

After all, your broker will probably be handling the bulk of your life's savings.

If what you are really looking for is some help in starting your investment program, or if you want to make sure your investments are on track, consider using a financial planner rather than a broker. Many financial planners work on a fee-only basis, and will discuss your investments in return for an hourly fee. Periodically using a financial planner may turn out to be much cheaper than trading through a broker. (Refer to Chapter 1 for advice on finding a reliable financial planner.)

THE DO-IT-YOURSELF APPROACH

You may, on the other hand, feel that you do not need any help at all. If so, you can save yourself a bundle of money when you buy and sell securities. You can pick no-load mutual funds, which are mutual funds that either do not charge a sales commission or charge only a small one. No-load funds are typically sold directly by a mutual fund company. In contrast, the load funds sold through brokers levy up-front fees of as much as 8.5%.

You can also use a discount broker rather than a full-service broker. That way, you will typically pay 60% less in commissions when buying and selling individual stocks. Some discount brokers will save you even more. Discount brokers fall into two camps: regular discount brokers, such as San Francisco's Charles Schwab, Boston's Fidelity Brokerage, and New York's Quick & Reilly; and so-called deep discounters. The deep discounters include Boston's Brown & Company; R. J. Forbes Group of Melville, New York; Kennedy, Cabot & Company of Beverly Hills, California; New York's National Discount Brokers; and Pacific Brokerage Services of Los Angeles. Deep discounters often charge just half of what regular discounters charge. But there is a trade-off. Regular discounters generally handle a broader selection of securities, including precious metals, mutual funds, and commodities, and they sometimes offer services not available from deep discounters.

HOW TO FIND A BROKER YOU CAN TRUST

You may come across a broker because you received a recommendation from a friend, or because the broker called you out of the blue to solicit your business, or because you attended a financial seminar given by the broker. These are all perfectly legitimate ways of hearing about a broker. But before you agree to buy anything, run two checks.

The first check involves contacting your state securities department. (You can find the phone number or address in Appendix A.) Ask one of the department's employees to help you check out the broker and his or her employer by tapping into the Central Registration Depository, a computer database that keeps tabs on anybody registered to sell securities. The database will tell you about the broker's education, employment history, and any legal troubles. Not only do you want a broker who is squeaky clean, but you also want one who is experienced and does not constantly jump from one firm to the next.

For the second check, you will have to rely on your own judgment. Arrange to sit down with the broker, and see what happens. Does the broker find out as much about you as possible, and then talk about developing an investment plan that will help you meet your financial goals? Or does the broker just try to sell you a few investments? You clearly want a broker who really wants to help you, rather than one who is purely geared toward generating commissions by flogging the fund of the month or the stock of the day.

CONSIDER THE COSTS

If you avoid brokers and instead invest on your own, you can save on brokerage commissions when buying and selling stocks, bonds, and mutual funds. But the costs of investing do not stop with commissions.

Investors also have to contend with such items as annual mutual fund expenses, account-maintenance fees, and trading spreads—not to mention the biggest investment expense of all, taxes. It is worth paying attention to investment costs, because that is one facet of investing that you really can control. When you pick a mutual fund or a stock, it is impossible to know whether you have a winning investment. But if you keep a tight lid on costs, you know for sure that you will improve your results. For instance, if you hold down the number of trades you make and how much you pay for those trades, you will clearly save on brokerage commissions.

Trading costs you may not think about include the so-called bid-ask spread, which is the gap between the price at which you can sell your stock or bond and the price at which you could buy the same security. The larger the spread, the more it costs to trade. This spread can be especially large with securities that are not actively traded. That is often the case with municipal bonds and the stocks of smaller companies.

With mutual funds, there are other costs to pay attention to. Funds fall into two camps, load and no-load, though it has become increasingly difficult to distinguish the two. No-load funds are sold directly to the public, while most load funds are sold through brokers. Load funds generally charge a sales commission either when you buy the fund or when you sell it.

Broker-sold funds have also taken to charging annual 12b-1 fees, which are used to compensate brokers. Some no-load funds also levy 12b-1 fees, and these fees go toward advertising and other marketing expenses. These 12b-1 fees are included in a fund's annual expenses. Annual expenses are charged by both load and no-load funds, and they cover such costs as shareholder servicing, advertising, and the fund manager's salary. Because many load funds now levy hefty 12b-1 fees, their expenses tend to be somewhat higher than those charged by no-load funds.

FUND EXPENSES CUT RETURNS

To find out about a fund's sales commissions and annual expenses, look in the fund's prospectus, which is the official sales document sent to prospective investors. Mutual fund annual expenses are expressed as a percentage of the fund's assets. Diversified U.S. stock funds generally charge expenses equal to around 1.3% or 1.4% of fund assets, whereas taxable bond funds typically have expense ratios of between 0.9% and 1%. These expenses directly reduce a fund's return, so it pays to stick with lower-cost funds. For instance, if a fund's portfolio earned 10% during the year and it had an expense ratio of 1%, the return to shareholders would be 9%; if the expense ratio were 2%, investors would receive only 8%.

Mutual funds and brokerage firms have also taken to charging account-maintenance fees. These fees are charged regardless of whether you do any trading. While these fees may seem relatively modest, they do add up, so you should be leery of having too many brokerage accounts and owning too many funds.

THE BEST WAY TO HOLD DOWN COSTS

The best way to hold down your investment costs is to become a tax-smart investor. How do you do that? For starters, make full use of tax-sheltered retirement accounts, such as 401(k) and 403(b) plans, Individual Retirement Accounts, Simplified Employee Pensions, and Keogh plans. With these retirement-savings plans, your investments will grow tax-deferred, and your contributions each year may also be tax-deductible.

How much is the tax deferral worth? Imagine two 25-year-olds, who each make a one-time investment of $1,000. One puts her money in a nondeductible IRA, while the other keeps it in a taxable account. Both investors see their money grow at 10% a year over the next 40 years. Each year, the taxable investor loses a third of his gains to federal and state taxes, but at age 65 he is still left with an impressive $13,200. But that is not nearly as impressive as the gain earned by the IRA investor. She cashes in her account at age 65 and is then hit with a massive tax bill on her 40 years of tax-deferred growth. But even after losing a third of her money to taxes, she still has $30,500 left.

If your employer offers a 401(k) or 403(b) plan, it should probably be the first place you funnel your retirement dollars. Not only will you get tax-deferred growth, but you also can fund these plans out of pretax dollars, thus lowering your current income tax bill. In addition, your employer may match all or part of your contributions.

Similarly, those who are self-employed or who work for a small business should make full use of their Keogh plan or Simplified Employee Pension, also know as a SEP or SEP-IRA. Keoghs and SEPs offer the twin benefits of tax deferral and tax deductibility. Even if you have a 401(k) or 403(b) plan at work, you can still use a Keogh or SEP if you have some income from moonlighting.

IRAs CAN BE ATTRACTIVE

After making full use of your 401(k), 403(b), Keogh, and SEP, turn your attention to your IRA. IRAs have become a less popular retirement savings vehicle, partly because contributions are limited to $2,000 a year and partly because contributions are no longer tax-deductible for many people. But IRAs also have some important advantages. Accounts are easy to set up and maintain and—unlike your employer's retirement plan—IRAs make possible an almost limitless number of investment choices. Indeed, IRAs can be a useful way of supplementing your employer's plan. If, for instance, your company plan does not include an emerging-markets fund, you can buy one using your IRA.

CONSIDER AN "INDEX" FUND

You can also obtain a good measure of tax-deferred growth by buying and holding stocks in a regular taxable account. Yes, you do have to pay income tax on any dividends those stocks pay. But you do not have to pay taxes on the capital gains that you have earned until you sell your stocks.

If you like the idea of buying and holding a portfolio of stocks, consider an index fund. These funds simply buy and hold the securities that comprise a particular market index, in an effort to match the index's performance. Because index funds usually sell a stock only if it is dropped from the index for one reason or another, such funds do not tend to generate large tax bills for their shareholders. Actively managed mutual funds, by contrast, often generate fairly large capital-gains distributions each year, on which shareholders then have to pay taxes.

Municipal bonds offer another way to keep Uncle Sam at bay. Municipal bonds kick off income that is usually exempt from federal taxes and, in some cases, state and local taxes as well. But do not buy municipals simply because you loathe paying taxes. If you are in a lower income tax bracket, you may be better off buying U.S. government bonds or corporate bonds and paying taxes on the interest. Moreover, municipals will not match the long-run performance of stocks, even with the taxes that will be due on your stock market gains.

STOCKS AND STOCK MUTUAL FUNDS

Stocks terrify investors. They should not.

The perils of stock market investing are well known. On any day that the stock market is open, you are likely to find at least one or two stocks that have been slapped down 15%, 20%, or even more. And while the victims are usually the stocks of smaller companies, major corporations are not immune to selling frenzy.

Sometimes, selling fever spreads throughout the entire market. On average, the broad U.S. stock market has posted a loss in one out of every three calendar years. Those market drops can be nerve-wracking for investors, especially those who are more accustomed to the safety and security of certificates of deposit and money market mutual funds.

But while the terror of stock market investing is well known, the virtues do not receive nearly enough attention. Stocks offer a way to participate in the economic growth and improving productivity of both the United States and foreign countries. As the economy grows and corporate profits rise, shareholders benefit through both higher dividend payouts and higher stock prices.

SOME MAJOR BENEFITS

Stocks are your best bet if you want long-run, inflation-beating returns. According to Ibbotson Associates, stocks have historically outpaced inflation by seven percentage points a year. Bonds have beaten inflation by only two percentage points, and Treasury bills have kept ahead by just half a percentage point. With the benefits of compounding, stock market investors can reasonably expect that the real, inflation-adjusted value of their money will double every ten years. But with bonds, history suggests you would have to wait 35 years to get the same result.

Stocks usually make money for investors as long as they are willing to hold on for at least five years. Since World War II, there have been just two five-calendar-year stretches (1970–74 and 1973–77) when you would have lost money owning the stocks that comprise the Standard & Poor's 500-stock index. As your time horizon lengthens, the odds of making money get even better.

TIME HEALS ALL WOUNDS

Stock market returns fluctuate sharply over the short run. But if you stick with stocks for at least five years, you should have a good shot at making decent money. The following chart shows annualized five-year total returns since World War II for the Standard & Poor's 500-stock index. The average annual return over this period was 11.9%.

YEAR		RETURN (%)
1946–50		9.9
1947–51		16.7
1948–52		19.4
1949–53		17.9
1950–54		23.9
1951–55		23.9
1952–56		20.2
1953–57		13.6
1954–58		22.3
1955–59		15.0
1956–60		8.9
1957–61		12.8
1958–62		13.3
1959–63		9.9
1960–64		10.7
1961–65		13.3
1962–66		5.7
1963–67		12.4
1964–68		10.2
1965–69		5.0
1966–70		3.3
1967–71		8.4
1968–72		7.5
1969–73		2.0
1970–74		–2.4
1971–75		3.2

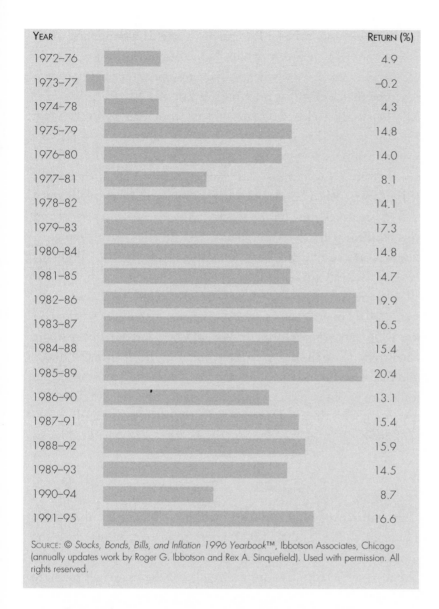

YEAR		RETURN (%)
1972–76		4.9
1973–77		–0.2
1974–78		4.3
1975–79		14.8
1976–80		14.0
1977–81		8.1
1978–82		14.1
1979–83		17.3
1980–84		14.8
1981–85		14.7
1982–86		19.9
1983–87		16.5
1984–88		15.4
1985–89		20.4
1986–90		13.1
1987–91		15.4
1988–92		15.9
1989–93		14.5
1990–94		8.7
1991–95		16.6

SOURCE: © *Stocks, Bonds, Bills, and Inflation 1996 Yearbook™*, Ibbotson Associates, Chicago (annually updates work by Roger G. Ibbotson and Rex A. Sinquefield). Used with permission. All rights reserved.

Stocks are also a great investment for people who want a reliable, steadily rising stream of income. In fact, dividends have typically accounted for half of the long-run total return earned by stock market investors. Because many companies regularly raise the dividends they pay to shareholders, the income kicked off by stocks tends to rise in most years. Historically, dividend increases have easily outstripped the inflation rate.

A stock's dividend measured as a percentage of the stock's price is called its "dividend yield." When you first buy a stock, its dividend yield will usually be far lower than the yield on bonds and often less than the yield on Treasury bills. Nonetheless, stocks—with their steadily rising stream of dividends—are in some ways a better source of income than either Treasury bills or bonds.

Treasury bill yields fluctuate widely from year to year. Since 1926, the payout has risen in 38 years and fallen in 30 years, according to Ibbotson Associates. Anybody who tried to live off the interest from Treasury bills could suffer sharp swings in their standard of living. With bonds, the interest you earn holds steady until the bond matures. But unlike stock dividends, the interest stream from bonds usually does not rise along with the cost of living, so those who try to live off the income from their bonds will gradually be squeezed by inflation.

To ensure you get the benefits of stocks, though, you have to have enough of them and you have to have time. The fewer stocks you own, the greater the chance that you will be badly hurt by a single rotten stock. The shorter your time horizon, the greater the likelihood that you will end up selling at a loss. As a result, most investors should aim to put together a well-diversified portfolio and then plan on sticking with the stock market for at least five years, and preferably longer.

SO MANY CHOICES

When putting together a stock portfolio, you have an unenviable amount of choice. Some 11,000 equity securities are listed on the New York Stock Exchange, the American Stock Exchange, and the Nasdaq Stock Market. Venture abroad, and the list grows by more than 50,000.

The choice is even more bewildering than it might initially seem. To begin with, there is common stock, which gives investors an ownership interest in a company. Common stock is what most people mean when they talk about stocks, but some companies also issue other types of securities. These include preferred stock and convertible bonds, which appeal to more conservative investors because they kick off a higher yield than the company's regular shares. Preferred stock gets its name because holders receive preferential treatment in certain areas. For example, preferred shareholders stand in line ahead of common-stock holders in case a company goes bust and its assets are liquidated. Convertible bonds are bonds that can be converted into a fixed amount of the issuer's common stock. Some preferred shares are also convertible into common stock. (If a preferred stock does not have a conversion feature, it is often more like a bond than a stock, and thus it offers little or no chance for capital gains.)

You can also invest in stocks by buying stock mutual funds. A fund will usually hold at least 20 stocks and will often own 100 or more. To buy a mutual fund, you usually purchase shares from the fund company itself, either with the help of a broker or by going directly to the fund. But some mutual funds are themselves listed on one of the stock exchanges. These are known as "closed-end" funds. A closed-end fund issues a fixed number of shares in an initial public offering. After the offering, the fund is closed to new investors and its shares are listed on a stock exchange. Thereafter, those who want to get in or out of the fund must buy or sell the publicly traded stock.

Many closed-end funds invest in bonds, so even though these funds are listed on the stock exchange, their performance is driven by events in the bond market. Similarly, the stock market offers the chance to invest in hard assets; you can purchase energy stocks, gold companies, and real estate investment trusts that often perform quite differently from regular stocks.

MUTUAL FUNDS VERSUS INDIVIDUAL STOCKS

At first blush, stock mutual funds appear to be a sorry group. Most funds fail to beat the stock market averages, not because their managers are incompetent, but because their performance is dragged down by trading costs and annual fund expenses. In addition, stock funds typically keep between 5% and 10% of their portfolios in cash, which tends to hold back performance when stock prices are rising.

Yet in recent years, stock funds have exploded in popularity because they offer a number of advantages over buying individual stocks:

• Finding a well-run fund is relatively easy.
• You receive the benefits of professional money management.

- Funds offer the chance to buy a broadly diversified portfolio for as little as $1,000.

- While funds may not beat the averages, they usually do not lag too far behind. If you buy a well-diversified fund run by a respected manager, you can be fairly confident that you will get the long-run benefits of stock market investing. For those who are trying to accumulate the huge sums needed to retire or send their children to college, that can be a great comfort.

Picking individual stocks is a riskier affair. While many stock funds own over 100 different stocks, individual investors generally just do not have the money to own more than 100 shares of 15 or 20 companies. Although there is a good chance that these 15 or 20 companies might together beat the market averages, there is also the risk that the stocks could trail the market badly.

It is also extremely difficult for most investors to diversify into foreign stocks if they stick with individual issues. They tend to lack familiarity with overseas markets and the differences in accounting systems and corporate disclosure requirements. The costs of buying and selling individual stocks in overseas markets also tend to be high. Some foreign companies trade in the United States as American Depositary Receipts (ADRs). But it can be tricky to build a well-diversified portfolio using ADRs. As a result, even die-hard stock-picking fanatics tend to use mutual funds when investing in foreign stocks. If you want a stock fund that invests exclusively abroad, buy an "international" fund rather than a "global" fund. Global funds own U.S. as well as overseas companies, whereas international funds purchase only overseas stocks.

By buying individual stocks, you will save on fund sales commissions and annual fund expenses. But you still have to contend with your own trading costs. Although you can keep your brokerage commissions low by using a discount broker, you are unlikely to trade as cheaply as a mutual fund, which typically pays rock-bottom institutional commission rates.

Buying individual stocks does have one clear-cut advantage, however. By sticking with individual stocks, you have much greater control over your annual tax bill. Each year, mutual funds pass on their investment gains to shareholders in the form of income and capital-gains distributions. Most investors choose to reinvest these distributions in additional fund shares. Nonetheless, they still have to pay taxes on these distributions. It is very difficult to know ahead of time just how big these distributions will be.

By contrast, if you own individual stocks, you can decide when to take profits and, thus, when you will pay taxes. You might, for instance, want to sell a stock. But you might decide to delay selling the position until after December 31, postponing the need to pay capital-gains taxes for an entire year.

DIVIDEND REINVESTMENT PLANS

If you own only 100 or 200 shares of a company, your quarterly dividend checks may be so small that they would not even cover a stockbroker's commission, yet alone allow you to buy more shares. What should you do? Some shareholders sign up for a company's dividend reinvestment plan.

With these plans, your quarterly dividends are automatically reinvested in additional shares—including fractional shares—at no commission. You can also make additional cash investments, usually on a monthly basis and often for as little as $10. Some companies even allow you to reinvest your dividends and make optional cash investments at a discount to the market price.

But despite the benefits, dividend reinvestment plans are not for everybody. While they might seem like a good way for small investors to build a substantial stock portfolio, you usually cannot enroll in a plan unless you own at least one or two shares, which can be costly to acquire.

Once in the plan, you can never be sure what price you will receive when you reinvest your dividends and make cash purchases. Because your investments often purchase fractional shares, the tax accounting can be messy. And when you finally decide to sell, you either have to ask the company to offload the shares—which means the selling price is uncertain—or you must sell the shares yourself, which means requesting a stock certificate and then waiting a few weeks for it to arrive.

If you are intrigued by dividend reinvestment plans, two good sources of information are the *Directory of Companies Offering Dividend Reinvestment Plans* (published by Evergreen Enterprises, Laurel, Maryland) and Standard & Poor's *Directory of Dividend Reinvestment Plans* (McGraw-Hill, New York).

How to Find a Winning Stock Fund

Before trying to pick funds, you first must decide what sort of funds you want to own. And that means deciding just how much financial complexity you are willing to endure.

You could, for instance, settle for a single fund that offers broad stock market exposure, including a smattering of blue-chip stocks, small-company stocks and foreign stocks. These sorts of funds are offered by many of the major fund groups, including Fidelity Investments, T. Rowe Price Associates, and Vanguard Group. Alternatively, you could build your own diversified portfolio by purchasing a large-company stock fund, a small-company stock fund, and a foreign fund.

Mutual fund junkies could go even further, by buying even more specialized funds. For instance, you could purchase two large-company stock funds, one that specializes in growth companies (which promise rapid earnings increases) and another that sticks with value stocks (which appear cheap when compared with current earnings or corporate assets). On Wall Street, the growth and value investment styles often go in and out of vogue at different times, so you can smooth out your portfolio's performance by owning both a large-company growth fund and a large-company value fund. You could also split your small-stock money between growth and value funds.

For foreign exposure, you might want to divide your money between a foreign-stock fund that invests in developed markets and another that confines itself to the emerging-stock markets of developing countries. Put it all together, and a full-fledged portfolio might include a large-company growth fund, a large-company value fund, a small-company growth fund, a small-company value fund, a foreign-stock fund, and an emerging-markets fund.

Once you have decided what sort of funds you want to own, picking the funds to build your desired portfolio becomes fairly easy. When selecting each fund for your portfolio, you have to consider three main issues:

• Will the fund perform well?

• How much will you pay to get that performance?

• How wild will the share price gyrations be along the way?

The cost issue is the easiest. When picking a stock fund, you want to make sure that the costs are not so high that the fund is unlikely to be a good investment. That means favoring funds that have moderate expenses and thinking twice before paying a sales commission to buy a fund. Diversified U.S. stock funds charge annual expenses of about 1.4%, on average. Small-company stock funds generally have higher expenses, as do foreign-stock funds. In general, try to avoid funds that have expenses that are higher than the industry average for the particular type of fund you want.

After you have taken a look at cost, consider risk. By owning a

PUTTING IT ALL TOGETHER

Here's what a well-diversified stock fund portfolio might look like. The portfolio does not include any bond funds or money market funds—which you may want to add, depending on your tolerance for risk.

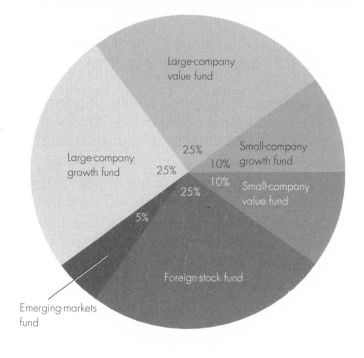

Large-company value fund

Large-company growth fund

Small-company growth fund

Small-company value fund

Foreign-stock fund

Emerging-markets fund

25%

25%

10%

10%

25%

5%

diversified group of funds, you will reduce your portfolio's overall price gyrations. You can fine-tune your portfolio even further by favoring more sedate funds.

How do you know which funds are more sedate? Look at how a fund is classified. Growth-and-income funds and equity-income funds, which focus on dividend-paying stocks, are often less erratic in their performance than funds that are categorized as "growth," "aggressive growth," or "capital appreciation."

You can also get a quick fix on a fund's risk level by looking at its year-by-year performance record. In particular, look at how the fund performed in years of market turmoil, such as 1987, 1990, and 1994. If a fund's loss in any one year seems unbearably large, scratch it from your list and consider other options.

To obtain year-by-year performance figures, contact the fund or look at one of the mutual fund directories at your local library. Among the leading publications are *Morningstar Mutual Funds*, CDA/Wiesenberger's *Investment Companies Yearbook*, and *The Value Line Mutual Fund Survey*. These publications also include risk ratings, such as "beta" (which measures a fund's price gyrations relative to those of the overall market) and "standard deviation" (which shows how much a fund's monthly return has strayed from its average return).

Once you have found funds with reasonable expenses and risk profiles you like, consider their track records. Funds with stellar records often fall from grace, so it is worth taking the time to check out a fund thoroughly before buying it.

Start by comparing the fund's record with the records of other funds that have a similar investment style. Thus, foreign-stock funds should be stacked up against other foreign funds, and a small-company value fund should be measured against other small-company value funds. Compare the funds' records over three, five, and ten years.

Also look at each fund's year-by-year record, to make sure that its long-term record is not built on one or two years of fabulous performance. Finally, find out if the fund manager responsible for the fund's record is still at the fund's helm. While some stock funds are run by a team of portfolio managers, most are run by a single stock-picker. To find out who runs a fund and how long that person has held the job, call the fund company or look in the fund's prospectus.

Even if a fund has all the hallmarks of a mutual fund superstar, there is every chance that it could turn out to be a miserable performer. As a consequence, once you buy a stock fund, keep close tabs on its performance. If its results lag behind those of similar funds for more than two or three years, consider selling. You should also consider selling if the fund's manager leaves.

Because of these risks, and because of the evidence that most stock funds fail to beat the market, many investors are turning to index funds. An index fund simply buys the stocks that make up a particular market index, in an effort to match the index's performance. Most index funds have very low annual expenses, incur only modest trading costs, and stay fully invested in stocks at all times. As a result, their performance is very similar to the market averages—and noticeably better than many actively managed stock funds.

Index funds are available that track the performance of large-company stocks, small-company stocks, foreign stocks, and even emerging markets, so it is possible to construct an entire portfolio using these funds. The biggest purveyor of index funds is the Vanguard Group, though most major fund companies now offer at least one index fund.

How to Find a Winning Stock

Just as mutual fund managers use different investment styles, so you should consider adopting your own strategy for picking individual stocks. And just as professional money managers go through rough patches, so your strategy will not always work. But if you are consistent, thorough, and patient, you should be able to earn decent returns over time.

What is the best strategy for you? Here are three popular stock-picking methods worth considering. Each of them can be implemented using your daily newspaper and a company's annual report, which you can order by calling the firm's investor-relations department. It is also helpful to study *The Value Line Investment Survey*, which can often be found at larger public libraries. *Value Line* includes historical financial data, earnings estimates, and brief analyses for over

2,000 publicly traded companies. If you use a full-service broker, you can also ask for the firm's latest research reports on the companies that interest you.

• **Value investing**. Value investors are the bargain hunters of the stock market. If you clip coupons, shy away from brand-name merchandise, and buy only used cars, you have the temperament of a value investor.

Value investors do not trust in bold predictions about a company's future earnings growth. Instead, they like to buy dirt cheap, beaten-up stocks that have been given up for dead by the rest of the stock market. Value investors often get their best bargains by buying on bad news, so keep an eye on the headlines.

To find value stocks, look for companies with low "price-earnings ratios"—companies whose shares are cheap compared with the company's current earnings. You can find out a company's price-to-earnings multiple, usually expressed as its P/E, by looking at the stock tables in many major newspapers. A typical value stock might trade at less than ten times the company's earnings over the past 12 months.

Value investors also look for stocks that are cheap compared with the company's "book value." Book value, which is the difference between a company's assets and its liabilities, represents the amount of money, expressed on a per-share basis, that has been invested in the company in the form of start-up capital, public stock offerings, and retained earnings. A stock's "price-to-book" value can be figured out by comparing the company's stock price to its book value, which is published in the firm's annual report. Value stocks often trade at or below book value.

Rich dividend yields are also important to value investors. Dividends account for half of the stock market's long-run total return, so if you buy stock with a 5% or higher yield, you start out with an edge over other stock market investors.

As with price-to-earnings ratios, stock dividend yields are published daily by many major newspapers. But before buying a high-yield stock, try to make sure that the dividend is safe. One method is to compare the dividend with the company's earnings. Check that the company is not paying an annual dividend equal to more than

80% of its earnings per share. If the dividend is too high, it could be cut if the company's earnings falter.

The biggest drawback with value investing is that dirt cheap companies can simply stay cheap—or get even cheaper. Value investors often buy cheap stocks, hoping that either the earnings growth picks up or the company is taken over or broken up. But if neither happens, there is every chance that the company's shares will continue to languish.

• **Dividend growth.** Unlike value investors, dividend-growth investors do not focus on a stock's current dividend yield. Instead, they are looking for companies that have a history of regularly raising their dividends. Some companies can boast of increasing their dividends every year for 15 years, 20 years, or even longer. Those are just the sort of companies that dividend-growth investors like to buy.

Why do they find these companies attractive? A regularly rising dividend is often the sign of a successful company, for two reasons. First, a company cannot regularly raise its dividend unless its operations are generating ever greater quantities of cash. Second, if a company can boost its dividend year after year, that suggests that the company operates in a relatively friendly business environment and has been able to grow in good times and bad. As a result, there is a fair chance that the company will be able to continue to raise its dividend in the future.

You can spot a rising-dividend company by flipping through *Value Line* or looking in a company's annual report. Once you have identified one of these companies, try to figure out why it has grown steadily in the past and ask yourself whether that is likely to continue. Even if you feel sure that the dividend will keep growing, you should not automatically buy the stock. Instead, take a look at the company's price-to-earnings ratio. While you do not need to be as parsimonious as a value investor, you do want to make sure that the stock's price-to-earnings ratio is not too rich.

WHAT IS A P/E?

The price-to-earnings ratio, or P/E, is possibly the most popular way of valuing stocks. A stock's P/E is commonly figured by dividing the current share price by the company's per-share earnings over the past 12 months. This information is published daily in the stock tables of many major newspapers. If, for instance, a company earned $1 per share over the past year and its stock trades at $15, the company is trading at a P/E of 15. The lower the price and the higher the earnings, the lower the P/E will be.

A more sophisticated approach used by many professional investment analysts is to divide the current share price by the company's expected earnings over the coming 12 months. Indeed, a company's current stock price often reflects not only what has already happened but what knowledgeable investors expect to happen.

• **Growth that you know.** This brand of investing has been popularized by Peter Lynch, the celebrated money manager who ran Fidelity Magellan Fund for 13 fabulously successful years. The idea is to invest in companies that produce products or services you know well and that you believe have a good chance for future growth.

If you love a new frozen dinner, read the package to see who makes it. If your child is begging for a new toy, find out the name of the manufacturer. If your company is suddenly losing sales to an upstart rival, check to see if the rival is publicly traded.

Once you have spotted a good candidate that is publicly traded, find out if other investors have already discovered it. To do that, compare the company's price-to-earnings ratio with its recent or likely earnings growth rate. Ideally, you want to buy a company with a price-to-earnings ratio that is lower than its earnings growth rate. For instance, if a company's earnings have been growing at 18% a year, it might be worth buying if the stock is at 16 times earnings, but not if the P/E is 20.

If the company is currently unprofitable, it might be worth calling the company and talking to the person in charge of investor relations. At smaller companies, this is often one of the senior officers. Ask when the company expects to turn a profit, how fast it thinks sales will grow, and what sort of competition the company faces. While some companies will be less than honest, many will discuss their business prospects with a surprising amount of candor.

INVESTING IN BONDS AND BOND FUNDS

Bonds are prized by investors because of one compelling virtue: They kick off far more immediate income than the two other major financial assets, stocks and cash. For retirees and others trying to live off their investments, that can be an irresistible quality.

But you should view bonds as more than just a rich source of income. Instead, consider the roles that bonds can play in your portfolio.

Bonds, in the guise of tax-free municipal bonds, are one of the last great tax shelters. Municipal bonds are issued by state and local governments. The interest from most municipal bonds is exempt from federal taxes and, in many cases, state and local taxes as well. Because of the tax advantage, municipal bonds generally have lower yields than Treasury or corporate bonds. But despite the lower yields, municipals are often an attractive investment for those in higher tax brackets. This is especially so if you live in high-tax states like California, Massachusetts, and New York. An investor in one of these states can usually save on both federal income taxes and state and local income taxes by buying bonds that are issued within the state.

Treasury bonds and U.S. savings bonds offer a modest tax advantage, too. The interest from these bonds is exempt from state and local taxes. In addition, the federal tax on interest from savings bonds is not due until the bonds are redeemed. The new inflation-indexed Treasury bonds that the government intended to introduce in 1996 promise investors returns guaranteed to protect them from inflation—an assurance that no other domestic investment can give.

Bonds can also help you diversify your investments. Bond prices generally bounce around less than stock prices, and bonds sometimes hold steady or even climb when stock prices are falling. As a result, adding a small position in bonds can help to dampen the price gyrations of a stock portfolio without sacrificing too much in portfolio performance.

Sometimes, bonds will be your single best investment choice, especially if you have a financial goal coming up in the near future. Bonds offer higher yields than supersafe investments but are generally much less erratic in their performance than stocks. As a result, they are probably your best bet if you have a goal that lies 18 months to five years away. Indeed, if you pick your bonds carefully and hold them until they mature, you can be almost certain of what your investment return is going to be.

For instance, suppose you have a son who will be entering college in three years. To help pay for the first semester's tuition, you purchase a bond whose maturity date coincides with the date when you will need the money. Because you plan on holding the bond until maturity, you know exactly what your investment gain will be. You will receive a specified rate of interest each year until the bond matures, at which time you will get back the bond's face value (also

READING THE RATINGS

Any bond with an A rating from the major credit-rating agencies should be able to weather an economic downturn without any financial difficulty. But if a bond receives some sort of B rating, it is quite possible that the issuer could default on its interest payments. That is especially so if a bond is rated below Baa or BBB. These bonds are considered below investment grade and—reflecting their shaky standing—are often called "junk bonds."

MOODY'S	STANDARD & POOR'S	MEANING
Aaa	AAA	Highest quality
Aa	AA	High quality
A	A	Upper-medium quality
Baa	BBB	Medium quality
Ba, B	BB, B	Below investment grade
Caa, Ca, C	CCC, CC, C	Highly speculative
———-	D	In default

known as the redemption value or par value). For instance, if you paid $10,000 to buy a three-year bond that trades at par value and has a yield of 7%, you would receive $700 every year for three years, until the bond matures. Upon maturity, the bond's issuer would return your $10,000.

Sound simple? Unfortunately, bond investing is not always as easy as this example suggests. In particular, bond investors have to contend with four major problems.

• **Defaults.** Corporations and government authorities sometimes default on their interest payments. For bondholders, that leads to a double whammy: They suffer a loss of income, and the price of their bonds will usually plunge.

One way of judging default risk is to look at a bond's credit rating. These ratings are made by independent agencies, such as Moody's Investors Service and Standard & Poor's Ratings Group. Under the Standard & Poor's system, for instance, the highest-quality corporate and municipal bonds are rated AAA. These bonds are believed to be almost as safe as bonds issued by the U.S. Treasury, which are considered risk-free. Indeed, the chance of default is considered slim for any bond that has a rating of BBB or above.

If a bond is rated below BBB, however, the chance of default is considered much greater. These low-rated bonds are often known as high-yield, or junk, bonds. Because the junk-bond market is so treacherous, smaller investors generally buy junk-bond funds rather than individual securities. These funds often boast far higher yields than other bond funds. But as with any bond investment, the high yield is a sign of high risk. In the case of junk-bond funds, the seductively high dividend payouts compensate investors for the risk that some of the bonds in their fund may default each year.

• **Rising interest rates.** While defaults are the biggest fear of bond investors, they are not the only way you can lose money. You can also suffer a loss if interest rates rise.

Bond prices move in the opposite direction from interest rates. When interest rates fall, bond prices climb. But when rates rise, this causes the price of bonds to fall. The further a bond is from its maturity date, the harder it will be hit by an interest-rate rise and the more it will benefit from an interest-rate drop.

If you buy a bond at par value and rates subsequently rise, you will not lose any money, providing you hold the bond until the maturity date. But if you sell prior to maturity, you could end up receiving far less than the bond's face value.

That can be a particular problem for retirees, who may occasionally want to sell some of their bonds to get extra income. One solution is to stick with shorter-term bonds. History suggests that a five-year bond (or a fund that owns them) will pay you almost as much interest as a long bond, but with only a fraction of the price gyrations.

• **High investment costs.** Even if the bond market is buoyant, you could still get a lousy price if you try to sell your bonds before they mature. That is because the bond market is dominated by large institutional investors, which typically trade in lots of $100,000 and up. If you have only $10,000 of bonds to sell, you may have to accept a below-market price in order to sell your bonds. To minimize this problem, you can call several brokerage firms in an effort to get the best possible price. But your best bet is to plan on buying bonds when they are first issued and then hold them to maturity. That way, you should cut down on brokerage commissions while also getting the same sort of price as far larger investors.

Bond fund investing can also be prohibitively expensive. Like other mutual funds, all bond funds levy annual expenses, and they may also charge a sales commission. Government and corporate bond funds typically charge around 0.95% a year in annual expenses, while tax-free municipal bond funds tend to charge around 0.8%. But some funds charge far less than these averages, so it pays to do some comparison shopping. A fund's expenses come straight out of the fund's dividend, thus eating into the income received by shareholders and reducing the fund's total return.

•**Early redemptions.** Some bonds can be "called," or paid off at face value before they mature. That can be a nasty problem for investors, especially if interest rates have dropped sharply. When you buy a new bond to replace the one that has been paid off, you may not be able to find a bond that pays nearly as much in interest. Or worse, you could suffer a real loss if you had bought your bond at a "premium," paying more than the face value in exchange for a higher-than-market interest rate.

Treasury bond investors do not have to worry about their bonds being called away before maturity. Just as Treasury bonds have no risk of default, newly issued Treasury bonds also have no "call risk."

Getting your money back early, however, can be a real problem with corporate, municipal, and mortgage bonds. Corporate and municipal bonds often have call provisions, which typically allow the issuer to pay these bonds off after ten years. Mortgage bonds are formed by pooling together home mortgages. Holders of the bonds receive interest and principal payments as homeowners pay down their mortgages. If homeowners refinance their mortgages or pay off their loans early, the holders of mortgage bonds will get back their money far sooner than they expected.

INDIVIDUAL BONDS VERSUS MUTUAL FUNDS

A bond eventually matures. A bond mutual fund never does. When deciding whether to buy an individual bond or a bond mutual fund, it is critical to understand that difference.

Suppose that you bought both a five-year bond and an intermediate-term bond fund that aims to hold bonds with an average maturity of five years. Will their performance be similar? Not at all. As time passes, the five-year bond will turn into a four-year bond, and then a three-year bond, and so on until it matures, at which point you will get back the bond's par value.

Meanwhile, what happens to the bond fund? Over the five years, it would continually readjust its portfolio to maintain an average maturity of around five years. As a result, the fund's record is likely to be significantly different from the individual bond's performance. While you cannot be sure which will perform better, this much is clear: You can reasonably expect your five-year bond to be redeemed at par at the end of the five years. Your intermediate-term bond fund, on the other hand, could finish the period worth far more or far less than you originally invested.

So when should you use bonds and when should you buy a fund? If you have a major expenditure coming up in the near future, and you can buy a Treasury bond whose maturity matches the date of the expenditure, then individual bonds are clearly a much safer bet than funds.

You should also buy individual bonds if you think interest rates are at an attractive level and you want to lock in that yield. By buying an individual bond, you will guarantee yourself a fixed stream of interest payments until the bond matures, no matter what happens to interest rates.

By contrast, a bond fund's dividend payout will tend to shrink as interest rates fall. That is not necessarily a bad sign. Indeed, at the same time that the fund's dividend is falling, you may well find that the fund's share price is rising. What you are losing on the dividend, you may be recouping through share-price appreciation.

Finally, investing in individual bonds can be much cheaper than bond fund investing, presuming you buy an individual bond when it is first issued and then hold it to maturity. Even a low-cost bond fund will probably charge annual expenses of 0.3% a year—a cost you will not incur if you buy individual bonds.

But while individual bonds offer a couple of advantages over bond funds, they are not your best bet if you think you might have to sell your bonds before they mature. Buying and selling individual bonds is surprisingly expensive for small investors. If you do not know when you will sell your bond investment, you are much better off buying a fund, which you can then sell easily and cheaply.

Bond funds are also a better bet if you have only a modest amount to invest. A mutual fund investor can buy a diversified bond portfolio for as little as $1,000. But you often need at least $5,000 or $10,000 to buy an individual bond, and even then you will have all your money riding on a single security.

In addition to offering professional management and broad diversification, bond funds are much more convenient than individual bonds. Once you have opened a fund account, you can often make additional investments of as little as $50 or $100. Funds allow you to reinvest your dividends automatically in additional fund shares. Many bond funds permit shareholders to write checks against their accounts. By contrast, holders of individual bonds cannot trade in very small amounts, which makes it difficult to reinvest interest payments and means investors have to sell an entire bond every time they want to raise cash.

Moreover, bond funds are usually the best way to go if you want to tap into more exotic areas of the bond market, such as mortgage-backed securities, high-yield junk bonds, foreign bonds, and emerging-market debt. Foreign-bond funds typically focus on the government and corporate bonds of developed countries, whereas emerging-market debt funds invest primarily in government bonds issued by developing countries.

How to Find a Winning Bond Fund

Bond funds come in a host of different flavors. Some funds buy taxable bonds; others stick with tax-free municipals. Some invest only in U.S. securities; others venture abroad. Some confine themselves to high-quality corporate, government, and municipal securities; others dabble in low-quality bonds, including junk bonds and low-grade municipals. Finally, some funds invest in bonds with 20 or more years to maturity, and others favor short-term bonds that will be redeemed in the next 2 to 3 years.

Which fund is right for you? It all depends on your investment goal and personal situation. The core of any bond fund portfolio should be a high-quality fund that invests in corporate, government, or municipal bonds. If you are in a high tax bracket, consider municipals. Otherwise, go for the higher yields offered by government and corporate funds. If you are sticking with taxable bonds, consider a bond-index fund, which tries to mimic the performance of one of the bond market indexes. These funds offer the advantage of broad diversification and rock-bottom expenses.

Buy shorter-term funds if you will need your money in the near future. But if you are willing to suffer some sharp share-price gyrations in return for a higher yield, consider putting some money in an intermediate- or longer-term bond fund.

What about junk-bond funds, foreign-bond funds, and emerging-market debt funds? These are best used as a way of adding spice to your core position in high-quality bonds. Junk, foreign bonds, and emerging-market debt can help boost your returns and diversify your bond holdings, thus smoothing out your bond portfolio's performance. But these funds make most sense for investors with substantial bond portfolios, who already have a big stake in high-quality bonds.

Once you have settled on the types of bond funds you want to buy, it is fairly easy to identify some good fund choices. When picking a stock fund, you should pay close attention to the fund's record. But when picking a bond fund, you should put at least as much emphasis on the fund's sales commission and annual expenses.

That is because most bond funds are highly specialized; for instance, they focus just on intermediate-term government bonds, or long-term municipals, or short-term corporate bonds. And funds that pursue the same investment objective tend to have very similar portfolios. The biggest factor distinguishing one fund from the other is cost.

Differences in costs can be very important to investors. Studies of bond fund performance suggest that high-cost bond funds are very unlikely to outperform low-cost funds. A bond fund that charges a sales commission or has annual expenses above 1% will find it extremely difficult to make more money for its shareholders than a no-load fund with annual expenses below 0.7%. This is especially true with funds that invest in high-quality government, municipal, and corporate bonds.

But the case for buying purely on cost is not quite so strong when it comes to junk-bond funds, emerging-market debt funds, and foreign-bond funds. With these funds, returns can vary sharply from fund to fund, and managers must deal with tricky issues, such as default risk and foreign-currency exposure. As a result, you should pay less attention to cost with these funds and give more weight to the fund manager's track record. Try to find a fund manager who not only has a good long-term record but has also performed well year after year.

How to Find a Winning Bond

If you are going to buy individual bonds, consider using five basic rules:

- Aim to buy bonds when they are first issued. That way, you should get a good price and save on brokerage commissions, because the sales commission on a newly issued bond is picked up by the issuer.

- Purchase only high-quality bonds, those that are rated AAA, AA, or A by Standard & Poor's and those that are rated Aaa, Aa, and A by Moody's. If you buy high-quality bonds, you do not have to worry too much about the bond's issuer defaulting on its interest payments.

- Check with your broker that the bond is not likely to be called earlier than you want.

- Plan on sticking with your bonds until they mature or are called, so you can avoid the perils of selling your bonds in the "secondary," or resale, market.

- Just in case you do have to sell before maturity, aim to buy the bonds of larger corporations and municipalities that regularly sell new securities. The secondary market for these bonds tends to be relatively active, so you are more likely to get a decent price for your bonds should you have to sell before maturity.

By following these rules, you will find yourself confined to three types of bonds: high-quality corporate bonds, tax-free municipal bonds, and Treasury securities. These are just the sort of bonds that should form the core of your bond portfolio.

If you favor simplicity, Treasurys are your best bet. Credit qual

BUYING TREASURY SECURITIES WITHOUT A BROKER

If you like Treasury bonds and bills, you will love the Federal Reserve. The Fed sells Treasury securities directly to the public, thus saving investors the commission they would pay if they went through a broker or a commercial bank.

The Federal Reserve offers these bonds and bills at regular auctions. Treasury bills, which are available with maturities of 13 weeks, 26 weeks, and one year, will cost you a minimum of $10,000. To purchase two-year and three-year Treasury notes, you need at least $5,000, but the minimum for longer-maturity bonds is just $1,000. If you are buying T-bills, you will need a cashier's check or a certified check from your bank; an ordinary bank check will do if you are buying notes or bonds. There is a $25 maintenance fee for accounts above $100,000.

Most individuals who buy through the so-called Treasury Direct program make "noncompetitive" tenders. That means that these buyers receive the average price and yield set through competitive bidding by the major institutional investors at the auction.

Buying through the Federal Reserve has one big drawback. If you want to sell before your bonds mature, the Fed will not do it for you. Instead, you must arrange to have your bonds transferred to a bank or broker, which is a hassle.

For more information on Treasury Direct, contact your nearest Federal Reserve bank or branch or call the Bureau of the Public Debt at 202-874-4000.

ZERO-COUPON BONDS

Zero-coupon bonds offer investors the unusual combination of wild short-term price swings and unrivaled long-term certainty. How so? It all has to do with the peculiar nature of these bonds.

Zero-coupon bonds do not pay any interest. Instead, investors buy the bonds at a discount to their final maturity value and then profit when this discount narrows. The narrowing of the discount represents the effective interest rate earned by investors. Because zero-coupon bonds do not kick off regular interest payments like other bonds, they react far more violently to changes in interest rates. When rates fall, zeros can post dramatic short-term gains. But those gains can quickly disappear when rates are rising.

While the short-term gyrations can be unnerving, zeros provide total certainty to those who buy them and hang on to maturity. You do not even have to worry about reinvesting interest payments as you do with a regular bond. You simply sit back and wait for the discount to narrow as the bond approaches maturity.

Though holders of zero-coupon bonds do not actually receive cash interest payments, they still have to pay taxes on each year's imputed income. As a result, unless you own zero-coupon municipal bonds, you may want to hold your zeros in a tax-sheltered retirement account.

ity is not an issue, and newly issued Treasury bonds are not callable. If you like the safety of government securities, you may also want to consider U.S. savings bonds. These can be bought for as little as $25, which is half the $50 minimum face value. U.S. savings bonds are available with no fee from many banks and financial institutions. Unlike Treasurys, savings bonds do not pay a fixed rate of interest, nor is the interest paid immediately. Instead, your interest builds up in the bond's price; you do not get the money until you cash in the bond.

A particularly useful strategy is known as "laddering" your portfolio. With this approach, you buy bonds with a variety of maturities so that as the individual bonds mature, they provide a stream of income that can help carry you through retirement or pay for each year of a child's college education.

You can follow the same strategy with municipal and corporate bonds, but it is trickier. Call provisions may come into play, and you could be hit with credit-quality problems. Your best bet is to work through a knowledgeable broker who can help you analyze new bond offerings and let you know when they are coming to market.

OTHER INVESTMENTS

The world of investing does not end with stocks, bonds, and supersafe cash investments. What about options, futures, limited partnerships, collectibles, precious metals, and exotic investment strategies like short selling?

Forget about them. Yes, each of these can generate handsome gains for knowledgeable investors. But for the rest of us, fancy investments and complicated strategies are often more likely to hurt our financial health than help it.

OPTIONS AND FUTURES

Options and futures attract two sorts of investors—the ultracautious and the overly confident. These so-called derivatives allow nervous investors to buy protection against the risk that their portfolios will be hurt by an adverse movement in the price of stocks, bonds, currencies, or commodities. Meanwhile, for aggressive investors, options and futures provide the opportunity to take on risk, in the hope of making outsized returns.

Futures and options contracts exist for a slew of financial and hard assets, including individual stocks, Treasury bonds, wheat, currencies, pork bellies, and the stocks that comprise stock market indexes. A futures contract is an obligation to buy or sell the underlying asset at a fixed price at a future date. Options contracts, meanwhile, give holders the right—but not the obligation—to buy ("call" options) or sell ("put" options) the underlying asset.

If you purchase an options contract, the most you can lose is the price you paid for the option. Your losses can be much greater if you enter into a futures contract, or if you sell an options contract. When you sell an options contract, you are agreeing to buy the underlying asset from, or sell the asset to, the person who bought the put or call contract that you sold.

But for all of these investors, whether they are entering into futures contracts or buying or selling options, the prospects are not great. Options and futures are a zero-sum game, which means that for every dollar made there is a dollar lost. But even that overstates the odds. Why? The broker stands in the middle, taking a piece of the action.

SHORT SELLING

Short selling, which involves betting that a particular company's stock will fall in price, is a game where the odds are heavily stacked against the investor. Stock prices rise over time. As a result, if you bet that an individual company will drop in price, you better be very lucky or very smart—or you could end up losing your shirt.

When you sell a stock short, you borrow the desired number of shares from a brokerage firm and then immediately sell them. If the shares fall in price, you will be able to buy them back at a lower price and return the securities to the brokerage firm. Your gain is equal to the difference between the price you originally sold the shares for and the price you paid when you repurchased the stock. In the best outcome, the company goes bankrupt, the stock becomes worthless, and you pocket the entire amount that you received on the initial sale.

But if that potential gain seems impressive, consider the size of your potential losses. Although a stock can fall no further than zero, its potential rise is unlimited—and so, too, are your losses. The history of Wall Street is filled with instances of savvy investors who stubbornly insisted that a company's shares were overvalued; they ended up paying dearly for their obstinacy.

PRECIOUS METALS

For centuries, gold was used as money. Today, some see gold as an alternative to paper money. When the value of a currency seems imperiled, either because of rapid inflation or political crises, investors often bid up the price of gold.

Why do some investors flock to gold at these times? Over long periods, an ounce of gold has proved to be a remarkable store of value; it is an asset that maintains its real, inflation-adjusted purchasing power through all kinds of economic and political turmoil.

But unless you astutely time your purchases and sales, all you can expect from gold is to keep up with the rate of inflation over the long haul. Because gold does not tend to generate a positive real rate of return, some investment advisers suggest substituting a mix of real estate securities, basic-materials companies, energy stocks, and gold. That mix can often be found in sector funds that specialize in natural resources. Like gold, these other hard-asset investments tend to do well in times of inflation, but they can also generate decent long-run returns.

There is a trade-off, however. Gold prices typically rise rapidly when inflation scares the market, whereas the reaction of real estate, basic materials, and energy stocks is more muted. Gold will also tend to react to political and economic crises, while other inflation hedges may not respond at all.

Despite the diversification benefits, many investors should probably shy away from both gold and other hard assets. If you own your home, you effectively have a large investment in real estate and thus substantial exposure to hard assets. It may not make sense to take on even more exposure to hard assets, unless you have a very large portfolio or you feel the need for the psychological comfort that comes from owning gold and other hard assets.

Limited Partnerships

Limited partnerships, many of which were conceived as a way of helping investors pay less in income taxes, have proved far more effective as a way of producing lousy returns.

Partnerships were popular in the 1970s and 1980s as vehicles for investing in real estate, oil and gas, movie deals, nursing homes, equipment leases, and a host of other businesses. As a limited partner, you would share in the partnership's profits, but your losses would be limited to the amount you originally invested. The partnerships were supposed to help investors achieve above-average returns and, in some cases, cut their current tax bills.

Congress, however, has curbed the tax write-offs that limited partners can take. And decent investment returns have proved elusive, thanks to hefty fees and a history of rotten management. The result? Many disgusted investors would love to get rid of their partnerships. But even that is a problem. If you try to sell a limited partnership in the informal secondary market, you may receive significantly less than the partnership's real worth.

Art and Other Collectibles

Collectibles—like other hard assets such as real estate and gold—tend to do well when financial assets like stocks and bonds do poorly. Why? High inflation, which can be so devastating to stock and bond prices, tends to boost the price of hard assets.

But if you are turning to hard assets purely for investment purposes, the poorest choice may well be collectibles, such as antiques, baseball cards, gems, rare books, art, coins, and stamps. Buying, holding, and selling collectibles can be a costly process.

If you own an antique desk, for instance, you may need to have it restored or repaired. You may also want to buy insurance, in case the desk is stolen or destroyed by fire. Should you decide to sell, you may not be able to unload the desk quickly and, when you finally do find a buyer, you will never be sure whether you have received a good price. Getting accurate prices for collectibles is difficult because many collectibles are "one-of-a-kind" pieces and because there is no central market for them.

So if you buy collectibles, buy them because you like to see them gracing your home. And if you happen to make money, consider it an added bonus.

3

FINDING YOUR WAY THROUGH THE INSURANCE MAZE

$

Almost everybody seems to have some complaint about insurance. Maybe it is a hefty bill for coverage. Maybe it is the claim for a child's $75 doctor visit, or a $500 fender bender, that the insurer simply refuses to pay. Or maybe it is just the aggravation, such as attempting to decipher a policy written in inscrutable jargon or trying to get a straight answer from an agent who is apparently ready to say virtually anything to get your business.

Most people recognize, though, that insurance is an indispensable component—some might say a necessary evil—in managing their financial and family affairs responsibly. Look beyond the small-potato stuff. The real payoff from insurance comes if and when something truly bad happens—if you have an extended hospitalization, or your home burns to the ground, or the family breadwinner dies.

Insurance is an invaluable tool that limits the financial impact of such painful life events. Even policies on which you never collect a dime, such as a homeowner's policy on which you never file a claim, dramatically reduce your financial risks. Having an adequate insurance safety net lets you focus on more pleasurable aspects of life.

Fiddling with insurance coverage is no fun, of course. But it does not have to be an ordeal. And there is a big benefit to poking around in what may be a musty corner of your financial house: Many people have less insurance coverage than they need and are paying far too much for what they do have. This chapter discusses the principal types of insurance you purchase for yourself and your family; medical insurance and other types of coverage provided at work and by government programs, such as Medicare, are discussed in Chapter 4.

THINK BIG—BIG LOSSES, THAT IS

In buying any kind of insurance, the guiding principle should be to think catastrophe. You might like a policy that will cover every small loss. What you absolutely need, however, is enough coverage for the worst things that could happen. On an auto policy, for instance, coverage for towing after an accident might be nice (or unnecessary, if you get free towing as a member of an auto club). But plentiful coverage for bodily injury, including injury caused to you by an uninsured driver, is essential.

Check your existing policies every few years to make sure the coverage is still sufficient. Remember the last time you looked in the insurance folder in your home filing cabinet? If not, then there is a good chance you are seriously underinsured. With the increase in construction costs, your homeowner's policy might not provide a big enough benefit to rebuild your home if it were completely destroyed. A life insurance policy that seemed generous five years ago, when your living expenses were lower, might be woefully inadequate to maintain your family's lifestyle if you died tomorrow.

There may also be some financial risks that you have given too little thought. For instance, what if you were hit with a huge court judgment because someone was injured on your property or by a car you were driving? Some liability insurance, which pays such expenses, is included in auto and homeowner's policies. But many people should buy extra coverage. An "umbrella" liability policy of $1 million or more can cost a modest $100 to $300 a year.

Two other types of insurance are also worth considering, although they are unfortunately quite expensive. Employees who do not receive disability coverage at work should look at private policies that can help pay household bills if they are laid up and unable to work for an extended time. People approaching retirement should weigh the costs and benefits of long-term-care policies, which can help pay nursing-home costs.

GET MORE FOR YOUR MONEY

Most people are lousy insurance consumers. They do not shop when they buy, and they do not understand what they have. That seems to suit many insurance companies and agents just fine. But with surprisingly little effort, many people can either cut their insurance costs dramatically or get a much-needed increase in coverage without paying more.

How? By fine-tuning existing policies, switching to a different type of policy, or moving to a different insurer.

With auto and homeowner's policies, you probably know that you can trim the premium by raising the deductibles—the amount of loss you must pay before the insurance kicks in. For the biggest potential savings, though, check how much other insurers would charge for the same type of coverage. The range of prices may astound you. If you are unknowingly dealing with a high-cost insurer, switching companies may cut your auto or homeowner's insurance bill in half.

Insurers also offer a host of discounts for which you might be eligible if you would only ask. There can be savings just for consolidating your auto and home coverage with a single insurer.

With life insurance, meanwhile, the key to savings is making certain you have the right type of policy. Change may be in order if you need a lot more coverage than you have, but you are already struggling to pay the bills. Many insurance agents push "cash-value" policies, such as "whole life" and "universal life," that combine a death benefit with a tax-favored savings account. Those policies are ideal for some people. But they are not right for buyers, such as many couples with young children, who need lots of insurance but have only limited cash.

For the maximum protection at the lowest current cost, consider "term" policies, which provide only a death benefit. You should also compare prices. A few calls to local agents and 800-number services can help you find the most attractively priced products, whether you are buying a new policy or checking up on a term policy you already have.

KNOW WHAT NOT TO DO

Controlling insurance costs also means not wasting your money on unnecessary or duplicative coverage. If you have decent medical coverage, for instance, do not buy an extra policy that pays only if you come down with one particular disease, such as cancer.

Do not put much stock in accidental-death-and-dismemberment insurance, which pays if you are killed or maimed in an accident. Your family will need the same amount of money whether you lose your life in a car crash or a cancer ward. Make sure you have that amount of insurance and you can skip the accidental-death coverage.

Above all, when buying life insurance, do not let yourself be led astray by an agent whose financial interests are contrary to your own. Many life insurance agents provide invaluable and objective advice. But some others recommend unnecessary or inappropriate insurance to collect hefty sales commissions that typically equal 50% to 100% of your first-year payment.

In recent years, the life insurance industry has been rocked by scandals in which agents misrepresented policies as retirement-savings plans. Other unscrupulous agents convinced policyholders to make costly swaps of one policy for another. Far too often, agents exaggerate the advantages of their wares and downplay the risks that a policy will not perform as projected.

In buying life insurance, stay focused on its primary purpose—to provide for dependents in case of a breadwinner's early death. As a general rule, do not buy life insurance as an investment. Keep the agent's financial interest—and your own—in mind. You will find additional tips and a worksheet to help you figure out just how much coverage you really need in the Buyer's Guide to Life Insurance, Appendix C.

INSURANCE DECISIONS THROUGH THE AGES

At every stage of life, you will probably have several types of insurance. Your age plays a big role in determining which coverages are most important—and also most costly—at any given time.

If you are a young parent, for instance, life insurance is crucial. Thankfully, in your 20s and 30s, life insurance is also cheap, because the risk of imminent death is low. Decisions about life insurance can be tougher in later decades, when coverage costs much more.

The auto insurance bill will give you indigestion in your early 20s—and again when your children become old enough to drive. Changes in your personal circumstances and rising prices will probably require you to increase your homeowner's insurance and liability protection as you age. If you are in your 60s, for instance, you probably have far more assets to insure against physical damage and the financial risk of a lawsuit than you did when you lived in a bare-bones apartment in your 20s.

The following sections look at key insurance issues for people of different ages.

Your 20s and 30s

For people just starting out, the steepest insurance bill is often for auto coverage. You do not yet have a big home to insure. Life insurance, if needed, is much cheaper than it will be 20 or 30 years from now. But the auto insurance bill can be a real budget buster, particularly if you are an unmarried man under age 25. Because such drivers tend to have more accidents, insurers charge them far more than other drivers with the same cars and coverage amounts.

Do not skimp on the important liability portion of an auto policy, which pays if you cause an accident or are sued. Many states require drivers to have a minimum level of liability insurance, such as $20,000 per person injured, with a maximum $40,000 per accident. That is simply not enough given today's medical costs and hefty court awards.

Aim for liability coverage of at least $100,000 per person and $300,000 per accident. It may cost as little as $100 a year to go from a bare minimum of coverage to a more reasonable level. Be sure you also have uninsured-motorist insurance, which pays if you are injured by a driver who does not have coverage.

Meanwhile, consider the potential insurance costs in deciding what type of car to buy or whether to buy a new one at all. Insurance costs are typically higher on more expensive cars, which are more costly to repair or replace. Sports cars tend to be costly to insure because they are attractive to thieves and to buyers whose driving habits often lead to accidents.

You can save hundreds of dollars on auto insurance simply by sticking with an old clunker a while longer. The collision and comprehensive portions of a policy, which pay when your car is damaged or stolen, cost less on an older car. If a car is more than five to eight years old, you might want to drop those optional coverages altogether.

The most important way to keep auto insurance costs down is to drive carefully. A clean driving record will get you the most favorable, or "preferred," rates. If you already have an accident or a few speeding tickets to your name, aim to keep your driving record clean for a few years and then shop for a better deal. In about ten

CONSIDER INSURANCE COSTS WHEN SHOPPING FOR A CAR

It is smart to check current insurance rates before buying a car. This list shows 1995 models for which drivers were charged the highest and lowest premiums by State Farm.

HIGHEST	LOWEST
Porsche 911	KIA Sephia
Chevrolet Corvette ZR1	Ford Aspire (two-door and four-door)
Mercedes SL600	Chevrolet Cavalier (four-door)
Porsche 928	Saturn station wagon
Mercedes S600 (two-door and four-door)	Dodge/Plymouth mini-van
BMW 850CSi	Subaru Justy 4-wheel drive (four-door)
Mercedes SL500	Ford F150 pickup truck
Mercedes SL320	Saturn SL (four-door)
Chevrolet Corvette	Ford Escort station wagon
Porsche 968	Ford Taurus station wagon

SOURCE: State Farm Insurance Companies.

states, including New York and Texas, all drivers can get a discount on their auto insurance by successfully completing a driver-improvement class. Many other states provide discounts for people aged 55 or older. Check with your agent or a local American Automobile Association club.

HOME SWEET (RENTED) HOME

If you are renting an apartment, you need a renter's policy that protects your household possessions and also provides liability coverage. Without it, you could suffer a sizable loss if your apartment were burglarized or if part of the dining room ceiling came crashing down on your brand-new table. A renter's policy may cost only $100 to $300 a year.

When you buy a home, the mortgage lender will insist that you buy homeowner's coverage. While selecting the right policy will probably be a low priority in the last-minute buying-and-moving rush, try to compare charges from at least three insurers. Consider reviewing your options a few months later, when life has calmed down a bit.

Whether you are a renter or homeowner, pay a little extra to insure your possessions for their replacement cost rather than "actual cash value." If a plumbing leak destroyed your five-year-old sofa, a replacement-cost policy would give you enough money to take to the furniture store. In contrast, a policy that paid only the current value of that well-used sofa would leave you short of cash for a new one.

Remember to increase your homeowner's coverage if you enhance the value of your home. You will need much more coverage if that two-bedroom starter home has gained a new master-bedroom suite and a big deck.

Use the camcorder you bought to film the new baby to detail your home improvements and inventory your personal possessions. If you do not have a camcorder, borrow or rent one for a day. A video home tour is an easy project for a rainy afternoon (even though you may feel a little silly), and it will go a long way to substantiate a claim in the event of any loss.

DO NOT PROCRASTINATE

If you are a new parent, your biggest insurance concern should be life insurance. You may need more now than you will at any point later in life. Unfortunately, it is extremely easy to put off buying life insurance. There is no one requiring you to buy the stuff, as there typically is with auto and homeowner's coverage, and nobody likes to think about death. But if you have children or other family members who are dependent on your income, do not let yourself off the hook.

Making an informed selection of life insurance can be much easier than you think. You can do the job yourself, without leaving your home. The worksheet in the Buyer's Guide to Life Insurance, Appendix C, can help you estimate, in just a few minutes, how big a policy to buy. Spend a half hour on the telephone, and you can have several proposals for low-cost coverage headed to your mailbox.

People who need a lot of coverage but do not have a lot of cash should buy term insurance, which is essentially a promise from an insurer to pay a set death benefit if you die while the policy is in force. The cost will go up as you age and the odds of imminent death increase. But for now, a term policy will provide several times more coverage for a given annual payment than a cash-value policy, which incorporates both a death benefit and a tax-deferred savings component.

People who have sufficient cash flow and will need coverage for at least 15 or 20 years may want to consider a cash-value plan such as whole or universal life. A key appeal of such policies is that the premiums may remain level for life.

But where cash-value life insurance is concerned, a few warnings are in order. Never buy a smaller death benefit than you need simply to get coverage in the form of cash value. Skip the cash-value policy if buying it means you will not have enough money to take advantage of a company retirement-savings plan with a matching contribution from your employer. Buy a cash-value policy only if you are sure you will stick with it: Because of sales commissions paid to the agent, you will take a financial beating if you drop the policy in the first several years.

If you do not have any disability coverage at work, consider buy-

20s–30s

- Beef up auto liability protection.

- Insure possessions for replacement cost.

- Assess life insurance needs.

- Consider low-cost term life.

- Check disability coverage.

ing an individual policy. Also think about disability coverage when you are deciding what type of life insurance to buy. Buying term life insurance and a disability policy could be a wiser move than buying cash-value life insurance and no disability.

Your 40s and 50s

Life events, such as the purchase of a new home or a child reaching driving age, bring insurance issues and costs into sharp focus. But the simple passage of time, the steady pressure of inflation, and changes in your lifestyle and goals all affect your coverage. You should review your insurance every few years for adequacy and cost.

In checking your homeowner's coverage, the watchword is inflation. Some policies have an automatic inflation adjustment that increases the coverage as construction costs go up. If your policy does not have such a feature, and you have not boosted your coverage in years, you may be seriously underinsured.

Your homeowner's coverage should be equal or close to the cost of totally rebuilding your home. Although having enough coverage is obviously critical in a devastating loss, it can also be important if your home suffers lesser damage. If a kitchen fire causes $25,000 in damage, and your coverage is less than 80% of the home's replacement cost, the insurer may pay less than the full amount of any loss.

An insurance agent may be able to estimate the replacement cost of your home by doing some quick math based on the square footage of your home and local construction costs. If the home is very valuable or has many unusual features, consider hiring a property appraiser. Ask your agent about guaranteed-replacement-cost coverage that might pay some rebuilding costs in excess of the policy face amount.

One common mistake people make on their homeowner's coverage is failing to pay attention to the "internal limits"—caps on how much the policy will pay for losses involving items such as jewelry, furs, artwork, silverware, and Oriental rugs. It is not unusual for a family to have $10,000 or more in jewelry but a policy that limits jewelry payouts to $2,500. Policy "endorsements" or separate "floater" policies that boost coverage of jewelry or other valuables are simple solutions. The insurer will probably demand a separate appraisal for each covered item, which is always a good idea.

Make sure your home's contents are insured for their replacement cost, not the lower actual cash value.

TEEN DRIVERS? GROAN

If you have children of driving age, your auto insurance premiums have no doubt soared. Some companies offer discounts to students who earn good grades, take a driver's education course, or go to college more than 100 miles from home—without taking the car along. In any event, consider having your teens earn the money to cover your higher insurance premiums.

Meanwhile, think about lawsuit risk in looking at both your home and auto policies. Twenty years ago, if you had been sued, there probably would have been precious few assets to which someone could lay claim. That is probably not the case today. To protect what you have, consider beefing up the "liability" component of both auto and home policies. That is the insurance that pays if you cause an accident or are sued. You should probably also augment those coverages with an umbrella liability policy of $1 million or more, which might cost as little as $100 to $300 a year.

It usually pays to consolidate your home, auto, and related coverages with a single insurance company. Many insurers offer discounts to people who purchase coverage for more than one car or who carry multiple types of policies. An insurer may sell umbrella liability policies only to people who hold both auto and home policies from that particular company.

But do some shopping, particularly if you have not reviewed your insurance since buying a home or car several years ago. There can be dramatic differences in price.

Make sure you have disability insurance, since these are high earning years. Look into buying an individual policy if you do not have long-term disability coverage at work. Also consider buying a disability policy now if you are planning to leave a secure job to start a new venture on your own. It may be impossible to buy disability coverage in your business's first few years.

LOOKING AT LIFE INSURANCE

You may need to make some tough decisions about life insurance. Coverage is much more expensive than it was when you were in your 20s and 30s. To get the most out of your insurance dollars, give careful thought to how long you will need coverage.

Over the years, your need for life insurance may have fallen or increased, depending on your finances and family circumstances. Some people in their late 40s are counting the months until the kids finish college. Others are still changing diapers. While the first group may soon see their life insurance needs decrease, the second will probably need a lot of coverage for at least another 20 years.

If you own pure-protection term insurance, and you are in good health, you might save money by switching to another insurer. A "level-premium" term policy with premiums that will remain the same for the next ten years might be the lowest-cost way to maintain coverage until your 12-year-old finishes college.

If you expect to need coverage for at least 15 or 20 more years, though, consider switching from term to a cash-value policy that includes both a death benefit and a savings component. In later years, term insurance can become unaffordable. In contrast, while the premium for a cash-value plan is usually several times higher initially, it may remain level for life. Most term policies give holders the right to convert to a cash-value plan at the same insurer, regardless of your health. If you are in tip-top shape, though, you may find a better deal or more attractive policy elsewhere.

There are special opportunities, but also risks, for people who have owned cash-value policies for years. You may have accumulated substantial savings that you could now tap, through policy loans, to pay college bills or meet other expenses. Just make sure you understand the terms before you borrow. On some policies, the return credited to your cash value is reduced when you borrow, so that the charge for borrowing is really higher than it first appears.

Whether or not you plan to borrow, make sure your cash-value

COMPARING LIFE INSURANCE COSTS

First-year premiums for annual-renewable-term insurance are much lower than those for whole-life policies, but premiums for term policies rise each year while whole-life premiums may remain level for life. These rates are for $250,000 of coverage for nonsmokers in excellent health.

	MEN		WOMEN	
AGE	TERM LIFE ($)	WHOLE LIFE ($)	TERM LIFE ($)	WHOLE LIFE ($)
25	288	2,350	240	2,003
35	290	3,333	245	2,773
45	455	5,113	373	4,088
55	1,005	7,520	808	5,498
65	3,678	13,098	2,835	9,218

NOTE: These rates were effective as of November 1995. Required cash payments may actually be less, depending on the insurer's investment results and operating expenses.
SOURCE: © 1995 Northwestern Mutual Life Insurance Co.

policy is performing as you expected. Some people who bought in the late 1980s and have not heard from their agents since could be in for an unpleasant surprise: Because interest rates tumbled following the purchase, those policies could expire years earlier than expected or require more payments than expected.

Ask the agent or insurer for an in-force illustration—a computer printout showing how the policy will perform in future years if insurance charges and interest rates remain at current levels. But be wary of agents suggesting you replace one cash-value policy with another. Such switches generate big commissions for agents, but they are often not in the policyholder's best interest.

Even if your need for insurance has shrunk, do not be too quick to drop existing cash-value policies. Once in place, they are usually good investments. And, if you have accumulated significant wealth, insurance may be useful to help your family pay any estate taxes that would be due at your death. Consider moving life insurance policies to a trust to remove the death benefit from your taxable estate.

As you approach retirement age, you may also want to think about buying a long-term-care policy. Such insurance can cover the potentially bankrupting cost of an extended nursing-home stay. But the policies themselves are quite expensive.

40s–50s

- Reassess homeowner's coverage.

- Add umbrella liability policy.

- Consider cash-value life.

- Evaluate disability protection.

- Look into long-term-care policy.

Your 60s and Beyond

Over a period of decades, you have probably accumulated substantial financial assets, personal possessions, and real estate. Review your insurance every few years to make sure those holdings are adequately protected.

Your homeowner's coverage, for instance, should be equal or close to your home's replacement cost, the cost to rebuild after a total loss. Even if you have a smaller loss, some insurers will not pay the full amount unless your policy is for at least 80% of the home's replacement cost. See if your agent can estimate replacement cost using your home's square footage and local building costs. If your home is exceptionally valuable or has noteworthy architectural features, consider hiring an independent property appraiser. For an additional measure of security, ask your agent about "guaranteed-replacement-cost" coverage, which might pay even more than the policy's stated amount in the event of a devastating loss.

Also be sure that you have sufficient coverage—and the right kind of coverage—on your household possessions. Contents are typically covered up to half of the insurance on the house. But coverage of artwork, antiques, jewelry, and some other valuables is subject to internal limits that may be only $2,500 or so. Beef up insurance on your valuables with policy endorsements or separate floater policies.

It is worth paying a little extra to have your possessions insured for their replacement cost, not the lower cash value. Make sure you can document the value of major appliances, big furniture purchases, and valuables, whether with videotapes, photographs, or receipts and appraisals. Store that documentation in a safe-deposit box.

Be certain to review your liability coverage. Without adequate liability coverage, the wealth you have accumulated over your lifetime could be depleted by a lawsuit. Augmenting the existing coverage under your homeowner's and auto policies with an umbrella policy of $1 million or more can cost just a few hundred dollars.

AUTO INSURANCE IDEAS

People in their 60s and beyond sometimes have a hard time finding auto insurance. Compared with people in their 40s and 50s, they tend to have more motor vehicle violations and accidents for each mile driven. That reflects physiological changes, such as slowed reflexes and impaired vision.

If you are having trouble finding coverage, look into the insurance sponsored by the American Association of Retired Persons (AARP), the Washington-based association for people age 50 and older. The AARP also sponsors defensive-driving courses for older Americans, offered nationwide under the name "55 Alive." Other organizations, including American Automobile Association clubs, offer classes, too. In addition to making you a safer driver, such a course could save you money: A majority of states require insurers to give discounts to older drivers who complete such programs, and some insurers do so voluntarily.

At age 65, you are eligible for Medicare, but that government program will not pay all of your medical bills. To plug the holes, many Medicare recipients buy supplemental "Medigap" policies. You can learn more about Medicare and Medigap in Chapter 4.

Many older Americans are deeply fearful of seeing their hard-earned wealth eaten up by an extended nursing-home stay—which would not be covered by Medicare or a Medigap plan. One option is to buy a long-term-care policy that can help pay for nursing homes, home health care, and related services. But such coverage is quite expensive. If you sign up at age 65, a policy might cost $1,000 to $3,000 a year. The policies also have numerous limitations, such as fixed daily payments for nursing-home care that may fall far short of actual costs in your area. Long-term-care policies probably make the most sense for married couples who are concerned that one person's nursing-home confinement would leave the other one strapped. Very wealthy people can skip the coverage and "self-insure" for the financial risk of a nursing-home stay.

Some people in their 60s and beyond may want to tap the savings they have accumulated in cash-value life insurance policies. Options include taking policy loans, surrendering part or all of the coverage, and switching some dollars into an immediate annuity—

an insurance contract that would pay a fixed sum each month for
life.

If you do not need the money, though, it generally makes sense
to hang on to an older cash-value policy. You could face a big income tax bill on the investment gains within the policy if you drop
the coverage now. In contrast, if you hold the policy to death, all
the investment gains escape income tax. As a result, your heirs would
probably receive more money than if you dropped the insurance and
invested the proceeds in bonds or bank certificates of deposit. You
might want to convert to "paid-up" status, which would reduce the
death benefit but eliminate the need to pay further premiums.

A PITCH TO AVOID

If you are about to retire and collect a company pension, an insurance agent may suggest you buy life insurance to augment your
retirement income. Most pension plans offer a certain monthly payment for your lifetime or a reduced sum that will continue in full
or in part for a surviving spouse. The insurance pitch says: Take the
pension for your lifetime only and cover your spouse through insurance. The problem with this "pension-maximization" idea is
that, in many cases, the numbers simply do not work out because
the insurance is just too expensive. You could be putting your spouse
at risk.

Meanwhile, many well-off retirees are being encouraged to buy additional life insurance policies to pay estate taxes. The federal estate
tax, with a current top rate of 55%, is due whenever someone dies
leaving more than $600,000 to people other than a surviving spouse;
state levies vary. The hot insurance product is "second-to-die" coverage that pays only when both the husband and wife have died.

Before buying additional coverage, review your options thoroughly with an estate-planning attorney and other advisers. Life insurance can be useful in providing cash to pay taxes when family
wealth is tied up in a small business or real estate. Insurance can also
be a good way to pass money to your heirs, largely because of the
income tax benefits.

But watch out for marketing hype. You may not need insurance
to pay estate taxes if you hold lots of marketable securities that could

60s +

- Add endorsements to
  insure valuables.

- Get umbrella liability
  coverage.

- Take a defensive-
  driving course.

- Hang on to cash-
  value life.

- Consider a life
  insurance trust.

be easily sold. Although life insurance can be a good investment for your heirs, it may not be as wonderful as the commission-hungry seller says. There are also various estate-planning techniques that can reduce the potential estate-tax burden. (Several such strategies are explained in Chapter 5.)

Note that insurance death benefits are usually included in calculating your taxable estate. To avoid that, consult your attorney and accountant about moving existing policies into a life insurance trust. You also should generally purchase any new policies through a trust.

FINDING AN INSURER YOU CAN RELY ON

Insurance is a funny product in that you may pay premiums for many years, even decades, without receiving anything tangible in return. Indeed, you buy many kinds of insurance hoping you will never have to file a claim. What you are buying is protection. For your insurance dollars to be well spent, you must deal with companies that are financially strong. You want to be able to count on the companies to pay up, if and when you file a claim.

Insurance-company failures are relatively rare, but they do occur. Of more than 4,000 U.S. insurers, perhaps 50 mostly very small companies might fail in a typical year. There have also been some big and frightening collapses. Executive Life Insurance of Los Angeles and Mutual Benefit Life Insurance of Newark, New Jersey, are two major life insurers that crashed in the early 1990s because of troubled investments.

You may be able to collect on a claim even if your insurer goes belly-up. Every state has a "guaranty fund" that collects money from healthy insurers to pay claims filed by policyholders of insolvent insurers. You should not rely on those mechanisms, however, because there are limits on how much you can collect, as well as other problems.

The bottom line is that whatever kind of insurance you need, you should look into an insurer's financial stability when you buy a policy and review its condition periodically in future years. Unless you are a financial analyst by trade, you probably will not be able to make any sense of an insurer's financial statements. But you also should not simply take an agent's word that the company he or she represents is in excellent shape. Instead, check the ratings an insurer has received from one or more professional rating agencies.

A WHO'S WHO OF RATERS

For decades, the primary source of insurance-company ratings has been the specialized insurance-ratings firm A. M. Best. Mention the word "ratings" to insurance professionals, and they usually think first of Best. Best changed its rating system in the early 1990s after the firm was criticized for being overly generous with its top grades.

Four other significant players have entered the insurance-rating business. One is Weiss Ratings, a relatively new firm that has sometimes been criticized for being overly negative in its assessments. The other three entrants are well known for their ratings of bonds and other securities: Duff & Phelps, Moody's Investors Service, and Standard & Poor's.

Of the various raters, some insurance specialists put the most faith in the bond-rating firms. But only a limited number of mostly large insurers are rated by those firms, in part because companies pay steep fees to be rated. (Standard & Poor's, in addition to its full "claims-paying-ability" ratings, has less rigorous "quantitative" ratings for a large number of insurers.)

All five ratings firms supply ratings over the phone, and the three bond-rating firms do so for free. Their phone numbers and the applicable fees are listed in Appendix A. You may also find some of the raters' materials, such as the massive two-volume *Best's Insurance Reports,* in your local library.

HOW HIGH IS HIGH ENOUGH?

Whatever kind of insurance you are buying, get it from a company with relatively high ratings. Although a good rating is no guarantee that a company is healthy today—or that it will still be in good shape next year—it is your best bet. Given the large number of insurers in this country, you should be able to find a highly rated company that offers the coverage you want at an acceptable price.

But be careful in looking at ratings. A particular letter grade may not mean the same thing it did when you were in high school. It may also not mean the same thing at one rating service as it does at another.

For instance, an "A" grade is the second-highest rating given out by Weiss, just one notch down from "A+." That is the way you probably remember it from your student days. But an "A" is the sixth-highest rating under the systems used by Standard & Poor's and Duff & Phelps. An "A" is the third-highest rating at Best.

As a general rule, many insurance specialists like to see a rating of "A" or higher from Best. Some set their standards even higher

COMPARING INSURANCE RATINGS

These are the letter grades handed out by the five major insurance-rating services, listed from the highest to the lowest. A rating that is a particular number of notches down from the top at one service may not be exactly equivalent to a rating that is equally far down the scale at another firm.

BEST	DUFF & PHELPS	MOODY'S	STANDARD & POOR'S*	WEISS
A++	AAA	Aaa	AAA	A+
A+	AA+	Aa1	AA+	A
A	AA	Aa2	AA	A−
A−	AA−	Aa3	AA−	B+
B++	A+	A1	A+	B
B+	A	A2	A	B−
B	A−	A3	A−	C+
B−	BBB+	Baa1	BBB+	C
C++	BBB	Baa2	BBB	C−
C+	BBB−	Baa3	BBB−	D+
C	BB+	Ba1	BB+	D
C−	BB	Ba2	BB	D−
D	BB−	Ba3	BB−	E+
E	B+	B1	B+	E
F	B	B2	B	E−
	B−	B3	B−	F
	CCC	Caa	CCC	
	DD	Ca	R	
		C		

*Standard & Poor's also assigns "quantitative" ratings, identified by a "q" after the letter grade, to insurers that have not requested a full "claims-paying-ability" rating. The quantitative ratings are derived solely from analysis of public financial statements, whereas the claims-paying-ability ratings also reflect discussions with management and access to confidential information.

when the product in question is cash-value life insurance, which incorporates a savings element as well as a death benefit. For cash value, they might look for an "A++" or "A+" from Best, as well as a top rating or next-to-top rating from at least one of the other services.

There are some good reasons to be extra choosy when buying cash-value coverage. For one thing, you may accumulate tens of thousands of dollars of savings in such a policy over the years, and you want that money to be secure. When insurance companies have failed, holders have sometimes been denied access to those funds for an extended time. (In contrast, death benefits are usually paid fairly promptly.)

Another reason to be especially picky is that switching insurers later can be costly. Insurers make it expensive to drop one company's cash-value policy for another's because they need your business for several years in order to recoup the steep up-front sales commissions they pay to agents. Finally, if you buy cash-value insurance from a highly rated company, and the rating is cut a couple of notches, you can take comfort in the fact that the company will still carry a solid rating.

INSURING YOUR CAR AND YOUR HOME

Whether you are buying a new insurance policy to protect your car or your home, or you are evaluating existing coverage, the task can be surprisingly easy—and yet deliver dramatic savings. Looking at automobile and home insurance at the same time is a good idea, since you can typically get a discount by consolidating your business with a single insurer.

The first step is deciding on the appropriate types and levels of coverage. Once that is done, you are ready to compare what various insurers have to offer. Although one insurance policy looks very much like another, there can be huge differences in price. If you have inadvertently been dealing with a high-priced insurer, a few phone calls or visits may be all it takes to make a big chunk of your annual insurance expense disappear.

Insurance for Your Car

Your automobile insurance policy is actually several different coverages rolled into one. Some are required by state law, or by lenders, while others are at your discretion. You can mix and match the types of coverage and also the amounts. Understanding the various pieces is the first step in buying or reviewing a policy. Here is a look at the most important parts of the coverage you should have.

Liability Coverage

The standard auto policy has two liability sections that compensate other people if you cause an accident. Bodily injury liability pays if someone is hurt or killed. Property-damage liability kicks in if you damage someone else's car or other property.

This insurance protects you from what could be enormous damages and legal costs in the terrible event that you are responsible for a serious accident. It also protects you by paying legal defense costs if you are wrongly accused of being at fault. If a claim is filed against you, your insurer will decide if it should be paid, negotiated, or defended in court.

Your liability coverage applies in situations where your car is driven by you, by a member of your immediate family, or by someone else who has your permission. You are also covered while driving someone else's car.

A majority of states require drivers to have liability insurance, but the mandated minimum is often far too low. For instance, the state minimum might require bodily injury coverage of $20,000 per person, up to $40,000 per accident, and property coverage of $10,000. To limit your financial risk, buy more generous coverage of at least $100,000 per person, up to $300,000 per accident, and $50,000 of property damage. (Some insurers have a per-accident maximum with no per-person limit, which provides more protection.) Consider buying an umbrella liability policy as well.

UNINSURED-MOTORIST COVERAGE

If you were seriously hurt in an accident caused by another driver, you could potentially collect from that person's liability coverage for your pain and suffering and lost wages. But what if the other driver did not have insurance? What if it were a hit-and-run accident? You could be on your own. Protecting you in such cases is the purpose of uninsured-motorist coverage, which may be combined with underinsured-motorist coverage. Even if such coverage is not required by your state, buy it. Select the same level of protection you have on the liability portion of your policy.

MEDICAL PAYMENTS

Special coverage for medical bills pays your doctor and hospital bills after an accident, regardless of who was at fault. It covers your passengers as well, and also incidents in which you as a pedestrian are hit by a car. In some states, this coverage is called personal-injury protection, or PIP, and it may also cover lost wages and other items besides medical bills.

Medical coverage is optional in some states. You may not need it if you have good medical insurance. The broader "personal-injury" coverage is usually required in so-called no-fault states, which have laws requiring that your auto-related injuries be covered by your own auto policy, regardless of who causes an accident. Under no-fault laws, there are typically limits on your ability to sue after an accident.

COLLISION AND COMPREHENSIVE

Collision insurance covers damage to your car when it collides with something else. Comprehensive insurance pays if the car is stolen or vandalized or otherwise damaged. Together, they can account for a third or a half of your annual insurance bill. These coverages are not required by law. But they usually are required by lenders when they make an auto loan and by lessors, under car leasing arrangements.

Each coverage has a deductible—the amount of loss you must pay out of pocket before the insurance kicks in. You can save some

STRENGTHENING THE SAFETY NET: AUTO INSURANCE

This illustration shows how a hypothetical Chicago motorist could get better catastrophic coverage with only a negligible increase in cost by fine-tuning his policy.

CURRENT ANNUAL PREMIUM	$1,509
Boost bodily injury coverage to $100,000 per person/ $300,000 per accident from $50,000/$100,000	+62
Boost uninsured-motorist coverage to $100,000/ $300,000 from $50,000/$100,000	+50
Raise collision deductible to $250 from $100	−44
Raise comprehensive deductible to $250 from $50	−60
ANNUAL PREMIUM FOR IMPROVED POLICY	$1,517

NOTE: This illustration uses 1995 rates as they might apply to one hypothetical motorist in a particular set of circumstances. Individual circumstances vary, and you will need to talk with an insurance agent to see what your own premium would be at today's rates. SOURCE: Allstate Insurance Company.

money on your annual premiums by raising those deductibles. For instance, raising your collision deductible from $200 to $500 might cut your collision-insurance charge by 15%.

If your once-new car is now at least five to eight years old, you might consider dropping collision and comprehensive coverage altogether. In the event your car is damaged or stolen, the insurer will pay no more than the car's current value. That value is obviously quite a bit less than it was when you first drove the car off the dealer's lot.

In weighing possible changes in deductibles and optional coverage, gather all the facts and then decide what feels right to you. Your agent can tell you the cost of each level of coverage and may also be able to tell you the market value of an older car. If not, check newspaper ads or see if your library has reference books listing such values.

INSURANCE FOR YOUR HOME AND POSSESSIONS

A tree limb crashes into your living room during a severe storm. Or a thief makes off with a diamond ring and other jewelry worth thousands of dollars. Or the boy next door breaks his arm falling off your back porch, and his parents file a lawsuit.

Any one of these events would cause heartache and disrupt your life. The expenses you would have to pay out of your own pocket should be limited, though, if you have a well-chosen and up-to-date home insurance policy. Unfortunately, too many people do not have the right coverage. Some find the holes in their insurance only when they suffer a devastating loss in a disaster such as Hurricane Andrew in 1992 or the Midwest floods of 1993. You should check the adequacy of your home coverage every few years.

PROTECTING THE HOUSE ITSELF

A primary part of your homeowner's policy covers damage to the house itself from perils such as fire, theft, wind, hail, and falling objects. Your coverage should be equal or close to your home's replacement cost—the amount it would cost to rebuild totally today. Less coverage could leave you short of funds to rebuild in the event of a devastating loss. At some insurers, coverage below 80% of replacement cost could leave you out thousands of dollars in the wake of a smaller loss.

How so? Let's say your house would cost $120,000 to rebuild, and you have a $60,000 insurance policy. You suffer a $20,000 loss when that tree limb crashes into the living room. Because your policy fails the 80% test, your insurer might refuse to pay the full amount of that $20,000 loss. It might pay only 50% of your loss, or $10,000, because the coverage on the house is 50% of replacement cost.

Unless you are a building contractor, you probably have no idea of your home's replacement cost. Ask your agent or hire an independent property appraiser for help. You might also ask a contractor or the local builders association for average construction costs per square foot. A home's resale price often exceeds the rebuilding cost, because the price includes the land. But some fine older homes would cost more to reconstruct than they would command at sale.

To trim costs, consider raising your deductible—the amount of loss you pay out of pocket before the insurance kicks in. Going to a $500 deductible from $250 might cut your bill by 10%.

Some policies include a handy feature that increases coverage annually, in line with building-cost inflation. (You should review the policy amount anyway every few years, to make sure it is appropriate.)

You should also ask about guaranteed-replacement-cost coverage that will pay rebuilding costs even in excess of the policy's face amount. Such policies are becoming more common, and in some cases they may cost the same or even less than the usual replacement policy. But guaranteed-replacement-cost policies are usually not available for older homes and those that fail to meet certain other criteria. Payment is often capped at 120% or 150% of the policy amount. An insurer may require you to carry a larger dollar amount of coverage than you do now.

Some home insurance buyers may not be able to get standard replacement-cost coverage. You may be limited to coverage for your home's market value if you live in a high-crime area, or rent out a home to others, or own a fine older home whose replacement cost would far exceed the current market value.

INSURING THE STUFF INSIDE

Household possessions are typically covered for at least 50% of the overall policy amount, which is sufficient for most people. But your policy may cover furniture and other possessions only at their actual cash value. What you want is replacement-cost coverage on contents, which can boost your bill by 10% or 15%. While the ten-year-old table and chairs in your kitchen are probably quite functional, their actual cash value is not much. In the event of a fire or other loss, you would want enough money to buy new items.

Many homeowners should also upgrade the standard contents coverage in another way—by adding policy endorsements or separate floater policies for jewelry and other valuables. That is because home insurance typically has internal limits on how much coverage is provided for such items as jewelry, furs, computers, silver, antiques, stamp and coin collections, and Oriental rugs. Your jewelry coverage, for instance, might be only $2,500—a level easily exceeded if a thief makes off with a diamond engagement ring and a few other pieces.

A floater will increase the scope of your coverage as well as the dollar amount. Under a standard home policy, your jewelry is insured against theft but not against accidental loss. By contrast, a floater will pay if the clasp on your emerald necklace breaks and the piece slips off unnoticed while you are dancing at your cousin's wedding. The insurer will probably require appraisals for each item, which is always a smart idea.

LIMITING LAWSUIT RISK

The liability portion of your home policy comes to the rescue when your young neighbor breaks his arm after that tumble from your porch. Such coverage pays others when you are legally responsible for their losses. It also pays your legal defense costs.

Having sufficient liability coverage is critical to protect your accumulated wealth. A typical homeowner's policy includes $100,000 in coverage, with higher limits available for an extra charge. You might also augment the liability coverage in both your home and auto policies by buying a separate umbrella liability policy.

UNCOVERED CATASTROPHES

Among the risks not covered by the standard home policy are earthquakes and floods. If you live in an area where there is not much risk of such catastrophes, you do not have to give them a lot of thought. But homeowners who are at risk should buy the special coverage that will protect their financial well-being if Mother Nature goes on a rampage. While the premiums for this insurance are often steep, do not roll the dice when your family home is at stake. The types of disasters you have seen on television really could happen to you.

Earthquake coverage is offered by insurers as an add-on to a regular homeowner's policy. Insurers write flood insurance as participants in the government-subsidized National Flood Insurance Program, which is administered by the Federal Emergency Management Agency.

HOME INSURANCE FOR PEOPLE WHO RENT

If you rent an apartment or house, you still need home insurance just as much as those who own. While you do not need to insure the building against damage, you do need the two other key components of a homeowner's policy: coverage of household contents and liability insurance that pays if you are sued.

Cost is no excuse not to have renter's coverage. A policy might cost $100 to $300 a year. As with homeowner's coverage, it is worth paying a little more to insure your possessions for replacement cost, not actual cash value. And consider policy endorsements or separate floater policies to beef up coverage of jewelry or other valuables.

CONDO AND CO-OP COVERAGE

There are special home insurance policies for owners of condominiums and co-operatives. And there are unique insurance issues for these people to consider.

In particular, condo and co-op owners need to find out whether they are responsible for built-in items, such as plumbing fixtures and kitchen cabinets, or whether those are covered under a master policy that insures the overall structure and common areas. Check the condo association bylaws or the co-op's proprietary lease. Make sure you get the coverage you need on your individual policy.

As with other home policies, it is worth paying a little more to insure your possessions for replacement cost, not actual cash value. Also consider policy endorsements or separate floater policies to beef up coverage of jewelry or other valuables.

BE ABLE TO PROVE IT

Buying adequate insurance is not enough. Do not pat yourself on the back unless you also have records to document the condition and quantity of your household goods in the event of a loss.

Perhaps the easiest and most comprehensive documentation is a home-video tour of your abode, complete with a look inside closets, kitchen cabinets, and drawers. Other options include photographs, home-inventory software, and inventory worksheets supplied by agents and insurers.

Make a point of saving receipts for major purchases. Appraisals for your jewelry and other valuables are good to have and are usually required if you buy additional coverage for those items. Be sure

STRENGTHENING THE SAFETY NET: HOME INSURANCE

A few smart moves can mean better coverage for your home and your household possessions, as well as a stronger financial defense against lawsuits. This example, using 1995 rates from State Farm, is for a home in Indianapolis currently insured for $150,000 of replacement-cost coverage.

CURRENT ANNUAL PREMIUM	$653
Switch to replacement coverage, instead of actual-cash-value coverage, on contents	+78
Add $5,000 jewelry endorsement	+29
Raise liability coverage to $300,000 from $100,000	+10
Raise deductible to $500 from $250	−111
ANNUAL PREMIUM FOR REVISED HOMEOWNER'S POLICY*	$659

*An even better option: If this home qualifies for guaranteed-replacement-cost insurance, the premium for the same amount of coverage would be a much lower $528.
SOURCE: State Farm Insurance Companies.

to store your documentation outside the house—a safe-deposit box is a good place.

AN UMBRELLA FOR EXTRA PROTECTION

Liability insurance is a key component of both your home and auto policies. It pays if you are responsible for someone else's losses—not only the losses themselves but also your legal defense costs, including your legal fees if you are unjustly sued. But with lawsuits today that seek damages of $1 million or more, even from people who are not wealthy, the basic liability coverage included in your auto and home policies probably is not enough.

There is an easy and not-too-expensive way to protect your wealth more fully from lawsuit risk: an umbrella liability policy. An umbrella policy provides additional coverage of $1 million or more. If your auto policy provides $300,000 of liability coverage, for instance, a $1 million umbrella would boost your auto-related liability protection to $1.3 million. It would likewise augment the liability portion of your home policy. Umbrella policies also usually cover some risks not covered by auto and home policies, such as libel, slander, and invasion of privacy.

The price of this important extra measure of protection is relatively modest. A $1 million umbrella typically costs $100 to $300 a year. You might pay $200 to $500 a year for a $2 million policy.

Many insurers require people buying umbrella liability policies also to buy auto and home policies from them. Insurers usually specify minimum levels of liability coverage you must carry in those underlying policies before they will sell an umbrella to go on top.

SHOPPING FOR AUTO AND HOME COVERAGE

It is easy to compare different insurers' charges for auto and home insurance—and maybe reap significant savings—once you have decided on the particular types and levels of coverage you need. Price is not the only consideration, though, in picking a company. You want a financially strong company, as evidenced by high ratings. And you want a company that is not just able, but also willing, to pay. Some insurers are only too happy to take their customers' premium checks but turn ugly when somebody files a claim.

There are a couple of valuable resources that can help you make a smart selection without spending a lot of time. One is your state insurance department. (You will find addresses and phone numbers in Appendix A.) These regulatory agencies can tell you which insurers are most active in your state. Many publish shoppers' guides and surveys that show what different insurers charge for similar coverage.

Perhaps even more valuable, the insurance departments keep track of consumer complaints. Many publish annual surveys that rank auto and home insurers by the volume of complaints (as a percentage of each insurer's business in the state). Other departments will supply some complaint information over the phone.

Consumer Reports magazine is another good source of information about how insurers treat policyholders when they file claims. The magazine publishes articles every few years that rate insurers for claims-related service, based on surveys of the magazine's readers. Your library should have back issues. (Auto insurance was covered in October 1995 and home insurance in October 1993. To check if there is anything more recent, ask your library or call *Consumer Reports* at 914-378-2000.)

SOME COMPANIES TO CONSIDER

You might start your shopping with a couple of very familiar names: State Farm and Allstate. State Farm Insurance of Bloomington, Illinois, and Allstate Insurance of Northbrook, Illinois, are the biggest companies selling property and liability insurance in this country. They tend to offer reasonable, although not bargain-basement, rates, and they also earn decent grades for service and financial strength. State Farm and Allstate each sell through local agents who represent only State Farm or Allstate. Call or visit the agents nearest you.

But do not stop at that. Next, pick up the phone and dial a few toll-free 800 numbers. You may be able to find even cheaper coverage through one of a small number of companies, including charge-card powerhouse American Express, that sell insurance by telephone and mail. Direct marketing saves companies money, and they can pass that savings along to policyholders as lower premiums. You do not have to forgo good service, either. Direct writers Amica Mutual Insurance and USAA (United Services Automobile Association) received top grades for customer service in the *Consumer Reports* rankings.

Be forewarned, though: Insurers that sell direct tend to be very picky. Some deal only with buyers who meet certain criteria. You will be asked many questions. At some companies, you might be rejected flat out for auto coverage if you have one or more accidents on your driving record.

You might also contact a local independent agent who represents multiple insurers. Policies sold through independent agents tend to be more expensive because of the agents' higher commissions. If your current policy was obtained through an independent agent, you can probably save money by taking your business elsewhere. On the other hand, an independent agent can shop your business with a number

CALLING FOR COVERAGE

Here are four insurers that sell auto and home insurance direct to consumers by phone and mail.

- **American Express, New York**
  800-842-3344

- **Amica Mutual Insurance, Providence, R.I.**
  Referral by existing Amica policyholder is preferred but not required.
  800-242-6422

- **GEICO, Washington, D.C.**
  800-841-3000

- **USAA, San Antonio, Texas**
  Sells only to current and former military officers and their families. USAA stands for United Services Automobile Association.
  800-531-8080

of companies. That can sometimes be very helpful. If you have a poor driving record, for instance, an independent agent can obtain auto insurance quotes from a couple of companies that specialize in substandard risks.

ASK ABOUT DISCOUNTS

When you shop for new coverage or review what you have, be sure to ask about discounts. Most insurers offer a bevy of discounts that can reduce your annual charges. The specifics vary from company to company, but there are numerous possibilities. With auto policies, for instance, there are usually discounts for customers who are insuring more than one car or who have not had an accident in the past three years. There are discounts in most states for older drivers—and in some states, for all drivers—who take a defensive-driving course. Vehicles with antitheft devices, airbags, or antilock brakes often qualify for discounts. There are also discounts for students with good grades and for young drivers who have taken driver's education courses. And if the young driver in your family has gone off to college more than 100 miles away and left your car at home, call your insurance agent—that is another reason for a discount.

With home insurance, you will find that smoke detectors, fire extinguishers, burglar alarms, and deadbolt locks often qualify for a discount. So might banishing all smokers from the premises. Customers who buy auto and home coverage from the same insurer and longtime policyholders also often qualify for discounts.

LIFE INSURANCE

There is a lot of value in life insurance. There are also lots of problems in the way it is sold.

Life insurance is a wonderful way to minimize financial risk. The primary reason to buy it is to provide for your dependents. Do you have a spouse or young children depending on your income? A life insurance policy can provide a lump sum after your death to replace the income you would have contributed to the family for years to come.

Like other types of coverage, life insurance is all about odds. At age 30 or 40, the probability of your imminent death is slim. That is why it does not cost much to assure what agents call an "instant estate" for your family if you are among the unlucky few who die so young. For a 35-year-old man, a $250,000 policy might cost just $200 to $300 for the first year.

As for the problems, just consider the industry truism that "life insurance is sold, not bought." Most of us would rather not think about our own mortality. Few people seek out agents or insurers to buy coverage, even when they clearly need it. Many rebuff agents who call. To surmount those hurdles, companies pay agents hefty commissions, equal to between 50% and 100% of the first-year policy charge, to pester and persuade people to buy. Some agents get the job done by explaining the benefits of their wares forthrightly. Others play fast and loose with the truth. While this hard-sell system has led many people to buy much-needed coverage they would never otherwise have obtained, it has also persuaded too many people to buy coverage that is unnecessary, the wrong type, or too costly.

You do not need to be among that put-upon crowd. Having made it this far into this book, you are obviously a self-starter where personal finance is concerned. The secret to being a smart life insurance consumer is simple: You need to understand the product and decide what you want before you hit the market. Watch out for inflated marketing claims. If you proceed in logical steps, getting the right coverage at the right price can be much easier than you might think. The following sections can help you figure out how much life insurance you need, what kind you should have, and how to evaluate your existing coverage. You can find additional tips and a useful worksheet in the Buyer's Guide to Life Insurance, Appendix C.

OTHER REASONS TO BUY

Most families should not buy life insurance for any reason other than replacing a breadwinner's income in the event of early death. If an agent suggests a cash-value policy—one that combines a death benefit with a savings component— as an investment or as a retirement-savings vehicle, you should generally say no. Unless you need the insurance protection, you are probably wasting your money.

Still, there are some other legitimate uses of insurance for people in particular circumstances. Among them:

- **Continuation of a small business.** If two people own a business jointly, they have to plan for family needs and business continuation in the event one person dies. Life insurance can assure each partner enough cash to buy the other's interest from surviving family members in the event of a death.

- **Estate planning for affluent individuals.** If a person's wealth is tied up in a small business or in real estate, insurance can provide ready cash to pay the estate taxes that will be due at death. Heirs will not be forced to dispose of hard-to-sell assets at fire-sale prices.

- **An investment for heirs.** For affluent individuals with large sums that they are sure they will not touch, buying a cash-value policy might provide more cash to beneficiaries than buying bonds or other securities because of the significant income tax advantages of life insurance.

If any of these reasons seems appropriate for you, proceed with care. Commission-hungry agents routinely overhype life insurance as some sort of magic estate-planning tool for the wealthy. Get an unbiased second opinion from an attorney or fee-only financial adviser who has no business dealings with the insurance agent. (Also, see Chapter 5 for some estate-planning strategies that will not make your insurance agent rich.)

How Much Is Enough?

Deciding on an appropriate amount of coverage is the first step in buying life insurance or evaluating your current coverage. While you can easily have too little, you may have too much. If fact, it is just possible that you do not need life insurance at all.

The primary use of life insurance—the one we focus on in this book—is to provide money your dependents can tap immediately and over the years if you should die tomorrow. If no one would be financially harmed by your death, you probably do not need any life insurance. You may well be in this position if you are a 20-something single with no children. As a general rule, there is also no need to buy insurance on a child's life.

But if there are people depending on your income, you do need life insurance. It is important to make sure you have enough. A policy with too small a death benefit could cause severe hardship for your family in the event of your death. Never skimp on the amount of coverage in order to buy more expensive types of policies that offer a savings component as well as the basic death benefit.

At the same time, it is important to make sure you do not have too much life insurance. A policy with a death benefit that is unnecessarily large eats up dollars that might be better devoted to retirement savings or other important goals.

NO MAGIC NUMBER

Unfortunately, there are no hard-and-fast rules on how much life insurance is enough. A few years ago, *The Wall Street Journal* asked ten financial advisers and agents to make recommendations for a hypothetical 45-year-old man with a wife and two children. The suggestions ranged all the way from $250,000 of coverage to $1.2 million.

Still, deciding how much life insurance to carry does not have to be as frustrating as such widely disparate suggestions imply. The key is to accept that there is not a single magic number. Play around with some numbers yourself or with professional assistance. Scrutinize and vary the assumptions used. Then go ahead and buy coverage without further delay. Any thoughtful decision about how much insurance to buy is probably better than no decision at all.

One approach is to use an old rule of thumb that life insurance should equal five to seven times—some say ten times—a person's annual salary. One variation of that basic guide is to maintain coverage equal to four times pay, plus another two times pay for each child to be raised and educated, minus your investment and pension assets.

TRY THE WORKSHEET

Such multiples provide only ballpark figures, though, and they may be totally inappropriate for a particular family's needs and goals.

BENEFITS FROM UNCLE SAM

While most people think of Social Security as a source of retirement income, the government program might also provide significant income for your family in the event of your death. Social Security survivor benefits can reduce the amount of life insurance you need to buy.

The biggest monthly benefit is paid when covered workers die leaving minor children. Each child is entitled to a benefit if unmarried and under age 18, or under age 19 if still in high school. There is also a benefit for a surviving spouse taking care of children who are under age 16 or disabled. The average benefit paid to a surviving spouse with one or more minor children is about $1,400 a month.

Social Security benefits to survivors generally stop if the children reach maturity before the surviving spouse reaches retirement age. Later on, though, your surviving spouse can collect a retirement benefit based on your work record; those benefits are available when the surviving spouse reaches age 60, or age 50 if he or she is disabled. To receive a personal estimate of all the Social Security benefits for which you are eligible, call the Social Security Administration (800-772-1213) and ask for a Form SA-7004-SM.

Many advisers and insurance sellers use detailed worksheets or computer programs to help people calculate their insurance needs. You can do an abbreviated version of such an analysis using the worksheet in the Buyer's Guide to Life Insurance, Appendix C.

If you are married, you and your spouse should each do a separate calculation of your insurance needs. Do not overlook a spouse who stays at home to care for children. In many families, it makes sense to purchase some insurance on the life of the stay-at-home parent. If that individual died, the surviving job-holding spouse would face new expenses for child care and household services. An insurance policy could also supply a ready sum for college bills or other family goals.

TYPES OF LIFE INSURANCE

People trying to sell life insurance often have definite ideas about the type of policy you should buy. You may hear about the wonders of cash-value coverage and the horrors of competing term policies—or the exact opposite. As a consumer, you should be wary of any salesperson who presents this product choice as a battle between good and evil. The two principal types of life insurance are indeed very different. Term policies, which are generally much cheaper to begin with, provide a payment upon death. Cash-value policies not only provide a death benefit but also include a savings component.

There is no absolute right or wrong for all buyers. Among the factors life insurance buyers need to consider are how much they can afford to spend, how long they will need the coverage, and how much effort they want to devote to buying the insurance.

In general, term is the right choice if cash is tight or if your need for insurance will last no more than 15 or 20 years. It is also by far the simpler of the two products. Cash value can be a better choice for people who will need insurance longer than 15 or 20 years or all the way to their full life expectancy. But many agents push cash-value coverage because the higher premiums translate into higher commissions.

It does not have to be an either-or decision, though. Some people find their needs best met by a mix of term and cash-value coverage.

TERM INSURANCE

As the name suggests, term insurance is a promise from an insurer to pay a certain sum to your beneficiaries if you die during the term when coverage is in effect. It is pure protection, with no savings element mixed in. Many people buy term because it is much less complex and, initially, far less expensive than cash-value coverage, which does include a savings or investment account.

Term is a cheap way to get a lot of coverage when you are relatively young. Many people simply cannot afford to buy the full death benefit they need in the form of cash-value coverage. So term coverage is obviously the way to go.

But if you own a term policy, your insurance bills will go up as you grow older and the odds of imminent death increase. People who save a lot of money during their working years may not need life insurance coverage in retirement. But for people who need or want coverage for more than 15 or 20 years or all the way to their full life expectancy, term is usually not the right choice. In your 60s and later years, term coverage can be prohibitively expensive. Some policies cannot even be renewed past age 70.

Most term policies give holders the right to convert to a cash-value policy at the same company without having to take a medical exam. Some people who have a long-term need but limited cash may want to select a term plan with the intention of converting to cash-value coverage later on.

There are two basic types of term life to consider.

• **Annual-renewable term.** The simplest type of term coverage is annual-renewable term, or ART, on which the premiums go up each year. Different insurance companies take very different approaches in pricing this plain-vanilla product. One company might start with a super-low first-year rate, which then ratchets up sharply in subsequent years. Another might charge a higher premium in year one but raise the charge in more modest increments after that.

You usually do not know for certain, however, what the future-year charges will be. Many insurers guarantee the annual-term charge for just the first year. Beyond that, you will typically be shown a schedule of "projected" or "current" charges the insurer expects to levy in future years. Insurance companies retain the right to raise prices all the way to the much higher "guaranteed" charges—although few have actually done so.

• **Level-premium term.** Some of the hottest-selling term insurance policies in recent years have been level-premium policies that come with charges that are projected—and often guaranteed—to remain the same for 5, 10, 15, or even 20 years at a time. In the year you purchase a level-premium term policy, it often costs more than an annual-renewable one. But if held for the full level-premium period, a level-premium policy is usually the cheapest coverage to be found.

Level-premium policies are an ideal choice for insurance buyers who know their need will end at a particular time, such as when a child will graduate from college. If the charge is guaranteed for the full period, you lock in your cost.

But there is also a big risk in most level-premium term policies. If a policyholder wants to continue coverage beyond the level-premium period, and his or her health has deteriorated, premiums

COMPARING TERM POLICIES

A 40-year-old man who needs $250,000 of life insurance for ten years could save money by buying a ten-year level-premium term policy rather than annual-renewable term. But he should be prepared for a giant leap in the premium if he decides to keep the coverage longer and if his health is then impaired.

POLICY YEAR	PREMIUM ($)		
	ANNUAL-RENEWABLE	LEVEL-PREMIUM	
1	328	310	
2	345	310	
3	368	310	
4	393	310	
5	423	310	
6	455	310	
7	490	310	
8	528	310	
9	568	310	
10	610	310	
		STAYS HEALTHY	HEALTH IMPAIRED
11	655	623	1,288
12	705	623	1,398
13	760	623	1,525
14	823	623	1,668
15	903	623	1,833

NOTE: Based on mid-1995 prices from two major insurers.
SOURCE: Compulife®. Compulife is a registered trademark of Compulife Software, Inc.

will skyrocket. That is because most level-premium policies are what are known as re-entry policies. At the end of the initial level-premium period, holders who pass a medical exam can re-enter the coverage at what are expected to be favorable rates. In many cases they would simply be buying a new policy from the same insurer. People who are in poor health can continue the existing policy, but the charges are typically horrendous.

CASH-VALUE INSURANCE

A cash-value policy is like term insurance plus something else—a built-in savings or investment account. The accumulating cash value in the savings component is what gives these policies their name.

Fundamentally, a cash-value policy is simply a convenient way to pay for a lifetime of term insurance coverage. In the year you buy a cash-value policy, it will cost several times more than term. In essence, you are overpaying for the basic insurance protection. But the premium is usually intended—and sometimes guaranteed—to remain level for life. The early-year overpayments are used to defray the high cost of coverage later on and to reduce the amount of coverage you need.

Say you buy a policy with an unchanging $100,000 death benefit. After a few decades, you might have $50,000 of accumulated cash value and only $50,000 of pure protection. Within the policy, the charge for each $1,000 of protection goes up steadily with age, just as the price of term does.

A policy's cash value earns interest or accumulates other investment gains. You can take some or all of those dollars if you drop the policy. You can also tap those accumulating dollars by taking a policy loan, although a loan reduces the death benefit the policy would pay if you died tomorrow.

When you buy a cash-value policy, certain levels of death benefit and cash value are guaranteed by the insurance company. The insurer usually also projects higher levels of death benefit and cash value, but whether they materialize depends on future investment returns and policy expenses.

Consider cash-value insurance if you will need coverage for many years and you can afford the premium it takes to buy the amount of death benefit you need. Such coverage is the life insurance of choice for people who want or need to have coverage in place for their full life expectancy.

Some people disparage cash-value coverage by saying that consumers do better to "buy term and invest the difference." The term-and-invest strategy makes sense for a short-term insurance need. But

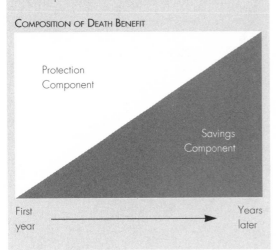

UNDERSTANDING CASH-VALUE INSURANCE

With many cash-value policies, the annual premium and the death benefit stay the same from year to year. But the composition of the death benefit changes, as shown in this simplified diagram: Over time, you accumulate more and more dollars of savings or "cash value," and you buy less and less protection from the insurer.

COMPOSITION OF DEATH BENEFIT

Protection
Component

Savings
Component

First
year

Years
later

over a period of 20 or 30 years, or longer, buying cash-value insurance may be a better deal. You may end up with more cash if you surrender a cash-value policy after a couple of decades than if you had used equivalent annual sums to buy term and invest. That is because cash-value policies enjoy certain income tax advantages: Investment gains are not taxed until you surrender a policy. And they escape income taxation entirely if you hold the policy to death.

But do not scrimp on the amount of coverage you need so that you can afford to buy a cash-value policy. Many people simply do not have the money required to buy sufficient coverage in cash-value form—or to buy term and invest the difference. For them, the answer is a term policy. They can go a long way toward meeting their investment needs by putting as much as they can afford into tax-advantaged retirement-savings plans at work and making smart use of other tax-favored options, including Individual Retirement Accounts. (Chapter 2 has many tips on how to invest a small nest egg.)

Also understand that cash value is the policy of choice for most commission-paid sellers. Whether an agent sells term or cash value, the commission is usually 50% to 100% of your first-year payment. But because you will pay several times more initially for cash value than for term, the agent will collect several times more commission for the same amount of protection.

Within the broad category of cash-value coverage are some distinctly varied product designs:

• **Whole life.** The old standard and still the biggest-selling form of cash-value life is whole life. This type of cash-value plan usually has the highest annual charges but also the strongest guarantees for the buyer. If you keep paying the specified premium year after year, you are usually guaranteed coverage for your whole life.

• **Universal life.** Flexibility is one of the major attributes of universal life. You can skip a payment or vary the amount that you pay. You can pay lower premiums than you would with whole life, although you may find in later years those premiums are not enough to keep the policy going for life. Universal-life and whole-life policies should perform similarly over long periods of time if you pay the same premiums into each.

• **Variable life.** When companies sell whole-life and universal-life policies, they typically invest in bonds and credit interest to your cash value each year. With a variable-life policy, you allocate your accumulated dollars among a variety of investment accounts, called "subaccounts," that are comparable to stock and bond mutual funds. Each year, the value of those holdings can go up or down. Variable life has gained in popularity in recent years, although it still attracts fewer dollars than whole life and universal. Many variable policies are actually of the variable-universal variety, meaning they offer both investment choice and payment flexibility. Buy variable life only if you are inclined to invest much of your cash value in common stocks. Watch out for exorbitant fees.

WHAT ABOUT THOSE EXTRAS?

Whether you buy term or cash-value coverage, there are several add-ons, or riders, that an agent or company representative may urge you to buy. With many of these extras, the best answer is no.

For instance, an accidental-death-and-dismemberment (ADD) rider will deliver a souped-up benefit to your loved ones if you die in an accident rather than from disease. But why would they need more? Buy the right amount of regular life insurance and say no to ADD.

A child rider on your policy will provide some insurance on your minor child's life. But there is generally no need for children to have life insurance. Most children do not provide income that their families would need to replace in the event of a tragic death.

On the other hand, one rider that is probably worth considering is the "disability waiver of premium." This one will continue your life insurance coverage, without requiring you to make premium payments, if you become disabled. You should probably buy this rider if your regular disability insurance is skimpy or nonexistent.

CASH-VALUE CAVEATS

While cash-value coverage has a lot going for it, there are substantial risks. One big risk is that you can take a financial beating if you buy a typical cash-value plan from an agent and drop the coverage a few years later. When you drop a cash-value plan, you can walk away with some accumulated cash value, called the "surrender value." But some policies have practically no surrender value even after you have made sizable payments for three or four years. That is because much of what you pay in the first few years is used to pay the agent's commission.

Industry statistics suggest that one-third of whole-life policies are dropped within five years. Policy surrenders cost consumers huge sums—perhaps as much as $6 billion a year, according to an estimate by the Consumer Federation of America.

Meanwhile, there are other risks related to the complexity of a cash-value policy's protection-and-savings design. Most consumers simply do not understand what they are buying. Some agents overstate the attractiveness of such policies as investments. And some understate the risk that people may have to pay higher premiums or pay for more years than projected if future interest rates and insurance charges are less favorable than assumed.

Buy a cash-value policy only if you are going to take the time to make sure you understand what you are buying. You can avoid most commission-related charges and much of the marketing hype by buying "low-load" policies from a small number of insurers that deal directly with consumers. (You can find them listed in the Buyer's Guide to Life Insurance, Appendix C.)

SHOPPING FOR COVERAGE

Once you have decided on the appropriate amount and general type of life insurance to buy, the actual process of shopping does not have to be an ordeal.

Buying term is particularly easy. First, fine-tune the types of term to consider based on how long you need the coverage. After that, gathering a handful of quotes to compare can be as simple as spending a half hour on the phone. Buying cash-value coverage does not have to be much trickier. Seek out one or two local agents. Or use your newly acquired insurance savvy to buy a low-load high-performance policy from a company that bypasses the agent community and markets direct. (You can find tips on buying both term and cash-value policies in the Buyer's Guide to Life Insurance, Appendix C.)

Whatever type of coverage you are buying, you need to check the ratings on the insurer's financial strength, as explained earlier in this chapter. And you have to consider how your insurance tab will be affected by your health, your hobbies, and whether or not you smoke.

A LOT DEPENDS ON YOU

Are you very healthy? Or not so healthy? Do you fly a private plane or have other high-risk hobbies? Do you smoke?

With life insurance, as with other types of coverage, insurers set their premiums based on how likely you are to file a claim. The old pay more than the young. Women pay less than men of the same age because women tend to live longer. Beyond that, many life insurance companies offer reduced rates to buyers whose health and lifestyles make them likely to live longer than others of the same age and sex. They charge higher rates for smokers than nonsmokers because of the attendant health risks. The highest rates, at each age and sex, are charged people with significant health problems that put them at particular risk.

If you are a nonsmoker in good health, you might qualify for attractively priced coverage as a preferred risk. Companies compete aggressively for the business of people they perceive to be the best risks. You have to watch out, though, because some agents will quote attractive rates without specifying that those charges assume you qualify as a preferred risk. A company might have outstanding preferred rates but set its standards so high that very few applicants make it.

In general, you will not qualify for preferred rates if you are overweight, if you have medical problems, such as high blood pressure, or if you engage in a hazardous activity, such as motorcycle racing or flying a private plane. Some other criteria may come as a surprise. Some insurers exclude people who have gotten more than a couple of speeding tickets in recent years. Others rule out people who are healthy but who have had an immediate relative die before age 60 of a heart attack or other specified ailment.

You could also be denied preferred status because of conditions you are not aware of, such as a high cholesterol level uncovered through a blood test. When you apply for coverage, insurers typically dispatch a medical technician to collect blood and urine specimens and to check your blood pressure, height, and weight. The insurer might pay for a complete physical by a doctor if the applicant is older and seeking a very large policy.

As you narrow down the insurers you are considering, you should ask the agent or insurer for the requirements to get preferred rates. Some people may want to ask for both preferred and standard rates.

HELP FOR THE HARD-TO-INSURE

What if you are definitely not in great shape? The good news is that life insurance is available even for people with some pretty serious

ailments. The bad news is it may take a little effort to find a willing insurer at a reasonable price.

While many people can purchase life insurance on their own,
without an agent, that is usually not the best
route for people in impaired health. You should
ask one or two local agents to recommend an
agent who specializes in "substandard" or "impaired" risks.

You want someone who knows which insurers specialize in such business and, within that
group, which insurers are likely to quote the best
rates for a particular impairment. One company
may be considerably friendlier to diabetics than
another, for instance. The agent might discuss your medical history
with representatives of various companies before actually filing a formal application.

> ## THE COST OF SMOKING
>
> There is an obvious way that millions of people
> could cut their life insurance bills sharply. All
> they have to do is stop smoking. On a term pol-
> icy, where the savings is most visible, a non-
> smoker might pay half as much as a smoker. To
> qualify as a nonsmoker, you may have to be free
> of tobacco for one to three years. Companies
> sometimes offer nonsmoker rates, on a trial
> basis, if you promise to quit.

EVALUATING YOUR EXISTING COVERAGE

No one wants to spend a lot of time thinking about life insurance.
Unfortunately, life insurance is not something that can be safely
tucked away and forgotten. Over time, your needs change. A particular policy may turn out to have been a poor choice. Or it may
now be possible to get comparable coverage for less money.

It is smart to review your life insurance every few years. If you
cannot remember the last time you even thought about your coverage, here are seven reasons to dig out your policies and related papers and take a fresh look:

1. You may be underinsured or overinsured. Think about the reason you
bought a policy in the first place and how your circumstances may
have changed. Then fill out the worksheet in the Buyer's Guide to
Life Insurance, Appendix C.

2. You may be paying too much. Prices for term coverage, the simplest
form of life insurance, vary widely. If you bought years ago, it is
worthwhile—and also easy—to compare the cost of your coverage
with what you would have to pay for a new policy. You might save

a lot of money on a new policy if you are a very healthy nonsmoker and you bought your current policy before insurers divided nonsmokers into preferred and standard risks.

Before you check with other insurers, pull out the listing of projected premiums you received when you bought your policy and check the most recent bill to verify that your insurance company is sticking to that schedule. Or you can ask your agent or insurer for an in-force illustration showing projected future premiums.

3. You may need coverage for a longer time. Changing family circumstances, such as a new child, may mean that some adjustments in your term coverage are in order. You may be better off with a new policy if your current term plan will require you to pass a physical exam within the next few years to continue coverage at reasonable rates.

If you know your need for insurance will end at a particular date, you might lock in a low cost over your holding period by buying a term policy on which the premiums will remain level for 5, 10, 15, or even 20 years. Meanwhile, term holders who need coverage for more than 20 years or to life expectancy should probably switch to a cash-value policy whose premiums may remain level for life.

4. Your cash-value plan may be strapped for cash. People who bought whole life or universal life several years ago, when interest rates were much higher, may be in for a real surprise. There are significant consequences to the slower-than-projected growth of cash value.

In the case of universal life, the current annual premium may not be sufficient to keep the coverage in force for life. Many whole-life holders who had been told their premiums would vanish after, say, ten years may find that payments are due for years longer. (Even in the best of cases, the premiums do not really vanish: Instead, earnings within the policy are used to pay future premiums.) Find out where you stand by asking your agent or insurer for an in-force illustration.

5. Beneficiaries may be out of date. The person you named years ago to receive the policy benefit at your death may not be the same person you would want to receive the money today. An old policy might name a former spouse, for example, to whom you no longer have a financial obligation. You can file a simple form with the agent or insurer to make a change.

6. *You might be able to cut taxes.* Affluent policyholders may do well to shift ownership of their policies to a life insurance trust. At your death, if you own a policy, the death benefit is included in your estate and potentially subject to steep estate taxes. Assets transferred to a trust escape that bite. Discuss benefits and legal costs with an estate-planning attorney.

7. *Your insurer may have weakened.* Insurance-company failures have been relatively rare. But financial advisers say policyholders should periodically check their insurers' financial-health ratings by asking the agent or checking one or more rating agencies. If you own term insurance and are in good health, you can probably move from a low-rated company to a higher-rated one without much cost. But you should carefully consider costs before replacing one cash-value plan with another. Moreover, even in insolvencies, death benefits have usually been paid.

DO NOT RUSH TO REPLACE

In switching from one insurer to another, you should never cancel the existing policy until you have the new one in hand. You should be wary of switching at all, though, if your current coverage is a cash-value variety, such as a whole-life or universal policy.

Many people with cash-value life insurance have been taken advantage of in recent years by unscrupulous agents sometimes dubbed "replacement artists." These agents generate big commissions for themselves by persuading policyholders to drop one cash-value policy for another. The commissions make swaps terribly costly—and usually leave policyholders worse off.

As a general rule, you should be very suspicious of any commissioned salesperson who tells you that your policy is a poor performer—or that the company is going down the drain. You certainly cannot trust an agent trying to sell you a policy from Company B to give you a unbiased opinion of where you stand with Company A.

Still, replacing one cash-value policy with another does occasionally make sense. Moving from one cash-value insurer to another may be worthwhile if your current company's health has deteriorated severely. It can also make sense to switch if your current policy is a dog. For instance, an insurer might be paying particularly stingy interest on your universal policy while extracting exorbitant fees.

While you can gauge a company's financial health by checking its ratings, evaluating its performance is tougher. Cash-value policies are complex protection-plus-savings creations, and insurance companies provide hardly any information about how their products perform.

PUT IT IN WRITING

Is an insurance agent nagging you to replace an old policy with a new one? Ask the agent to put the rationale for the switch in writing—and also to obtain written comment from the insurer he or she is representing. Then indicate that you will seek the view of your current insurer.

Having these comments should help you make an informed decision. But you might not get that far: Sometimes the agent suggesting replacement just slinks away.

The first step is to ask the agent or insurer for an in-force illustration—a computer printout showing what will happen to the cash value and the death benefit in future years if policy interest rates and death-benefit charges remain at current levels. Ask the agent or insurer for help in interpreting this projection.

You might also get a second opinion from another agent whom you trust or from a fee-paid insurance adviser. Another excellent option, particularly if the policy is not large enough to merit paying steep fees, is to obtain a rate-of-return analysis. These are available for $45 from the Consumer Federation of America in Washington, D.C. (202-387-6121). Working from an in-force illustration, the consumer group makes some assumptions about reasonable expense charges and then estimates the return on the policy's cash value.

QUANTIFY THE COSTS

Anyone considering replacing an existing cash-value policy with another should carefully tally the costs involved. If the old policy is fewer than ten years old, there may be substantial surrender charges. Those charges may be either clearly disclosed or reflected in the slow growth of the policy's savings component. Meanwhile, if the new policy is sold by a commission-paid agent, the commissions may exert a drag on cash-value growth for ten or more years to come.

Convinced that you should replace your current policy? That does not mean you have to run into the arms of another agent. You can avoid steep commission charges on the new policy by buying low-load coverage from one of a handful of insurers that market direct by telephone and mail. They are listed in the Buyer's Guide to Life Insurance, Appendix C.

HEALTH COVERAGE

Many people receive medical benefits from an employer or from the government. In your working years, a good health plan is one of the most valuable employee benefits a company can offer. From age 65 on, a significant portion of your medical expenses may be covered by the government Medicare program. But what do you do if you are self-employed or otherwise on your own where obtaining medical insurance is concerned?

Medical coverage is a type of insurance most people simply must have. Without sufficient coverage, the expense of a major illness could be bankrupting. Unfortunately, the insurance itself is painfully expensive: Even if you are in great shape, you might have to pay thousands of dollars each year to provide comprehensive medical coverage for yourself and your family.

To spend your health-coverage dollars wisely, you should consider various options, including traditional medical insurance policies and health maintenance organizations, or HMOs. You may be able to save money by signing up for a policy with high deductibles or by purchasing a group policy through a professional organization or state-authorized purchasing pool. Finding health coverage is toughest for those who need it most—people with significant medical problems. But there are places to look.

TRADITIONAL INSURANCE VERSUS MANAGED CARE

There are two basic types of health coverage you can buy: traditional health insurance policies and managed-care plans, such as those offered by health maintenance organizations.

With traditional coverage, you see the doctors of your choice and submit bills for reimbursement. A typical plan pays 80% of covered doctor and hospital expenses after you pay an annual deductible. There is usually a maximum amount, perhaps $1,000 or more, that you might have to pay out of your own pocket in any given year. Note that the cap does not apply to expenses that exceed what your insurer judges to be "reasonable and customary."

Managed care is often cheaper, but you give up some flexibility. If you join an HMO, for example, you might pay only $10 or $15 to see a participating doctor. There may be no charge for a hospital stay. But, except in case of emergency, you typically have no coverage at all if you see a medical professional who is not on that organization's roster.

HMOs offer a big plus for families with young children: They usually cover regular physicals and immunizations that are not covered by many traditional plans. You also avoid the annoying and time-consuming chore of filing insurance claims. A potentially big negative with HMOs, though, is that you are covered for treatment by a specialist only if you are referred to that provider by your primary physician.

Other managed-care options include "preferred-provider organizations" and "point-of-service" plans. These are hybrids that combine attributes of traditional insurance and of HMOs. For instance, a plan might charge the low per-visit price of an HMO if you use participating providers but also cover 70% of care if you turn to nonparticipating doctors and hospitals.

WEIGHING THE OPTIONS

Is traditional coverage or a managed-care plan the right choice for you? That depends.

If you are adamant about not changing doctors and not restricting your flexibility, you will probably want traditional insurance. With so many doctors signing up with managed-care plans, though, you might find a plan that includes most of your current doctors. Also note that many traditional plans are moving in the managed-care direction: They are requiring policyholders to get advance clearance for nonemergency surgery and for psychotherapy.

In looking at HMOs, take a close look at each plan's list of participating providers. Having a primary physician and pediatrician located nearby is a priority for many families. You probably do not want to drive 30 minutes to see a doctor each time your child has an earache.

For many people, cost is the major consideration in what type of plan to select. First, review your medical bills for the past few years to see what your annual expenses have been. Then, in weighing traditional insurance against managed care, estimate what you might pay in a typical year under each design. You need to consider both the stated cost of coverage as well as sums you are likely to end up paying yourself for services that are not covered.

You can lower the cost of traditional insurance coverage by agreeing to pay more bills yourself. You might accept a higher annual deductible, say $1,000 per person rather than $250 or $500. Alternatively, rather than having an insurer pay 80% of expenses above the deductible, you might arrange for only 50% co-insurance. Shifting to 50% co-insurance can cut your premium significantly, even if you keep the same maximum amount that you would pay each year before the insurer begins paying in full.

BE PREPARED FOR THE WORST

Make sure you have sufficient catastrophic coverage. A medical insurance plan should have a lifetime maximum of at least $1 million—and preferably no ceiling at all.

One item to examine closely is the coverage for any "pre-existing" medical conditions. Under many insurance plans, expenses related to problems that you have at the time you buy coverage are not covered for as long as a year or more. Some insurers do not exclude pre-existing conditions but are more picky about whom they will cover.

SAVE YOUR MONEY

Some types of medical insurance are not good choices for long-term, comprehensive coverage:

- **Short-term policies.** These cover you for only a period of months, presumably until you find a job with health benefits. These may make sense in some limited circumstances, if you are confident you have only a short-term need. There is often no coverage of pre-existing conditions.

- **"Bare-bones."** These policies, which are available in some states, do not cover most doctor visits. They go into effect if the insured person needs major surgery or has a sudden serious illness. Even then, though, benefits are limited. For better catastrophic coverage, buy a standard policy with a high deductible.

- **"Hospital-indemnity" plans.** These pay a fixed daily amount, say $50 or $75, if you are hospitalized. Such coverage is cheap and for a good reason: The set dollar payments would make barely a dent in the cost of a typical hospital stay.

- **Dread-disease policies.** These pay only if you are diagnosed with cancer or other specified ailments. Benefits are limited, and the policies do not pay anything if you are felled by an accident or an illness that is not on the list. This is definitely a type of insurance to skip.

A landmark health-insurance law, key provisions of which take effect in 1997, will make medical coverage available to millions of workers who switch or leave their jobs, even if they have pre-existing health problems. For example, if you switch jobs, moving from one employer-sponsored health plan to another, the Health Insurance Portability and Accountability Act requires that your new employer provide coverage to you and any family members who were covered under your former plan. You still may face a waiting period before your new coverage takes effect if you have a pre-existing health problem. But the waiting period will be limited to a year and may be much shorter, depending on how long you were covered under your previous plan.

The new law also provides that workers who leave a company where they had health benefits but who have no new employer in sight will also be able to get individual health insurance if they meet certain requirements. But states and insurance companies will have a good deal of flexibility in determining how to provide that coverage and how much it will cost. (You will find more information on the new law in Chapter 4.)

WHERE TO LOOK

To gather information and prices for health coverage, you might start with the obvious sources: Call local agents who sell medical policies. You might get quotes on HMO coverage from agents as well, or you can call local HMOs to see if they deal direct. Do not stop there, though. There are a few other sources to which you should turn as well.

To get a quick idea of costs for individual policies, call Quotesmith, a Darien, Illinois, firm that maintains an extensive database of insurance products and acts as an agent (800-556-9393). At no cost, Quotesmith will supply a long list of policies and prices based on factors such as your age, sex, and where you live. You get a detailed description of policy terms and limitations for one or more of the products.

Many states and localities have established buying pools through which self-employed people and small businesses join together to buy coverage. Premiums for such a group plan may be far cheaper than going out to buy individual coverage on your own. To find a local purchasing pool, try your Chamber of Commerce or your state insurance department. (See Appendix A for addresses and phone numbers of the state regulatory offices.)

You might also be able to obtain an attractive group policy through a professional association or trade group to which you belong. Do not assume group coverage is always better, though. Be sure to examine the actual coverage provided by any plan.

Consumer Reports magazine has published useful articles in past years evaluating health insurance policies and HMOs. To see how recently the magazine has covered those topics, check your local library or call *Consumer Reports* at 914-378-2000. Check your state insurance department for materials such as a buyer's guide, a price survey, or a report on the volume of consumer complaints it has received about various insurers.

You might also ask your state insurance department about health-coverage options for people with chronic conditions or a history of serious illness. Many states have enacted reforms to help such buyers find coverage. A small number of states, including New York, New Jersey, and Vermont, require insurers to provide coverage to anyone willing to pay their rates. About half the states provide "high-risk pools" for people whose health problems would otherwise bar them from getting coverage. People who buy insurance through these pools can expect to pay rates about 50% higher than standard policyholders.

Another alternative for people with health problems is Blue Cross/Blue Shield. In some states, Blue Cross/Blue Shield plans function as insurers of last resort, such as by holding annual open-enrollment periods when anyone who applies gets coverage. Some HMOs also offer open-enrollment programs.

DISABILITY INSURANCE

Many otherwise responsible people have a big hole in their insurance safety nets. While they may spend hours worrying about whether they have the right life insurance in case they die, they devote little or no time to figuring out what they would do to replace some of their income if disability caused by illness or accident left them unable to work and bring home a paycheck for an extended time.

In fact, most people who work should pay far more attention to disability coverage than they do. Although many large companies provide disability insurance as part of their benefit plans, the coverage is often limited. Many people do not qualify for disability benefits under Social Security.

Unfortunately, buying an individual disability policy is very expensive. A policy might cost a steep 2% to 3% of your salary. Disability coverage is also complex, and insurers have been making their policies less generous. Not everyone can even get individual disability coverage. For instance, part-time workers and people who have just started their own businesses may be out of luck.

As a result, you might decide to forgo supplemental coverage if your employer provides even limited disability coverage. But if you do not have any disability insurance, you certainly should consider buying an individual policy.

BUYING AN INDIVIDUAL POLICY

The first step is to check what coverage, if any, you receive at work. This is not "sick pay" or "short-term disability," which keeps your paychecks flowing when you are out for a few days or weeks. You want to find out about "long-term disability" coverage, which typically kicks in once you have been unable to work for six months. Many company plans will replace 60% of your pay, up to a certain ceiling. You need to find out how long that coverage lasts and how different types of disability are covered. (You can find more information on disability benefits provided by employers and Social Security in Chapter 4.)

If your employer does not provide disability coverage, or if you feel the amount would not be enough, the next step is to consider buying an individual policy. Disability plans are typically sold by agents who also sell life and health insurance.

FEATURES TO WATCH

There are several policy features, besides the dollar amount of coverage, that can have a big impact on the premium you are charged.

For instance, the maximum period for which benefits are payable can be as short as one year or as long as your lifetime. Many people opt for benefits to age 65.

Another variable is the waiting period before benefits begin. Coverage might kick in after just one month of disability or not for a year or longer. The longer the waiting period, the lower the premium. You might pick a waiting period of three months or six months, or even longer, if you have set aside an emergency fund that could pay your household expenses for a period of months.

Many individual disability policies are guaranteed renewable at least to age 65. That means the insurer cannot turn you away if your health deteriorates. But the insurer is usually not guaranteeing to renew coverage at the same premium. It retains the right to increase premiums for a broad class of policyholders as a group.

Insurance companies use the term "noncancelable" to refer to disability policies on which the insurer cannot raise the premium after the policy is purchased. Not all companies offer such coverage. At those that do, a policy that is noncancelable and guaranteed renewable might cost 20% more than one that is just guaranteed renewable.

DEFINITIONS ARE CRUCIAL

How is disability defined? That is a central consideration in looking at policies. In years past, many professionals opted for the Cadillac of disability plans, so-called own-occupation, or "own-occ," protection. Such coverage will pay full benefits if you cannot perform your stated occupation but are still able to work at a related, though lower-paying job.

In recent years, though, insurers have been losing money on such policies, and they have been making it harder to collect. For instance, an insurer denied benefits to a trial attorney who was stricken with panic attacks and could not enter a courtroom. The insurer told her she could still work as a lawyer and so was not considered disabled under the terms of her own-occupation policy.

To avoid this kind of surprise, ask the insurer for a letter spelling out its current and expected practices in determining disability. Will you qualify if you cannot perform the functions of your specialty but can perform related work in your field? Or will you qualify for benefits only if you cannot perform several functions in your field?

Also, check how long own-occupation benefits continue. Most policies say that after one, two, five, or more years, the own-occupation standard expires, and you will be entitled to benefits only if you cannot work in any occupation to which you are suited by training, background, education, and income.

Another option, rather than buying own-occupation coverage, is to go with a policy that defines disability based on what you earn. Such "residual" coverage defines disability as something that lowers your income. If you earn less in your own occupation (because you have changed your hours or duties) or earn less because you have shifted to a lower-paying field, you are entitled to disability benefits.

Some insurers have stopped writing own-occupation policies altogether. When you have a choice, skipping own-occupation coverage can cut your premium by as much as 20%.

WAYS TO GET CHEAPER COVERAGE

Here are three other strategies to trim the bill for individual disability coverage:

- **Do not buy more coverage than you can collect.** Insurance agents often try to sell disability policies for as much as 80% of an individual's income. But the maximum anyone can collect from all sources is 80%, including benefits from an employer and the government. If you are covered by your employer's policy for 60% of your salary, any supplemental policy you buy will replace only 20% of your salary. In most cases, you should buy only that lesser amount of supplemental coverage.

- **Say no to COLA.** Insurance agents earn an extra commission on cost-of-living-adjustment, or COLA, riders, which is one reason they push them so hard. But the COLA riders on disability plans are usually a bad deal for the policyholder. A COLA rider might cost 15% to 40% more a year but be designed to pay only an extra 5% a year after one full year of disability.

- **Convert your policy when you are older.** Some insurance companies allow policyholders to convert to a five-year policy from a policy meant to last until age 65. So, when you reach your late 50s, ask your insurer to convert the policy to the five-year version, giving you the same coverage at a better price. You could save several thousand dollars a year in premiums.

LONG-TERM-CARE INSURANCE

You might think twice before booking a hotel room for $150 or $200 a day. But you could be saddled with such lofty charges, day in and day out, if you were confined to a nursing home for an extended stay. And in most cases, those costs are not covered by medical insurance or by the federal Medicare program for those age 65 and older.

Does that mean you should buy one of the special long-term-care policies insurers are selling? Not necessarily. This is a relatively new type of insurance. The cost tends to be high: If you buy at age 65, a policy might cost $1,000 to $3,000 or even more each year. And the coverage is often limited.

In general, affluent people who could afford to pay for a long nursing-home stay should skip long-term-care insurance. Many people with limited resources simply cannot afford the insurance.

The logical buyers, according to some insurance specialists, are people whose assets, excluding a home, are between $100,000 and $1 million. Within that population, long-term-care insurance probably makes the most sense for couples who fear that a nursing-home confinement for one person would leave the other strapped.

BENEFITS AND COSTS

Long-term-care policies are usually sold by agents who sell other medical and life insurance coverage. A growing number of employers also have begun to offer long-term-care insurance. (Employees generally have had to pay the full cost of such coverage, but this may change because of new tax breaks for employers that subsidize long-term-care premiums.) The policies typically cover not just nursing-home stays but also home care and other services for people with disabling conditions. Most plans pay a fixed dollar amount for each day of care. For instance, a policy might pay $100 a day when you are in a nursing home and $50 a day toward in-home care.

The levels of coverage available vary widely, from the stripped-down to the superdeluxe. A low-end policy might pay $50 a day for nursing-home care, for up to two years, and only after you have paid for 100 days of nursing-home care with your own money. A high-end policy might offer a bigger daily benefit of $150 and adjust that benefit regularly to keep up with inflation. The deductible period for which you must pay might be only 20 days, and there might be no limit on the number of years for which you can collect benefits.

Premiums for long-term-care policies are usually designed to stay level for life, but that is not guaranteed. Insurers retain the right to increase rates for any broad category of policyholders. Many insurers entered the long-term-care market just in the past decade, and consumer advocates are worried they may have priced the product too low. If claims exceed insurers' expectations, policyholders could see big rate increases down the road. Starting in 1997, premiums individuals pay for long-term-care insurance, up to certain limits, are tax-deductible if they and other reimbursed medical expenses exceed 7.5% of adjusted gross income.

SOME KEY FEATURES

In buying long-term-care coverage, like any other type of insurance, you should check offerings from several companies with solid financial-strength ratings. Weigh various combinations of policy provisions to find a mix that will give you adequate coverage at an affordable price.

Do not skimp on the daily benefit amounts. The nursing-home payment should be high enough to cover current charges in your community. You can find out what those are by calling a few local facilities or a local government agency on aging. The benefit should increase 5% or so each year (ideally, on a compounded basis) to keep up with inflation.

To keep insurance charges affordable, focus on the time periods for which benefits are paid. For instance, buy a policy that requires you to pay the first 100 days of nursing-home care yourself. Maybe opt for three to five years of nursing-home coverage rather than an unlimited period. While 65-year-olds have about a 40% lifetime risk of entering a nursing home, according to one study, many nursing-home stays are brief. Only about 10% of people age 65 will stay for five or more years.

Buyers should pay close attention to the conditions that must be

WHERE TO LEARN MORE ABOUT IT

Following are three places to turn for additional information on long-term-care insurance.

- **United Seniors Health Cooperative**

  This nonprofit group publishes a useful book, *Long-Term Care: A Dollar and Sense Guide*, $12.50.

  1331 H Street NW, Suite 500
  Washington, DC 20005-4706
  202-393-6222

- **American Association of Retired Persons**

  This membership organization for seniors offers another useful book, *Before You Buy: A Guide to Long-Term Care Insurance*. No charge.

  601 E Street NW
  Washington, DC 20049

- **Government Services**

  States run free health insurance counseling programs for seniors that also provide information on long-term-care insurance. Contact your state insurance department or area agency on aging. (Insurance departments are listed in Appendix A. For your local agency on aging, check the phone book or call 800-677-1116.)

met under a policy before benefits are paid. In the late 1980s, earlier generations of long-term-care policies were widely criticized for being too restrictive. Although today's policies are much better, there are still significant variations in the triggers for benefit payments. Many start paying benefits only when someone is considered dependent in two or more "activities of daily living," such as eating, bathing, and dressing. But some policies consider a person dependent only if he or she needs direct help every time an activity is performed; others require the person to need only assistance or supervision.

Benefits should also be triggered by "cognitive impairment." People with Alzheimer's disease or related ailments may be physically able to perform many tasks but may need supervision to protect themselves and others from harm. Avoid policies that require care to be "medically necessary" or that cover custodial care only if a person has first received skilled-nursing care.

4

MAKING
THE MOST OF
YOUR
BENEFITS

$

M ost people know, at least intuitively, that such benefits as employer-provided health care coverage and Social Security contribute enormously to their financial well-being and security. But too often, they do not explore all the ways they can maximize those benefits in their current finances and in planning for the future. As a result, they rob themselves of the equivalent of hundreds, even thousands, of dollars a year.

Employee-benefit plans are one of the most valuable sources of tax breaks and savings opportunities most people have. They are also usually the chief source of medical coverage and life insurance for working Americans and their families. For retirees, Social Security and Medicare provide a crucial financial and medical safety net. Although few can expect to live on Social Security alone when they retire, it typically provides about a quarter of the retirement income for people who earned in the $60,000 range during their working lives. Medicare provides thorough medical coverage for 95% of the nation's elderly.

But taking full advantage of company and government benefits has never been more complicated. The complexity of benefit plans has increased significantly over the past decade, so managing them has become almost as much of a chore as doing your taxes. You may already be making a half dozen decisions about your retirement plan, such as whether to participate, how much to contribute, which investments to choose, and how much to allocate to each category. You may also have to choose among a handful of health insurance plans and make decisions about life insurance, disability coverage, and other benefits.

WHAT EMPLOYEES GET

Paid vacations, life insurance, and medical care are common employee benefits, but paid maternity leave is rare.

EMPLOYEE BENEFIT	FULL-TIME EMPLOYEES* RECEIVING BENEFIT
Paid vacations	97%
Paid holidays	91%
Life insurance	91%
Medical care	82%
Paid sick leave	65%
Dental care	62%
Unpaid maternity leave	60%
Defined-benefit retirement plans**	56%
Unpaid paternity leave	53%
Reimbursement accounts	52%
Defined-contribution retirement plans**	49%
Sickness and accident insurance	44%
Long-term disability insurance	41%
Paid personal leave	21%
Flexible-benefit plans	12%
Paid maternity leave	3%
Stock-purchase plans	2%
Paid paternity leave	1%

*At U.S. businesses with 100 or more employees.
**Many employees participate in both defined-benefit and defined-contribution retirement plans.
SOURCE: Employee Benefit Research Institute. *EBRI Databook on Employee Benefits*, 3d ed. (Washington, D.C.: Employee Benefit Research Institute, 1995).

Similarly, getting the most out of Social Security and Medicare requires retirees and those approaching retirement to learn the intricate rules that govern those programs. You must decide the best time to start collecting Social Security, taking into account how your benefits would be affected if you continued to work part-time during retirement, and how to coordinate Social Security and Medicare with the rest of your retirement plan.

EMPLOYERS ARE SHIFTING COSTS

The primary reason for the growing complexity of company benefit plans is cost. Employers are retooling their plans to shift more of the cost to employees and to taxpayers. To save on pension costs, employers are replacing or augmenting traditional retirement plans with savings plans, such as 401(k)s, to which employees must contribute themselves in order to build a retirement nest egg.

Not only must employees fund their own retirement accounts, but they also must become, in effect, their own pension managers. They have to choose the right investments, make their own investing decisions, and keep an eye on the costs of the investments in their plans. When they retire, they are responsible for a dozen decisions about how to handle their retirement-plan money.

Medical benefits are becoming as complex as retirement benefits, and for the same reason: cost control. To save on medical expenses, employers are raising deductibles, the amount employees pay before the health coverage kicks in, and co-payments, the portion of each medical bill employees must bear on their own. They are also tightening eligibility requirements, excluding more pre-existing conditions, adding more caps on treatment, and denying claims of employees who fail to follow the procedures spelled out in the fine print of their medical plans. A growing number of employers are also requiring that employees pay higher health premiums if they smoke, are overweight, or have particular health problems.

But the biggest change in employer-provided medical coverage is the trend toward "managed care." The most common form of managed care is the health maintenance organization, or HMO. HMOs limit your choice of doctors to those affiliated with the individual HMO. But the premiums are lower than for traditional "fee-for-service" health care plans, and the charge for each doctor visit is generally only $5 to $15. More and more companies also offer "point-of-service" plans and "preferred-provider organizations" that combine some of the features of an HMO and a traditional fee-for-service plan.

Employers are also taking an axe to the medical benefits they provide retirees. In some cases, they no longer provide assistance to retirees in buying insurance to fill the gaps in Medicare coverage. Some employers are dropping coverage for early retirees, leaving them to find and fund their own health insurance until Medicare kicks in at age 65.

SOME VALUABLE ADDITIONS

To help take the sting out of benefit rollbacks, employers are adding options that cost them little, including flexible work schedules (compressed work weeks, job sharing, flexible hours); reimbursement for health-club fees; day-care referrals; and flexible spending accounts, which enable employees to use pretax dollars to pay for unreimbursed medical expenses and day care. Some of these newer benefits can be quite valuable to employees who use them properly.

If you are fortunate enough to be among the top executive ranks, the company benefits picture looks far more generous. For the highest-paid executives, many companies continue to provide supplemental medical plans for their families, with no deductibles and co-payments, full coverage for preventive and diagnostic treatment, and free physicals. Elite earners are also more likely to have an assortment of "top-hat" pension plans, which supplement what they receive in their regular pension and retirement plans.

Whether you are a top executive with extra benefits or a regular employee with shrinking coverage, you will come out ahead if you know your options. With all the cost shifting, new choices, and restrictions, it pays to invest some time in understanding your benefit plan.

Similarly, it is important to know what you can expect from Social Security and Medicare. That is especially true in light of the growing talk about cutbacks to help rein in government spending. Already, the age at which full Social Security benefits can be collected is gradually being pushed back to save money. Suggestions for further cost cutting include means testing, which would lower benefits for retirees with incomes above a certain level. Many also expect that the cost-of-living increases Social Security recipients now enjoy will be curtailed, at least for future retirees. Meanwhile, the payroll tax that workers and employers pay to fund Social Security benefits is likely to rise.

The biggest anticipated change in Medicare is increased use of managed care. As with the managed-care plans used by more and more corporate employers, retirees would have to see doctors who are part of a network of care providers and would generally need a physician's referral to see specialists. In addition, most experts predict that the patient's share of Medicare-covered expenses will rise. Finally, Medicare beneficiaries who make six-figure incomes in retirement can expect to have to pay the full premium for Medicare Part B, the portion that pays physicians. Recipients currently pay about one-fourth of the full cost of the premium, regardless of income.

BENEFITS DECISIONS THROUGH THE AGES

The only way to ensure that you are making the most of your employee benefits is to sit down with the information provided by your employer and see how it applies to your own individual and family circumstances. Retirees and people nearing retirement should also familiarize themselves with the rules of Social Security and Medicare.

If this sounds about as alluring as writing your will, take heart: A little time examining your benefits and considering how to use them better could really pay off. To make the process as painless as possible, the following sections highlight some of the things that are likely to be of particular interest to people in various age brackets. As you read the one that applies to you, you might make some notes about things to discuss with your employee-benefit representative.

Your 20s and 30s

Younger employees tend to pay the least attention to their company benefits since they are usually healthy, have fewer family responsibilities, and are not yet worried about retirement. But people in their 20s and 30s can often earn an instant payoff in tax savings and other rewards by taking better advantage of what their employers offer.

For starters, if your employer has a retirement-savings plan, such as a 401(k), make sure you are enrolled in it and start making contributions, no matter how meager. Saving as little as $50 a month can make a big difference. Some employers kick in 50 cents for every dollar an employee saves, up to a certain amount. That is like getting an instant 50% return on your investment. And tax-free compounding over time will really make your small stash grow. Moreover, you will receive an immediate payoff at tax time because the money contributed lowers your taxable income.

If you are worried about locking the money up until retirement, consider this: Most plans allow you to borrow as much as 50% of the account balance and pay yourself back, at a low interest rate, over time. So the money will be there if you need help with the down payment on a home or a financial emergency. (Chapter 2 gives you many ideas about how to invest the money in your retirement-savings plan.)

Younger employees should be sure to set up "medical-reimbursement accounts," if there is the chance to do so. Also called "medical-spending accounts" and "flexible spending accounts," these accounts allow you to have pretax dollars (typically, as much as $2,000 or $3,000 a year) withheld from your salary to pay for un-reimbursed medical expenses. Eligible expenses may include the deductible portion of your medical bills and any uncovered expenses, such as routine physicals, eye exams, and contact lenses.

TAX-FREE CONTRIBUTIONS

The beauty of the medical-reimbursement account is that the government picks up part of the tab, because the money you contribute is free from federal income tax, most states' income taxes, and Social Security and Medicare taxes. So, if your combined tax rate is 40%, you reduce your take-home pay by only 60 cents for every dollar you contribute to these accounts.

Working parents can earn a similar break on child-care expenses by taking advantage of the "dependent-care accounts" that many employers offer. You can have up to $5,000 deducted from your pre-tax salary each year to cover the cost of day care, summer camp, and preschool and after-school care for children under age 13, so that you—or you and your spouse if you are married—can continue to work. You can also use these accounts to cover eligible expenses incurred in caring for a dependent elder.

The federal government also allows parents a 20% to 30% tax credit for eligible dependent-care expenses. But you cannot use a child-care account and get the federal tax credit for the same child-care dollars. Financial planners figure that company child-care accounts are a better deal for families with incomes of roughly $25,000 or more.

Medical insurance coverage is a huge money-saving benefit for millions of workers. Many younger employees choose managed care, which often costs less than traditional health coverage as long as you see doctors on the plan's roster. Managed care is known for its low-cost or free preventive care, which is a big help for young families who know they will be using extensive immunization, pediatric, and other preventive services that come with having a new family. Such services are not covered by many traditional insurance plans.

20s–30s

- Enroll in 401(k) and contribute.

- Set up medical-spending account.

- Consider higher medical deductible.

- Look into family benefits.

- Check Social Security records.

HIGHER MAY BE BETTER

Single, healthy people who have a choice between a medical plan with high deductibles and one with low deductibles may be better off choosing the one with higher deductibles, since they are less likely to incur large medical expenses. The higher the deductible you agree to, the lower your monthly premiums. Families, too, should run the numbers to see if a higher deductible plan makes sense. If you can predict ahead of time how much of the deductible you will actually spend, you could put that amount into a tax-free medical-spending account and come out ahead.

Maternity benefits are crucial for young couples starting families.

If you are planning to take advantage of your company's maternity benefits, be sure to read the plan document carefully. Companies are adding restrictions to their coverage to save money, which means they are authorizing shorter hospital visits and may not pay for certain tests unless the mother is age 35 or over. Pay particular attention to special provisions that require preapproval for some procedures, such as ultrasound or Caesarean sections, and to deadlines for signing the baby up for coverage. Mistakes could cost you thousands of dollars.

Finally, get into the habit of checking to see that the Social Security Administration is accurately recording your earnings, which it will someday use to calculate your benefits. This is particularly important for women who marry and change their names. Call the Social Security Administration (800-772-1213) and ask for Form SSA-7004-SM, Request for Earnings and Benefit Estimate Statement.

YOUR 40S AND 50S

Employee benefits can be of great help in dealing with some of the most pressing demands faced by people in their 40s and 50s: saving for their own retirement, providing reliable medical coverage for themselves and their families, shoring up their financial safety nets, and, perhaps, trying to assist aging parents. Some who waited until later to start families are often still struggling with child-care expenses.

If your employer offers a retirement-savings plan, such as a 401(k), take advantage of these peak earning years to cram as much money as you can into that plan. If you think you cannot afford to save more because you are still putting the kids through school, for example, reconsider. This is your last chance to build the savings you will need to carry you through, perhaps, 20 or 25 years of retirement. Tap other sources to pay tuition costs, such as home-equity loans.

Retirement-savings plans at work are a good choice for your limited investment dollars because the money is withheld from your pretax pay. As a result, the contributions will not pinch your budget like most other investments you could make. People in a combined 40% federal and state tax bracket, for instance, would see their take-home pay go down by only 60 cents for every dollar they put into a 401(k). In addition, some employers kick in 50 cents for every dollar an employee saves, up to a certain amount. That is like getting an immediate 50% return on your investment. And tax-free compounding over time will really make your nest egg grow. If you can afford it, consider also making after-tax contributions. (See Chapter 2 for some smart ideas about how to invest your retirement-savings money.)

BETTER TO BORROW

Many employers' 401(k) plans allow withdrawals for severe financial hardship, such as medical bills and college tuition, but you should resist the temptation. Hardship withdrawals are subject to income tax and, generally, a 10% federal penalty for people under age 59½. Instead, take a loan from your plan. You can usually borrow as much as half of the money in your account, up to $50,000. You pay yourself back, plus interest at a low rate, over a period of several years.

Review your medical coverage and take a fresh look at managed care. Many people in their 40s and 50s have grown accustomed to traditional medical plans that let them select their own doctors and reimburse them for about 80% of eligible expenses. But the cost of such coverage has been going up. You may be able to lower your health care costs significantly by switching to a "point-of-service" plan, a type of managed care that is being offered by more and more employers. Such plans charge you only $5 to $15 per doctor visit if you use doctors who participate in the plan's network of providers. You still have the option to go outside the network for care, although you would be reimbursed for only about 70% of the expenses you incurred. Check to see if your family doctor has become affiliated with one of the managed-care plans your employer uses.

Another way you may be able to cut the cost of your medical coverage is to choose a health care plan with a higher deductible—the amount you pay before the plan starts reimbursing you for eligible expenses. If you have a choice between a plan with a deductible of, say, $400 for a family and one with a $1,000 deductible, the plan with the higher deductible will have a lower premium. Over the course of a year, that could more than offset the higher deductible.

STRETCHING YOUR HEALTH CARE DOLLARS

You have yet another way to shave the cost of medical care if your employer offers a medical-reimbursement account. Also known as "medical-spending accounts" and "flexible spending accounts," these accounts allow you to have pretax dollars (typically, as much as $2,000 or $3,000 a year) withheld from your salary to pay for un-reimbursed medical expenses. Eligible expenses may include the deductible portion of your medical bills and any uncovered expenses, such as routine physicals, eye exams, and contact lenses. The money you contribute is free from federal income tax and most states' income taxes. Also, your contribution lowers the amount of your income that is subject to the Social Security and Medicare taxes. As a result, each dollar contributed to such an account would reduce the take-home pay of someone with a combined tax rate of 40% by only 60 cents.

Working parents and people providing care for aging parents can earn a similar break by taking advantage of the dependent-care accounts that many employers offer. You can have up to $5,000 deducted from your pretax salary each year to cover eligible expenses related to caring for a child or a dependent elder.

You should also review your disability insurance. If you become disabled, many companies will automatically pay as much as 100% of your salary for three to six months. Thereafter, long-term disability kicks in—if you have the coverage. Some companies require that you pay for a percentage of the premiums, often through payroll deduction. These are usually low, and having some coverage is worth it. If you have a choice between paying for premiums with pretax or after-tax dollars, it makes more sense to pay with after-tax dollars. That way, if you become disabled, the benefits you receive will be tax-free under the tax law.

Do you have enough life insurance? Many company life insurance plans pay death benefits equivalent to one to two years' salary, but employees frequently have the option of purchasing extra term in-

40s–50s

- Contribute to retirement plan.

- Consider managed care.

- Use "flexible spending account."

- Review disability coverage.

- Weigh costs of job switching.

surance. Your company's optional term insurance can be a good deal, but you may be able to buy the same or better coverage for less money on your own. (Chapter 3 and the Buyer's Guide to Life Insurance, Appendix C, help you figure out how much coverage you need and give you some useful hints on how to buy it.)

AN OFFER YOU CAN REFUSE?

Once you reach age 50, your employer may tempt you to retire early by offering a sweetened pension and other inducements. Weigh such a proposal carefully. You have many years ahead of you, and paying for such a lengthy retirement can be very expensive. Generally, the best candidates for early retirement are people who have substantial savings outside of their companies' retirement plans. (The Guide to Retirement Planning, Appendix D, has a section on evaluating an early-retirement offer that should help you make an informed decision.)

Also consider the potential costs, as well as the advantages, of a mid-career job switch, particularly if your employer has a traditional pension plan that promises retirement payments based on your age, years of service, and pay immediately before retirement. Moving to another employer in mid-career can sharply reduce the pension income a person will collect later on. Assuming the same pattern of pay increases over an employee's career and identical pension plans, spending 25 years at a single company will produce far more pension income than spending 12 years at one company and 13 at another.

To find out how much you can expect, check the annual benefit statement that most large employers send to employees or ask your benefits department for help. If you are age 50 or older, you probably should obtain a projection of what your benefit might be at age 65, assuming you keep working until then.

Check with the Social Security Administration, too, to make sure it is accurately recording your earnings, which it will someday use to calculate your benefits. This is particularly important for women who marry and change their names. Call the Social Security Administration (800-772-1213) and ask for Form SSA-7004-SM, Request for Earnings and Benefit Estimate Statement.

YOUR 60S AND BEYOND

You might think that a lifetime of employment would make it easier for people nearing retirement to handle benefit issues. The reality, however, is just the opposite. As you near retirement, you have more decisions to make, and the stakes are higher.

Unlike younger employees, those in their 60s do not have the luxury of decades of employment to recover from the wrong decisions. Poor choices in the final years of full-time earnings could lead you to pay tens of thousands of dollars more in taxes and to lose some Social Security and medical coverage.

If you are considering an early-retirement offer, for instance, make sure a guarantee of medical coverage is built in. Although older workers are more likely than younger employees to receive some form of retiree medical coverage, they cannot count on it. Employers are now cutting back on this benefit to save money. A. Foster Higgins, a consulting firm in Princeton, New Jersey, found that in recent years 7% of large employers have scrapped health care coverage for future retirees, and 3% have eliminated it for current retirees. Of those that still provide it, 23% have increased employee contributions, such as requiring early retirees to pay a higher share of the premium, make higher co-payments, or even pay any future premium increases.

Employees who might find themselves out of a job before age 63½ need to be especially cautious. Medicare—the government health coverage you have paid for through payroll taxes—does not kick in until age 65. If you lose your job, your employer is required by a federal law known as COBRA to let you pay for your group medical plan coverage, at cost, plus 2%, for 18 months. But this coverage can cost $5,000 or more annually for a family, and after it runs out, you probably will be on your own. (The Guide to Retirement Planning, Appendix D, has a section on evaluating an early-retirement offer that should help you make an informed decision.)

GIVING YOURSELF MORE TIME

You might well consider working a couple of years longer than you had planned. For one thing, the longer you work, the fewer years you will need to rely on your savings to pay bills. Working another year or two will give you more time to stash additional money into savings plans.

But perhaps the most significant and least recognized payoff for delaying retirement is the higher benefit usually available to employees covered by traditional "defined-benefit" pension plans. Such plans, which deliver set annual payments based on a retiree's age, years of service, and pay, cover about 60% of Americans who work for large companies. Many people can increase their pension checks by 25%, 50%, or even 100% just by staying on the job a few more years.

As you near retirement, think seriously about when to start collecting Social Security. You can get full benefits beginning at age 65, assuming that you were born before 1938, or start collecting a smaller benefit at age 62. But if you are still employed, your Social Security benefit may be reduced until you reach age 70.

SUPPLEMENTING MEDICARE

You should also start thinking about Medicare, the government health plan for senior citizens. Many people will find that Medicare provides better coverage than they have had on the job. But there are also gaps: Medicare leaves patients to pay for numerous costs, such as 20% of doctor bills and various deductibles. Some people have employer-paid coverage that will supplement Medicare. A growing number of others find they can get more complete care in retirement by joining health maintenance organizations.

Most seniors buy supplemental health insurance coverage known as "Medigap." There are ten standard Medigap policies, which are regulated by the states. But premiums for exactly the same policy sometimes vary drastically from insurer to insurer, so comparison shopping can really pay off.

People in their 60s should also pay attention to the finer points of taking money out of personal and employer-sponsored retirement plans. This can be tricky for those who have been fortunate enough to accumulate a variety of tax-advantaged and taxable accounts.

60s +

- Check medical coverage.

- Consider delaying retirement.

- Review Social Security decisions.

- Evaluate "Medigap" policies.

- Coordinate savings-plan withdrawals.

Couples with separate retirement plans who retire at different times can face particularly complicated questions. Review benefit-plan options with your human resources department, then with a good financial adviser. (The section on tapping retirement assets in the Guide to Retirement Planning, Appendix D, should help.)

MAXIMIZING YOUR RETIREMENT BENEFITS

The greatest changes in benefit plans are taking place in corporate retirement plans. Many employees can no longer count on receiving a traditional pension when they retire, with a monthly check based on their age, salary, and length of service. Thousands of employers have terminated such traditional "defined-benefit" pension plans in the past decade. Thousands more are cutting back on the amounts they contribute and making it harder to qualify for benefits.

Instead of traditional pensions, employees are more and more likely to have employer-sponsored retirement-savings plans, such as 401(k) plans, that make employees responsible for funding their own nest eggs and deciding how to invest the money. It is an enormous task, one that requires millions of employees to shoulder a huge responsibility for their retirement well-being.

Meanwhile, Social Security is coming under growing scrutiny as Washington struggles to find a politically acceptable way to deal with the mounting financial strain on the government retirement program.

As the debate over what to do heats up, current retirees and those who will retire in the next few years probably have little to worry about. Lawmakers are unlikely to tamper with benefits of current recipients or of those who will soon begin receiving benefits. People in their 20s, 30s, and early-to-mid-40s should pay close attention to the various proposals and make their feelings known to their elected representatives. But they should recognize that they will have years to adjust their retirement plans for any changes that are implemented.

Those with the biggest stakes are probably the people in their late 40s and early 50s, who are apt to become the leading edge of those affected by any new rules. For them, keeping close tabs on changes in Social Security benefits will be essential so that they can adjust their expectations and plans—perhaps by delaying retirement or continuing to work part-time.

The changes in company and government retirement programs make it crucial that retirees and those planning for retirement become familiar with the rules governing their benefits and that they think seriously about how to coordinate withdrawals from their various retirement plans. These include not only company plans and Social Security but also tax-advantaged Individual Retirement Accounts and ordinary taxable investment portfolios. Decisions can become especially complicated for married couples, who may have separate retirement plans of various types and retire at different times.

This section should help you identify the important areas to focus on and provide useful advice on getting the most out of corporate retirement plans, retirement plans for the self-employed and small businesses, and Social Security. You should also consult the Guide to Retirement Planning, Appendix D, which includes a handy retirement-planning worksheet and detailed help on sifting through the choices retirees have to make about tapping their assets. But retirement is also one of those times in life when it can be well worth hiring a professional financial adviser. Check the information on financial planners in Chapter 1 to help you find a good one and take the time to proceed with care: Retirees contemplating what to do with their life savings and accumulated benefits are too often easy prey for charlatans and unwitting victims of incompetence.

TRADITIONAL PENSION PLANS

Although traditional pension plans are becoming less common, they still cover about 60% of Americans who work for large companies.

If you are one of them, you can expect to receive a fixed, monthly check after you retire, generally for as long as you live.

A pension might replace as much as a third of your final pay if you retire at age 65 after 30 years of service. But you will not receive much if you move around in your career—even if you have pensions from two or three employers. The pension benefit is typically paltry if you stay at a company for fewer than ten years.

Part of the reason is "vesting." In order to qualify for a pension, you have to become vested, which means you have the right to collect a pension benefit at a specific age, even if you have left the job by then. If you joined a private company plan after 1988, the minimum vesting schedule is 100% vesting after five years, or 20% vested after two or three years and fully vested after seven years. Some employers vest sooner, whereas government plans may require you to be on the job ten years or longer before you are vested.

If you leave a job before you are vested, you forfeit the money you would have been entitled to. If you continue working after age 65, federal laws require that your pension keep on growing until you actually retire.

But assuming you get beyond the basic vesting requirement, the fundamental determinant of how big your pension check will be is the formula used by your employer. Payouts from traditional pension plans are usually based on a formula that includes your age, your pay, and your length of service. As a result, people who retire after many years with the same employer typically receive big pension checks, whereas people who jump from job to job get very little even if they are fully vested.

The last few years of employment are particularly important. In fact, many people can increase their pension checks enormously by staying on the job a few more years. Consider a hypothetical 55-year-old manager earning $70,000 after 25 years at one company. Under a typical pension formula, this person could retire now and collect $13,900 a year. But if he stayed on the job just two more years, with annual salary increases of 5%, his yearly check would be 40% bigger: $19,400. A five-year delay, to age 60, would more than double the manager's annual pension to $30,500.

RETIRE LATER, COLLECT MORE

If you are covered by a traditional pension plan, delaying retirement for a few years may produce a dramatic increase in your annual pension benefit. This is how a 55-year-old earning $70,000 after 25 years at one company might fare under a typical plan design.

RETIREMENT AGE	ANNUAL BENEFIT ($)
55	13,922
60	30,460
61	33,049
62	35,821
63	38,787
64	41,961
65	45,355

SOURCE: The Ayco Company L.P., Albany, N.Y.

Delaying retirement typically boosts the pension payout because participants accumulate more years of service and may also see an increase in the "final pay" used in the pension formula. Moreover, most pension plans have a provision that reduces the payments to employees who retire early—typically, before age 60 or 62—because, on average, those early retirees will be collecting pension checks for more years. Delaying retirement shrinks or eliminates that early-retirement penalty.

To find out how much you can expect, check the annual benefit statement that most large employers send to employees or ask your benefits department for help. If you are age 50 or older, you probably should request a projection of what your benefit might be at age 65, assuming you keep working until then.

When it comes time to tap your accumulated pension benefits, these traditional plans typically offer the choice of taking the money in monthly amounts over your life (a "single-

BEWARE OF "PENSION MAX"

If you are about to retire and collect a company pension, an insurance agent may suggest that you buy life insurance to augment your retirement income—a strategy called "pension maximization." Most pension plans offer a certain monthly payment for your lifetime or a reduced sum that will continue in full or part for a surviving spouse. The insurance pitch says to take the pension for your lifetime only and cover your spouse through insurance.

But the cost of life insurance is so high at retirement age that few people can afford to buy enough to provide much for a survivor. As a result, most people should just say no. You could be putting your spouse at risk.

life annuity") or over your life and your spouse's life (a "joint-and-survivor annuity"). Experts usually recommend that you take the joint-and-survivor option, to ensure greater security in retirement. After all, your pension check is something you cannot afford to outlive.

A growing number of employers also give retiring employees the option of receiving their pension money in a single, lump-sum check. And when given the choice, employees overwhelmingly choose the lump sum. But if you simply take the money and run, you will have to manage it astutely to make it last your lifetime and provide for your loved ones after you die—or hire someone to do the job for you and trust that they have the skill. Because of the complexity, some advisers recommend that you receive your pension money as a monthly annuity that you and your spouse cannot outlive. Alternatively, you may be able to take part of the money as a lump sum and put the rest toward an annuity.

401(k)s, 403(b)s, and Profit-Sharing Plans

For a growing number of people, an employer-provided retirement plan means a "defined-contribution" plan. Employees or their employers contribute a certain amount each year—the defined contribution—to a tax-advantaged retirement-savings account in which the money is managed by the employees themselves. How much an employee receives at retirement depends not just on how much was contributed over the years but also on how successful the individual employee was in managing the money.

Most of these newfangled retirement plans are "salary-reduction" plans that employees fund themselves by having money withheld from their salaries. The most common and best-known salary-reduction plan, used by more than 90% of large employers, is the 401(k). There are also 403(b) plans for employees of colleges, hospitals, school districts, and nonprofit organizations. Both types of plan, which are named for the sections of the tax code that authorize them, allow employees to have pretax dollars withheld from their pay and funneled into a variety of investment options. Investment gains are not taxed until the money is withdrawn.

Profit-sharing plans are fundamentally different in that the contributions are made by the employer, not the employee. Again, investment gains are not taxed until the money is withdrawn. And as with 401(k) and 403(b) plans, the employee's investment savvy is crucial in determining the size of the payments he or she will enjoy in retirement.

These retirement-savings accounts have some significant advantages over traditional pension plans. Foremost among these is "portability." While people with traditional pension plans may accumulate only meager retirement benefits if they move from job to job, or lose benefits entirely if they leave an employer before becoming vested, people with 401(k)s, 403(b)s, and profit-sharing plans are entitled to take their retirement savings with them when they change jobs. Also unlike traditional pension plans, these newer alternatives frequently allow participants to tap their savings through loans and "hardship" withdrawals.

But there are big drawbacks, as well. The responsibility for making their own investment decisions puts a big burden on employees, many of whom may be badly prepared for the challenge. If you are a participant in one of these plans and you have not already read about investing for retirement in Chapter 2, you owe it to yourself to do so.

People who work for employers with salary-reduction plans also have to take responsibility for contributing to the plans. This can seem like an impossible requirement to many people, especially lower-income employees and those whose family budgets are already stretched. But if they do not contribute, they often face the prospect of receiving no retirement benefit, since a salary-reduction plan is frequently an employer's only retirement plan.

Fortunately, contributing is not as onerous as some employees may believe, because the money is withheld from pretax pay. As a result, Uncle Sam subsidizes the contributions by lowering your tax bill. For someone who pays 30% in federal and state income taxes, for instance, a $1,000 contribution to a 401(k) or 403(b) plan would lower take-home pay by only $700.

PRIMARY PLAN

Defined-contribution plans, such as 401(k)s, are replacing traditional defined-benefit pension plans as the primary employer-sponsored retirement plan for many American workers.

Primary retirement plan cited by workers participating in employer-provided retirement plans:

	1988	1993
Defined-benefit plans	56.7%	38.2%
Defined-contribution plans	25.8%	49.8%

SOURCE: Paul Yakoboski et al., *Employment-Based Retirement Income Benefits: Analysis of the April 1993 Current Population Survey* (Washington, D.C.: Employee Benefit Research Institute, September 1994).

Moreover, with 401(k) plans, many corporate employers will match your contribution, up to certain limits. A typical formula is for an employer to match 50% of what you put in, up to 6% of your salary. Rather than matching your contributions with cash, many employers use company stock.

Here is a look at these three major types of retirement-savings plans in more detail.

• **401(k) plans.** In theory, you can make pretax contributions equal to as much as 15% of your salary, to an annual maximum that is subject to adjustment each year. The ceiling for contributions was about $9,500 in 1996. In reality, the maximum contribution may be lower at your company. That is because of complex rules that prohibit higher-paid employees from contributing the full amount unless lower-paid employees also take advantage of the plan. (This rule was established to make sure the plans are not used only by highly paid employees.) Many 401(k) plans also allow you to make after-tax contributions. While these contributions will not lower your taxable income, earnings will grow tax-deferred until you take out the money.

You generally have a choice of allocating your savings among mutual funds, guaranteed investment contracts that pay a fixed rate, and company stock. Typically, you can switch among the investments throughout the year. Some employers allow switching annually, and some quarterly, but the trend is toward giving employees unlimited ability to move their money among investment choices. In many cases you can tap the money through hardship withdrawals or through loans.

When you leave your job, you can take all the money you contributed, plus earnings. But you may not be able to take the company's matching contributions unless you have worked at the company for a certain number of years.

• **403(b) plans.** These plans for teachers and others may also be called TSAs (Tax-Sheltered Accounts), or have generic titles, such as "tax shelters" or even simply "savings plans." In general, you can contribute as much as 25% of pay, up to an annual maximum that is subject to adjustment each year. The ceiling in 1996 was about $9,500. Although complex restrictions may reduce that amount (check with your employer), the annual contribution can be much higher in special circumstances. Many 403(b) plans allow you to make additional catch-up contributions if you are nearing retirement and have not taken full advantage of the plan in the past.

Only two types of investments are allowed in 403(b) plans: mutual funds and annuities, which are investment contracts issued by insurance companies. How much money you end up with depends on the investments you choose and the quality of those investments. But schoolteachers, as well as about a third of other nonprofit employees, often have a big advantage over people with 401(k) plans: They can transfer the accumulated savings in their plans to individual 403(b) custodial accounts, even without employer approval. That can be a significant privilege if the annuities in an employer's menu of selections are poor performers.

When you leave your job, you can take all the money you contributed, plus earnings. Meanwhile, you can tap the money through hardship withdrawals or, in some cases, loans.

• **Profit-sharing plans.** As you might guess from the name, profit-sharing retirement plans are accounts set up for employees to which employers shuttle a share of the company's profits. In a typical plan, employers decide once a year how much of a contribution they will make to a master profit-sharing account, which is divvied up among all eligible employees. Employers usually contribute as much as 15% of each worker's pay, but no more than $30,000 per employee. Many profit-sharing plans also allow you to make after-tax contributions. These contributions will not lower your taxable income, but earnings will grow tax-deferred until you take out the money.

Although employers sometimes designate a trustee to invest the profit-sharing money, the trend at medium and large companies is to allow more employee investment discretion. In such cases, the plan is arranged much like a 401(k), allowing employees to allocate the money among three or more investments, such as mutual funds, company stock, and guaranteed investment contracts.

Employers can make employees wait a few years before they are entitled to 100% of their account should they leave. The waiting period is known as "vesting." A company could say, for example, that after three years employees are 20% vested, then 40% vested after four years, and so on until the seventh year, when they are 100% vested. Alternatively, companies could say that employees are not vested until they have been in the plan for five years, at which point they are entitled to 100% of the proceeds. Companies often come up with their own shorter vesting schedules. Employees must be fully vested once they reach the plan's normal retirement age, however.

Employees can borrow from profit-sharing plans if their employers allow it, and when they retire or leave the company, they can take the money with them. They can also take withdrawals as permitted by the plan for hardships.

TRANSFERRING MONEY WHEN YOU LEAVE

One of the nicest features of 401(k), 403(b), and profit-sharing plans is that you can take your accumulated retirement money with you when you change jobs. And if you transfer the money into a new employer's retirement plan or an Individual Retirement Account, you avoid having all that money hit with taxes until you withdraw it in retirement.

But it is vitally important that you transfer the money correctly. If the money goes to you, rather than to another retirement plan, 20% of it will be withheld for income taxes. Even if you move the remaining 80% into another plan or an IRA within a 60-day time limit, the 20% that was withheld will be treated as a "distribution," and you will owe tax on it— and, generally, a penalty, too, if you are not yet age 59½ Or you will have to come up with an amount equal to the 20% that was withheld, put it into your IRA on time, then file for a refund of the withheld dollars at tax time.

Fortunately, there is a much, much simpler alternative. All you have to do is arrange for what is known as a "direct transfer." The employer's plan administrator is required to give you details about how to transfer the plan funds or stock proceeds directly into an IRA or a new employer's plan 30 days before you receive your money from the plan. Essentially, the money is

TAKING YOUR LUMPS

Taxes and penalties gobble up a substantial portion of the money withdrawn in a lump sum from 401(k)s, 403(b)s, and profit-sharing plans before you reach age 59½

	TAX BRACKET	
	28%	31%
Lump-sum distribution	$100,000	$100,000
20% mandatory tax withholding at time of payment	$20,000	$20,000
10% penalty tax	$10,000	$10,000
Remaining federal income tax due*	$8,000	$11,000
Amount actually received	$62,000	$59,000

*Amount above the 20% withheld; does not include state tax.
SOURCE: Hewitt Associates.

transferred directly to the IRA or the new employer's plan without your ever seeing it. Brokerage firms, mutual fund companies, and others eager for your IRA business will be only too happy to help.

Another tip: If you are putting the money into an IRA but think you might some day want to roll it into another employer's plan, ask to set up what is known as a "conduit IRA." Do not mix the money with any other IRA contributions you might have made; you cannot transfer IRA dollars that have been commingled into a new employer's retirement plan.

GO EASY ON GICs

People who participate in retirement-savings plans at work generally have a choice of putting their accumulating retirement money in a handful of investment choices, including various types of mutual funds, their employers' stock, and guaranteed investment contracts, or "GICs." Despite the range of choice, the employee's preference in retirement-plan investments is disappointingly predictable: Too many simply direct their money into GICs and forget about it.

Offered by insurance companies or banks, GICs promise to pay a fixed rate of return for a year or more. The interest rate is typically a little lower than what you might receive on bond funds but higher than what you would get in a money market fund. And the principal is guaranteed by the insurers and banks that issue the GICs.

But while GICs do have a place in many retirement-plan accounts (they can be a good alternative to bond funds, for instance), most employees should restrain their desire for what looks like a sure thing. Over the long run, GICs are unlikely to provide the healthy inflation-beating returns you will need to fund a comfortable retirement. Most employees would be better off in stock funds, which hold out the prospect of higher, long-term returns. You can find help on smart retirement-plan investing in Chapter 2.

THE PAIN OF HARDSHIP WITHDRAWALS

When people run short of cash, they often cast a longing eye on money stashed in their company retirement plans. Unlike old-fashioned pensions, today's increasingly popular 401(k), 403(b), and profit-sharing plans generally do make it possible to pull the money out early. But do it the wrong way, and you will lose a substantial portion of your nest egg to taxes and penalties.

What is the wrong way? A "hardship withdrawal." Most employers allow withdrawals for severe financial hardship, such as medical bills, tuition, expenses to prevent eviction or foreclosure, and costs for the purchase of a principal residence. But if you make a hardship withdrawal, you will owe taxes on all the money, at your current tax rate. You will also probably have to pay a 10% federal penalty on all the money withdrawn if you are under age 59½. (The only exceptions are if you use the money to pay unreimbursed medical expenses exceeding 7.5% of adjusted gross income, become totally disabled, or are age 55 or over and retired.)

But there generally is an alternative. People who participate in 401(k), 403(b), and profit-sharing plans can usually borrow from their retirement accounts, then pay themselves back over a period of years through payroll deductions. The interest you pay yourself is usually a percentage point or so above the prime rate, which is the base rate banks use in setting rates on many loans to consumers and small businesses. There is one caveat: If you leave your job for any reason, the loan must usually be repaid at once, or it will be treated as a withdrawal and taxed.

Participants in some 401(k), 403(b), and profit-sharing plans can begin receiving periodic payments based on their life expectancy before they retire. While you pay tax on the money as you receive it, you escape the 10% penalty that applies to most withdrawals before age 59½. But once you start receiving annual payments, you cannot stop them without incurring a penalty until you have reached 59½, or have received the payments for five years, whichever is longer.

A WHOLE LOT OF BORROWING

The following chart shows the percentage of retirement plans offered by large employers with loans outstanding to various percentages of plan participants.

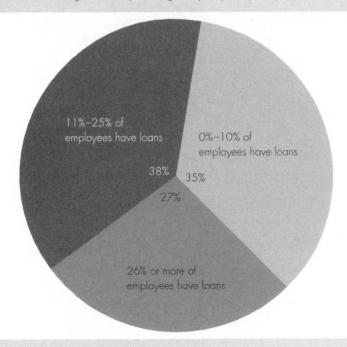

SOURCE: William M. Mercer, Incorporated.

OTHER EMPLOYER PLANS

Significant numbers of people are covered by employer-sponsored plans that differ from those discussed previously in this section. Among the most common are "457" plans for state, county, and municipal employees, "employee stock ownership plans" that give workers an investment interest in their employers, and supplemental retirement plans for key executives.

Here is a look at the basics of these plans.

• **457 plans.** These plans, which take their name from the section of the tax code that authorizes them, are simple salary-reduction plans. Employees can defer receiving some of their income, generally one-third of compensation, up to an annual ceiling, which was $7,500 in 1996. This lowers their taxable income, and the money grows tax-deferred until the employee changes jobs or retires.

Generally, employees can choose to allocate their 457 plan money among a selection of mutual funds and variable annuities. Employees also often have had the option of keeping the money in a general investment account run by their employer. But money in an employer's general account is subject to the credit risk of the employer. If the employer gets into financial trouble, as Orange County, California, did in 1994, employees may receive a lower payout than they were expecting. New rules require state and local governments to hold 457 plan money in separate accounts by 1999.

A significant difference between 457 plans and 401(k), 403(b), and profit-sharing plans is that employees who change jobs or retire cannot roll their money into Individual Retirement Accounts. But they usually can leave it in their old plan, where it can continue to remain untaxed until taken out.

Both loans and hardship withdrawals may be allowed. If you take a hardship withdrawal, the money will be fully taxable, but it will not be subject to the 10% federal tax penalty that generally applies to withdrawals from retirement savings plans before age 59½.

• **Employee stock ownership plans.** ESOPs are retirement-savings accounts, generally funded by employers, that invest in the employer's own stock. Proponents say they give workers an incentive to do a good job, since theoretically their retirement benefits will rise the harder they work. But most retirement experts agree that having your nest egg shackled to the fortunes of your employer is exceedingly risky, making ESOPs alone a dangerous basket for all your retirement eggs. If the company stock tanks, so do your retirement dollars.

No matter how promising the company stock seems, employees in ESOPs should diversify at their first opportunity. By law, employers must let employees in an ESOP sell the stock in the plan and put it into more-diversified investments after they have reached age 55 and have been in the ESOP at least ten years. At that time, your employer must let you sell up to 25% of the stock. Five years later, your employer must allow you the option of diversifying up to half of the plan's value. Some employers allow workers to diversify their ESOP even sooner, such as when they have been at the company for five years and are at least 40 years old.

If there is no market for the shares when it comes time for you to withdraw them for retirement, your company must buy them from you at a price set by an appraiser. Some companies, often closely held ones, do not let workers take the stock with them. Instead, they require departing workers to give them the right to buy the shares as a way of keeping ownership rights at a controllable core.

• **Supplemental retirement plans.** Executives at most large companies have retirement plans that supplement the pensions or retirement-savings plans offered to the rank and file. These supplemental plans are generally known as Supplemental Executive Retirement Plans, or SERPs. They include "excess" plans, which calculate what the executive would have been able to obtain using pension and retirement-savings plans formulas if no government limits were imposed on 401(k) or other retirement plans. SERPs are also called "top-hat" plans, since they are paid only to elite earners. It is also common for executives to elect not to receive their bonus but to instead have it added to a SERP.

Unlike traditional pension plans or such alternatives as 401(k)s, SERPs are usually not funded. Rather, they exist as promises to pay from the company's reserves or general assets. Consequently, they are a less certain form of pay than other types of retirement benefits that are subject to strict funding requirements. Sometimes employers will secure their promise with corporate-owned life insurance or through a trust.

These plans are called "nonqualified plans" because they do not qualify for the special tax treatment that pensions, 401(k), profit-sharing, and certain other employer plans enjoy. For instance, when you receive the money, you cannot roll it into an Individual Retirement Account, where it could grow tax-deferred. Instead, you will owe taxes on the sum right away.

PLANS FOR THE SELF-EMPLOYED AND SMALL BUSINESSES

Some people are on their own when it comes to retirement planning because they are their own bosses. Without a corporate employer's pension plan or 401(k) to fall back on, they have to fend for themselves. People who work for such entrepreneurs are also affected by the choices they make. Here is a look at two alternatives.

• **Simplified Employee Pensions.** Self-employed people can save hefty chunks of their earnings through a Simplified Employee Pension, or SEP. Also referred to as SEP-IRAs, because they are essentially turbo-charged Individual Retirement Accounts, they allow self-employed people to make annual contributions of about 13% of their net income, up to a certain dollar amount ($22,500 in 1996).

In general, any self-employment income qualifies, whether it is from moonlighting, consulting, freelance writing, or director's fees. The contribution is tax-deductible, and the money grows tax-deferred.

You have plenty of time to decide if you want to contribute to a SEP. You can deduct a SEP contribution for the previous year as long as you set up the account, and make your contribution, by the deadline for filing your tax return for that year. Unlike normal IRAs, if you get an extension of time to file your income taxes, you can take until the extended deadline—October 15 in some cases—to set up and add to your SEP.

SEPs, which are offered by banks and thrifts, credit unions, mutual fund companies, and brokerage firms, also require very little paperwork. But if you hire employees, you will have to contribute to the plan for them as you do for yourself, or you must discontinue the plan.

If you work for a small business run by someone with a SEP, you may have to wait until you have been there for three of the last five years before your employer begins making SEP contributions on your behalf. Employers can also skip contributions in some years if times are hard. But when your employer does make contributions, they can amount to up to 15% of your pay, to a certain maximum ($22,500 in 1996).

Typically, employees have control over how they invest the money in SEP accounts, and the plans are very portable: You own the assets and can tap them at any time once the contribution is made. Of course, like other tax-deferred retirement plans, if you withdraw the money before age 59½, the sums will generally be hit with income taxes and a 10% penalty. You cannot borrow from a SEP.

• **Savings Incentive Match Plans for Employees.** Starting in 1997, firms with 100 or fewer employees can offer this simplified type of retirement-savings plan, which is known appropriately as SIMPLE. The plan enables employees to set aside pre-tax dollars in special accounts to which employers also contribute. Employees may contribute a percentage of salary up to an annual limit, which is $6,000 in 1997. Employers are generally required to match workers' contributions up to 3% of pay, or put in 2% of pay for all workers whether or not they participate. The money grows tax-deferred until withdrawn. As with other tax-deferred retirement plans, withdrawals before age 59½ are generally subject to a 10% penalty. But the penalty increases to 25% for withdrawals during an employee's first two years of participation.

• **Keogh plans.** These retirement plans let you contribute as much as 20% of net self-employment income and deduct that amount when figuring your income taxes. The money then grows tax-deferred until withdrawn, usually at retirement. As with SEPs, any self-employment income qualifies, be it from your own business or occasional freelance work. While you have until April 15 or your extended filing due date to actually put the money in, the deadline for setting up the account for the year is December 31.

There are two types of Keogh plans. For most people, the best one is probably a "profit-sharing" Keogh. These let you contribute and deduct as much as about 13% of net profit from self-employment, up to a certain dollar limit ($22,500 in 1996). You can change the contribution amount every year or interrupt contributions. That flexibility is great for people who are not sure what their income and contributions will be.

"Money-purchase" Keoghs allow people to contribute as much as 20% of self-employment income, to a maximum that in 1996 was $30,000. But these plans are trickier, because you have to elect an amount to contribute every year, with a minimum of 3% of income, and keep to that schedule. If you do not make the payment, the tax penalty can be steep.

If you hire employees, you generally have to contribute the same amount for them as you do for yourself. If you cannot manage that, you will have to terminate the plan or it will be disqualified.

If you work for a small business that offers a Keogh plan, your employer will decide for you how much is put in each year. Your employer, not you, is also responsible for funding the plan, but may wait until you have two years of consecutive service before starting to make contributions on your behalf. Depending on how the plan was set up, you may or may not have control over how the money is invested; but if the plan is a "self-directed" one and was established though a mutual fund company, you probably can invest in any of its funds.

If the plan is a profit-sharing Keogh, your employer is permitted to put in as much as 15% of your pay, up to a dollar limit that was $22,500 in 1996. But your employer also has the flexibility to forgo contributions in some years. If the plan is a money-purchase Keogh, your employer could potentially contribute up to 25% of your pay, subject to a limit that was $30,000 in 1996. Money-purchase plans, which are usually set up in addition to profit-sharing Keoghs to maximize retirement savings, lock employers into contributing the same percentage of your income each year.

With either kind of Keogh, your employer could make you wait out a vesting period of up to seven years before you are entitled to the proceeds—although once you reach the plan's normal retirement age you must be treated as 100% vested. You can generally tap the assets only when you leave the company, or sometimes if you have a hardship for which the plan allows withdrawals. You also cannot take loans against the proceeds of most Keoghs.

But when you are finally eligible to tap the money in your Keogh, you can roll it into an IRA if you want to let the proceeds continue to grow tax-deferred. If you take it out without rolling it over, you may be able to figure the income tax by using a special forward-averaging method that reduces the amount you have to pay.

SOCIAL SECURITY

Even if you are too young to be receiving Social Security benefits, you are probably already part of the system. In fact, more than 12% of your salary up to a certain limit is regularly handed over to the government so that when you retire, or if you become disabled, you will be entitled to monthly income until you die. In 1996, the Social Security tax was collected from all workers' salaries up to $62,700; that limit rises each year with inflation. Half of the tax is paid by your employer, the other half by you. If you are self-employed, the whole burden is on you.

Currently, workers who reach age 65 and have generated enough Social Security credits over their working lives are eligible to start collecting their full Social Security benefits. Generally speaking, working for ten years will garner you enough credits. Workers can collect a reduced benefit starting at age 62.

But the traditional retirement age is being moved up gradually for people who were born after 1937. Someone born in 1938, for example, will have to wait until they are age 65 and two months before they can collect full Social Security benefits. Those born in 1939 must hit 65 and four months, and so on. Ultimately, those who were born after 1959 will be entitled to their full Social Security benefits only if they wait until they are 67 years old to start collecting. They can still start at age 62 if they choose, but their monthly payout will be reduced if they do not wait until 67.

HOW MUCH WILL YOU GET?

The Social Security formula is designed so that if you have average earnings (about $25,000 a person for the mid-1990s) your whole working life and retire at age 65, your Social Security payments will equal about 40% of your earnings just before you retire. Those earning the full salary subject to Social Security tax ($62,700 in 1996) or more will generally receive a quarter or less of their salary in Social Security benefits. Those who earn the minimum wage might get more than 50% of their pay in Social Security benefits when they retire.

The benefit you receive is ratcheted up each year according to a cost-of-living index, which is based on the rate of inflation. For example, people who retired at age 65 in 1993 and received an average monthly benefit of $679 got a cost-of-living increase to $698 a month in 1994.

To obtain an estimate of how much Social Security you may ultimately be entitled to, call the Social Security Administration (800-772-1213) and ask for Form SSA-7004-SM.

WHEN CAN YOU COLLECT?

Although many people consider 65 the age you start receiving Social Security benefits, you could choose to start taking them at age 62. But if you do so, your monthly benefit will be reduced from what it would have been had you waited. And while your payment will rise with inflation, the reduction itself is a permanent one. For instance, say you retired at age 62 and received $960 a month. By the time you reached age 65, your monthly benefit might be around $1,050, depending on the cost-of-living increases you received. But if you had waited to retire until age 65, you would have have gotten about $1,200 a month in 1995.

Still, you may find that delaying benefits would be a mistake, especially if you have to start withdrawing money from retirement-savings accounts, thereby giving up years of tax-deferred growth.

There is another consideration: If you have been the family's main breadwinner and your spouse is younger, you may want to put off taking Social Security until age 65. If you take Social Security early, your spouse will receive a reduced survivor benefit upon your death.

Also, if you delay taking your Social Security benefit until, say, age 70, you will receive a monthly benefit that is higher than what the maximum would have been at age 65. Those born before 1938, for example, will have 3% to 6.5% a year added to their benefit for each year they delay up to age 70. Younger people will receive even bigger annual increases in their benefits if they delay taking Social Security when the time comes.

What If You Keep Working?

If you are between the ages of 62 and 70 and keep working, you can still receive Social Security, but your benefits will be reduced if your wages exceed a certain dollar amount that changes annually. People under age 65 lost $1 in benefits for every $2 of earned income above $8,280 in 1996. Those age 65 through 69 lost $1 in benefits for every $3 of earned income above $12,500 in 1996; the amount that Social Security recipients in this age group can earn without losing benefits rises to $13,500 in 1997 and continues to rise in subsequent years until it hits $30,000 in 2002. Those age 70 and over can earn what they please without losing any Social Security benefits. (The income limits do not apply to investment income—so-called unearned income.)

If you decide to keep working and collect a reduced benefit, the Social Security Administration will boost your benefit once you stop working, or turn 70, to make up for some or all of the benefits you lose now.

Uncle Sam Gives—and Uncle Sam (Sometimes) Takes

Most Social Security recipients do not have to pay income tax on the payments they receive because their income is less than $25,000 ($32,000 if married). But those whose income exceeds that threshold—about 22% of

FICA IS NOT A PLANT

That cryptic "FICA" you see on your pay stub where the various deductions from your gross wages are listed represents the payroll taxes employees pay for Social Security and Medicare. FICA stands for Federal Insurance Contributions Act.

Social Security claims 6.2% of your salary up to a certain dollar limit that changes every year. In 1996, Social Security applied to the first $62,700 of salary. In addition, there is a 1.45% tax to fund hospital services for Medicare beneficiaries; this levy applies to all of your salary, no matter how high.

Whatever your combined Social Security and Medicare tax, your employer is assessed an equal amount. Self-employed people pay both the employee's and the employer's portion, all lumped together and called self-employment taxes.

recipients—do have to pay income tax on some part of their benefits.

Caution: This becomes tricky because the government takes a very broad view of what constitutes income for purposes of deciding whether you have exceeded the threshold. Income from all sources is counted, including tax-exempt municipal bond interest and half of your Social Security benefit.

The percentage of benefits subject to tax varies quite a bit depending on income. But no more than 85% of anyone's benefits will be taxable. The instructions accompanying your annual tax forms include a worksheet to help you figure out how much of your Social Security benefit is subject to tax.

EMPLOYER-PROVIDED HEALTH CARE COVERAGE

If your employer has a health care plan, consider yourself lucky. Buying medical insurance on your own that would provide coverage equal to the group coverage major American employers offer through their employee-benefit plans would cost thousands of dollars a year. But making the most efficient use of this valuable benefit is becoming increasingly complicated.

Today's corporate health plans typically offer a choice of either traditional fee-for-service medical coverage or managed care, such as health maintenance organizations (HMOs), point-of-service plans, and preferred-provider organizations. In some cases, employers still pick up the full cost of the coverage for employees and eligible family members, but the trend is toward requiring employees to bear a growing share of the cost.

Traditional coverage lets you pick your own doctors, but it is also the most expensive. Such plans usually reimburse you for about 80% of eligible expenses after you have paid the annual "deductible"— the amount, usually a few hundred dollars, that employees must pay themselves before the health plan kicks in.

HMOs limit your choice of doctors to the individual HMO's

specific roster, but they cost less in monthly premiums, there is almost never a deductible, and the charge per doctor visit is only $5 to $15. Point-of-service plans and preferred-provider organizations charge the low per-visit price of an HMO if you use doctors who participate in the plan's network of providers, and they generally reimburse you for about 70% or so of the costs if you go outside the network for care.

Deciding which type of coverage to pick requires employees to balance their own needs and budgets against the range of services, restrictions, and costs of each plan.

TRADITIONAL PLANS AND MANAGED CARE

Given the choice, most employees, especially older workers and those with continuing health problems, prefer to have the freedom to see doctors of their own choosing, to get unlimited second opinions and tests, and to see specialists as they feel it is necessary. Traditional fee-for-service medical coverage has been the health care plan of choice for many of these people.

But as such care has become more and more expensive over the years, employers have been shifting more and more of the costs to employees. This trend is likely to continue. Look for higher deductibles and bigger co-payments. You can also expect more restrictions on treatment, exclusions for pre-existing conditions, and caps on what the plans will pay for certain things.

As a result, it can be smart to look into managed care. If you have researched this option in the past and decided against switching from a traditional health care plan, it may be worthwhile to reconsider. For one thing, your own doctor may have joined one of the managed-care groups your company offers. Seeing the trend toward managed care as inevitable, many physicians have been signing up with existing plans or forming groups of their own.

Point-of-service plans and some preferred-provider organizations also give employees more flexibility than the HMO you may have rejected a few years ago. You could probably cut your health care costs significantly by opting for a preferred-provider or point-of-service plan and using its network of doctors for most of your care. You would still have the right to see out-of-network specialists of your choosing if the need arose, at somewhat higher cost to you.

EMPLOYER-PROVIDED HEALTH COVERAGE

More and more employers are offering managed-care health plans.

TYPE OF HEALTH PLAN	PERCENTAGE OF EMPLOYERS OFFERING SUCH PLANS*
Traditional fee-for-service	61%
Preferred-provider organizations	47%
Point-of-service	22%
Health maintenance organizations	80%

*Many employers offer a variety of plans.
SOURCE: Hewitt Associates.

Many managed-care plans will now allow women to visit their obstetricians or gynecologists without having to go through a primary-care doctor—a physician who acts as a sort of gatekeeper, deciding which other doctors managed-care patients may see and when. In some cases, in fact, a woman's gynecologist may now be her primary-care doctor.

But do not switch to managed care until you check with your employer about whether you would lose any benefits by doing so. While HMOs are generous in covering general preventive medicine, they may place limits on such care as psychiatry or services for children away at college. Bear in mind, too, that managed care is just that: There often are incentives for doctors to keep expensive tests and procedures to a minimum. If you are especially cautious about your health and do not mind footing part of the bill for just-to-be-sure tests, you may be happier sticking with fee-for-service care.

Still, even traditional health care plans now often require some procedures, especially surgery, to be preapproved before the insurer will pay for them. And if your doctor or hospital charges fees that are well over the costs the insurer considers "reasonable and customary," you may find that the insurer will not foot as much of the bill as you thought.

COORDINATING FAMILY COVERAGE

Husbands and wives who both have a choice of health-coverage options at work need to sit down and figure out what combination of plans will give them the most comprehensive coverage at the least cost. It may be, for instance, that one of the plans provides maternity benefits that are clearly superior. For a couple thinking about starting a family, that alone may be reason enough to choose coverage under a particular plan.

But the days when spouses could submit the same doctors' bills to both employers' plans and finagle 100% reimbursement are virtually gone. Today, most employers coordinate coverage so that at best you will get the maximum benefit of the better of the two plans.

Consider a two-career couple who elected coverage for both spouses under both company health plans. The standard procedure today would be to submit bills incurred by each spouse first to his or her own health care plan as the primary insurer. The portion of the expense not covered by the primary insurer would then be submitted to the other spouse's health plan for consideration.

For instance, assume that the wife's plan would provide reimbursement for 70% of a $100 doctor's bill incurred by her and that the husband's plan would provide 80% reimbursement. If the wife had satisfied her deductible requirement, her plan would pay her $70. The couple would then submit the bill and the information on reimbursement to the husband's health care plan. If the wife had satisfied any deductible requirement under her husband's plan, it would send her $10—the amount necessary to bring the total amount of reimbursement from the two health care plans up to the level provided by the better of the two plans.

Many employers are encouraging workers not to include their spouses and other dependents when signing up for health care. As long as an employee's family members have some other coverage, these employers pay bonuses for leaving them off the plan. The payments are typically around $60 a month for an individual and $85 for a family. Some people have found that this is a good deal. They take the bonus and opt for coverage as individuals under their own companies' plans, while their spouses get coverage for themselves, plus the kids if they have any, under the plan of the spouses' company.

Some working couples find it better for the whole family to be covered under one spouse's plan. That might not be the best option, though, if it turns out that a wife's plan will charge a penalty for covering the whole family when the husband could have received his own coverage at his job. It is also important to ask what would happen if the spouse whose employer provided the health care coverage lost his or her job. In most cases, the other spouse would be allowed to rejoin his or her own company's plan and include other family members as dependents. But there could be some restrictions on someone needing to enroll on short notice.

Both spouses should examine the alternatives thoroughly with their benefits departments before acting. Some large companies are giving their employees software so they can use personal computers to help them make all the complicated choices involved in picking the right health plan.

MATERNITY BENEFITS

Maternity care is an expensive benefit for employers, and many are limiting the coverage they offer. Couples who are thinking about starting families should review their options carefully before pregnancy. A woman who has been covered under her employer's HMO plan, for example, might find that she could get more generous benefits by selecting another option on her employer's benefits menu. Or she may want to elect coverage under her spouse's traditional fee-for-service plan. Employers usually allow employees to switch health plans only once a year, often in November or December.

Some health plans at small companies simply do not pay for routine pregnancy care, which can cost upwards of $4,500. Such bare-bones plans may pay only if a delivery requires emergency measures or other extraordinary care. Even at companies that do cover pregnancy care, preapproval is often required for certain procedures. In some cases, such tests as ultrasound or amniocentesis are covered only if the patient is over age 35 or has a family history of genetic disorders. Other plans limit the number of covered ultrasound tests to one or two.

Employer health care plans are also limiting the amount of time mothers and infants may remain in the hospital after birth. Without prior approval, most plans now pay for only one or two days after a vaginal delivery, or three to four days after a Caesarean section. Moreover, their definitions of what constitutes a "day" vary. In some cases, as long as the mother and child are in bed by, say, noon or midnight, they have completed one day. That leaves many mothers slated for discharge only 12 hours or so after delivery. Several states have worked to require insurers to cover at least two days.

Most plans will cover any care the baby needs right after delivery as long as the parents sign up the baby as a dependent within 30 to 60 days. There may be a separate deductible of several hundred dollars for the new baby, however. If you wait too long to sign up your newborn, you run the risk that any health problems your baby has might be considered a pre-existing condition, which many insurers will not cover until after a year-long waiting period, and some will not cover at all.

Once the mother is home, many plans pay for a visiting nurse's services. Nurses check the baby for conditions such as jaundice, answer parenting questions, and sometimes provide breast-feeding instructions.

EMPLOYEE-ASSISTANCE PROGRAMS (EAP)

Most major employers offer employee-assistance programs for workers suffering from alcoholism, drug addiction, job stress, depression, family woes, and other problems. Employees are encouraged to contact EAP counselors for a referral to a therapist or just to "unload."

Some companies run their own internal EAPs, but about 80% are run by managed-care companies that use the services as gatekeepers for mental-health benefits. Before employees can see outside psychotherapists, they have to persuade an EAP counselor—often a social worker—that they qualify.

For people fortunate enough to work for companies with good employee-assistance programs, the help available can be a real blessing. Keep in mind, though, that using these services may compromise your privacy. Although employees are given written assurance that their records are confidential, there are a number of instances in which this is not the case. The most common of these is if you file a workers' compensation claim or sue your employer.

Mental-Health Benefits

Most large employers offer mental-health benefits, which may include coverage for counseling with a psychologist, treatment by a psychiatrist, hospitalization, and drug and alcohol treatment. But as with regular medical care, costs are rising and employers are cutting back.

Employers with old-fashioned fee-for-service plans allow employees to choose their own practitioners and will typically pay a percentage of the cost of visits, up to a specified dollar amount, or number of visits, each year. Managed-care plans usually authorize an employee or dependent to make 20 visits a year to one of the practitioners in the managed-care network. But after the first five or so visits, the employee or covered family member must get approval from a case manager for continued treatment. Depending on the provider, it may be difficult to win approval for more than five or ten visits. Some companies that offer traditional fee-for-service coverage for other medical care have switched to a managed-care approach for mental-health benefits.

Employees who are reimbursed for visits to psychotherapists should be aware that they may not have as much confidentiality as they think. Managed-care programs require therapists to report to insurance-company clerks about the nature of the treatment, typically in great detail. That information goes into unregulated insurance-company databases. Although insurers insist that the information is kept strictly confidential, there is no way for employees to know if it is.

What If You Lose Employer Coverage?

If you have felt locked into your job because of the health benefits, or suddenly find yourself out of work and have no new employer in sight to provide coverage, do not panic. You may have more options than you realize, especially with the enactment in 1996 of the landmark Health Insurance Portability and Accountability Act. The law guarantees health insurance coverage for millions of Americans who switch or leave their jobs. It also shortens the exclusion periods for pre-existing health problems that employer-sponsored plans and insurers can impose on eligible workers. Those requirements will begin to become effective in July 1997.

The law will offer protection to workers in several situations. If you switch jobs, moving from one employer-sponsored health plan to another, the new employer must provide coverage to you and any family members who were covered under your former employer's plan. If you have a pre-existing health problem, you still may have to face a waiting period before your new coverage takes effect. But that waiting period will be limited to a year and may be further shortened by the number of months you were covered under your previous plan. For example, if you have a heart condition but had been covered under your previous employer's plan for six months, your new employer's plan could impose only a six-month waiting period.

Some employer plans have excluded pregnancy as a pre-existing condition. Under the new law, they may no longer do that, nor may they exclude newborns or newly adopted children.

Still, the new protections leave plenty of gaps. For one thing, in order to be credited for prior coverage to shorten any pre-existing waiting periods under a new employer's plan, you must not have gone without qualifying coverage for more than 63 days. Moreover, because the portability provisions apply to plan years beginning after June 30, 1997, some plans might not have to conform to the new rules until 1998. If you are on the job market before then, be sure to ask any prospective employers about when you would be eligible for full coverage under their health plans.

If you have any reason to think you will go without group coverage for more than two months, you may want to elect what is known as COBRA coverage. With COBRA coverage, departing employees can extend the coverage they were getting at work for 18 months after leaving. You will have to pay the premiums yourself, but you will pay the same group rates your employer pays, plus a surcharge of 2%.

COBRA coverage is particularly important if you leave a company with health benefits to start your own business or to work on a freelance basis. Under the new law, you would have a guarantee of individual coverage as long as you had been under a group plan for at least 18 months and, if you had been eligible for COBRA, exhausted those benefits. But states and insurance companies will have a good deal of flexibility in determining how to provide individual coverage and how much it will cost.

If you are highly confident you are going to be without coverage from a new employer for only a short time, you could consider a short-term policy that covers you for only about three months or so. These policies tend to be significantly cheaper than either COBRA coverage or a standard individual health-care policy, but they do not pay for care associated with pre-existing conditions, such as diabetes or pregnancies. For a longer-term solution, some people who elect COBRA coverage may be able to continue with the plan after the initial 18 months by paying nongroup rates. But this is often an expensive option.

If you have no new employer in sight, you will have to shop for the cheapest policy you can find. Many self-employed people and workers who have not been covered under a group plan are not guaranteed coverage under the new law. If you are among such employees, you may have a difficult time even finding a medical policy if you are old or have any pre-existing conditions. But you still have options.

For starters, if you are self-employed, you will be able to deduct a greater percentage of your health-care expenses under the new law. That percentage will be phased in, increasing from 30% to 40% in 1997; 45% in 1998 through 2002; 50% in 2003; 60% in 2004; 70% in 2005; and ultimately reaching 80% in 2006. Many self-employed people and workers at small companies also may be able to purchase health insurance through new tax-deductible medical savings accounts.

Individual insurance policies often are very expensive, costing thousands of dollars a year. You may be able to keep premiums down by agreeing to pay a higher deductible or larger co-payment. Some insurers might lower the quoted premiums if you cite your healthy behavior, like the fact that you are a nonsmoker. You may also be able to get better rates with a group or association plan through your

MEDICAL SAVINGS ACCOUNTS

Under the Health Insurance Portability and Accountability Act of 1996, more than a million people could become part of an experiment to test the controversial concept of medical savings accounts. These are private, tax-favored accounts that are to be used to pay for routine health costs. The accounts are coupled with high-deductible medical policies to cover big-ticket medical expenses.

Starting in 1997, tax-deductible medical savings accounts will be available for people who work for companies with 50 or fewer employees and for people who are self-employed. People who participate will have to be covered by high-deductible insurance policies with annual deductibles of $1,500 to $2,250 for a single person and $3,000 to $4,500 for a family. The project will set limits on the total out-of-pocket medical expenses that a person could face in a given year, with a maximum of $3,000 for a single person and $5,500 for a family. But those caps apply only to services covered by the health-insurance plan.

Both employers and employees may make tax-deductible contributions to the accounts, but not both in the same year. The maximum contribution an employee may deduct—or have excluded from income and wages if the employer makes the contribution—is 65% of the annual deductible for a single person and 75% of the annual deductible for a family. Earnings on the money in the accounts, as well as sums withdrawn to pay medical bills, will not be taxed. Withdrawals for nonmedical bills will be subject to income tax—plus an extra 15% penalty for people under 65.

The pilot project will limit the number of medical savings accounts to 750,000 over a four-year period. To expand the availability of the accounts beyond the year 2000, Congress will have to vote its approval. But, even if Congress does not vote to expand the program, people with accounts will be permitted to keep them and contribute to them indefinitely.

local Chamber of Commerce or a professional or trade organization to which you belong.

HMOs or other managed-care plans also may offer a less expensive alternative to an individual policy, although many still do not offer individual memberships. With an HMO, too, you are restricted to using an approved roster of doctors and hospitals.

If you have health problems, see if your state has rules requiring insurers to provide coverage for anyone willing to pay the rates the insurer sets. Only a few states have rules to make sure the insurance you are offered is affordable.

About half the states provide "high-risk" pools for people who cannot get coverage because of health problems. Premiums generally are at least 50% more expensive than other individual policies. Another alternative may be a Blue Cross/Blue Shield plan. In many states, these plans act as insurers of last resort, holding open enrollment periods each year with coverage for anyone who applies. (You can find out more about buying your own health insurance in Chapter 3.)

WHAT IS COBRA COVERAGE?

When you leave a company that employs at least 20 workers, the Consolidated Omnibus Budget Reconciliation Act of 1985 requires that you be allowed to continue your former employer's health coverage for 18 months at your own expense. You pay the same group rates your employer receives, plus a surcharge of 2%. You are entitled to this COBRA coverage whether you quit, are laid off, or are fired (unless you are fired for gross misconduct). If you or a family member is disabled within 60 days of leaving, you are entitled to the coverage for 29 months, although you may have to pay a surcharge of up to 50% of the premium.

It is not just employees who have the right to elect COBRA coverage. You may be entitled to it if you are left without company-provided health insurance coverage because of the death of a spouse or a parent whose employer included you as a dependent, or because that covered employee becomes eligible for Medicare. In such cases, the coverage can often last for 36 months rather than the normal 18 months.

Divorcing spouses have a right to pay for their own policy if their ex's coverage was all they had. But, although the spouse with the coverage is supposed to tell the plan administrator about the divorce so the other spouse will be informed of his or her rights, sometimes the ex never gets the word until he or she falls sick and has to fight for coverage.

You have 60 days after being notified of your right to COBRA coverage or after your regular coverage would terminate, whichever is later, to decide whether to elect the coverage. If you are relatively healthy and do not have any pre-existing conditions, you may find it cheaper to buy an individual policy. That is because people picking up COBRA coverage cannot change the terms of their employers' plans and, thus, may end up paying for more services than they need.

THE INS AND OUTS OF MEDICARE AND MEDIGAP

It is not unusual for people who receive Medicare when they retire to find that it provides more generous health care coverage than they ever had while they were working. Medicare is the government-sponsored health program that covers people who have reached age 65. People with certain long-term disabilities or kidney ailments may also qualify for Medicare before they reach age 65.

Medicare coverage is divided into two parts. The first, known as "Part A," is free and provides hospitalization insurance. Medicare "Part B" is optional coverage that pays for medical services other than hospital stays—services such as doctor's visits, medical equipment, and medical tests. Participants pay a monthly premium that changes annually. (In 1996, it was $42.50.) For most seniors, the price is right—95% of all those eligible for Medicare Part B sign up for it.

When you start collecting Social Security retirement benefits, you will receive a Medicare card in the mail. If you retire at age 62 and start collecting Social Security, you should get your Medicare card automatically when you turn 65. If you delay getting Social Security, you generally should apply for Medicare yourself within a seven-month period around your 65th birthday. If you miss that deadline you may pay a penalty when you finally want to enroll, and you will have to wait until the first quarter of the next year, when Medicare has its general enrollment period.

Unfortunately, as comprehensive as Medicare is, it leaves some hefty costs on the shoulders of beneficiaries. You have to pay 20% of all doctor's visits, plus a portion of the cost for hospital stays—a share that grows the longer you are there. Then there are some incidental costs that add up, such as the first three pints of blood you might need. Medicare does not cover prescription drug costs at all.

As a result, many retirees buy another insurance policy known as Medigap, which picks up such expenses when the time comes. There are ten standard Medigap policies, but premiums for exactly the same policy can vary drastically from insurer to insurer. So it is important to shop.

Because of the added complexity, some people who turn 65 and are still covered by an employer-provided health plan may want to delay joining Medicare. That way they can avoid unnecessary duplication and stick with the coverage they know. Be sure to notify Medicare of your wishes.

UNDERSTANDING THE BASICS

Medicare generally works like most other insurance, only on a more controlled scale. You can go to any doctor you choose, but Medicare will pay that doctor only a set sum for any given visit or procedure. Doctors who agree to be satisfied with the Medicare-set amount for their services are said to "accept assignment." Other doctors will take you but charge you more than what Medicare will reimburse. Such nonassignment doctors are not legally allowed to charge you fees more than 15% higher than the Medicare limit.

Providers who accept assignment must send your claims to Medicare for you. They also have to include the information on any Medigap coverage you might have, which is then forwarded to the carrier you chose for Medigap.

Some people eligible for Medicare choose to join managed-care arrangements that are reimbursed slightly differently. Instead of going to the doctors of their choice, these people choose to limit themselves to seeing doctors or hospitals on a roster maintained by the managed-care group—either a health maintenance organization or some other plan. The plans vary a great deal in their rules about whether patients may occasionally see a doctor who is not part of the program and how much patients must pay if they do see a nonprogram physician.

You may still pay Part B premiums if you join an HMO or other managed-care plan, but it is unnecessary to buy a separate Medigap policy.

FILLING THE GAPS

It is clear pretty quickly once you start investigating Medicare that there is much that is not covered. Knowing this, many people buy special Medigap policies to pay for uncovered expenses. There are ten standard Medigap policies, simply dubbed "A" through "J," and each covers a different array of Medicare-omitted costs.

Each of the ten policies pays the patient's portion of the basic hospital and doctors' costs not covered by Medicare, including daily charges for hospital stays and 20% of doctors' bills. They all also

COMPARING MEDIGAP BENEFITS

The ten basic Medigap policies offer a broad range of coverage.

WHAT THE POLICY PAYS FOR:	TYPE OF POLICY									
	A	B	C	D	E	F	G	H	I	J
Basic Medicare cost sharing	•	•	•	•	•	•	•	•	•	•
Hospital deductible ($716 in 1995)		•	•	•	•	•	•	•	•	•
Skilled nursing-home co-payments			•	•	•	•	•	•	•	•
Medical-services deductible ($100)			•			•				•
Foreign travel emergencies			•	•	•	•	•	•	•	•
At-home recovery assistance				•			•		•	•
Excess doctor charges						100%	80%		100%	100%
Preventive screening					•					•
Outpatient prescription drugs*								(1)	(2)	(3)

*50% after $250 deductible
[1]$1,250 maximum
[2]$1,250 maximum
[3]$3,000 maximum
NOTE: Some choices may be unavailable in Delaware, Massachusetts, Minnesota, New York, Pennsylvania, Vermont, and Wisconsin.
SOURCES: United Seniors Health Cooperative; Prudential Insurance Company of America–AARP Group Health Insurance Program.

pay 100% of the cost of 365 days of hospitalization over a policy-holder's lifetime.

Policy "A" covers only those basics, while the other nine each go further in some way. Some pay the deductible for each spell in the hospital; some pay 50% of your prescription drug costs, up to a $3,000 annual maximum; some pay for emergency coverage for out-of-country travel; and some cover as much as $1,600 of personal home care following an illness or surgery. The Cadillac of Medigap, the "J" plan, also reimburses policyholders for their annual deductible for doctors' visits and as much as $120 of health screenings or preventive services.

The content of the policies is strictly regulated by state law. Although there are some minor state-to-state differences, a policy A sold by one insurer within a given state must cover the exact same things as any other policy A offered in that state. Still, premiums for the exact same coverage from different insurers can vary widely. In fact, comparison shopping may save you 50% or more.

You want to make the best buying decision you can the first time because you may not get a second chance. While insurers must accept anyone applying for Medigap within the first six months after joining Medicare Part B, after that, they can reject practically any applicant they predict will use a lot of benefits. As a result, if you later develop health problems that a new insurer does not want to cover, you may not be able to switch to a less expensive or more comprehensive policy.

BUYING TIPS

Social or professional organizations catering to seniors often offer group policy rates that can be much cheaper than you would get on your own. The American Association of Retired Persons offers policies in most states that are often particular bargains for older people.

In selecting policies, consider what benefits you are going to need. Someone who always visits doctors who charge no more than Medicare-set fees might find that paying extra for plans F or G, which reimburse policyholders for doctors' charges above Medicare's limits, could be wasteful. A cheaper C or D policy might provide all you really need.

Ask how the prices are set. Premiums that are priced based on a person's "attained age," for instance, usually rise every year, so that while they might look cheap for a 65-year-old now, years later the policy may be prohibitively expensive. A more expensive policy with premiums that stay relatively stable over the long run could be the better deal. To get a sense of what the policy will cost down the road, look at the policy's "outline of coverage" or the premium schedule from the insurance company.

Buying Medigap coverage from an insurer that offers electronic billing can save money. Many insurers also offer automatic claims handling, called "crossover billing," which means Medicare automatically sends bills to the Medigap carrier. That way you will not pay a bill and later forget to file for reimbursement.

GETTING ADDITIONAL INFORMATION

The U.S. Health Care Financing Administration, which administers the Medicare program, offers two free resources that answer many of the questions people usually have about Medicare and Medigap: *The Medicare Handbook*, which is considered the bible of Medicare, and *Guide to Health Insurance for People with Medicare*. These popular books are updated annually and become harder to find as the year progresses. To get copies, if available, call 800-772-1213. Or check your local library.

Another good source of information is the United Seniors Health Cooperative, 1331 H Street NW, #500, Washington, DC 20005-4706.

WHEN YOU ARE UNABLE TO WORK

What happens to your salary if you get cancer, have a stroke, are hit by a car, or suffer from some other sickness or injury that leaves you temporarily—or permanently—unable to work? If you are lucky, you are protected by group disability coverage, a workplace benefit that typically pays 60% of your salary while you are disabled. According to Department of Labor figures, about half of all companies with more than 100 employees offer this long-term disability coverage.

For most employees, this coverage is the only thing that keeps a paycheck coming in while they are laid up. But qualifying for benefits has become more difficult in recent years. Citing the need to control costs, employers are adding restrictions, including caps on what they will pay for certain conditions. That makes it all the more important for employees to take a close look at how their disability benefits work. If your employer does not provide disability coverage, or if you feel the amount provided would not be enough to meet your needs, consider buying an individual policy. This is an expensive option, though, and relatively few people have such coverage. (You can find some helpful tips about individual disability coverage in Chapter 3.)

GROUP DISABILITY DETAILS

At most companies, if you are disabled for a few days or weeks, you are on "sick leave," and your paycheck continues to roll in as usual. Some employers may also apply vacation days toward your sick leave.

After sick leave expires, many employers offer short-term disability coverage. This typically covers 40% to 70% of your salary, depending on how long you've worked at a company and other factors, and it may last for 30 days to six months. Payments are reduced by any amounts you receive from Social Security and are taxable as income. Depending on your plan, short-term disability may start on the day your sick leave expires or on the first day of hospitalization.

If you are disabled longer than 180 days, long-term disability kicks in; it generally covers 60% of pay, up to a specified ceiling. Many plans will pay the benefit for two years if you cannot work at your occupation. Thereafter, most will continue paying the benefit only if you are considered too disabled to work at any occupation. If that is the case, the plans usually pay benefits until age 65. (If you are older than 65, coverage usually lasts five years.) As with short-term disability, payments are reduced by any amounts you receive from Social Security and (unless you paid the premiums yourself) are taxable as income.

If your employer does offer disability coverage, it is vital to know whether it is automatic or optional. If the coverage is optional, sign up for it. Also ask whether you can purchase supplemental coverage. If you are a new employee, you may not qualify for coverage until you have been at the company for a year.

SOCIAL SECURITY DISABILITY INCOME

If you have a total disability that is expected to last at least a year or result in death, you may receive Social Security Disability Income benefits. Benefits, which are based on recipients' salaries, average $661 a month, and the maximum payment is about $1,200 a month. You apply for benefits through your local Social Security office, but do not assume payments are a sure thing. So stringent are the requirements, in fact, that 42% of applicants are initially rejected.

It is also crucial to know how your employer's plan defines "disability." Some companies will agree that you are disabled only if you qualify for Social Security disability payments.

Also find out what conditions are excluded or restricted. Disability coverage for "mental and nervous disorders" is usually limited to two years or less. As with health coverage, employers can also install lifetime caps that restrict the total amount a plan will pay.

WORKERS' COMPENSATION

If you suffer a work-related illness or injury, you may be entitled to "workers' compensation," which most employers are required to buy. This coverage provides medical coverage and a percentage of your pay until you are back on your feet, regardless of whose fault the injury was.

But there are drawbacks to workers' compensation. Employers that provide it are immune from lawsuits, so you cannot recover money for pain and suffering, even if you lose an arm and a leg, your eyesight, or suffer other permanent damage because of employer negligence.

And collecting benefits is not easy. In recent years, insurers have raised the price of premiums they charge employers. In turn, employers have successfully argued for changes in state laws making it more difficult for injured workers to collect benefits.

Insurers say they are swamped with claims for emotional stress and repetitive-motion injuries, and they say they are the victims of fraud perpetrated largely by medical providers. Many employers say their employees improperly claim their injuries are job-related, knowing they will receive medical treatment that is 100% reimbursed rather than what they would receive under their medical plan, assuming they have one.

Given this climate, here are some things to keep in mind when filing a workers' compensation claim:

• Report injuries right away and get immediate medical care. Delaying treatment weakens your injury claim.

- File a workers' compensation claim immediately. While you may have as long as two years to file a claim, depending on your state, you are better off getting the paperwork rolling as soon as possible.

- Expect a thorough investigation. Insurance carriers aggressively investigate the validity of claims and may operate on the assumption that you are lying until proven otherwise. This is less likely to happen if you have a tangible injury and more likely if you file claims for back pain, emotional stress, or repetitive-motion injuries.

The Family and Medical Leave Act

If you have been a full-time worker for at least 12 months at a company with 50 or more workers, you are entitled to take an unpaid 12 weeks off each year for the birth of a child; caring for a newborn; adopting a baby or taking in a foster child; caring for a parent, spouse, or child with a "serious health condition"; or caring for your own serious health condition.

Employers have the right to require that you use up any unused paid time off, such as vacation or sick days. If you have three weeks of unused paid leave, for instance, your boss could require that you take it and then get nine weeks of unpaid leave under the act. This rule applies only to unused vacation time: Employers cannot shorten your 12 weeks because you took your family to Disney World earlier in the year.

It may be possible to get a better deal. Nearly a third of large employers offer more generous time-off policies in some situations than is required by the federal act. An employer might allow workers to be out longer than 12 weeks at management's discretion, for example, or might pay for part of a maternity leave. Some states also have rules that are more generous than the federal rules.

When you come back from leave, your boss must give you your same job or an equivalent one, unless you cannot do the old job because of health problems. If you worry your employer will try to shunt you to a less favorable slot when you come back to work, get a doctor's note saying the medical problem you had will not keep you from working at your old job.

OTHER BENEFITS

As employers cut back on retirement and medical benefits to save money, they are adding a plethora of other offerings.

Some of these newer "benefits" are not really benefits at all in the traditional sense because they are paid for by the employees themselves. For instance, many employers are offering employees the opportunity to purchase additional types of life insurance, long-term-care policies, homeowner's insurance, and other financial products through payroll deduction. Although this may be convenient, it may not be a good deal. For one thing, you may not really need the product. Or you may be able to find something better for less money on your own. In any case, keep in mind that the fact that your employer is offering a particular financial product through payroll deduction does not necessarily mean that your employer has screened it.

At the same time, employers are also offering some additional benefits that can be very appealing to employees. These include flexible work schedules, or "flex time," extra days off, and medical and child-care reimbursement accounts that allow employees to pay for medical and child-care expenses with pretax dollars.

"Cafeteria" Plans

"Cafeteria" plans have nothing to do with food. Instead, they are "flexible-benefit plans" that give employees a certain number of "credits" and a menu of benefit options on which to spend them. The list may include medical coverage, life insurance, disability coverage, vacation days, and dental care. Employees who do not want a particular benefit can spend more on another or collect the difference in cash.

Taking the cash will not make you rich: Opting out of all the benefit offerings might bring you $600 or so. And you probably cannot decline medical coverage unless you can prove you are covered elsewhere.

But the flexibility can be useful. A young, healthy person who is unlikely to have more than basic medical bills might save credits by opting for a low-cost health maintenance organization and spend them on extra vacation days. A woman who is planning to have a child in the year ahead might cut back on vacation and boost her medical coverage by picking an option that will lower her out-of-pocket expenses or give her more choice in selecting doctors and hospitals. A middle-aged man might choose a medical option with a higher deductible, thus lowering the monthly cost of coverage, and use the credits he saves to add to his retirement savings or to pay for long-term-care coverage.

Another feature of cafeteria plans is that they generally let employees pay their share of benefit costs with pretax dollars. This is a mixed blessing. On the one hand, it is like having Uncle Sam subsidize your benefit payments, because each dollar deducted from your salary for benefits reduces your taxable income. Thus, a person who pays 40% in taxes would pay only 60 cents for each dollar of benefits. On the other hand, employees of companies that adopt cafeteria plans are generally being asked to pay more of the cost of their benefits. The flexibility is sort of the "spoon full of sugar" that helps the medicine go down. Using pretax dollars to pay for the employees' share of the costs also lowers employees' income for purposes of accruing Social Security benefits. While this may not affect higher-paid earners, those with low salaries may find that it erodes their Social Security accruals.

FLEXIBLE SPENDING ACCOUNTS

Flexible spending accounts can save you money on medical expenses that are not covered by your health plan and on dependent-care expenses, such as child-care or elder-care fees. You elect to have part of each paycheck shunted into special accounts—sometimes called medical-reimbursement or savings accounts, child- or dependent-care accounts, and flexible savings accounts. Then, as you incur el-

LET UNCLE SAM HELP

When you have pretax dollars withheld from your pay to fund a flexible spending account for medical or dependent-care expenses, the tax savings reduces your out-of-pocket cost every time the account reimburses you for an eligible expense.

Your Income and Family Status	Medical or Child-Care Expense Reimbursed from Flexible Spending Account ($)	Your Out-of-Pocket Cost ($)
$25,000/Single	100.00	77.35
$40,000/Family of four	500.00	386.75
$40,000/Family of four	2,500.00	1,933.75
$60,000/Single	250.00	160.88
$80,000/Family of four	700.00	493.85
$80,000/Family of four	5,000.00	3,527.50
$100,000/Single	1,000.00	675.50

Note: Out-of-pocket costs reflect savings on federal income tax and Social Security and Medicare taxes, using 1995 rates. Depending on your state, you may save additional amounts in state taxes.
Source: © 1995 Buck Consultants, Inc.

igible expenses over the year, you receive reimbursements from the accounts.

The plans save you money because your contributions to the special accounts are withheld from your salary, lowering the amount of your income that is subject to federal income tax, Social Security or Medicare tax, and most states' income taxes. Because of the tax savings, each dollar you put in is really worth much more. If your combined tax rate is 40%, for instance, each dollar you contribute costs you only 60 cents. Using the accounts is simple. When you incur expenses, you submit the bills to the account administrator, who reimburses you from your account.

Employers usually set limits of $2,000 to $3,000 for medical-reimbursement accounts, which you can use to pay for such things as the deductible portion of your medical bills and any uncovered expenses, such as routine physicals, eye exams and contact lenses, and mental-health counseling.

By law, working couples and single parents can save as much as $5,000 per family annually in a dependent-care account to cover the cost of babysitting, day care, summer camp, preschool, and after-school care for children under age 13, and the cost of care for a dependent elder. The expenses must be necessary so that you—and your spouse, if you are married—can continue working. Thus, nighttime babysitting is not covered, unless you work at night.

You cannot use a dependent-care account and also get the federal child-care tax credit for the same child-care dollars. Financial advisers figure that dependent-care accounts are a better deal for families with incomes of roughly $25,000 or more.

With medical-reimbursement accounts, you do not have to wait to accumulate the money in order to have it paid out. For instance, say you agreed to have $1,000 taken from your pay over the year for your medical-savings account, and you incur $900 in unreimbursed expenses in January. When you submit the unreimbursed expenses, the full $900 will be paid to you, even though you will not accumulate the savings until the year is almost over. (This generous provision does not apply to dependent-care accounts.)

What happens if you leave your job before accumulating enough money in your medical-savings account to cover the expenses for which you have been reimbursed? Your employer absorbs the cost.

But there is a risk for employees in medical-savings accounts and dependent-care accounts: If you do not spend the money by the end of the year, you forfeit it. So it is important to estimate carefully how much you are likely to spend in the coming year on medical costs, including insurance deductibles or co-payments, eye care, routine physicals, dental visits, or mental-health therapy. Similarly, tally what you will definitely spend for the care of your children under age 13, or in some cases a dependent parent, in order for you to be able to work. Keep in mind that if you claim reimbursement for child-care or elder-care expenses, federal law will require you to report names, addresses, and Social Security numbers of the caregivers on your income tax return.

STOCK-PURCHASE PLANS

How would you like to make a quick 15% return?

That is not only possible but also easy for employees at the many companies with employee stock-purchase plans. Typically, employees can buy as much as $10,000 of their company's stock at a discount of generally 15% from its market value.

Employees are given a chance to join the program each year, either by making a cash purchase or by having a certain percentage of their salary withheld each pay period over six months to one or two years. Although employees frequently flip the stock as soon as they buy it, those in the highest tax brackets might want to wait more than a year to sell, since their profits may qualify for more favorable tax treatment.

5

HANDLING FAMILY FINANCES AND ESTATE PLANNING

$

Strip away all the extras, and financial planning is about fundamental family things—providing your kids with a good education or being able to help take care of your aging parents, having the money to visit your grandchildren or being able to leave something when you die.

That has never been easy, but it is more complicated than ever these days. With many people delaying marriage and children, and with the rise of second marriages and second families, many people are having to deal with toddlers and aging parents at the same time. Some are struggling to pay for their kids' education just as they begin their own retirements. Some even have children and grandchildren starting college at the same time.

Still, the basic rules of family financial planning do not change. Families need to balance current lifestyle against such future needs as the down payment on a home, college tuition, or retirement. That means developing a good understanding of cash flow, investing regularly, and creating a safety net—just in case.

The tools for doing all this are straightforward. Every family needs a system of budgeting, some stocks or stock mutual funds for growth, some fixed-income investments to offset stock market volatility, and some insurance and a rainy-day fund to protect against the unexpected. A will, by itself or combined with some sort of trust, takes care of the rest.

BALANCING COMPETING DEMANDS

The reality of family and finances is seldom simple. Mixing family and money can be highly emotional. Money, like sex, is traditionally viewed as a subject not to be discussed with children. Many children, on the other hand, often feel they have some claim on their parents' assets for everything from college tuition to the down payment on a house.

The problem is trying to balance the needs and desires of one family member against another without creating ill will. What happens when one child wants to go to graduate school and the other needs money for a house? What happens if your parents fall ill just as you are closing on your new home?

This family balancing act is easier if there is good communication about money between parents and children. That does not mean you should show your kids your tax returns. But you should make a point of including them in family discussions about money when appropriate.

Once they are old enough to understand, children should be included in financial decisions that affect them. Tell them early on that if they want a car they will have to pay for it themselves. Make sure they know it if the only way you can afford the Ivy League is for them to get a scholarship. Or make it clear that they will have to earn money to help pay their college living expenses. They may not like you very much for these discussions, but if you do not bring it up until their expectations have already been set, they will be upset—and justifiably so.

INTERGENERATIONAL COMMUNICATION

The need for good communication does not stop when children are grown. Adult children need to understand their parents' estate plans, particularly if they will eventually serve as executors. Knowing what parents intend also makes it easier for children to make their own plans. After all, you do not want your children waiting around for an inheritance that may not exist. Nor do you want them to inherit $1 million having given nary a thought to what they will do with the money.

Broaching these subjects may feel like entering an emotional minefield, but keep in mind that such conversations are almost always harder for the children to initiate. Kids do not want to feel greedy or grasping, and many are uncomfortable discussing the eventuality of their parents' deaths. Parents do their children a big favor when they take the first step.

Even then, it may be hard for one generation to empathize with the concerns of the other. Each stage of life brings its own worries. Estate-tax avoidance is not a high priority for a 25-year-old, whereas retirees are not likely to remember how hard it was to save for a bigger house.

Whatever the stage, keep a long-term view. The decision you make today will certainly lead to the bill you pay tomorrow. Sending the kids to private school, for example, will probably lead to private college. That may preclude early retirement or a family vacation home. Indeed, everything is a trade-off. How you spend your money is your choice. But if you choose to do one thing now, it may well mean that there is something else you will not be able to do later.

INHERITANCE EXPECTATIONS

Baby boomers expect to give more than they receive.

Likely to receive an inheritance	62%
Likely to leave an inheritance	93%
Feel they are deserving of an inheritance	60%
Feel children are deserving of an inheritance	86%
Feel parents are obligated to leave them an inheritance	16%
Feel they are obligated to leave children an inheritance	54%
Parents have discussed inheritance with them	54%
Have discussed inheritance with their children	25%

SOURCE: First Interstate Bank Trust and Private Client Services Group.

PROVIDING FOR YOUR FAMILY
THROUGH THE AGES

Family financial concerns tend to change with the passage of years. For a young couple just starting a family, finding a way to pay for today's necessities while putting something aside for that newborn's college education can be an enormous challenge. People in their middle years often face a tug of war between the needs of their kids, their parents, and themselves. Estate planning is frequently a large concern for retirees.

But at every stage of life, handling financial demands is a balancing act. The following sections deal with the major issues in family finance for people who are just starting out, watching their families grow up, and looking forward to a long and healthy retirement.

YOUR 20S AND 30S

First there is the stuff you have to do. Then there is the stuff you should do. When you are just starting out, the stuff you should do usually takes a backseat.

Newlyweds who are struggling with balancing their new joint checking account, for example, are not thinking about writing wills, setting up investment plans, or buying life insurance. When children arrive, however, the far-off future suddenly moves nearer. You know you ought to be doing something about college funding and estate planning. But your family's disposable income has just been slashed, either because you are paying for child care or because one spouse has stopped working to take care of the children. Then comes the realization of what a child really costs. It is not just the necessities like diapers, milk, and babysitters. It is also the things you want for your child, such as piano lessons and summer camp. Meanwhile, college looms large as the black hole of family finances.

It is time to take a deep breath and start from the beginning. If you have not done so yet, make sure you have an adequate reserve fund covering three to six months of living expenses. This is the money you will use for emergencies, so it has to be accessible. Certificates of deposit, money market mutual funds, and short-term U.S. Treasurys are all reasonable choices. (For a closer look at the principal options, refer to Chapter 1.)

Now, discipline yourself about investing. Decide how much you can afford to invest every week or every month, and then do it. One way to start is by setting up an automatic investment plan. Some employers allow you to buy company stock or U.S. savings bonds through a payroll-deduction plan. Or you can set up an automatic investment program to buy mutual funds by having the money taken directly out of your bank account. If your regular investment program can make use of tax-advantaged options, such as a 401(k) retirement-savings plan at work, your money will grow even faster.

Once you have kids, it makes sense to start socking away money for their education as soon as possible. For instance, parents with a newborn who save $310 a month can accumulate $150,000 by the time that child starts college—assuming an 8% annual return. But if they wait until the child is ten, they would have to set aside $1,113 a month to reach the same total. There are several simple, no-fee ways for parents to accomplish their college saving, including making regular investments in no-load mutual funds. (Chapter 2 has a number of suggestions about how to make the most out of a small investment portfolio.)

A TAX BREAK YOU MAY NOT WANT

It may make sense to put some investments in the child's name because children get a tax break on some of their unearned income. Exactly how much of their income qualifies for special tax treatment is subject to adjustment annually, but in 1996 the amount was $1,300. That is equivalent to a return of about 7% on an $18,600 investment. Uncle Sam collects nothing on the first half of the qualifying amount—$650 in 1996. The second half is taxed at 15%, which is typically a lot lower than what Mom and Dad pay. Unearned income above the qualifying amount is taxed at the parents' rate until the child turns 14.

But putting money in a child's name can work against you when your youngster starts applying for college financial aid. That is because college-aid formulas are based on children using a much higher percentage of their assets to pay for education. Moreover, whether you are saving for college or just trying to give your child a nice nest egg, there is no guarantee that money will be used for that purpose. Once the child turns 18 or 21—depending on the state in which you live—he or she can spend the money on a Porsche, a trip to Europe, or some new love interest.

Indeed, it is important to remember that kids are not born with money-management skills. They need to be taught how to handle money, use credit, and make investments. Start the instruction early with something simple, such as an allowance in their elementary school years, and expand to include bank accounts, credit cards, and investments as they mature.

Do not overlook holiday and birthday gifts as a way to promote financial education. Stocks and mutual funds, if selected to match a child's interests, are a good way to spark enthusiasm for investing. You might look at Reebok International or Nike for your young athlete, or Microsoft for your budding computer jock. Some companies even offer special perks that appeal to young shareholders.

Some parents even start family investment clubs. Children help research investment options and decide where the monthly investments will go. The National Association of Investors Corporation in Madison Heights, Michigan (810-583-6242), can provide information on how to set up such a club.

KID APPEAL

These three companies offer stockholder perks that seem bound to tickle young investors.

- **Wm. Wrigley Jr.**
  Sends shareholders a box of gum for the holidays.

- **Tandy**
  Offers shareholders Christmastime discounts on purchases at its Radio Shack and other electronics stores.

- **Walt Disney**
  Gives shareholders a discount on its Magic Kingdom Card, which entitles holders to 10%–30% discounts on various attractions and resort facilities. Annual meetings feature previews of movies and other entertainment.

YOU MUST PICK A GUARDIAN

For most people, estate planning at this stage of life is relatively straightforward. You need a will. If you have minor children, you also need to choose a guardian for them in case something happens to you and your spouse, and you need to decide how they should inherit your estate. Do not let the difficulty of choosing a guardian keep you from completing the job. You can always go back and name someone else later. Be certain to consult with the person you select before naming them. While there is little chance that person will ever have to take over for you, you do not want the assignment to be a surprise.

Hand in hand with the will goes life insurance. If you have children, you must have it. This is not a place to skimp. You need to insure both parents, even if only one draws a salary. A spouse who stays home to bring up the children may not bring in any money, but the services provided are extremely costly should you have to replace them. (For suggestions on getting the insurance coverage you need at a price you can afford, see Chapter 3 and the Buyer's Guide to Life Insurance, Appendix C.)

YOUR 40S AND 50S

By the time you reach your 40s and 50s, you have already learned that children are expensive. Hang on. They are going to become more expensive. If that is not enough, you may soon learn how much your aging parents can cost.

This is a period of great compromise. The number of demands on your resources is way up, and many of those demands suddenly seem to carry very high price tags. For many people, the biggest crunch will be their children's college tuition bills. Few manage to save enough to cover the entire expense, which already can run $25,000 a year and more. Scholarships, loans, and other sources of tuition money will probably be essential.

One good place to look is your house. If mortgage rates are low, you can take money out of your house by refinancing with a mortgage that is larger than your current balance outstanding. Home-equity loans, which typically carry much lower interest rates than many other types of loans, are another possibility. With both types of mortgage debt, the interest you pay is generally tax-deductible.

GET THE KIDS TO HELP

Before you start reworking your finances, though, it is important to remember that you do not have to shoulder the cost of college alone. You can ask the kids to help. In fact, it is a good idea. Provide an amount that is comfortable for you and have the college-bound student take out a separate loan to cover the rest. This not only reduces the size of your financial burden, but it also helps your kids understand the value of what they are getting.

Children may not be the only drain on your resources. Aging parents may also be growing costly. There is little you can do to prepare for these expenses, since you do not know when or even if parents will need your help. But the costs can quickly skyrocket once they do. Folks who feel the need to do something overt can buy their parents a long-term-care insurance policy. This would protect against future nursing-home costs. But because these policies are very expensive and may never be needed, it may be wiser to take your chances, standing by in case you are needed. (You can find more information on long-term-care insurance in Chapter 3.)

As the tug of war heats up, do not ignore your own needs. You cannot afford to be too selfless. These are the years when you should be accumulating most of your retirement savings. You need to be investing on a regular basis so that your funds have an opportunity to grow.

You also need to be thinking about estate planning. A simple will is probably no longer sufficient. Many people in this age group have estates that are big enough that they will be taxed by Uncle Sam when they die. Although the entire estate can pass tax-free to the surviving spouse, when he or she dies, federal estate taxes will take 37% to 55% of anything over $600,000, including life insurance death benefits. That makes it important to take steps, often relatively simple ones, to try to reduce the tax bite.

Those steps frequently include shifting assets out of joint ownership, creating reciprocal "bypass" trusts, and possibly setting up a

40s–50s

- Tap home equity to help pay for college.

- Have children share college costs.

- Keep tabs on parents' needs.

- Do not neglect retirement savings.

- Review estate plan.

life insurance trust. This basic plan allows both you and your spouse to make full use of the exemption that allows $600,000 in every estate to pass free of federal estate taxes. By taking assets out of joint ownership and making sure that as much as $600,000 of them will go into a trust for the benefit of your surviving spouse and children, you preserve your exemption by "bypassing" your spouse's estate.

Creating a trust for your life insurance keeps the death benefit out of your estate altogether. That can save you a bundle. In a large estate, estate taxes on a million-dollar life insurance policy, for example, can cut the effective death benefit to only $450,000.

YOUR 60s AND BEYOND

There is a light at the end of the tunnel. If you are lucky, the kids are on their own, the mortgage is paid off, and there is money in the bank. But you are not off the hook yet.

Just when you feel you can kick back and relax, do not be surprised if one of the kids announces that he or she is getting married—or getting divorced and coming back to live with you. Or maybe help is needed with the down payment of a house or braces for your grandchildren. Even when children do not ask, there are things you want to be able to do to make their lives easier.

But while it is nice to help when you can, you will not do anyone any favors by being too generous. Indeed, the best thing you can do for your children is to arrange your finances so that you will not become a burden to them. That by itself is no small accomplishment. You also need to make sure that you are providing your kids with needed information. Talk to them about the myriad "what ifs" that can develop at this stage—illness, disability, and death. Tell your children who your advisers are. Make sure all the necessary documents are drawn up and that the children know both where to find them and what to do with them.

Among the necessary documents is a durable power of attorney. Drafted with the help of a good lawyer, this document allows the child to do such things as sign tax returns and make financial decisions for the parent. Make sure you have the right kind of power of attorney. Unlike some other kinds, a "durable" power of attorney is worded so that it remains in effect even if a parent becomes incompetent. Equally important is a health care power of attorney, which delegates the right to make health care decisions. Rules vary from state to state, but often a living will is incorporated into the document, outlining specifically what measures would be acceptable to prolong life.

MAKE SURE OTHERS KNOW

The third item is a list of assets and where they can be found. Include everything from life insurance policies to bank accounts to pension plans. The Personal Financial Inventory in Appendix B will help you remember what information you need to provide and organize it in a way that will be most useful to other family members. Just fill in the information, put the list in your files, and leave a copy with your lawyer or in the safe-deposit box.

Even if most of your assets are already in a trust, a will is important. It specifies your wishes after death. It names your executor and divides any assets that remain in your estate. This is where you make sure your niece gets the family china and your grandson gets your vintage Ford.

If you have many assets or special concerns, your use of trusts may expand. You may want to establish a marital trust, allowing you to place some restrictions on the part of your estate that will pass directly to your spouse. This would allow you to do such things as choose advisers to help your spouse manage the money or make sure those assets stay in your family should your spouse eventually remarry. A similar arrangement, structured as a so-called living trust, may even make sense before you die if you or your spouse is infirm. Such a trust would address issues such as who pays the bills in the event that both are ill or incompetent. Trusts have also been used to shelter assets so that people can qualify for Medicaid when they need nursing-home care. But changes in the law make it unlikely that such trusts will be of much use in the future.

Once you have your affairs in order, do not overlook the pleasure of seeing your heirs use some of your assets while you are alive. Uncle Sam lets you give as much as $10,000 a year to each of an unlimited number of people without triggering a gift tax. If you are

60s +

- Talk to kids about your wishes.

- Update estate plan.

- Draft a power of attorney.

- Write a living will.

- Consider gifts to family.

married, you and your spouse can each give $10,000 to the same person for a total of $20,000 a year. In some circumstances, you can give even more. You can, for example, pay tuition bills for grandchildren, even if they are two or three times the $10,000 annual limit. That is because you can make gifts of unlimited amounts to pay tuition bills or medical bills, as long as the check is made payable directly to the school or the medical provider.

PLANNING YOUR ESTATE

You will never know how good your estate plan is because you will not be around to see how it works. But it is likely to be the one part of your financial planning that has the greatest long-term effect on your family. If crafted with care, you can create a series of documents that will preserve more of your estate, provide your family with greater flexibility, and make sure that assets do not inadvertently end up in some unintended place.

But that is not an easy task. Overlooking even seemingly small details can thwart your best intentions, in some cases creating a probate quagmire that can tie up your estate for years. If you fail to take all the reasonable possibilities into account, the real-life consequences may be far different from what you intended.

That is why the first step in any estate plan is to ask all the potential "what if" questions. Consider not only the size of your assets and the impact of taxes but also what your family's financial and emotional needs are likely to be. Remember, you can inflict great pain from the grave if you slight someone in your will. The fallout can go far beyond hurt feelings to contested wills and even long-term family conflicts.

Typically, the amount of estate planning you need is directly proportionate to both the amount of money you have and the complexity of your family relationships. This is not a place for do-it-yourselfers. While some software companies market computer programs that let you do your own legal work, creating trusts is complicated, and there are many ways to trip up. You want knowledgeable, professional help.

YOU MUST HAVE A WILL

A will names your executor and specifies how you want your assets distributed. In simple estates, this is where you make sure the kids get the house, that Aunt Tillie's silver goes to the ladies' club, and that each of the grandchildren gets a small nest egg. Even if you have a series of carefully crafted trusts to handle who gets what, you still need a will in case you overlook something. Common items left out of trusts—accidentally or on purpose—include houses, checking accounts, inheritances, recent investments, and loans made to other people.

Wills can be simple documents, but they must be written. You cannot, for example, make a videotape. They also must be dated so the court can determine the most recent will. Strict rules govern the signing and witnessing of wills, and failure to follow them can invalidate a will.

Just having a properly executed will, however, does not mean your property will go where you say. Other factors can come into play. If you and your daughter own your home jointly with rights of survivorship, for example, that property will pass directly to her, even if your will says it should be divided evenly among all three of your children. Likewise, if you want to disinherit your spouse by leaving everything to your children, you will have a tough time. Most states give surviving spouses the right to claim a significant portion—typically a third—of any estate.

Wills take on added importance if you have young children. That is because they name the guardian who will look after your children if something happens to you and your spouse. This can be an emotionally loaded issue, since husband and wife may have different ideas about which relatives or friends would do the best job. Just naming the guardian, however,

THINGS TO REMEMBER WHEN DRAFTING A WILL

Although drafting a will can be a fairly simple matter, it is essential to get proper legal advice. There are strict rules governing wills, and even simple mistakes can cause big problems. Here are some things to keep in mind.

- If you have a house in New Jersey, a vacation home on Cape Cod, and a condo in Palm Beach, your will is going to be subject to probate in three different states, unless the properties are owned by a trust or other entity.

- You cannot leave a videotape for a will. Wills must be written and dated. Strict rules govern signing and witnessing, and failure to follow them can invalidate a will.

- Do not assume someone will agree to serve as either executor or guardian for your children. Always ask, and remember to name backups.

- If you want to disinherit your children, say so in the will. If you simply leave them out, many states will assume you forgot them and they will inherit as if you had never written a will.

is not enough. You must also decide how your minor children will inherit. If you simply name your children as the beneficiaries of your will, for example, they will inherit outright. The problem is that minor children cannot own anything you leave them. Instead, the court will oversee the assets until the children turn 18 or 21, depending on the state. Then, as a birthday present, they gain full control of the money to do with whatever they please.

A TRUST FUND FOR THE KIDS

Many attorneys recommend that any assets inherited by children go into a trust. This approach gives you a say not only in how the money should be spent but also at what age the children finally gain control. Attorneys commonly recommend that at least one trustee should be someone other than the children's guardian, preferably a banker or other professional trustee. Why? If the money is grossly mishandled, use of a professional trustee gives your children some recourse through the courts.

To avoid creating financial conflicts between guardian and trustee, you can be very specific about how the trustee should spend that money. You can specify that money be available for anything from child care to helping the guardian buy a bigger house to make room for your kids. In some cases, you might even want the trustee to provide funds for your guardian's children. One example would be paying for the private school education of both sets of children to avoid potential jealousies.

TRUSTS ARE NOT ONLY FOR THE RICH

If mention of the term "trust fund" conjures up images of mansions, yachts, and indolent wealth, think again. Once the province of the very rich, trusts have found their way into the lives of many families who have never thought of themselves as wealthy. Escalating housing prices and booming investment markets have helped push more and more estates above the federal estate-tax exemption. At the same time, longer life spans, second marriages, and lawsuits have more people looking for ways to protect and manage family assets.

Trusts come in two basic flavors: "revocable" and "irrevocable." Revocable trusts can be changed at any time, and typically the person who sets up the trust can be both a trustee and a beneficiary. As such, the trust is basically invisible for tax purposes; any taxable events are reported on the tax forms of the person who sets up the trust. Irrevocable trusts cannot be changed once established, and they are generally considered separate tax entities. Not only are these trusts subject to high tax rates on undistributed income, but moving assets into such trusts can have gift-tax consequences.

Within these two basic categories, there are myriad variations. Trusts are classified according to when they are created, who benefits, how assets are distributed, or any of a number of other characteristics. They often do not fall into neat categories because trusts can serve multiple purposes. None offers a simple magic solution to estate planning or any other problem. Here is a look at some of the more common types of trusts.

• **Credit-shelter or "bypass" trust.** This is, perhaps, the most common estate-planning trust. It is designed to allow married couples— who can leave everything to each other tax-free—to take full advantage of the exemption that allows $600,000 in every estate to pass free of federal estate taxes. If you and your spouse have a $1.2 million estate, for example, each of you can leave everything to the other without triggering estate taxes. But if the value of the estate is still $1.2 million when the survivor dies, the tax collector will get $235,000—the estate tax on the amount in excess of $600,000. Alternatively, each of you could leave $600,000 in a credit-shelter trust to be used by the survivor and eventually passed to the kids. That way, there would be no estate tax at all.

• **Disclaimer trust.** This is for the couple who do not yet have enough assets to need a credit-shelter trust but may need one in the future. A surgeon who will soon finish paying off college loans might want to take this approach. Here, the surviving spouse is left everything but has the right to disclaim some portion of the estate. Anything disclaimed would go into a credit-shelter trust. This technique provides the surviving spouse with the flexibility to shelter wealth from estate taxes, if there is any wealth to be sheltered. But

THE FEDERAL ESTATE-TAX BITE

Uncle Sam takes a rapidly growing share once estates exceed $600,000, the amount that escapes federal estate taxes under the "unified credit."

TAXABLE ESTATE	TAX AFTER UNIFIED CREDIT	TOP MARGINAL RATE
$600,000	0	0
$700,000	$37,000	37%
$1,000,000	$153,000	41%
$1,500,000	$363,000	45%
$2,000,000	$588,000	49%
$5,000,000	$2,198,000	55%
$10,000,000	$4,948,000	55%
Over $10 million		55%*

*An additional 5% tax is imposed on estates over $10 million to phase out the unified credit and the progressive rates; estates over $21,040,000 pay a flat rate of 55% on every dollar.

if the estate does not grow as expected, the survivor is not locked into a trust structure.

• **Marital-deduction trust.** This is a trust you can use to leave your spouse any money that does not go into a credit-shelter trust. No matter the amount, it is free of estate tax when you die, since it qualifies for the marital deduction. Why put the money into a trust rather than leaving it outright to your spouse? The primary reason is to make sure your money stays in your family. Leave your assets to your spouse outright, and a remarriage after your death would give somebody else a claim on those assets. A trust lets you keep the assets separate. A marital trust also lets you establish certain terms and conditions. Rather than making your spouse trustee, for example, you could name someone with more financial experience, if you wish.

• **Q-TIP trust.** Perhaps the most popular form of marital trust is the "qualified terminable interest property" trust, or Q-TIP. Here, the surviving spouse receives all trust income, which must be distributed at least once a year, and sometimes access to the principal as well. But when the spouse dies, the assets go to whomever you specified in the trust documents. The trust assets are then taxed as part of the surviving spouse's estate. Q-TIPs work particularly well for some couples with kids from a previous marriage. The Q-TIP provides income to the surviving spouse, but the underlying assets eventually go to the kids. But do not try this if the first kids and the new spouse are the same age. The kids will not see a penny until the spouse dies, an event they might not live to see.

• **Living trust.** This is typically a revocable trust formed while you are alive. Well-structured estate plans often start with a living trust that becomes irrevocable at death, dividing itself into several other types of trusts, such as the credit-shelter trust. By transferring assets into a trust that survives you, you typically can avoid court probate upon your death and speed distribution of your assets. That can be an important strategy in a state like California, where probate fees kick in on anything over $60,000 gross value. By themselves, however, living trusts do not avoid taxes. They need to be combined with other trusts.

SOME TRUSTS ARE FOR THE WEALTHY

Estate-planning techniques range from the straightforward to the very complex. The very wealthy have great motivation to try more sophisticated techniques. With the tax collector getting as much as $55 out of every $100, people with very large estates can easily justify the legal fees and headaches of layering complicated trusts one on the other.

But make no mistake about it, these sophisticated estate-planning techniques are not things to be entered into lightly. Typically, they require you to part with something of value, such as a life insurance policy, a house, or a stock portfolio. The idea is that in giving up direct control of an asset, there will be a future benefit, often in the form of lower estate or gift taxes.

Here is a look at five such techniques. Some work well for a wide range of wealth. Others are only for the extremely rich. But all five must be carefully crafted and properly monitored. That means not only asking all the potential "what if" questions but also making sure that all the members of your estate-planning team—attorney, accountant, financial adviser, and insurance agent—work together.

• **Life insurance trust.** Putting life insurance into an irrevocable trust for the benefit of children or spouse keeps the death benefit out of your estate. That can translate into big savings on estate taxes. You either provide money for premium payments or transfer an existing policy to the trust. If you take the transfer route, however, you must live at least three years for the policy to be outside your estate. Although a life insurance trust is a common estate-planning tool, it requires careful monitoring so that it does not run afoul of gift-tax rules.

Basically, these rules allow everyone to give away $10,000 a year to an unlimited number of people. Exceed that amount, and you begin eating away at the lifetime "unified credit" that allows you to pass along $600,000 free of federal estate or gift taxes. Exceed that $600,000 limit, and you owe gift tax. The difficulty with a life insurance trust is that gifts to an irrevocable trust do not usually qualify for the $10,000 annual exclusion. Estate-planning specialists have a way around this problem that includes limiting the size of the annual transfer to a prescribed formula and giving beneficiaries a brief window when they can take that amount for some other use.

• **Qualified personal residence trust.** Also known as a QPRT, this trust allows you to take your home or vacation home out of your estate. You give your home to a trust but continue to live in it for a term of, say, ten years. At the end of that time, the home belongs to the continuing trust or to the trust beneficiaries, depending on how the trust is written. Any gift tax you might incur from giving your home away is adjusted substantially downward by the fact that you have retained residential rights to the house. Transfer a $500,000 house to a QPRT, for example, and depending on the terms of your trust, your gift might be valued at only $250,000. If you die before the term of the trust expires, however, the home will be considered part of your estate.

Some estate planners take this technique further, having donors buy the home back from the trust at the end of the term. Using the previous example, you would end up with $500,000 cash in the QPRT—an asset that could not be transferred there otherwise. But your gift, for gift-tax purposes, would still be valued at only $250,000. From a tax point of view, this buyback technique is also advantageous, particularly if the heirs are likely to sell the home. If passed on through the QPRT, the home's tax basis would be what-ever the donor paid for it. That could mean big capital-gains taxes for the heirs. But if inherited through the estate, the heirs would have a more advantageous stepped-up basis set at the time of death.

• **Charitable remainder trust.** This trust lets you leave assets to a favored charity, earn a tax break, but retain income for life. Chari-table remainder trusts work best for people who are rich on paper because of an appreciated asset, such as land or a stock bought long ago, but who need to have additional cash to live on. While selling the asset might generate a lot of money, these people would give up a sizable chunk of it in capital-gains taxes.

With a charitable remainder trust, they can give the asset to a char-ity, which can sell the property—paying no tax. Then, with the pro-ceeds of the sale, the charity sets up an annuity that pays the donor a regular income. There is one big drawback, though. Once you have given the asset away, it is gone. That means your children will not inherit it. That is why many people take some income from the trust, give it to their kids, and let them buy a life insurance policy to make up for the asset that they now will not inherit.

• **Charitable lead trust.** This works the exact opposite way of a char-itable remainder trust. Here, a trust pays a charity income from a donated asset for a set number of years. When the term is up, the principal goes to the donor's beneficiaries with reduced estate or gift taxes. Setup and operating costs, however, preclude the use of this type of trust unless the assets involved are substantial. This is a ve-hicle for the very wealthy, allowing them a way to keep an asset in the family but greatly reducing the cost of passing it on.

• **Generation-skipping trust.** People who want to leave a lot of money to their grandchildren need to think about generation-skipping trusts. That is because the government imposes a flat 55% tax on everything in excess of $1 million that you leave to your grandchildren's generation. It is Uncle Sam's way of making up for losing the opportunity to levy estate taxes on the middle generation. Generation-skipping trusts can be used at the time of death, much like a credit-shelter trust, to preserve the $1 million generation-skipping tax exemption for both members of a couple. More commonly, they are used to increase the value of that exemption. Put $100,000 into an irrevocable generation-skipping trust early on, and it will use up one-tenth of your lifetime exemption. Even if that money grows to $2 million, the entire amount is sheltered from the generation-skipping tax.

PUTTING IT ALL TOGETHER

How you use these various techniques to put together an estate plan depends on your own individual circumstances and preferences. The variations are endless. Here's one possible scenario.

You have a $1 million estate. In your will, you leave all of your tangible property to your spouse. Your revocable living trust becomes irrevocable on your death and divides into two parts. The first is a credit-shelter trust of $600,000 set up for the benefit of your spouse and then passing to your children. The remaining $400,000 would go to a Q-TIP trust for your spouse and then pass to your children.

No estate taxes would be due at your death. The $400,000 in the Q-TIP would be taxed on your spouse's death if that estate exceeded $600,000.

In larger estates, that same living trust could establish a number of more sophisticated trusts. Some possibilities are charitable lead trusts, which grant income from a trust to a charity for a specified period of time, and generation-skipping trusts, designed to reduce the impact of the generation-skipping tax.

The terms of the trusts you create will determine how they are administered. You can, for example, determine when children gain access to trust funds. You can even specify how trust money should be invested. Or you can grant special powers to your trustees to make these decisions. A "sprinkling power," for example, lets the trustee make distributions to beneficiaries as needed. You could grant your spouse special powers of election in a Q-TIP trust so that he or she can, in part, determine who the final beneficiaries are.

FINDING GOOD LEGAL ADVICE

The legal world is a place of specialists. Whether you are drawing up a new will, buying a house, getting a divorce, or wrangling with the IRS, one lawyer cannot do it all. Just as you would not ask a gastroenterologist to treat your heart problems, you should not be asking your real estate attorney to draw up your will. Finding the right specialist can save you both time and money, since someone current on the issues affecting you will not need to do special research for your case.

You also need to consider the size of the law firm. Large firms with hundreds of attorneys tend to cater to the corporate client, and their fees are typically much higher. Most people will find small law firms a better fit, both for the scope of their problems and the size of their pocketbooks. If you have some special problems and need a high level of expertise, however, you may be able to find it only at a larger firm.

Having limited the scope of your search, you now need a list of prospective attorneys. Word-of-mouth referrals from relatives, friends, and coworkers can be valuable. So can local bar associations, which often provide a free referral service. You can also conduct your own search by going to any large public library and checking the *Martindale-Hubbell Law Directory* for your state.

Once you have your list, call your state bar association to check out your prospects. Ask if there are any complaints filed against the lawyers or if they have ever been disciplined for improper or questionable conduct. Then make appointments to meet with your prospects. Take careful note of the way you are treated by the lawyer and office staff during your interview. It is indicative of the way you will be treated once you are a client.

As part of your interview, make sure you understand how you will be billed. If your lawyer charges by the hour, ask for a reasonable estimate of how many hours your case is expected to take. Many lawyers request a retainer to cover a set number of hours of work. Retainer agreements should always be carefully reviewed. Do not be afraid to question any terms you find objectionable.

If your lawyer charges a flat fee, make sure you understand exactly what services are included and which ones are not. That way you will not be surprised to find a larger-than-expected bill because of "extras" that you thought were part of the package.

ASKING THE RIGHT QUESTIONS

These questions, suggested by New York attorney Alice Griffin, author of the book *How to Find the Right Lawyer*, will help you focus on some of the key issues when you are interviewing lawyers.

- How long have you practiced your specialty?
- What are the names of other lawyers in this specialty who can serve as references?
- What are the names of clients who can serve as references?
- What, if any, problems do you think my case presents?
- How much will your services cost?
- If a retainer is required, what are the terms?
- If a flat fee is charged, will my case require more than what is included in the package deal?

SOURCE: *How to Find the Right Lawyer*, 2d ed. Copyright 1996 by Alice Griffin. Available from Cakewalk Press, P.O. Box 1536-DJ, New York, NY 10276, for $13.95 postpaid.

Finding a Trustee

Picking a person or organization to manage the trusts set up to administer your assets after death is a common stumbling block in estate planning. You want someone who will be a sound administrator, a wise investor, and responsive to the needs of your beneficiaries. But it can be tough to find a trustee with all those characteristics.

People with large and complicated estates often opt for professionals, such as banks, but lackluster performance and personnel turnover are common complaints. People of more modest means commonly select close friends or relatives, but they may lack the necessary investment skills.

But big changes are afoot. For one thing, a revision of the "prudent-investor rule," which sets trust investment standards, is now working its way through the states and has already been enacted in a few. The revised rule, developed by a committee of trust experts, dramatically changes the way trustees must invest. Just as important, it will allow individual trustees to delegate investment responsibilities they formerly had to shoulder alone.

That should make the search for a trustee an easier task for many. No longer will you have to find one person with all the characteristics of a good trustee. Under the new rule, you only have to find someone you trust who knows how to delegate if necessary. At the same time, investment companies, such as mutual fund giant Fidelity Investments and brokerage-industry powerhouse Merrill Lynch, are aggressively positioning themselves in the trust market. One reason for this is that a whopping $10 trillion is expected to pass from one generation to the next by the year 2040, according to a Cornell University study. That should translate into a lot of trust funds.

MORE CHOICES

The investment firms' expansion into the trust market, combined with the revision of the prudent-investor rule, means that people will have more options both for the choice of trustees and the way those trustees can operate. Here is why. The old rule, embodied in the laws of many states, basically says a trustee, as a prudent investor, must pay attention to widely accepted investment-industry standards. But those standards became ossified, and some states even adopted lists of investments that were considered safe.

The revised rule recognizes not only that beating the market is very difficult but also that a diversified portfolio greatly reduces risk and boosts return. As such, a trustee must now diversify trust investments or have a good reason for not doing so. Bans on investments that were once deemed too risky—stock options or international stocks, for example—are also being eliminated. Now it is the portfolio—not the individual investments—that is important.

What about poor Uncle Harry who is overseeing the family trust fund but lacks the kind of investing expertise now required? Under the new rule, the Uncle Harrys of the country are told to get help, be it in the form of hiring an investment manager or even turning to mutual funds. He is not off the hook entirely, however, since he must make the selection with care and can be held accountable for a bad choice.

Such delegation was previously allowed if specifically written into a trust. But now it will be generally accepted practice. That means your trustee will have the option, whether you specifically write it into your trust or not. There will be many professionals lining up to provide the necessary assistance. Some may be mutual fund companies or investment advisers who seek to work with the investment part of a trust. Many trust companies, on the other hand, will be looking to convince people that professional trustees are a better alternative.

THINGS TO REMEMBER

Here are some things to keep in mind when selecting a trustee.

- Consider naming more than one trustee and including at least one professional. The professional can provide financial accountability, while a close friend or family member can provide sensitivity to the beneficiaries' needs.

- You can write performance guidelines into your trust, allowing beneficiaries to change trustees if they fail to meet some reasonable performance standard.

- Consider naming a "trust protector." A protector, often a trusted family friend, can discharge a trustee under some circumstances or even veto certain trustee decisions.

- You may want specifically to allow a change of trustee should beneficiaries move out of state. A trust with a California trustee, for example, might owe income tax in California even though the beneficiaries now live in a state, such as Texas, without an income tax.

- Wording a trust agreement so that an individual trustee does not have to retain a bond—a kind of insurance policy that protects against embezzlement or misuse of funds—may be penny-wise and pound-foolish.

YOUR CHILDREN AND MONEY

Children and money just seem to go together. While no loving parent ever looks at his or her child in terms of dollar signs, there is no question that having children is an enormous financial responsibility for families at every income level. Juggling the dollars to pay for medical bills, food, clothes, toys, entertainment, transportation, and education is seldom easy. But the job can be much more manageable if you do some planning.

Your Bundle of Joy Will Cost You a Bundle

Add up the diapers, the sneakers, the breakfast cereal, the toys, the nursery school, the piano lessons, the bicycles, the summer camp, the birthday parties, the blue jeans, the haircuts, the use of the family car, the stereo equipment, and the prom clothes. What you will find is no surprise. Children are expensive.

Just how expensive is tough to calculate. Not only is it hard to know whether the kids or the grown-ups ate the Cheerios, but also the amount spent varies according to the income of the family, the order of birth, where the family lives, how many children are in the family, and whether the parents are divorced. Moreover, some parents are extravagant spenders, while others find ways to make do comfortably with far less.

But if you really want some estimate of what your little bundle of joy may end up costing, try these government figures on for size. In families that make more than $55,500 a year, a child born in 1994 will cost his or her parents $198,060 by the age of 18, according to a study by the U.S. Department of Agriculture. That is before taking inflation into account.

Many people will spend more because these numbers are for the second of two children in a family of four. If you are talking about an only child, the costs go up a whopping 26%, since the cost of the crib, the family car, and the bigger house are not spread over more than one child. An only child, according to these government estimates, will cost $249,556. And if you happen to live in the urban West, add another 4.4% onto the total.

Of course, if you have more than two children, you will be spreading the expense and lowering your cost per child. Indeed, those with three or more children will spend roughly 22% less on each child.

These numbers, however, do not give the whole picture. They do not include the cost of prenatal care or childbirth. Nor are the expenses of college tuition, room, and board—which can be $25,000 a year or more—part of that total.

Where does the money go? Housing gets the biggest share—some $71,550 of the $198,060. Food ranks second at $30,960, with it costing almost $2,200 a year to feed a child by the age of 15. Clothing for newborns and toddlers costs $600 a year, but that figure nearly doubles by the time the child reaches 15.

Taking into account the indirect costs, such as the lost career opportunities and the forgone earnings that result from taking time to rear children, researchers have found that costs can actually be more than double these estimates, says Mark Lino, author of the report. "But people continue to have children," he says. "They must be worth it."

Teaching Your Kids about Money

If it seems you spend your whole life telling your kids why they cannot have those $95 sneakers or that new bike, think ahead. Requests for parental handouts are just going to become bigger as the kids grow older and move from bikes to cars to college to home down payments. Parents who are not particularly happy about the way their children look at money need to tackle the problem head on. If their kids do not learn basic money skills, they will have a rude shock when they finally move out on their own. Or worse yet, they will come right back to Mom and Dad, asking for more handouts.

Like brushing teeth, financial responsibility is a habit easiest established when children are young. But it is a long-term project that takes a lot of parental time and patience. It means including kids on financial decisions that involve them and being willing to let them make their own mistakes.

For the most part, schools will take care of the elementary money concepts, such as counting money and making change. Parents who want to tackle the next level, however, will find it is a struggle just to attract their kids' attention. You cannot simply sit down and say, "Let's talk about money." You have to give them a reason to want to listen.

That means an allowance. Having control over their own money is probably the best way for children to learn. Before you set up their weekly allotment, think about what you want them to learn. Important lessons are taught both in the way the allowance arrives and where it goes. Many parents, for example, tie the weekly payday to family chores; others give a basic allowance but provide extra money in exchange for household responsibilities. The idea is to link work and money so that you dispel any notion that money grows on trees.

GIVE YOUR KID A RAISE

How much you pay is an important consideration. You may not accomplish all you hope if you hold the purse strings too tightly. An allowance of a dollar a week, for example, may keep a ten-year-old in candy and comic books. But if you want that youngster to be responsible and start saving for more substantial purchases—maybe a new bike or a portable tape player—you have to raise the stakes. If you want to include even longer-range goals, such as saving for college, you really have to make the weekly stipend meaningful.

Some parents match the allowance to the age of the child, giving one dollar for each year. Others use different formulas. But the idea is to give a big enough allowance so that your child is not always looking for the next handout. How might you set up an allowance for that ten-year-old? In exchange for, say, $10 a week, your child might have certain household duties, such as doing the dinner dishes, cleaning the bathroom, walking the dog, and taking out the garbage.

WHAT KIDS GET

About half of all children surveyed by *Zillions* magazine received a regular allowance. But kids without allowances got about the same amount of total money, thanks to extra cash from parents or payment for chores. Still, those with no allowance were both more likely to run out of money by the end of the week and less likely to have saved.

	Weekly Allowance	Extra Cash	Total
Ages 9–10	$3	$4	$7
Ages 11–12	$5	$8	$13
Ages 13–14	$5	$15	$20

Source: "The *Zillions* Allowance Survey." Copyright 1995 by Consumers Union of U.S., Inc., Yonkers, NY 10703-1057. Reprinted by permission from *Zillions for kids from Consumer Reports* magazine, April/May, 1995.

The weekly allowance might then be divided into several parts. The first could be spent immediately; the second would be earmarked for some much coveted item, such as new skates or a video game. If you want to teach a longer view on savings, have your child put a third of that $10 weekly allowance away for college.

But, you say, $520 a year is a lot for a ten-year-old to manage! You would be right if the amount were handed over in a lump sum. But by dividing the amount into manageable chunks and directing its use, you teach that ten-year-old how to handle money and make financial decisions. And you may find that it really is not costing you more.

If your ten-year-old saved a third of his $10 weekly allowance for college, he would be putting aside $173 a year. This teaches the discipline of long-term saving, but it also helps the child become an active participant in paying for that education. Another $173 would go toward stuff that you might very well end up buying your child anyway—skates, video games, or bike equipment. But by passing along the money as an allowance, you would be helping your child learn how to set goals and budget. You may even find your kids becoming educated consumers, carefully reading product reviews and comparing prices. The final $3.33 a week is totally discretionary. That comes to a couple of packs of gum, a comic book, and a soft drink or two. But once again, you may only be shifting purchases that you already make for your child. It is just that by having the child do the paying, you start to convey the message that a few candy bars can add up.

Some parents may skew the allocation, making less money available for immediate gratification. Some may want the children to allocate part of their weekly allowance for charity; others might levy a family tax on the entire amount and put it toward a family vacation or other family purchase. Still others may establish a "junior 401(k)," in which they match any long-term amount the child saves. The variations are endless. The important thing is to create a system that both you and your children like so that you will stick with it.

EXPERIENCE FOR SMALL INVESTORS

Once a child is saving, it is time to look at investments. Savings accounts are usually the first step, and some banks offer programs for young savers with low minimum initial deposits. Admittedly, the return on passbook accounts is not much. But a bank account makes children feel important, and it gives them a good way to watch their money grow.

Mutual funds are a good next step, providing a way to diversify even a kid-sized portfolio. Mutual funds also generate mail, a seemingly endless supply of statements that you can use to help teach your children how to follow their investments. Some funds actively target the children's market through Uniform Gifts to Minors Act and Uniform Transfers to Minors Act accounts. Stein Roe & Farnham's SteinRoe Young Investor Fund, for example, not only buys stocks that appeal to kids, such as Coca Cola, but also provides kid-friendly literature about the portfolio. Others appeal to kid-sized budgets with low investment minimums. Several funds have only a $250 minimum for a child's account, accepting additional investments of $50 or more. Some funds require even lower initial investments, or waive them entirely, if you set up an automatic investment program: A set amount—as little as $50 in some cases—is taken directly from your child's bank account each month.

Individual stocks do something a mutual fund often cannot. They catch a child's attention. While your 12-year-old may have a hard time relating to a growth-stock fund that owns 25 different stocks, chances are he or she will understand Coca-Cola, Nike, or Walt Disney. When the annual report comes for a company that is of interest, at least part of it may actually be read.

Once your children have a handle on the basics, you must be willing to let them make their own decisions. That may mean mistakes. You may suggest that they sell a stock as the market changes. But if they decide to hold and take a beating, they will have learned a valuable lesson.

Lengthening the time between allowances is another way of shifting more responsibility onto older kids. Moving from a small weekly allowance to a larger monthly allowance by the time the child is in high school teaches budgeting. You may also want to expand the allowance to include such things as clothing. Again, though, you have to be willing to live with the choices your child makes. When your daughter, who needs new shoes, decides that she wants to blow her entire clothing allowance on some high-priced jeans, do not bail her out. You are teaching her that people make choices with their money, and that some choices are better than others.

Meanwhile, do not shy away from open discussion about other financial issues. Kids today are faced with decisions on matters their parents never had to think about. That means they have both more opportunities and more ways of making mistakes.

LEARNING TO BORROW AND REPAY

Credit cards have become ubiquitous. If you do not teach your children about them, they may discover plastic all on their own in high school. Many young people are directly solicited by credit card companies without the knowledge of their parents. They may sign up without really understanding the commitment that they have made. That can lead to big debts at an early age. You can start with an automatic-teller-machine card, giving kids access to some of their own money in a savings account. Then move on to credit cards, explaining their use as loans that must be repaid. To make sure they understand the concept, you can even loan children money for some important purchase and charge them interest.

Taxes can be part of the financial education process, too. By the time they are teenagers, kids can help to prepare their own taxes. If you can sit them down and walk them through the tax form, it will not be such a shock when they have to do their returns themselves. It will also give them some idea of exactly how big a bite taxes can take. Of course, letting them help prepare their tax returns means your children will become well aware of any investments that you have made in their names. That money will be theirs when they turn 18 or 21, depending on the state you live in. If you do not want them to know the details of this nest egg, perhaps you should postpone the lesson on taxes.

Retirement may seem far away, but it is never too young to start saving. Any child who earns money can open an Individual Retirement Account, annually contributing an amount equal to what he or she earns up to a maximum of $2,000. The principle is the same whether you are talking about a 6-year-old child model, a 10-year-old with a paper route, or an 18-year-old working at McDonald's. By tucking the money away and letting it grow tax-deferred for 40 or 50 years, a few thousand dollars can grow into a significant nest egg.

Chances are, however, that your teenager will need some significant incentive to put money into a retirement account that generally cannot be touched without penalty before age 59½. One way is to set up a matching program, so that a child who puts $500 into an IRA will receive an additional $500 for the IRA from you. You may want to fund the IRA even if your child chooses not to contribute at all. Put $2,000 into an IRA for your 18-year-old son and continue funding the account until he turns 24. If the IRA earns a 10% return—the average historical return on stocks—your son will have more than $1 million when he turns 65.

INVESTING FOR A CHILD

Children cannot own investments directly, but they can own them through special custodial accounts. There are two types of custodial accounts—one created under the Uniform Gifts to Minors Act (UGMA) and the other created under the Uniform Transfers to Minors Act (UTMA). The child is the owner under either account, but the custodian manages the assets until the child reaches the age of majority. State law determines both the type of account and the age when the child gains control of the assets.

Here is a listing of the terms in different states.

		TYPE OF ACCOUNT	
STATE	AGE OF MAJORITY	UTMA	UGMA
Alabama	21	•	
Alaska	18*	•	
Arizona	21	•	
Arkansas	21	•	
California	18*	•	
Colorado	21	•	
Connecticut	18		•
Delaware	18*		•
District of Columbia	18	•	
Florida	21	•	
Georgia	21	•	
Hawaii	21	•	
Idaho	21	•	

STATE	AGE OF MAJORITY	TYPE OF ACCOUNT	
		UTMA	UGMA
Illinois	21	•	
Indiana	21	•	
Iowa	21	•	
Kansas	21	•	
Kentucky	18	•	
Louisiana	18	•	
Maine	18*	•	
Maryland	21	•	
Massachusetts	21	•	
Michigan	18		•
Minnesota	21	•	
Mississippi	21		•
Missouri	21	•	
Montana	21	•	
Nebraska	19	•	
Nevada	18	•	
New Hampshire	21	•	
New Jersey	21	•	
New Mexico	21	•	
New York	18		•
North Carolina	21	•	
North Dakota	21	•	
Ohio	21	•	
Oklahoma	18	•	
Oregon	21	•	
Pennsylvania	21	•	
Rhode Island	18	•	
South Carolina	18		•
South Dakota	18	•	
Tennessee	18		•
Texas	18		•
Utah	21	•	
Vermont	18		•
Virginia	21	•	
Washington	21	•	
West Virginia	21	•	
Wisconsin	21	•	
Wyoming	21	•	

*Donor may designate that the custodianship terminate at an age greater than 18 but not more than 21.
SOURCE: Liberty Financial Companies, Inc.

SAVING FOR COLLEGE

You probably did not pay cash for your house. And chances are, you will not be able to pay cash for your kids' college education. With tuition bills at many private colleges running $25,000 a year and more, many families already find there is no way they can come up with the full amount out of savings. If your child will not be ready for college for another 5, 10, or 15 years, you can expect the tab to be considerably higher.

How are you going to swing it? By using a combination of savings, current income, financial aid, and loans. The mix, of course, will vary. The larger your income, the less financial aid you will get. The bigger your savings, the fewer loans you will need. There are typically three parts to any college plan. The first starts early, often when your child is just a newborn. This is when you start putting money away on a regular basis, investing for the long term.

No matter how conscientious you are, however, savings alone will often not be enough. You need to have a borrowing plan to shift costs you cannot cover into the future. You also need to do financial-aid planning. Indeed, knowing the rules of financial aid can affect even your earliest planning choices.

KEEPING INVESTMENTS IN YOUR NAME

Take, for example, the decision of whose name to use—yours or your child's—when opening that college savings account. You can earn a tax break by putting the money in your child's name, but the strategy could end up costing you. That is because schools, in determining the family contribution to school costs, assess children's assets at 35% but assess a maximum of only 5.65% of the parents'. A $50,000 college savings fund in the child's name would be assessed $17,500 for the first year of college, but the same fund in the parents' name would be assessed at a maximum of only $2,825. The $14,675 difference would more than cover any tax savings the family might have received from being taxed at a lower rate over the years.

So where should you put all that college money? If you are looking to optimize your chances for financial aid, keep it in your name

COLLEGE SAVINGS CALCULATOR

Saving for college is easiest if you start early. This table will help you decide how much you need to save each month, depending on how long it is before your child enters college. Do not panic if the amount seems impossible. Most families finance college with some combination of savings, current income, financial aid, and loans. The point is to save at least something—and to begin saving as soon as possible.

| Years until Student Begins College | FOUR-YEAR COST | | MONTHLY SAVINGS | |
	Public	Private	Public	Private
1	$48,377	$102,965	$3,860	$8,216
2	51,280	109,143	1,964	4,181
3	54,356	115,691	1,332	2,835
4	57,618	122,633	1,016	2,162
5	61,075	129,991	826	1,757
6	64,739	137,790	699	1,487
7	68,624	146,058	608	1,294
8	72,741	154,821	540	1,149
9	77,106	164,111	487	1,036
10	81,732	173,957	444	945
11	86,636	184,395	409	870
12	91,834	195,458	379	807
13	97,344	207,186	354	754
14	103,185	219,617	333	708
15	109,376	232,794	314	668
16	115,938	246,762	297	633
17	122,895	261,567	283	602
18	130,268	277,261	270	574
19	138,084	293,897	258	548
20	146,369	311,531	247	525

NOTE: Four-year costs are based on College Board survey data for the 1995–96 year and include tuition, room and board, transportation, books, and other expenses, and assume in-state residency for public schools. Numbers are calculated from a 1997 base year, so that a child entering college in one year would enroll in the fall of 1998. The table assumes 6% annual increases in college costs and an 8% annual return on investments. The table also assumes that there are no additional investments or earnings once the child starts school, and that investments are made at the beginning of each year.

SOURCE: T. Rowe Price Associates, Inc.

in a separate account earmarked for college. This not only helps with financial aid but also keeps the money out of your children's hands when they turn 18 or 21. Invest it for long-term growth. With anything longer than a five- or ten-year time horizon, that means some sort of stock market investments. Add to it at regular intervals, perhaps using an automatic-investment program. Then, starting five years before the first tuition bill arrives, gradually shift it into safer investments, such as short-term U.S. Treasurys. That way you will be sure the money is there when you need it. (You can find many good ideas about investing for the long haul in Chapter 2.)

You may feel such planning is a waste of time because your child will never qualify for financial aid, but do not be so sure. College financial-aid officers say it can be a big mistake for anyone to assume they will not qualify. At Harvard University, people with incomes above $100,000 have received aid, though the average family income of aid recipients is $60,000. There is also nothing to lose by trying for aid if admissions decisions are need-blind, as they are at Harvard.

Financial-aid officers chafe at the concept of financial-aid planning, complaining that it is unethical to manipulate a system designed to help those in need. Nonetheless, they admit that understanding the rules makes a big difference in whether you receive aid. Aid decisions for the first year of college, for example, are based on financial data from the year starting January 1 of your child's junior year of high school. The higher your income that year, the less aid you will qualify for. Thus, it makes sense to try to keep that amount as small as possible. If you plan to sell a big chunk of appreciated stock, sell it before the year starts so that the capital gains will not be counted in your aid application. If you earn a big yearly bonus, see if you can get it before the critical calendar year starts.

TIME FOR A CLOSE LOOK AT AID

The year your child is in the tenth grade is probably the time to take a closer look at financial aid. Financial-aid planning books available at many bookstores contain worksheets that will help you see if you will qualify. Even if you find that you have little chance, going through the worksheets is worthwhile because you can then do your planning knowing financial aid is unlikely. If you end up being ineligible for financial aid, for example, you may still be able to take advantage of your child's lower tax bracket. You can transfer appreciated assets, such as stock, to your child and let the child sell it. Taxes will still be calculated using your basis price, but any capital gains will be taxed at the child's much lower rate rather than yours.

Combine financial-aid planning with some good solid consumerism when looking at colleges. Look not only at the sticker price of the schools your child is considering but also their financial-aid track records. You should not necessarily rule out expensive schools, but it is a good idea to have a backup school that you can afford even if your child receives no financial aid.

If you are offered aid, but it is not all you hoped for, remember that it is not set in stone. Some schools even invite negotiation, saying they want to be competitive with other schools. Others, such as Harvard, shun the concept of negotiation but will reconsider their offers if presented with information not fully taken into account.

Loans are the final part of any college plan. Many people can tap the equity built up in their homes. Not only do home-equity loans carry relatively low interest rates, but interest costs can often be written off on your income taxes. You could also take a look at the borrowing terms of your employer's retirement-savings plan or consider a loan from an old cash-value life insurance policy that may allow you to borrow at interest rates as low as 3% or 4%.

STUDENT-LOAN OPTIONS

Before parents start borrowing, they should investigate student-loan options. For one thing, having the children do some of the borrowing gives them a stake in their own education. Moreover, student-loan terms can be extremely attractive, particularly if the child qualifies for financial aid.

Students with significant financial need may receive a 5% Perkins loan, which allows them to borrow up to $3,000 a year. Subsidized Stafford loans, on which the government pays the interest while the student is in school, are also awarded on the basis of need. Repayment begins six months after the student graduates or leaves school.

Even students with no proven financial need can borrow under the Stafford program. But they are responsible for loan interest during their school years. They can either pay off that interest while in school or add it to the total amount borrowed. Loan size under the Stafford program, however, is limited, with students able to borrow from $2,625 for the first year to as much as $5,500 beginning in the third undergraduate year. (For more information about loans for education, see Chapter 6.)

Finally, parents should remember to figure in the portion that comes from the students' own earnings. Financial-aid packages, in fact, typically include an expected student contribution. That is the money that a student has to earn during the college years to help pay tuition costs. At Harvard, for example, a student is expected to earn $1,900 during the summer and an additional $5,700 during the year. These jobs typically are on the college campus—such as doing research for a professor—and often can add an important dimension to the child's education.

YOUR PARENTS AND MONEY

Parents are the flip side of the family money equation. They taught you, paid your way, and gave you a helping hand. Their finances, however, have always been off-limits.

But at some point, you have to start taking an interest in their financial well-being. You need to make sure they have taken the steps that can ease the way when and if illness and disability strike. You need to understand what resources they have to provide for their own care. And you need to know how to intervene if you one day get an emergency call for help.

Mom and Dad, We Have to Talk

It is not that you really want to talk about it. It is certainly not something your parents want to discuss. But if you fail to address the "what ifs" of illness, disability, and death with your parents, you may have a rude awakening. You could find yourself scavenging for wills, insurance policies, and bank statements after they die. Or worse, you could find yourself without the basic tools to protect your parents' interests and carry out their wishes if they become seriously ill or incompetent.

Make no mistake about it: This can be an emotional minefield. It is important that you put yourself in your parents' shoes. You need a realistic understanding of what it costs your parents to live. Then factor in the fears and concerns—well founded or not—that influence your parents' money management.

One real fear some parents have is that their children want the money for themselves. Because most seniors worry about outliving their money, any attempt to change their money management may be greeted with suspicion. So do not start by trying to fiddle with their finances. Focus on the basic paperwork, which is often the best starting place.

THE ESSENTIAL DOCUMENTS

There are five basic documents that children and their aging parents need to address: a will, a durable power of attorney, a living will, a health care power of attorney, and a personal financial inventory. (These are the same documents you should not be without that are discussed in Chapter 1; you may want to refer to that chapter for more details.)

A durable power of attorney is a critical but often overlooked document. Drafted with the help of a good lawyer, this document would allow a child to do such things as sign tax returns, transfer assets into a trust, and make financial decisions for a parent who becomes incompetent. If worded properly, it could even allow a child to establish trusts and make gifts for a parent. Many parents do not want to give such power too soon for fear the kids will abuse it. One solution is to execute the durable power of attorney but leave it with a lawyer to be delivered when needed.

A durable power of attorney does not replace a will. For one thing, its power lapses upon death. In the absence of a will, or the appropriate trusts, the state will impose its own formula on distribution of the estate. In a second marriage, for instance, that means that the new spouse could receive some of the share intended for the children.

Your parents also ought to have a health care power of attorney delegating the right to make health care decisions for them if they are unable to make those decisions themselves. This should be coupled with a living will, outlining what type of measures they would find acceptable to prolong life.

The fifth document, the personal financial inventory, is a list of assets and where they can be found. That list should include not only bank accounts and stock certificates but also pension plans, insurance policies, and Individual Retirement Accounts. Do not forget things like money due, such as a loan made to a sister but never openly discussed. Even the mortgage coupon book should be on the list. (Just follow the sample Personal Financial Inventory in Appendix B.)

CONSIDER THE ALTERNATIVE

Parents may not like opening the books to their children. But consider the alternative of trying to reconstruct an estate with no guidelines. Attorneys tell stories of children finding stock certificates in the attic years after their parents' deaths, eying one another suspiciously over missing jewelry, or trying to reconstruct assets from parents' tax returns.

When making the list, parents should record the date of purchase and the purchase price of investments. This provides a basis price for tax purposes in case assets have to be sold as the parents grow older. Also remember that certain assets, such as brokerage accounts, may require their own powers of attorney, since some financial institutions do not honor a durable power of attorney.

While taking care of the paperwork, children may want to tackle funeral arrangements. This may be harder for the children to deal with than the parents, but it is important to find out if the parents have already bought burial plots or made arrangements with a specific funeral home. An informal discussion of the type of funeral they might like goes a long way to easing the burden when such decisions must actually be made.

Once the basics have been tackled, it may be easier for both children and parents to talk about financial planning. If investment changes are called for, children must be careful not to trample their parents' security in a search for higher returns. Money socked away in certificates of deposit, for example, may seem a less-than-optimum investment, but that does not mean the child should push to put that money into a riskier, higher-yielding investment. Indeed, advisers say that it often helps to bring in a third party if big changes are needed. Use of an impartial outsider tends to make it easier for the parent to accept the advice, since it can no longer be considered either judgmental or self-serving on the part of the child.

GETTING HELP IN A CRISIS

It is the phone call everyone dreads. An elderly parent, perhaps retired and living thousands of miles away, is seriously ill and needs your help. The details—not just medical but also financial and legal—can be overwhelming. But it is something more and more people are going to face. The population aged 75 and older—those most likely to need care—is expected to grow by 25% in the next decade to about 17 million individuals.

Years ago, adult children often took elderly parents into their homes, but that is not always possible these days. Children can live far away, so that taking in an elderly parent would mean moving them from familiar surroundings. Moreover, many women, who used to be the caregivers, are now in the workplace and unavailable to provide care for aging parents or in-laws.

Those problems are compounded by the fact that most people give little thought to the problem. Professionals who work with the elderly say that few of them make plans for how they will deal with a serious illness or disability. Their adult children may worry about the possibility, but they often are reluctant to bring it up.

Planning ahead helps, but there are places to turn even if you have not planned. County and local government, support groups, educational associations, and health care professionals are among those who can provide assistance, even for those whose parents are miles away. Although some things can be quite expensive—full-time care at home can easily come to $10,000 or more for just a few months, for instance—other services are available at little or no cost. Some things may be covered by insurance or government programs, such as Medicare.

The first step, professionals say, is to find out what is available in your parents' community. That does not always mean a nursing home. Home care, adult day care, or just housekeeping services and home delivery of meals may be all that is needed. If Mom or Dad is in the hospital, a social worker or discharge planner can help identify resources. If you are going it alone, local senior centers may have information. Other places to look include county or local departments for the aging. Local chapters of such organizations as the Alzheimer's Association often can provide referrals.

The information from these sources is usually free. The cost of services depends on what is needed, geographic location, and whether the patient is eligible for government assistance or has private insurance. For instance, adult day care—which may include social activities, supervised programs for Alzheimer's patients, meals, and even bathing—can range from just a few dollars a day for subsidized programs to $12 an hour for privately run facilities. It may be covered by private long-term-care insurance or by Medicaid, the joint state and federal program that provides health care for the poor.

Many senior centers offer hot meals at minimal cost. Such programs as Meals on Wheels, typically funded by local government and private contributions, deliver hot meals to the homebound elderly. There also are residential facilities where the elderly live independently but have access to meals and medical care when needed.

If you cannot be there to supervise your parents' care or make all the necessary arrangements, there is someone else who will do it for you for a fee. Private geriatric-care managers, who are often social workers or nurses, can do everything from arranging for home repairs or hot meals to hiring someone to care for Mom or Dad at home. They can help you find a nursing home. They may even provide counseling for patients and family members. Not inexpensive, these professionals usually charge $350 to $400 for an initial assessment. This includes a visit with the patient as well as an assessment of the patient's physical environment and medical and emotional needs. Additional services typically range from $20 to $150 an hour, depending on what type of service is needed.

In many cases, the biggest expense is daily care, be it at a nursing home or care at home. Nursing homes average $30,000 a year nationwide but can cost twice that or more in many urban areas. Full-time home care can be just as expensive. Medicare, the federally funded health care program for the elderly, and most supplemental insurance generally cover skilled nursing care or therapy after a hospital stay or an acute illness. Sometimes care has to be ordered by a doctor in order to be covered, so check with your parent's doctor.

Long-term custodial or personal care for patients with chronic conditions, such as Alzheimer's disease, usually is not covered by Medicare. It may be covered by private insurance or by Medicaid for those meeting income and asset limitations. Most people pay for it themselves.

You may need to get legal advice, either to qualify your parent for Medicaid, to review a will, or to be sure that ailing parents are cared for according to their wishes. If your aging parent has not yet signed both a power of attorney and a health care power of attorney, it is important that they to do so while they are still mentally competent.

WHERE TO TURN FOR HELP

You do not have to do it all. Here is a partial list of resources that can make it easier for you to help with the problems faced by aging parents.

- **County and Local Departments for the Aging**
  These government agencies can provide referrals for everything from meal service to nursing homes. Consult your local telephone directory for phone numbers and addresses.

- **National Association of Area Agencies on Aging**
  A Washington, D.C., group whose Eldercare Locator directs callers to appropriate state and local agencies or service providers (800-677-1116).

- **National Association of Professional Geriatric Care Managers**
  A Tucson, Ariz., organization that provides names of private-care managers in all parts of the country (520-881-8008).

- **National Academy of Elder Law Attorneys**
  A lawyers' association based in Tucson, Ariz., that provides guidelines for finding an attorney to help with estate planning, Medicaid issues, and other legal matters. A registry of attorneys in various states is available for $25 (520-881-4005).

- **Children of Aging Parents**
  A Levittown, Pa., organization that acts as a clearinghouse for information about caring for the elderly and provides contacts for support groups for adult children (800-227-7294).

In Death As in Life

If you think financial ties to parents end at death, think again. Chances are good you will be named executor when one or both of your parents die. Be forewarned: You probably will not thank them.

Executors have four basic responsibilities: locating and valuing assets, paying creditors, settling taxes, and finally distributing assets. Even in simple estates, that can mean a full year of wrestling with paperwork, tracking down assets, and filing papers. If estates become more complicated, executors may have to deal with six or more different sets of tax forms, make a variety of investment decisions, or even mediate disputes between heirs. If someone contests the will, the headaches increase exponentially.

Executors tackle these tasks saddled with two extra burdens. The first is the desire to live up to the trust of the deceased. The second is more concrete: the knowledge that if you mess up, you personally can be liable for everything from poor investments to underpaid taxes. That may not be a worry in estates where the executor is also the sole heir. But in estates with feuding heirs, such liability can become an overriding concern.

TIMETABLE FOR SETTLING AN ESTATE

The rules of estate settlement vary from state to state. Some states require lengthy probate proceedings, while others have procedures that are relatively quick and painless. Allowing for such variation, this list shows in general what an executor must do to settle an estate.

UPON DEATH

- Order death certificates.
- Find wills and other legal papers and send them to the attorney handling the estate.
- Compile a list of all heirs or others named in the will.
- Gather all financial records, making preliminary listings of the decedent's assets and liabilities.
- Safeguard all assets. Check on sufficiency of fire, liability, and casualty insurance. Cancel credit cards.
- Apply for Social Security death benefits and/or veterans benefits.
- File life insurance claims.

- Make sure bills, such as mortgage and insurance premiums, continue to be paid.
- Check on pension or other retirement-plan provisions.

INITIATE PROBATE

- Gather and file necessary documents in probate courts.
- Check on notification and publication requirements in your state.

ONCE EXECUTOR OR ADMINISTRATOR IS APPOINTED

- Apply for a tax identification number for the estate.
- Open a bank account and a custodian account for securities for the estate.
- Collect life insurance proceeds.
- Prepare an inventory of property, have assets valued, and file with the probate court if necessary.
- Distribute tangible property, such as furniture, if appropriate.
- Check on all tax-filing deadlines.

SIX MONTHS FOLLOWING DEATH

- Complete identification of all estate assets and liabilities.
- Pay remaining debts if the estate is solvent.

BY APRIL 15 OF THE YEAR FOLLOWING DEATH

- Prepare and file the decedent's federal and state income tax returns.

WITHIN NINE MONTHS OF DEATH

- Get appraisals on property, such as real estate, jewelry, or antiques.
- Determine cash needs of the estate and determine which assets must be sold to raise cash.
- Decide whether to claim executor's fee.
- Prepare and file estate taxes or file for an extension.

WITHIN ONE YEAR OF DEATH

- Consider partial distributions, including payment of any specific bequests.

TERMINATION OF ESTATE

- Distribute balance of estate, retaining a reserve sufficient for final income taxes and other fees.
- Prepare and file any final estate income tax returns.
- File the final probate account, if required under state law.
- Notify beneficiaries of tax basis of all property.
- Notify the IRS of termination of the estate.

The executor is formally appointed when the will is filed in probate court and approved. Then, armed with notarized death certificates and proper court authorization, the executor can open an estate bank account and gain access to investments and other assets. But wills are sometimes lost, or they are not properly executed, or they name people you cannot find, or they refer to assets that are not there. Having an experienced attorney makes it easier to navigate the testamentary waters.

WHAT IS INVOLVED

Among other things, the executor generally must give notice to everyone named in the will and everyone who would have inherited from the deceased if there had been no will. Lists of assets and their value also need to be compiled. Sometimes, artwork or jewelry must be appraised. For tax purposes, the value of these assets is set either at the time of death or six months later. But which date you choose is not arbitrary. You can take the later date only if it actually lowers estate taxes. You also cannot value part of the estate on one date and the rest on the other.

Though strictly bound by the terms of the will, executors still have many decisions to make. If they need money to pay taxes, they may have to decide whether to sell, say, the vacation home at the lake or a big chunk of the stock portfolio. They also have to decide when to distribute assets. And until they do distribute the assets, they must decide where to park any cash, making sure it is available when needed. Treasury bills are a usual place, offering executors a way to match maturity to tax payments and distributions. Just keeping the money flow straight can be difficult, particularly if in addition to estate funds, there are assets held in trust.

Perhaps the toughest part of being an executor comes with the distribution of assets. The executor can begin distributions well before the estate is settled, and the family often pressures the executor to do just that. But if there is not enough money left in the estate to pay all bills and taxes, that money may end up coming out of the executor's pocket.

One way to reduce any tension between the executor and the beneficiaries is simply to keep the beneficiaries up to date on what is happening. Even so, there can be contention, and one likely arena is distribution of personal possessions, such as furniture and jewelry. This process can be emotionally charged, particularly if the will is vague and there are children from two different marriages or animosity between siblings.

TAXES, TAXES, AND MORE TAXES

Taxes demand a lot of attention, particularly in a large estate. An executor may face six or more sets of tax returns. First there are the income taxes. Not only do federal, state, and sometimes city income taxes have to be paid for the last year that the deceased was alive but also for income earned by the estate. If the deceased had any trusts, tax filings will be required on that income, too.

In addition, federal estate taxes are due nine months after death on estates of more than $600,000. Then there are state estate or inheritance taxes. If the deceased owned property in another state, there will be another state tax return to file and probate proceedings in the other state, as well. All that means many people may want to add an accountant to the list of professionals they hire to help settle the estate.

For their efforts, executors may receive nothing more than a hearty handshake. They are entitled to a fee, typically ranging from 1% to 5% of the estate's value. But this fee—which often is set by the state—is taxable income. Thus, whether an executor charges a fee is often a tax issue. If the executor's personal income tax rates are lower than the estate's, then it probably makes sense to take the fee, particularly if there are no other heirs who might resent your getting this extra compensation. When the estate is under $600,000, the executor is probably better off to forgo the fee and simply inherit the money.

OTHER FAMILY MONEY MATTERS

Sometimes there are family strategies that seem to help everyone. Say you have a large sum of money in certificates of deposit coming due soon. Your kids are buying a house and need a mortgage. With a little creative thinking and a good lawyer, these two seemingly un-related circumstances can be turned into a family loan.

By lending directly to your children, you eliminate the middle-man. That means the kids can get a mortgage without paying points and application fees. The loan will take less time to process, and the interest rate can be below the rate commonly available from banks on 30-year, fixed-rate mortgages. At the same time, you can boost your own return considerably, because the rate you charge the kids is more than you could have earned by rolling over the CDs.

This kind of family finance is not for everyone. Some children are not a good credit risk, no matter how much you love them. Some parents would find it difficult to collect. Still, if both parties take the agreement seriously, family loans can be very advantageous. Indeed, the loan agreement can be crafted to reflect a variety of family needs.

If the kids, for example, wish to supplement their parents' income, they might pay a higher interest rate. Parents who want to help subsidize the children might charge a somewhat lower rate. Family loans can be arranged to finance everything from cars to college. In some cases, kids even loan money to their parents, helping the parents make ends meet without denting their pride.

PLAYING BY THE RULES

No matter how the loan is structured, it is important to observe the formalities. If you are making a mortgage loan, for example, the debt must be secured by your child's residence and the mortgage filed with local authorities in order for the child to deduct the mortgage interest on his or her income taxes. Without the necessary paperwork, you could also find other creditors—such as the holder of your child's home-equity loan—ahead of you in case of a default. The parent's name should appear on the title insurance policy, just as it would with a bank mortgage.

The interest rate you charge is not entirely up to you either. Each month, the federal government sets minimum rates—called the "applicable federal rates"—that must be charged on long-term, mid-term, and short-term intrafamily loans. If you charge less, the Internal Revenue Service can tax you on the interest you should have collected. That means if you gave your kids a 3% mortgage in August 1995, for example, the IRS could say you should have charged at least 6.56%—the rate at that time—and tax you on the interest you should have received. This is called "imputed interest."

The imputed interest rules have two exceptions. They do not apply on loans of up to $10,000 used to purchase non-income-producing property. Thus, you could give your son an interest-free $9,000 loan to buy a car without worrying about imputed interest. The second exception covers loans of up to $100,000 if the borrower's net investment income is under $1,000. You could loan your daughter $100,000 for medical school at below-market rates and not be liable for the imputed interest if the daughter's own investments produced less than $1,000. Even if her investment income exceeded that limit, the imputed interest on which you would have to pay income tax would be limited to the amount of her investment income.

Intrafamily loans can also run afoul of gift-tax rules, creating a potential double whammy for those who do not follow them. Interest that should have been charged on a below-market loan is viewed as a gift that could be taxed. As a practical matter, no gift tax is generally owed. That is because even a $100,000 loan will produce annual interest payments of under $10,000, the amount that one person can give another each year free of gift tax. In any case, do not forget to put the loan in writing, or the IRS may decide that the entire loan, not just the forgone interest, is a gift and subject to tax.

6

THE SMART WAYS TO DEAL WITH DEBT

$

"Neither a borrower nor a lender be," William Shakespeare wrote in *Hamlet* nearly 400 years ago. But in the late 20th century, life is not so simple. These days, the question usually is not whether to borrow, but how much and for what, under what terms—and how to pay it all back. Many people borrow substantial amounts, for a home, a car, a child's education, and even for such things as clothing and furniture.

Lenders want the business. Mailboxes are filled with credit card solicitations, and newspaper advertisements trumpet the rates on car loans, home-equity loans, and mortgages. All told, in early 1996 Americans owed more than $5 trillion, including more than $3 trillion in home mortgages.

Only you can decide how much debt you can manage. Although many mortgage companies and other lenders have guidelines to help them evaluate applications, such as the percentage of monthly income that can go to service debt, they tend to be overly simplistic. Just because someone is willing to lend you $100,000 does not mean you should sign on the dotted line.

Cash flow is more important than income in making monthly payments. When other expenses are high, spending even 10% of after-tax income to repay debt can be too much. Some people may be able to handle payments equal to 50%. Be honest with yourself about how much cash you have coming in every month, how much goes out, and how that may change in the months and years to come.

THE GOOD AND THE BAD

Debt generally can be divided into two categories. You might think of what you owe as necessary debt and unnecessary debt, or as investment debt and consumption debt. For some people, the issue could be whether or not interest is deductible from their income taxes, or whether the debt is used for an asset that will appreciate in value or one that will depreciate. But whatever the terminology, the bottom line is that there is good debt and there is bad debt.

Running up a lot of credit card debt, for instance, should be on everybody's list of no-nos. Interest rates may rise and fall over the years, but the average on credit cards usually remains close to 18%. That is often more than twice the going rate on other types of loans, and there is no tax deduction. Easy access to credit can also make it easy to overspend.

Borrowing to purchase a home is usually okay. You have to live somewhere, and even though the real estate market does fall into the doldrums from time to time, it is reasonable to expect the value of a home to appreciate over the years. College is a huge expense, and although you know you should have been saving since before your first child was born, the fact is that many people have to go into debt. At least a college diploma is an asset that usually generates income.

Beyond that, however, it can be hard to decide what falls into which category. Should you borrow to invest in the stock market, for example, or is that a bad idea? How about paying cash for that new car instead of borrowing the money? If you decide to finance, you could use tax-deductible home-equity debt or a low-rate auto loan. There is a place for credit cards, when properly managed.

THE GROWTH OF PERSONAL DEBT

The amount owed by American households, including home mortgages, doubled in the past decade. (In billions of dollars.)

Year*	Total Household Debt	Credit Cards
1986	$2,602.37	$135.83
1987	$2,858.95	$153.06
1988	$3,174.14	$174.27
1989	$3,496.10	$199.16
1990	$3,738.47	$223.52
1991	$3,919.53	$245.28
1992	$4,175.30	$258.08
1993	$4,452.60	$286.59
1994	$4,817.70	$334.50
1995	$5,151.69	$394.80

*Figures are year-end totals.
Source: DRI/McGraw-Hill.

How does an individual know what to do? The after-tax cost of the debt—determined by the interest rate, whether interest charges are tax-deductible, and the term of the loan—is a major factor, but it is not the only one. There are other things to consider that may vary with the type of debt. Different kinds of loans are discussed in detail later in this chapter, as are some special considerations for people in various age groups. But it is important to begin with a few basics:

• **Home mortgages.** Many people know something about mortgages, since it is unusual to be able to pay cash for a house. You probably know, for instance, that the interest is tax-deductible—and for most people it does not matter that this is true only on the first $1 million of mortgage debt. You may also know that there are 15-year, 20-year, and 30-year loans, some with interest rates that are fixed for the life of the loan, others with rates that change periodically. But how do you know which one is right for you? Top issues among those to consider are how long you plan to remain in your home and your tolerance for risk. Adjustable-rate loans typically have lower initial interest rates than fixed-rate loans, but payments could increase substantially if inflation heats up. Shorter-term loans have larger monthly payments, but they result in significant interest savings over time.

• **Home-equity debt.** Home-equity loans and lines of credit offer the attraction that interest payments are generally tax-deductible on borrowings up to $100,000. (This is in addition to the interest write-off you get on mortgage loans of up to $1 million.) Because they are secured by your home, rates are often lower than on many other loans. Home-equity loans usually are not hard to obtain if you have more than a 25% equity stake in your home, and you can use them for just about anything. But remember that these loans are secured by your home. If you cannot make the payments, you could find yourself homeless.

• **Credit cards.** Paying with plastic can be a big convenience, as long as you can pay the bill when it comes. Problems start when balances start to mount and interest charges accrue. Still, most people do carry a balance at some point, so it is important to know the terms of the cards you have. Some financial institutions offer rates well below the national average. There also are differences in fees and grace periods, or the time before interest starts accruing. People who usually carry balances on their cards should look for the lowest rate; those who regularly pay their balances in full should go for a card with no annual fee.

• **Car loans.** Buying a car these days can be confusing. Not only do you have to decide what kind of car you want and how much you can afford, but you must decide whether to take the dealer's financing or go to the bank, or whether to use tax-deductible home-equity debt or pull the money out of savings or investments and pay cash. Or, like more and more people these days, you might consider leasing. You probably want to steer clear of the six-year and seven-year car loans some lenders offer. Although the monthly payments would be lower than with shorter-term loans, your payment book might well outlive the car.

• **Investment debt.** Borrowing against the value of stocks and bonds, or buying securities "on margin," is among the more controversial forms of debt. Because of the risks involved, it is usually recommended only for sophisticated investors. Generally, an investor can borrow up to 50% of the value of stocks owned or up to 90% of the value of bonds, depending on the type of bond and its maturity. As with other collateralized loans, rates may be lower than on unsecured debt, but problems can arise when the market value of the securities falls below the level required to maintain sufficient collateral. The resulting "margin call" could require repayment of a significant portion of the loan within days or even hours.

• **College loans.** After a mortgage, loans to finance a college education are the second-largest debt many people have. Few families can afford the cost of college without some sort of loan. You can borrow directly from the federal government, from a bank, or from one of the private organizations that lend money for college or graduate school. Some loans are guaranteed by the federal government or by state agencies. Interest rates typically are lower than on other kinds of unsecured debt. Many student loans do not have to be repaid until after graduation. Parents generally have to begin repayment within a few months after the funds are disbursed.

MANAGING DEBT THROUGH THE AGES

Too many people tend to think about personal finance almost exclusively in terms of assets: How can they earn more on their savings or increase their investment returns? In doing so, they overlook the simple fact that there are two sides to everyone's personal balance sheet. Giving more attention to the liabilities, perhaps by using some savings to pay down a large credit card balance or by refinancing a home mortgage, can have an immediate, positive impact.

As with other aspects of personal finance, managing debt tends to involve different considerations at different stages of life. For a young, single person who is moving to a new city and starting that first real job, for instance, trying to juggle credit card bills and car payments while keeping up with college loans and the rent can be a real chore. As the years pass, and income and assets grow, home mortgages, home-equity loans, and margin accounts become the looming personal-debt issues. The following sections look at some of the more important considerations for people in various age groups.

Your 20s and 30s

It is easy to overuse credit when you are just starting out. There is that first apartment to furnish, clothes for your new job, and the temptation to treat yourself well now that you are finally earning some money. But you are also establishing a credit history, which means that it is important to pay your bills on time. Future lenders, when you are applying for a mortgage, a car loan, or other credit, will look at your record. If you learn to use credit wisely right from the start, you will avoid getting in over your head.

Limit yourself to just one bank credit card at first. Bank cards are accepted almost everywhere these days, including most department stores, and having fewer cards will make it easier to keep track of your spending. Many recent graduates have college loans to repay and may have to borrow to buy a car, which increases their monthly obligations.

Try to charge only what you can pay for every month. If you do carry a balance, pay as much as you can every month. Just making the minimum payment on a half dozen different credit cards can leave you paying double-digit interest rates for years. Some financial advisers say you should never let the balance outstanding exceed four weeks net pay. Pay off your college loans as quickly as possible, too. That will help you build a good credit record, and once those loans are out of the way, you will have more cash for things you might otherwise put on a credit card. Do not take on any new debt unless absolutely necessary.

Credit reporting agencies keep data on loans outstanding, credit cards you have, how much credit is available to you, and your payment history. The information is available to lenders, retail merchants, and other credit issuers. Borrowers with a good repayment history and not a lot of outstanding debt are more likely to receive a loan. This becomes especially important when you apply for a mortgage to buy your first home. Delinquencies, usually defined as payments that are more than 30 days late, remain on your record for seven years, bankruptcies for ten years. While one late payment on your Visa card probably will not ruin your chances of getting a mortgage, lenders do not like patterns of lateness.

You can obtain a copy of your credit report by contacting the three major agencies: Equifax, Experian, and Trans Union. It is usually a good idea to review these reports every couple of years and especially before you apply for a mortgage or a big loan, to make sure there are no inaccuracies.

When going for that first mortgage, finance no more than 80% of the purchase price if at all possible. The interest rate is likely to be a little lower, and you probably will not have to pay extra for mortgage insurance, which is insurance many homeowners are required to pay until the equity in their homes reaches about 20% of the amount of loan outstanding.

Young people on limited budgets generally will prefer a 30-year loan, because the payments are lower than on shorter-term loans. Family members may be willing to help out with a loan for the down payment, or for other purposes. If you do borrow from Mom and

20s–30s

- Stick to one or two credit cards.

- Pay bills promptly.

- Try for 20% down when buying a home.

- Consider a 30-year mortgage.

- Document terms of family loans.

Dad or other relatives, treat it as a business transaction. There should be a note, specifying an interest rate, and a repayment schedule. You may want to consult a lawyer to draw up the necessary documents. Interest should be at or near market rates to avoid tax consequences for the lender.

YOUR 40S AND 50S

These usually are your peak earning years. Ideally, that would make this a good time to start reducing your debt burden in preparation for retirement. But that probably will not be easy, because this is also the time when people trade up to a bigger and better house, purchase that bigger and better car, and send their kids off to college. Many middle-aged middle managers, laid off by big corporations, have to borrow to start or expand a business.

The middle years do offer opportunities for creative financing. People usually have more assets, including significant equity in a home, and lenders may be more liberal with borrowers who have established credit histories. Their higher income makes it easier to service the debt. One strategy worth thinking about is setting up an emergency home-equity line. You can do this at little or no cost at many banks, and there is no finance charge unless you actually draw on the money. Home-equity debt can be used for just about any purpose, and the interest you pay is generally tax-deductible.

Borrowing against a life insurance policy can also provide easy access to money at comparatively low rates, but remember why you purchased life insurance in the first place. If you do not pay back the loan quickly, you are diminishing the value of the policy for your survivors.

Loans from 401(k) or profit-sharing plans usually have a maximum term of five years and a fixed repayment schedule through payroll deduction. Rates typically are lower than on many other forms of debt. There is no tax deduction, but you are paying interest to yourself. The downside is that the amount you can borrow is limited, and if you are fired or quit your job, you may have to repay the loan quickly or face a tax penalty. And although you are paying yourself interest, your retirement funds might grow at a faster rate if fully invested. But if you really do need the money, borrowing is far superior to making a hardship withdrawal. (Refer to Chapter 4 for more information about tapping retirement-plan assets.)

If you want to borrow to start a new business, or you are considering taking out a loan so you can invest in someone else's business, think carefully before borrowing against the equity in your home. Many new businesses fail in a relatively short time, but you would still have to make payments on the loan or you could find yourself without a place to live.

Unless you are an especially sophisticated investor, it is also a good idea to avoid borrowing against the value of your stocks and bonds, or buying securities on margin. Problems can develop quickly if the market takes a sudden plunge; you might have to meet a margin call within days, even hours, or lose your investment.

Keep in mind that, in some significant ways, having a lot of debt is riskier now than when you were in your 20s. The potential for serious illness is greater, and middle-aged people who are laid off in corporate cutbacks and restructurings often have a hard time finding another job. Aging parents also may need financial assistance.

Do not let easy access to credit tempt you to take on more debt than you can handle. Buy cars with cash, if possible, and use your added income to pay off the debt you already have, starting with the most expensive. Credit card and other consumer debt, for instance, generally has the highest interest rates and is not tax-deductible. Then pay off home-equity lines of credit and try to pay down your mortgage, so you will not have to worry about making payments when you are retired. One way to cut your mortgage costs, if you do not want to refinance into a 15-year loan, is to make additional payments on an existing mortgage. Paying an extra $100 a month, or making one additional payment a year, can reduce the term of most mortgages by several years.

Your 60s and Beyond

In the best of all possible worlds, you would be debt-free as you enter retirement, but few people live in the best of all possible worlds. It is not unusual for people in their 60s and 70s to have mortgage pay-

40s–50s

- Pay off credit cards.
- Refinance mortgage.
- Buy car with cash.
- Set up emergency credit line.
- Avoid margin debt.

ments to make and car loans to repay. Some have business loans outstanding or may need to borrow to start a new business. A few, who waited until their 40s to start a family or who remarried in middle age and had a second family, are taking on debt to pay for a child's college education.

Some older people may borrow just for liquidity while assets in their retirement plans continue to grow tax-deferred; after all, individuals now in their 60s and 70s could live another 20 years. They may want to help their children or grandchildren financially, or take that dream-of-a-lifetime vacation while they still can.

Some things do not change when you are older, however. You still have to consider your cash flow and the cost of the debt. But there are special factors, too. To begin with, many older people simply are not comfortable with risk. And in these later years, when future income and cash flow may be uncertain, a healthy measure of caution is warranted. Fixed-rate loans are generally better than variable rates, and shorter-term debt is preferable to long-term debt.

Avoiding investment debt is probably wise when you are older because you may not have the time to achieve the rate of return necessary to offset the cost. Margin debt, or borrowing against the value of stocks and bonds in a portfolio, is particularly risky because of the possibility of a market downturn that would force you to put up additional collateral or sell the securities.

Many older people have substantial equity in a home, which gives them access to low-cost, tax-deductible home-equity debt, either a line of credit or a new mortgage. If you did not set up an emergency home-equity credit line earlier, it might be a good idea to do so now, before you retire. A home-equity credit line can be an excellent source of emergency money or funds to pay for home improvements and repairs. You can set these up at little or no cost at many banks, and there is no finance charge unless you actually draw on the money. But lenders will probably be more eager to accommodate you when you still have a full-time salary coming in.

Seniors with substantial equity in a home that is now much too big for their needs might consider selling and moving to a less expensive, more manageable home. This can both lower their costs and give them cash to help meet living expenses or add to reserves.

Another possibility some people might consider is a "reverse mortgage." This is a loan based on the equity a homeowner has accumulated, disbursed as a line of credit in monthly installments over a period of years or as a lump sum. The amount generally depends on the borrower's age and the amount of equity in the home. The older you are and the more your house is worth, the bigger the payments will be. But reverse-mortgage loans can be costly. Interest charges and other fees usually are financed as part of the loan and added to the balance. Only a few lenders offer reverse mortgages, and rates may be higher than on conventional mortgages. The house typically is sold to repay the loan when the borrower dies or moves out, which could leave little or nothing for the homeowner or the homeowner's heirs. Many seniors might want to look for less costly and less complicated sources of cash.

60s +

- Analyze future cash flow.
- Pay down debts.
- Opt for fixed rates.
- Do not invest on margin.
- Tap home equity if you must borrow.

DEBT COMES IN MANY DIFFERENT TYPES

Before you can determine how much debt you can handle, you have to understand how different kinds of loans work. Terms vary widely, which can dramatically alter the after-tax cost and your ability to repay what you borrow. The following sections explain the major details of the principal types of credit you are likely to encounter along life's path. They should also help you figure out what does and does not make sense for someone in your situation.

CREDIT CARDS

Credit cards may be the most common form of debt. Card issuers start signing up new customers when they are in college, or even in high school, before they have a job with the income to pay more than the minimum required. And these days, you can use credit cards just about anywhere—at the grocery store, the fast-food outlet, and the doctor's office, as well as at the hotels and restaurants that have accepted credit cards for years.

Most people carry several credit cards, and many seem to use them whenever they get a chance. Although some people regularly pay off the entire new balance each month, many others allow their balances to build month after month. Even the most diligent bill payers usually find that there are times when carrying a balance is unavoidable—after Christmas, perhaps, or a vacation.

Whatever the individual reasons, Americans owe some $400 billion in credit card debt. About 70% of us have balances outstanding, typically more than $1,800 per account. That gets expensive. Although most cards carry variable rates, the average rarely falls much below 18%. On the typical balance, that amounts to about $325 a year.

That should be sufficient motivation for you to take some time to understand the terms of the cards you have and make sure you are getting the best deal possible. A low interest rate is important, but other factors also affect the cost of a card. For example, some card issuers do not charge interest until 25 days after billing, whereas others start the meter immediately or when the charge is posted. Cash advances may carry higher rates than new purchases, and sometimes they carry additional fees.

EVEN FIXED RATES CAN CHANGE

You have to read the small print to find out all the details. About three-quarters of the bank cards outstanding carry variable rates. These variable rates are often linked to the prime rate—the base rate banks use for setting interest rates on many types of loans to consumers and small businesses. Some issuers use other benchmarks. Rates may be adjusted monthly, quarterly, or even annually. Even fixed rates do not offer any guarantees; they can be changed with 15 days' notice.

Some card issuers boast that they require only small minimum payments. That may seem attractive, but it usually is not. You may find yourself paying bills, and substantial interest charges, for many years. Even if you cannot pay the whole bill right away, you should always pay as much as you can as soon as possible.

When selecting a card, think about your bill-paying habits. It is generally best for people who tend to carry balances to look for the lowest rate. People who regularly pay their balances in full would do better to find a card with no annual fee. If you have two cards, consider having a low-rate card for purchases you will not be able to pay for right away and a no-fee card for charges you will pay as soon as the bill comes. That way you will avoid paying unnecessary interest, since many issuers charge interest immediately if you already have a balance.

Also be on the alert for special offers. The credit card business is very competitive, with issuers frequently offering inducements to attract new customers. You may not even have to switch to obtain better terms. Banks do not want to lose customers, and you may be able to have the fee waived on your current card or negotiate a lower rate just by calling the issuer and asking. Customer-service representatives often are authorized to offer a whole menu of low-rate or no-fee options, but you have to ask.

FINDING THE BEST DEALS NATIONWIDE

There are a number of sources to help you find the best deals nationwide. Among them are CardTrak, a monthly newsletter ($5 per issue; Box 1700, Frederick, MD 21702; 800-344-7714), and Bankcard Holders of America, a consumer-advocacy group ($4 for a low-interest-rate card list; 524 Branch Drive, Salem, VA 24153; 540-389-5445). *The Wall Street Journal* publishes a list of low-rate cards once a month (usually in the first ten days of the month) based on data from RAM Research, publisher of CardTrak.

Be careful to read any credit card solicitation that comes in the mail closely before signing up. Issuers offer a variety of incentives, including superlow rates for customers who transfer balances from another card. Those low-rate deals typically are for a limited time, however. Although many continue for a full year, some offers are good only for a few months. It is important to know what the rate

AN EASY WAY TO EARN 18%

Paying down the balance on your credit cards can give you a whopping 18% return—tax-free and with absolutely no risk.

It is simple arithmetic. With the typical interest rate on credit card balances around 18%, you are paying out $18 a year on every $100 you owe. Eliminate that debt, and you save all the money you would have had to pay out in interest. In effect, you have given yourself an 18% return. The only risk is that you will let those unpaid credit card balances build up again.

will be after the introductory offer expires. The card issuer should tell you what benchmark is used and what you would be paying at current interest rates.

You also should find out whether that low introductory rate applies to new purchases or just to balances you transfer from another card. Otherwise, you could be in for a big surprise when you receive your first bill. Do not be misled by a large maximum credit line touted in big print on the envelope: It may be far more than you are actually eligible for with your current income.

No matter what kind of deal you are offered, remember that you do not need more than one or two bank cards. Merchants and others who accept credit cards will generally take any of the major cards. What is more, having many cards increases the temptation to overspend.

Home Mortgages

The biggest debt most of us have is a mortgage, and we spend much of our adult lives paying it off. Yet in the excitement and stress of buying a home, few people really focus on finding the type of mortgage that best meets their needs. The choice can make an enormous difference in the cost over time. There are 15-year, 20-year, and 30-year loans, some with fixed rates and others with adjustable rates that change as often as every six months or as infrequently as after seven years. Under current tax law, interest on up to $1 million is tax-deductible.

Most people prefer the security of a fixed-rate loan—the kind of mortgage our parents and grandparents had—because they know exactly how much their monthly payment will be and can budget for it over the long term. The rates lenders charge on fixed-rate mortgages generally rise and fall in tandem with rates on 10-year and 30-year Treasury securities. But once the lender has locked in your rate, you can count on it remaining unchanged for the duration of your loan, regardless of what happens to market rates.

A GOOD CHOICE FOR SOME

Adjustable-rate mortgages, or ARMs, have their own advantages and are certainly worth considering if you have a tolerance for uncertainty. Typically, ARMs are cheaper than fixed-rate loans, to compensate borrowers for assuming some of the risk of rising rates. Although payments could increase substantially if interest rates rise, variable-rate loans can be a good choice for young people who are reasonably certain that their income will rise over time and for people who know they are going to move in a few years.

Interest rates on nearly half of all adjustable-rate mortgages are linked to rates on short-term Treasury securities, which usually are lower than on longer-term instruments; others are based on the Federal Home Loan Bank's cost-of-funds index or on such benchmarks as the London Interbank Offered Rate, the rate banks charge each other for loans in the London money market. The mortgage rate is usually about 2.75 to 3 percentage points above the index.

If you do consider an ARM, make sure you know which index the lender is using, where it is published so you can track it, and when adjustments are to be calculated. There have been cases of banks miscalculating periodic changes. Lenders also should provide historical data about the index used. Although that does not guarantee future performance, the magnitude of the variations over time should give you some idea of the risk you are taking.

Rates on adjustable-rate mortgages that adjust every six months

MORTGAGE INDEXES

Following are the different indexes used in calculating adjustable-rate mortgages.

- **Treasury Securities.** Generally, the auction average of six-month Treasury bills, or the yield on one-, three-, or five-year Treasury securities calculated on a constant-maturity basis. Six-month Treasury bills usually are used only with mortgages that are adjusted every six months.

- **Eleventh District Cost of Funds.** An index calculated by the Federal Home Loan Bank of San Francisco, 1 of 12 Federal Home Loan Banks. The index reflects the interest that savings institutions in Arizona, California, and Nevada pay on their sources of mortgage money. It is used more frequently by institutions on the West Coast.

- **LIBOR.** The London Interbank Offered Rate, the average interest rate banks charge each other for deposits in the London market. The six-month average is most commonly used for setting mortgage rates.

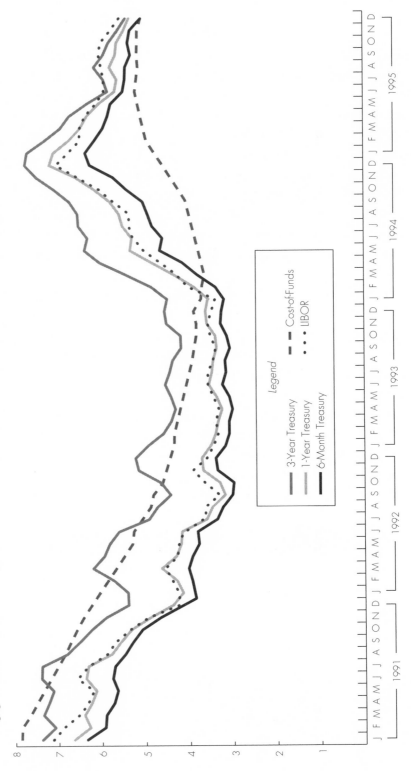

HOW THE INDEXES HAVE PERFORMED

Mortgages based on short-term Treasury indexes—six-month bills in particular—usually carry the lowest rates but can be the most variable.

Legend

— 3-Year Treasury
— 1-Year Treasury
— 6-Month Treasury
- - - Cost-of-Funds
· · · LIBOR

SOURCE: HSH Associates.

or a year usually can move a maximum of two percentage points a year and five or six percentage points over the life of the loan. Rates on mortgages that adjust less frequently may move as much as four percentage points on the first adjustment, after three, five, seven, or ten years. Typically, these loans adjust annually thereafter, with the same two-percentage-point limit as on other adjustable-rate mortgages.

Two percentage points can make a big difference in your monthly payment. On a 30-year $100,000 mortgage, for example, the difference between 7% and 9% would be nearly $150 a month. Indeed, you generally should not consider an ARM unless the rate is more than two percentage points lower than the fixed-rate mortgage. Otherwise, your savings could evaporate after only one year, with the prospect of even higher rates to come.

Whether you go for a fixed or an adjustable rate, a longer term or a shorter one, you can save money and reduce your risk by making a larger down payment. Some lenders will give you a mortgage equal to 95% of the value of your home. But on a $150,000 home, your payments on an 8.5% 30-year mortgage would be $173 more a month than if you put down 20%. That difference adds up to more than $62,000 over the term of the loan, nearly three times the amount of the additional down payment. By making a larger down payment, you also may be able to avoid having to buy mortgage insurance, which is insurance many homeowners are required to pay until the equity in their homes reaches about 20% of the amount of loan outstanding.

WHAT IT TAKES TO QUALIFY

When evaluating mortgage applications, lenders typically require that housing expenses, including real estate taxes and monthly maintenance payments on a cooperative apartment or condominium, not exceed 28% of the borrower's gross income. It used to be that taking an ARM, with a lower rate and lower monthly payments, would allow you to qualify for a bigger mortgage to buy a bigger and better home. These days, however, lenders generally make their decision based on the introductory rate plus two percentage points, requiring almost the same income levels as for a fixed-rate loan.

Shorter fixed-rate loans, such as 15- or 20-year mortgages, require larger monthly payments but offer significant savings in interest charges over the life of the loan. On a $100,000 mortgage at 9%, for instance, payments on a 15-year loan would be about $200 higher than on a 30-year loan, and the total savings would be more than $100,000. Interest rates are generally somewhat lower on 15-year loans, making the savings even greater. You will also be debt-free 10 or 15 years sooner, which makes these shorter-term mortgages a good choice for people nearing retirement or expecting to send a child to college in 15 to 20 years.

Those who do not qualify for a 15-year loan, or who do not want to commit to the higher payments every month, might consider adding something to the payments on a 30-year loan or making one extra payment a year. The equivalent of one extra payment a year could shorten a 30-year mortgage by 10 to 12 years. Some lenders offer the option of loans with biweekly payments—each equal to half of a regular monthly payment—that result in the equivalent of one extra payment a year.

Even if you have the cash flow for a 15-year loan, you might choose to take a 30-year mortgage with lower payments and invest the difference. You will come out ahead if you put the cash into something that generates an after-tax return greater than the after-tax cost of your mortgage. But remember that those returns are far from guaranteed, and you must have the self-discipline actually to invest the money month after month.

Refinancing Your Mortgage

Once you have a mortgage, do not stop paying attention to interest rates even if you never plan to move again. You might be able to save thousands of dollars a year by refinancing into a lower-cost loan. Refinancing is simply trading in your old mortgage, sometimes wrapping in a second mortgage or home-equity loan, for a new one. Usually, the new mortgage has a lower interest rate, although you may decide to refinance to shorten or lengthen the term of the loan or to convert from an adjustable to a fixed rate.

The savings can be substantial. Someone with a $150,000

30-year loan at 10%, for instance, would cut monthly payments by more than $200 with an 8% mortgage, for a $75,000-plus savings over the 30 years. If the term were shortened to 15 years at that same 8% rate, monthly payments would increase by about $120, but the homeowner would save more than $200,000 in interest by cutting the term of the loan in half.

WATCH THE COSTS

There usually are costs involved in refinancing, which can eat into the savings. For instance, there may be lawyers' fees and application fees, as well as fees for a new title search and appraisal. The biggest cost is usually the "points," the loan-origination fee that is based on a percentage of the total borrowed. These expenses can add up to 3% to 5% of the mortgage amount, or as much as $7,500 on a $150,000 loan.

The simplest way to figure out whether refinancing is worth it is to add up all the costs and divide the total by the amount you would save each month. The result is the number of months it will take you to break even. If you are likely to move before then, forget refinancing, no matter how much you would save each month.

If you have an adjustable-rate loan, there are other considerations. If rates are falling, the hassle and costs of refinancing may not be worth it. But it also could be a good time to lock in a fixed rate if you plan to stay where you are for a while.

The calculations become even more complicated when you have had a mortgage for a number of years and built up some equity. Because mortgages are structured so that payments in the first few years consist mostly of interest, refinancing could mean that it will be years before you start making a dent in the principal again. If you go from one 30-year loan into another, in effect extending your debt, you may reduce your monthly payment substantially, but you will pay thousands of dollars more in interest charges. The way to realize longer-term savings is with a 15-year or 20-year loan.

Say, for example, that you took out a $150,000 30-year mortgage at 10%, and you have been making monthly payments of $1,316.36 for ten years. If you refinanced the $136,470 balance into a new 30-year loan at 8%, the monthly payments would drop to $1,001.37.

But by extending your debt for an additional ten years, you would pay more than $40,000 in extra interest.

If, instead, you opted for a 20-year loan at the same 8% rate, your monthly payments would be $1,141.49, the mortgage would be paid off at the same time as the original loan, and you would save more than $40,000 in total interest charges. Refinancing that same balance into a 15-year 8% loan would save you a whopping $81,000 in total interest, you would be out of debt five years sooner, and your monthly payments would be $1,304.18—about what they were before.

TAX CONSIDERATIONS

There are tax considerations, too, in all refinancings. Because a lower interest rate means a smaller tax deduction for home mortgage interest, most people's actual after-tax savings will probably work out to about 70% of the pretax amount. In addition, points paid on refinancing, unlike those paid on the original mortgage, are not fully tax-deductible for the year they are paid. They must be amortized over the life of the loan.

Some lenders offer no-cost refinancing. These mortgages typically carry higher interest rates than standard loans, but if rates have fallen enough since you got your original mortgage, there still could be savings. There are also special programs for borrowers who have poor credit histories, although these, too, may charge higher interest rates.

It is often worthwhile to call your original lender first when you start the refinancing process. You may be able to negotiate a better deal than you have now without a new title search or appraisal. Also, some adjustable-rate mortgage loans can be converted to a fixed rate at little or no cost during a specified period, usually the first five years.

Because of the costs involved, the rule of thumb used to be that the new interest rate had to be at least two percentage points lower than the old to make refinancing worthwhile. But with no-cost or low-cost refinancing, a much smaller difference can result in savings. It pays to crunch the numbers both ways, however, because homeowners who reasonably expect to stay where they are for five years or longer may find that taking a lower rate and paying the costs is a better deal.

MORTGAGE REFINANCING CALCULATOR

When does it pay to refinance? Look at the following table and find the amount on the left that is closest to what it would cost to refinance your mortgage. Follow that row to the right, until you come to the column over the amount that is closest to what you would save each month by refinancing. The number where the cost row and the savings column intersect is the approximate number of months it will take for refinancing to begin paying off. Actual payback periods will be affected by tax considerations.

Costs of Refinancing ($)									
7,000	140	94	70	56	47	40	35	32	28
6,000	120	80	60	48	40	35	30	27	24
5,000	100	67	50	40	34	29	25	23	20
4,000	80	54	40	32	27	23	20	18	16
3,000	60	40	30	24	20	18	15	14	12
2,000	40	27	20	16	14	12	10	9	8
1,000	20	14	10	8	7	6	5	5	4
Monthly Savings ($)	50	75	100	125	150	175	200	225	250

HOME-EQUITY LOANS AND LINES OF CREDIT

Home-equity loans and lines of credit can be an easy and low-cost way for homeowners to borrow. Rates are often lower than on many other kinds of credit, and interest payments on up to $100,000 in home-equity debt, in addition to a mortgage, are generally tax-deductible.

Like mortgages, home-equity debt can carry either a fixed or a variable interest rate. Home-equity loans, which allow you to borrow a certain amount and pay it back over a specified term, generally carry fixed rates. Lines of credit, which allow you to draw upon them as needed, usually carry adjustable rates. Those adjustable rates are linked to an index, such as the prime lending rate, the benchmark banks use for many loans to individuals and small businesses.

Lenders often set a maximum loan amount of $100,000 because of the tax deductibility. Many limit total borrowing, including the balance on the original mortgage, to 75% of the market value of your home, although it is possible to find lenders that will let you borrow more.

VERSATILE DEBT

You can use home-equity debt to meet a multitude of needs. It may be a relatively low-cost source of cash for home improvements, buying a car, financing a child's education, or even starting a new business. You can also use a home-equity line of credit to augment your emergency reserve fund. With a line of credit that you can draw on as needed, you pay interest only on the money you are actually using.

The important thing is to pay back the loan as quickly as possible. Some people opt to use home-equity debt when purchasing a car because of its tax deductibility, for instance. But cars depreciate rapidly. If you do not pay off the debt in four years or less, just as you should an auto loan, you could end up making payments on a car that has lost a significant part of its original value while depleting the equity in your home.

Also be aware of the special risks to which you will subject yourself in using home-equity debt to provide the cash to start a new business. Many new businesses fail in the first few years, and if you borrow too much, you could find yourself without a business and without a home.

Also avoid the temptation to use a home-equity line like a checking account, to pay for such things as clothes and vacations. Sure, the rates are lower than on credit cards and interest payments are tax-deductible, but you are putting your house on the line. That new fur coat may keep you warm, but it will not replace the roof over your head if you cannot make the payments on your loan.

Indeed, the big risk in borrowing against the equity in your home is that property values will fall and you will find yourself owing more than the house is worth. You will not be able to sell without taking a big loss, and if you cannot make the payments on your loan, you risk foreclosure. Many homeowners in California and the Northeast found themselves in exactly that position in the early 1990s, and some literally walked away from their mortgages.

Still, home-equity loans and lines of credit have become increasingly popular in the past decade, making it possible for many homeowners to cope with significant expenses, such as a college education, more easily. The typical loan is about $40,000 or $50,000 and runs for 15 years. There was about $375 billion in home-equity loans and lines of credit outstanding in 1995.

Auto Loans

These days a car costs what a house did not too many years ago, and there are almost as many financing options as there are types of mortgages. The least expensive way to do it is to pay cash, although it probably will not feel that way when you write a check for $20,000 or more. For those of us who do not have that kind of money readily available, or have other plans for it, the options include dealer financing or an auto loan from a local bank or credit union. You might also consider a home-equity loan, which typically would allow you to deduct the interest payments. Then there is the possibility of leasing instead of buying.

Making the right choice is more than just figuring the monthly payments. A lease usually costs less per month than a loan, for instance, but unless you are someone who wants a new car every two or three years, it is usually cheaper over time to buy. Monthly payments on a five-year loan are lower than if you borrowed for three or four years, but the total cost, including interest, could be thousands of dollars more.

IMPORTANT CONSIDERATIONS

You must consider how long you plan to keep the car, how much you drive, and, of course, how much you can afford to pay. If you can afford to pay cash, there are no finance charges and you have full ownership of an asset that has value. There is an "opportunity cost"—the lost income from the cash you are using to buy the car—but you have to be sure that you would actually invest it. Even then, there is no guarantee that you would get an after-tax return that exceeded the cost of financing.

If you have to borrow, home-equity debt is usually the least expensive source of funds. Although rates may not be significantly lower than on new-car loans, the tax savings resulting from the deductibility of interest payments can be equal to 40% or more for

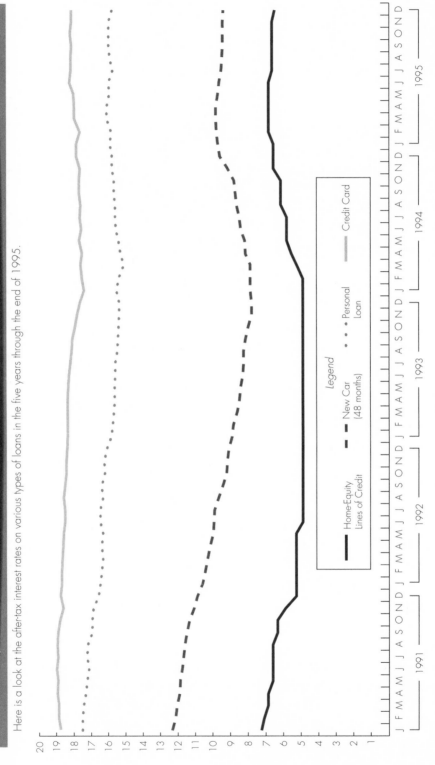

HOW BORROWING COSTS COMPARE

Here is a look at the after-tax interest rates on various types of loans in the five years through the end of 1995.

Legend

— Home-Equity Lines of Credit   - - New Car (48 months)   ••• Personal loan   — Credit Card

NOTE: Rates on home-equity lines of credit were calculated at 1.5 percentage points over the prime rate, not first-year introductory rates; after-tax rate assumes a 34% tax rate, including federal, state, and local levies. Interest on credit card debt, personal loans, and new car loans is not tax-deductible.

SOURCE: Bank Rate Monitor.

those in high tax brackets. But pay off the debt at least as quickly as you would an auto loan so you do not end up depleting the equity in your home.

Not everyone has access to home-equity debt, however, and even those who do should look into other low-cost sources of financing. Manufacturers eager to sell a particular model may offer what they call 0% financing, essentially a no-cost loan, or rates as low as 1.9% or 2.9%. Credit unions typically offer lower rates than banks or auto-financing companies. You may be able to find a better deal at your own bank.

Whatever the financing, first make sure you are getting the lowest possible price for the car. Even a no-cost loan may not be such a great deal if you are paying an inflated price. Try to negotiate a deal as close to the dealer's cost as possible before you discuss financing; several books listing dealer costs are available at bookstores. The smaller the amount you finance, and the shorter the length of the loan, the lower your cost will be. Although you always should look for the lowest rate, you also should make a down payment if at all possible and keep the loan to three or four years.

To figure out how much the car is really going to cost you, add up your monthly payments over the term of the loan, plus any down payment you make. The federal Truth-in-Lending law requires lenders to give you an annual percentage rate, which includes loan fees and other charges, as well as the interest rate. This is the total cost per year of the loan and the number you should use when making comparisons.

THE ALLURE OF LEASING

Leasing is simply another way of financing a car, which has grown in popularity in recent years in response to ever-rising sticker prices. Because the leasing company retains ownership of the vehicle, monthly payments are lower than on a standard auto loan. By some estimates, more than a quarter of all new cars purchased these days are leased, and the percentage is higher for more expensive cars.

Manufacturers like leasing because it keeps consumers coming back for a new car every three years or so. Consumers like it because they can drive a bigger and better car than they can afford to buy.

Keep in mind, however, that you will not own anything at the end of the lease. From a strictly financial point of view, a conventional loan is almost always better.

Still, there are other considerations. Sometimes, being able to walk away from a car you do not like after two or three years without having to worry about the resale market outweighs the cost. And if you like having an expensive new car every two or three years, leasing may be the way you can afford it.

BUY OR LEASE?

This worksheet shows the steps you need to take to compare the costs of leasing and financing an automobile. The example is an imported sedan leased for four years (payments of $299 per month) or purchased with a four-year loan at 9.25% (20% down; payments of $389.96 per month).

	YOUR CAR DEAL		EXAMPLE	
	LEASE	LOAN	LEASE	LOAN
Negotiated Price	═══	═══	$19,495	$19,495
License and Fees	___	___	530[1]	80
Sales Tax (cost × local rate)	+ ___	+ ___	+ 1,170	+ 1,170
Security Deposit	+ ___	+ 0	+ 200	+ 0
Down Payment	+ ___	+ ___	+ 0[2]	+ 3,899
TOTAL UP-FRONT COST	= ___	= ___	= 1,900[3]	= 5,149
Total Monthly Payments	+ ___	+ ___	+14,352	+18,718
Excess Mileage Charges	+ ___	+ 0	+ 750[4]	+ 0
Lost Interest or Investment Income (5% after-tax)	+ ___	+ ___	+ 140[5]	+ 840[5]
Refund of Security Deposit	− ___	− 0	− 200	− 0
TOTAL COST AFTER ____ MONTHS	= ___	= ___	=16,942	=24,707
Value of Auto Owned	− 0	− ___	− 0	− 9,975[6]
ACTUAL COST	= ___	= ___	=$16,942	=$14,732

[1]Example assumes acquisition fee of $450.
[2]Example assumes no capitalized cost reduction.
[3]Many leases require the first payment due at inception; if so, this may increase your up-front cost.
[4]5,000 miles at 15¢/mile.
[5]For the lease, lost interest/investment income is calculated on the $650 acquisition fee and security deposit; for the loan, it is calculated on the $3,899 down payment.
[6]Value of auto after four years based on residual value at the end of the lease.
NOTE: This example does not take into account the time value of money.
SOURCE: Arthur Andersen.

Typically, lease arrangements permit you to buy the vehicle at the end of the lease for the "residual value," which is an amount specified in the lease that is expected to approximate the vehicle's depreciated value at the end of the lease period. Manufacturers generally try to keep residuals high, which reduces the monthly payments and attracts customers. But setting the residual is a guessing game for manufacturers and leasing companies. If, at the end of the lease, the specified residual turns out to be higher than the vehicle's market value, you should walk away. You could buy a similar used car for less money. If the residual is equal to or lower than the market value, buying it could be a good deal. After all, you know that car—you really took care of it, and it probably has many good miles left on it. Even if you do not want to keep the car, you might consider buying it and then reselling it at a profit.

If you do lease, make sure that you have "gap" insurance—coverage for the difference between what you owe on the car and the amount your auto insurance will pay if the car is stolen or destroyed during the term of lease.

Also, make sure you know how much you are likely to drive each year. Most leases permit 15,000 miles annually, with extra charges at the end if you exceed that amount. If you drive much less, or much more, you probably should not lease unless you can negotiate the lease payment to reflect the difference at the outset.

Leases generally do not require any up-front payment other than a security deposit and the same title and registration fees you would pay if you were buying. You can reduce your cost, however, by putting some money down, known as a "capitalized cost reduction," just as you can cut financing costs on a purchase with a down payment.

INVESTMENT DEBT

Buying securities on margin, or borrowing against the value of stocks and bonds, is among the more controversial forms of debt because of the risks involved. If market prices rise, the leverage can dramatically increase the gains. But if prices fall, losses are magnified. Financial professionals usually recommend it only for sophisticated investors.

Generally, an investor can borrow up to 50% of the value of stocks owned or up to 90% of the value of bonds, depending on the type of bond and its maturity. As long as proceeds are used to purchase taxable securities, interest charges are tax-deductible to the extent that they are offset by taxable investment income. Rates usually are lower than on many other types of loans because the debt is secured.

Problems can arise when the market value of the securities falls below the level required to maintain sufficient collateral. The resulting margin call could require repayment of a significant portion of the loan within days or even hours, forcing an investor to sell securities at a loss.

Investment debt works like this: Say an investor wants to buy $10,000 of a stock that trades at $20 a share. If he paid cash, he could buy 500 shares. If the price then rose to $27, the investor would make a tidy profit of $3,500, a 35% return on his investment, excluding commission costs. But for the same $10,000, the investor could purchase 1,000 shares on margin. A price rise to $27 would produce a profit of $7,000, a whopping 70% return on the initial cash outlay.

THE GROWTH OF MARGIN DEBT

Investment debt doubled in the ten years through 1995.

Year	Amount
1986	$36,840
1987	$31,990
1988	$32,740
1989	$34,320
1990	$28,320
1991	$36,660
1992	$43,990
1993	$60,310
1994	$61,160
1995	$76,680

SOURCE: New York Stock Exchange.

That is the good news. Now look at what would happen if the price fell to $13 a share. If the investor had paid cash, he would lose $3,500—painful, but probably not devastating. But if he had bought the stock on margin, he would sustain a $7,000 loss and still owe the brokerage firm $10,000. That is not all. The margin investor would also be subject to a margin call because the $3,000 left in the account would no longer meet the brokerage firm's minimum equity requirements—usually 30% of market value. If the investor could not quickly come up with $900, the securities could be sold at a big loss to cover the debt.

Still, margin borrowing continues to grow. Although most people use the proceeds to purchase securities, the cash can be used for just about anything, including paying off high-cost credit card debt, starting a business, and sending a child to college. (Interest charges, however, are not tax-deductible when margin loans are used for these other purposes.) Rates are relatively low, and it is easy to borrow. Generally, all you have to do is write a check against your asset-management account at a brokerage firm. There usually is no fixed repayment schedule; the debt can remain outstanding indefinitely as long as the market value of the underlying investment continues to meet minimum requirements.

You can greatly reduce the risks of margin loans by paying back the debt quickly. Then if the stock or bond market plummets, you will not find yourself with an investment loss, a big loan, and a margin call to cope with. Indeed, many financial professionals say margin debt should be used only for short-term purposes because it is unlikely that you will be able to achieve a long-term investment return that exceeds the cost of financing.

EDUCATION LOANS

Many people are willing to lend you money to pay for college, which is a good thing because you are probably going to need it. Few of us can just sit down and write a check for tuition, room, and board. The cost of many private colleges is more than $25,000 a year and rising. Even parents who have been conscientiously putting money aside for years are finding that they just do not have enough.

Most scholarships and grants are need-based, and even when a financial-aid package includes a scholarship, it usually requires the student to work part-time and take out a loan, too. Awards based on academic merit typically cover only a small percentage of the cost of a year at college. It is no wonder that more than half the students at many private colleges (or their parents) have taken on debt to finance their education.

But just as with other kinds of debt, not all financing is equal, and the differences can significantly change the total cost of borrowing. Some loans are guaranteed by the federal government or by state agencies, whereas others are private. Interest rates and fees vary; some loans are for students only, and others are for parents. There may be family-income limits or maximum amounts that can be borrowed. Payback periods can be as short as 5 years or as long as 30.

SOMETHING FOR ALMOST EVERYONE

Almost everyone qualifies for at least one of the federal loan programs, which provide more than $25 billion a year to more than six million students. These loans may be made by banks or other institutions, guaranteed by a state agency, and insured by the federal government. A number of schools are now part of the Federal Direct Student Loan program, begun in 1994, under which the U.S. Department of Education makes loans through participating colleges and universities.

Most college financial-aid offices can give you information about government loan programs, as well as about private sources of funds. There is a toll-free telephone number for information about federal student aid (800-433-3243) and a single application for all federal programs that is also available from most college financial-aid offices.

The most popular of the government-guaranteed loans are Stafford loans, which generally provide a maximum of $5,500 a year to undergraduate students and more to graduate students. The interest rate is variable based on the three-month Treasury bill, to a maximum of 8.25%, and it is reset annually. The student is responsible for paying back Stafford loans. Repayment usually begins six months after graduation, although interest begins to accrue as soon as the loan is disbursed and is added to the principal amount.

HOW COLLEGE LOANS COMPARE

Here is a look at the major features of two popular government programs.

	STAFFORD LOANS	PLUS LOANS
Who Can Borrow	Undergraduate or graduate students enrolled at least part-time	Parents
Maximum Loan Amount	$5,500 for dependent undergraduates who have completed two years of study; $10,500 for independent undergraduates; $18,500 for graduate students	Cost of education, less other financial aid for which the student is eligible
Income Requirements	None; interest subsidies for students who demonstrate financial need	None; credit check required
Interest Rate	Variable, 8.25% maximum	Variable, to 9%
Repayment Begins	Six months after studies end; interest subsidized for needy students until payback begins	60 days after final disbursement

SOURCE: U.S. Department of Education.

Students whose family incomes fall below certain thresholds can receive subsidized loans, meaning that the federal government pays interest on the debt while they are in school.

Parents can apply for PLUS loans—Parent Loans to Undergraduate Students. These also carry a variable interest rate, which is linked to the one-year Treasury bill and capped at 9%. There are no income limitations for these loans, and parents can borrow up to the full cost of tuition, room, and board each year. Parents usually must begin to repay PLUS loans about 60 days after the money is received. Both PLUS and Stafford loans usually have a 10-year payback period, although it can be extended to 20 and even 30 years under certain circumstances.

Another possibility for parents who own a home is a home-equity loan. The rate may be somewhat lower than other sources of cash, and interest charges are tax-deductible on borrowings up to $100,000. Some schools will arrange home-equity loans to pay for college costs, but these loans usually can be used only to pay tuition and other costs, such as room and board. Many parents prefer to arrange home-equity loans themselves so they have the flexibility to use some of the proceeds for other purposes.

Not all parents can, or want to, take on mountains of debt to finance their children's education, however, and in many cases they should not do it. Because there are no income limitations on PLUS loans, it can be too easy to borrow more than you can pay back, especially if the payments extend into your retirement years. Home-equity loans could put your home at risk.

GREATER FLEXIBILITY

Private loans, which can be arranged through banks, thrifts, or other lenders, may offer the flexibility that government programs do not. They can be used to supplement the limited amounts available to students under the Stafford program, for example, and they may have a wider variety of payment and repayment options.

Just do not let easy access to credit become too tempting. Some young people graduate from college owing $30,000 to $40,000. If they go on to graduate or professional school, the total can top $100,000. It could be years before you have the income to pay back that much debt.

Although it is possible to consolidate loans and extend payback periods, the days when people could simply walk away from student loans are gone. The government will seize tax refunds or garnish wages to recover bad debts and will report deadbeats to credit agencies. You have to pay back the loans even if you do not complete your studies and never receive a degree.

But for those who manage debt wisely, college loans could turn out to be a good investment. Studies show that the difference in lifetime earnings of a high school graduate and a college graduate usually far exceeds the cost of borrowing.

PAYING IT BACK

The trouble with borrowing money is that you have to pay it back, a truth that becomes all too apparent to young people graduating from college and facing monthly payments of a couple of hundred dollars even before they buy a car or furnish an apartment. But while the prospects can seem bleak, there are ways to have student loans deferred, forgiven, restructured, refinanced, or consolidated.

It is not just new grads who can benefit, either. Anyone who still owes money on a student loan, which typically runs for ten years, may be able to get some financial breathing room if it is needed. The process is surprisingly easy. The U.S. Department of Education, for example, can consolidate loans from a variety of sources with a single application through its Direct Loan Consolidation Program (800-455-5889).

Through the consolidation program, you also can arrange to extend repayment schedules on government-guaranteed loans, in some cases to as long as 30 years. These programs generally are available to students and to parent-borrowers, although there may be fewer options for parents. You also can contact your lender directly.

Federal loan programs generally offer four repayment options, and you can switch back and forth depending on your circumstances:

- **Standard.** Borrowers must pay a fixed amount each month—at least $50—for up to ten years.

- **Income-contingent.** Monthly payments are based on the borrower's income and the loan amount; as the person's income rises or falls, so do the payments. Repayment can take up to 25 years. After that, any remaining balance will be forgiven, although borrowers have to pay income tax on amounts forgiven.

- **Graduated repayment.** Payments start low and increase every two years over 12 to 30 years.

- **Extended repayment.** Repayment may be stretched to as long as 30 years, depending on the loan amount.

Consolidation is attractive because it is often easier to budget for a single monthly payment. Sometimes a married couple may want to combine their loans. If you do decide to consolidate or restructure college loans, remember that just as with other kinds of debt, the cost of borrowing is determined by the interest rate and the term. If you have to refinance at a higher rate, or if you extend the payback period, you may be paying much more over time for the privilege of paying less each month now.

If you cannot find a job at all, if you are returning to school, or if you can demonstrate economic hardship, you may be eligible for a deferment, which postpones repayment. If the loan was subsidized, the government continues to pay interest during a deferment. Otherwise, interest continues to mount. You can make interest-only payments each month during a deferment, or the interest that accrues will be added to the balance of the loan.

With a forbearance, which is granted if you are willing but unable to meet your repayment schedule and you are not eligible for a deferment, payments are postponed or reduced. Interest continues to accrue and, if it is not paid, is added to the balance due.

The Student Loan Marketing Association (Sallie Mae), the quasi-governmental agency that holds and services student loans, offers similar options. Sallie Mae also gives borrowers a small interest-rate reduction if they make their monthly payments by direct electronic transfer from a bank account, and it gives a one-percentage-point reduction on the balance of the loan if borrowers make the first 48 scheduled payments on time. Private lenders may have their own loan consolidation programs.

It is important to contact your lender, or apply for a Direct Consolidation loan, as soon as you realize you may not be able to make payments as scheduled. It is easier to renegotiate terms before you start missing payments, and you cannot get a deferment or forbearance if your loan is in default. In general, loans are forgiven only in case of total disability or death, or in some instances bankruptcy. But certain teachers, child-care workers, and medical workers may qualify for cancellation of federal Perkins loans, which are low-interest loans for the exceptionally needy.

ESTABLISHING AND MAINTAINING CREDIT

The world seems to run on credit. But if you are just setting out on your own, starting over after a divorce or the death of a spouse, or trying to get back on your feet after bankruptcy or other financial problems, what do you do?

The first step toward establishing credit often is opening a checking or savings account at a local bank. Building a savings account is a good way to show potential lenders that you have the self-discipline to make regular payments on a loan. You also may be able to get a credit card from that same bank, and having an existing banking relationship may entitle you to a break on the interest rate or annual fee.

Credit card applications are pretty simple. They generally ask for your name and address, place of employment, and income. If you have lived at your current address or been at your job fewer than two years, you may have to give a previous address or employer. You may also be asked to list bank accounts and other credit cards or loans. Usually, you will be asked to document your income—in the form of pay stubs or tax returns—only if you are applying for a big loan, such as a mortgage.

Most credit applications are scored by computer, based on the issuer's guidelines for weighing such factors as length of employment, income, amount of credit available, and past payment history. Some issuers set strict standards, others are willing to consider high-risk accounts.

When applying for that first credit card, consider getting a so-called secured card. You will have to leave an offsetting balance equal to your credit line on deposit at the bank, but you will earn some interest income on it, and the interest rate on the card may be lower than it would be otherwise. Secured cards also may have a psychological advantage. Because you have to deposit cash equal to what you might charge, you are less likely to think of a credit card as free money. And you know you will always be able to pay the bill.

Secured cards may be the only choice for people with no credit history or those who are trying to reestablish themselves after past credit problems. Be careful, however. Some organizations that advertise secured credit cards are less than fully legitimate; what you will get is a card that entitles you to purchase items from their catalog. Try to deal only with banks or other known credit grantors.

If you cannot get a bank card, department store cards and gasoline credit cards may be easier to come by. If you pay your bills on time, you can begin to establish a credit history that can lead to more choices in the future. Just do not carry big unpaid balances on these cards—interest rates can be extremely high.

Recent college graduates planning to buy a new car should ask if they qualify for special lending deals. Eager to establish brand loyalty when people are starting careers, manufacturers may offer rebates or interest-rate discounts to recent graduates and may be willing to defer the first payment for several months. To qualify for a lower rate, you will generally have to be able to show a good credit history.

Even if you are just starting out, you should avoid seeking help from Mom and Dad. The only possible exception is the down payment on your first home, because it can be such a sizable amount and it helps reduce the cost of a mortgage. It should not be necessary for anyone to co-sign your loans and, indeed, you would not want a co-signer when you are trying to establish a credit history. The loan would be based on the co-signer's income, and the record would not reflect your ability to make the payments.

If you cannot obtain credit any other way, you might consider asking to be listed on someone else's account as an additional cardholder and paying the bills for the charges you incur. Make sure that credit reporting agencies know that you are responsible for payment.

Once you are started, limit your total debt, excluding a mortgage, to 15% or so of your gross income so the payments do not get out of hand. Do not let available credit—the amount you can borrow or charge on credit cards—exceed 30% to 40% of income.

CHECKING UP ON YOUR CREDIT RECORD

Once you have a credit card you have a credit record. Credit bureaus probably know where you live and work, whether you are single, married, or divorced, and, most important for them, how much you owe and whether you pay your bills on time. The information is based on regular reports from credit card issuers and other lenders.

Since lenders can easily obtain these records when you apply for credit, knowing what information credit agencies have collected on you and your financial habits can save a lot of time and headaches later. You do not want to wait, for instance, until after you have been turned down for a mortgage to find out that some credit bureau has you confused with your deadbeat cousin.

It is not hard to obtain a copy of your credit report. There are three major credit reporting agencies nationwide: Equifax, Experian (formerly TRW), and Trans Union. There are also regional and local firms. Experian offers consumers one free copy of its credit report each calendar year and charges about $8 for additional reports. Other agencies generally charge $8. But you can always get a free copy of your credit report if you have been denied credit within the past 60 days.

WHAT YOU WILL FIND

Contrary to popular belief, there is no actual credit rating in an individual file. Creditors generally report whether accounts are current, 30, 60, or 90 or more days late. Any payment that is more than 30 days late can be reported as delinquent, although most creditors wait until 60 days to begin reporting. Delinquencies and other bad debts generally remain on file seven years. There are also data from court records, such as bankruptcies, foreclosures, legal judgments, and tax liens. Bankruptcies can remain in your record for as long as ten years. Delinquent child-support payments show up occasionally, depending on the state, but there is no information about traffic infractions or even criminal activity.

Lenders use their own scoring systems to evaluate the information in the files to determine creditworthiness. A few late payments on your Visa card probably will not affect your chances of being approved for a loan, but a pattern of delinquencies or a foreclosure or personal bankruptcy certainly will.

It is a good idea to review your file every few years; you should do so especially before applying for a big loan such as a mortgage. That way you can correct any inaccuracies before you apply. Even if the adverse information is correct, potential lenders may be more sympathetic toward people who bring it to their attention and offer a reasonable explanation. Few of us have a perfect credit report.

Married people and young adults should make sure that all the accounts for which they are jointly and individually liable are correctly listed. Some credit grantors are reluctant to consider applicants with little or no credit history.

No one knows for sure how many errors there are in credit reports, but with 180 million credit-active Americans and 2 billion bits of data coming into credit bureaus each month, some inaccuracies are inevitable. These can range from an incorrect address or employment information to nonexistent court judgments or tax liens. Sometimes information about someone with the same name or a similar Social Security number can find its way onto the wrong credit report.

If you do find something you think is wrong on your credit report, notify the credit reporting agency in writing immediately. The agency will try to verify the information; if it cannot be verified it will be removed from your file. If the credit grantor insists that the information is correct, you can ask that it be reinvestigated. At that point, however, it may be better to contact the issuer directly to resolve the matter. Lenders generally do not want to antagonize customers or potential customers and often will accept your explanation.

HAVING YOUR SAY

If the disagreement cannot be resolved, or if adverse information on your credit report is the result of a dispute with a creditor or other unusual circumstances, you can put a 100-word statement in your credit file explaining the situation. Before you write the statement, however, remember that it will be read by potential lenders and maybe by potential employers. You may not want a potential lender to know that you were fired from a job, for example, or a possible employer to know that you were seriously ill for six months last year.

People who have been recently divorced need to be especially aware of what is in their credit reports because a divorce decree does not automatically sever your joint accounts. After reaching an agreement with your ex-spouse, you need to notify creditors about who is responsible for each account, and they will notify the credit bureaus.

You should always ask that closed or inactive accounts be removed from your file, even if they show no balance due. Potential lenders may consider available credit as money spent and turn down an application. If you do request changes in your credit report, you should check after a few months to make sure the information has been corrected. Any changes should automatically be reported to any business that received a copy of your credit report in the previous six months.

You can help ensure the accuracy of your credit report by being consistent with your name when you apply for credit. Although your Social Security number and your address are also used as identifiers, it is easier if you are always known as Jonathan Q. Public, rather than J. Q. Public, Jon Public, Jonathan Public, and J. Quincy Public. If you have a common name, it is always better to include a middle name or middle initial.

While all three major credit reporting agencies collect similar information, their files may not be identical. Ask for reports from all three. Equifax has a toll-free telephone number (800-685-1111) to request a copy of your report. You can find a local number for Trans Union in your telephone book or write to Trans Union National Consumer Disclosure Center, P.O. Box 390, Springfield, PA 19064-0390. Experian has a toll-free number (800-682-7654) for information on where to write, depending on whether you are asking for a free report, an additional report the same year, or a report after you have been denied credit.

If you are writing, be sure to provide your name, address, date of birth, Social Security number, and any additional identifying information, such as other recent addresses, that could be helpful. Do not forget to add Jr. or III or a middle initial if that is the way you are listed on your accounts.

If you are applying for a mortgage or other large loan, you can ask your lender which credit reporting agency it uses and ask for that report first. Local credit reporting agencies can usually be found in the Yellow Pages of your telephone book. The nationwide agencies recently automated their complaint-resolution system so that when a lender corrects inaccurate information in the files at one agency, it will be corrected at the others. But it still pays to check with all three because some lenders are not part of the automated system.

CREDIT COUNSELING AND BANKRUPTCY

It can happen to anyone, sometimes because of lost income or unusual medical expenses, and sometimes as a result of simple overspending. At some point in their lives, many people have trouble making ends meet. Indeed, financial planners tell tales of the potential client who owed $200,000 on 23 credit cards but wanted to plan his retirement, or the up-and-coming young executive earning $250,000 a year who was about to have his electricity cut off because he had not paid the bill.

If you are having trouble paying your bills, you owe it to yourself to get help. The best-known credit counseling organization is probably Consumer Credit Counseling Services (800-388-2227), a not-for-profit association with more than 1,000 offices around the country. For a small fee, or no fee at all, CCCS counselors can help you draw up a budget, negotiate an extended payment schedule with your creditors, or create a debt-management plan that stops collection efforts while you pay off as much as you can afford. More than a million consumers call CCCS for help each year. Some get help by phone or mail, and more than half go in for counseling.

DEVELOPING A PLAN

The first step usually is to look at income and spending and develop a budget. You will have to disclose the details of your financial situation. If you do need a debt-management plan, which generally requires concessions from creditors on fees, interest charges, or the amount owed, it will be noted on your credit report. You will make a single monthly payment to CCCS, which disburses payment to your creditors.

CCCS is largely funded by creditors, who are asked to return to the service 15% of the funds they collect from its clients. Counselors generally discourage bankruptcy filings wherever possible, although they may require you to cut up your credit cards.

Some local not-for-profit groups that are unaffiliated with CCCS may be more willing to consider a bankruptcy filing, or they may be more flexible about other issues. Some have a religious orientation, although they are not affiliated with a particular church. Like CCCS, they usually charge just a nominal fee and some services are free of charge.

These groups generally are regulated by the state banking department. Before signing on with anyone, you should check with state regulators and your local Better Business Bureau to make sure you are dealing with a reputable organization.

KEEP UP YOUR GUARD

Beware of so-called credit doctors, or credit-repair clinics, that charge big fees and promise to clean up your credit file. At best, they are doing only what you could do yourself for free. At worst, they can be outright fraudulent by creating fictitious files.

You also may be able to get free or low-cost help from social service agencies in your area, or from your employer's employee-assistance program. The U.S. Department of Agriculture's Cooperative Extension System has credit counseling services, which typically also receive some funding from states and counties. They may be located at your state university or at county offices.

The notation in your credit report that you have consulted one of these services is not all bad. By the time most people reach this point, they already have many negative entries in their files, and some creditors may like the fact that they are seeking help. In addition, collection agencies will stop calling, and you will not receive any tempting offers for more credit while you are getting back on your feet.

You can also call your creditors yourself. Especially if your financial difficulties are the result of illness or job loss, they may be surprisingly willing to reduce or postpone payments for a limited period. Most lenders would prefer getting less now and something later than getting nothing at all. But you should make these calls before your accounts are turned over to collection agencies, because once that happens lenders have less flexibility.

THE LAST RESORT

Filing for bankruptcy is not a step to be taken lightly. It will remain on your credit report for ten years, affecting your ability to get a mortgage, buy a car, and perhaps even rent an apartment or get a job. There is also the psychological effect of acknowledging that you cannot pay your bills.

Still, bankruptcy laws were designed to give people a chance to get a fresh start. Sometimes that is just what you need.

There are two different types of personal bankruptcy; they are known as Chapter 7 and Chapter 13, after the sections of the federal Bankruptcy Code that describe them. Under Chapter 7, you give up certain assets and ask the court to discharge your debts. Under Chapter 13, you set up a plan to repay your debts that must be approved by the court.

Whichever type you choose, a bankruptcy filing will stop the calls from bill collectors and halt creditor lawsuits and other efforts to get you to pay up, at least temporarily. If the bank is about to foreclose on your home or repossess your car, you will win some breathing room.

But there are certain obligations that even a bankruptcy filing will not eliminate. If you owe the Internal Revenue Service back taxes, for instance, in most cases you will still have to pay eventually. Child support and alimony payments must be kept current. Most student loans will have to be repaid. And if a friend or a relative has co-signed a loan, that person will be stuck with the payments unless you make arrangements to pay it off yourself.

KEEPING YOUR ASSETS

If you have regular income and could reasonably be expected to pay your debts over several years, Chapter 13 bankruptcy is a better choice. Indeed, a judge can dismiss a Chapter 7 filing if it is possible to meet most of your obligations through Chapter 13. Some creditors and future lenders may look more favorably on people who file under Chapter 13, and there is the benefit to your own psyche of knowing that you paid back what you owed. Under Chapter 13, you also can keep your assets, although you will have to use all income over and above basic living expenses to pay back debts. You have some control over how the debt is repaid because you develop the plan that is approved by the bankruptcy judge.

The maximum repayment period is five years. You will be required to list your debts in three classes: secured, unsecured, and taxes. You must repay your unsecured creditors at least as much as they would receive in a Chapter 7 bankruptcy.

In a Chapter 7 bankruptcy, you will have to turn over the full value of all your "nonexempt unencumbered assets" to a trustee, who will sell these assets to pay your debts. There are some variations by state, but usually you are allowed to keep your home and car up to a certain value, clothing and furniture, one television, tools you need for your business or trade, and some sporting equipment. If there are nonexempt assets you want to keep, you can give the trustee money instead, although few people filing under Chapter 7 are able to do that. Once the trustee has used what you have turned over to pay your debts, the remainder of what you owe is discharged, or erased, and you can start to reestablish your financial life. You cannot file under Chapter 7 again for six years.

A FEW LAWYERLY WORDS

Most people considering a bankruptcy filing consult with a lawyer, although it is possible to do it yourself with forms available at most federal courthouses and in a variety of self-help books. A lawyer can assist in the decision about which type of bankruptcy is better, suggest other options, or negotiate with your creditors. Sometimes a lawyer will use a possible bankruptcy filing as a tool to negotiate with creditors. Especially if you are considering a Chapter 7 filing, unsecured creditors may be willing to make concessions on interest charges, fees, and even the balance due in order to get a portion of what you owe rather than nothing.

If you do file for bankruptcy, do not be surprised if you start receiving credit card solicitations in the mail. Although many issuers shy away from people who have had credit problems, some think that bankruptcy makes you a better risk because you will not want to go through it again. If your spending habits got you in trouble once, however, be careful before you sign on the dotted line.

7

MANAGING THE REAL ESTATE BALANCING ACT

H ome ownership is often considered the cornerstone of the American dream. It is something that many people from middle- and upper-middle-class backgrounds have come to regard almost as a birthright, and something that many who are less well-off aspire to achieve. Some 63 million U.S. households own their own homes. Clearly, home ownership is a source of great pride to a great many people.

But buying a home is also a significant investment decision. That is true whether you are a first-time buyer, an experienced homeowner trading up to a larger place, or a retiree looking for a smaller, more manageable one. Americans have about $9.1 trillion invested in single-family homes, according to estimates by the Federal National Mortgage Association. Their equity, or the value of what they own outright after mortgage debt, amounts to about $5.4 trillion.

Viewed purely as a financial decision, buying a home almost seems to fly in the face of prudent financial management. Just think about it. Buying a home involves putting a substantial part of your net worth in a single asset. There is no diversification. Moreover, there are steep transaction costs and high maintenance expenses, and it can be next to impossible to get your money out in a hurry. Four out of five dollars paid to purchase this asset are usually borrowed.

It generally takes three decades to pay off the debt, and, at least in the early years, the payments can eat up nearly a third of a family's income.

THE DISCIPLINE OF MONTHLY PAYMENTS

But buying your own home has generally turned out to be a smart move in the long run—sheltering hard-earned dollars from the tax collector, providing a hedge against the ravages of inflation, building wealth, and providing security in retirement. Few things can rival the savings discipline of making mortgage payments month after month. Over time, the growing equity creates a nest egg that can be tapped for income in retirement or provide a handsome legacy for heirs.

The government puts some icing on the cake by making the interest payments tax-deductible. In effect, you have a government subsidy that enables you to pay off your mortgage in pretax dollars. The tax savings means that if the interest rate on a 30-year mortgage is 8%, the effective borrowing cost is just over 5.75% for someone in the 28% federal tax bracket—and less than 5% for those fortunate few whose high incomes put them in the 39.6% bracket. When you take state and local income taxes into account, the after-tax borrowing costs are even lower.

AN ENORMOUS INVESTMENT

The equity Americans have in their homes exceeds the value of their investments in stocks, bonds, mutual funds, or bank deposits.

Home Equity	$5.4 trillion
Stocks	$4.1 trillion
Bonds	$2.0 trillion
Mutual Fund Shares	$1.2 trillion
Bank Deposits and Money Market Funds	$3.5 trillion

NOTE: 1995 data.
SOURCES: Federal National Mortgage Association, DRI/McGraw-Hill.

Then there is the important matter of home prices, which have typically marched steadily higher through the years. During the past 150 years, owning one's home has produced a "real," or after-inflation, return of about 2.5% a year. In some periods, investments in property have returned much more. In the heat of the 1980s real estate boom, for instance, home prices in the explosive New York market doubled every three years. Even during the collapse of the commercial real estate market starting in the late 1980s, average U.S. home prices continued to advance about in line with inflation.

The fact that so much of the money used in buying a home is usually borrowed adds to the potential profit. It works like this: Typically, home buyers come up with about 20% of the purchase price as an initial down payment and take out a mortgage for the rest. That means that on a $100,000 home, the homeowner's out-of-pocket investment is $20,000. Now, assume that the market value of the home rises to $120,000 over five years. At that point, the homeowner could sell, pay off the mortgage, and have enough left over to cover the original down payment plus an additional $20,000. Through the magic of leverage, a 20% price gain becomes a 100% profit. (This leaves aside transaction costs and the principal paid down on the mortgage, but you get the idea.)

LOOK AT THE DOWNSIDE, TOO

All of this does, indeed, make a pretty compelling case for home ownership. But do not rush out to buy that dream house just yet. The decision to buy a home should not be made lightly. As millions of home buyers learned to their dismay in the late 1980s and early 1990s, it can be a money-losing proposition. Even while national home-price averages held up well, the median home price in ritzy Beverly Hills, California, fell nearly 30% between July 1990 and December 1993, before turning up slightly. Nearby Woodland Hills was even harder hit, with prices down more than 40% between 1990 and 1995, according to Case Shiller Weiss, a Cambridge, Massachusetts, consulting firm. Home prices in some Boston suburbs plunged about 35% in a five-year period.

When prices fall, the magic of leverage can become a nightmare. If a home's price were to fall 20% over five years, for instance, the owner's initial stake would be wiped out. If prices fell more than that, the owner could owe more than the house was worth. Owning a home can also be a constant drain on a family's financial resources. In adding up the costs, you have to include insurance, property taxes, maintenance, and repairs, in addition to monthly mortgage payments.

With so much at stake, it is essential that you do some research before buying a home. Indeed, you may find that it makes more sense to rent, depending on your financial resources, where you live, and how long you expect to be there.

If you are going to buy, begin with a cool-headed assessment of just how much you can afford. As a rule of thumb, most lenders limit monthly payments—including interest, principal, real estate taxes, and insurance—to 28% of monthly income before taxes. Using those guidelines, and assuming a 20% down payment and 30-year mortgage rates of about 8%, every $25,000 of annual income could support about $90,000 of home. Individual circumstances vary a great deal, however. Some people may be able to handle more; others should make do with less.

Select the area in which you are buying carefully. Consider the economic trends: You want a growing job market, with wages increasing as fast or faster than home prices. The pace of local home construction should not be excessive. Good local schools also shore up home values over time. Then narrow your search to a few neighborhoods or communities and start looking. Especially if you are a first-time buyer, try not to fall in love with any property. Sure, buying a home is an emotional experience. But it is also an enormous financial commitment, and the decision to buy should be based on a careful investment analysis. Keep that in mind, and the home you purchase will indeed be a source of pride and a comfortable place where you and your family can prosper.

REAL ESTATE DECISIONS THROUGH THE AGES

When you are young, scraping together that big pile of cash needed for the down payment is often the hardest part of becoming a homeowner. But it is far from the only issue first-time buyers must face—beginning with whether it might actually make more sense to rent. Even for seasoned homeowners, real estate decisions involve a number of difficult issues.

The following sections examine some of the most important considerations for people in their 20s and 30s, 40s and 50s, and 60s and beyond. Whatever your age, keep in mind that buying a home is the biggest investment decision most people ever make—and that once they have taken the plunge, their homes are their most valuable asset. You owe it to yourself and your family to make real estate decisions with special care.

Your 20s and 30s

While home ownership is a big part of the American dream, the costs can be an impossible burden when you are just starting out and even after you are well under way. That is even truer today than it was a generation ago, because home prices have outstripped salary increases over the past couple of decades. The average monthly payment on a mortgage now accounts for nearly a third of a homeowner's after-tax income, compared with less than a quarter of it in 1976. As affordability has slipped, the average age of first-time home buyers has edged up—to 32.1 in 1995 from 28 in 1976.

The only answer for many people is to rent. But even if you do have a choice, renting can be a better option than buying if you are not yet established in a career or do not know how long you will be in the same location. You will save yourself the struggle of coming up with that big down payment, and you will not have to worry about paying real estate taxes, repairing a leaky roof or a faulty boiler, and such mundane things as snow removal and garbage disposal. You also will not have to worry about the ups and downs of real estate values. Homeowners who bought in the late 1980s, when prices in some areas were jumping 25% a year or more, found to their dismay that prices can fall sharply, too. That is especially important to keep in mind if you are unsettled in your job, or if your work is apt to involve frequent transfers. If you buy and then relocate after a couple of years, you may not be able to recoup your costs.

AN ASSET YOU KNOW YOU WILL USE

Still, home ownership exerts a powerful pull on many people. More than half the renters questioned in a survey for the Federal National Mortgage Association said that buying a home is a very important personal priority. While buying a home used to be part of a package that included marriage and plans to start a family, other surveys show that nearly a third of the homes sold in some cities these days are bought by singles. Many people want to buy as soon as they can scrape together the down payment. And as long as prices at least remain stable, owning a home can be a good deal. At least a home is an asset you know you will use.

First-time home buyers are faced with a multitude of decisions, such as where to buy, how big a house they need, and how much to borrow. Before you even start looking, you need a firm idea of what you can afford. Typically, banks require that interest and principal payments on your mortgage, property taxes, and insurance payments together amount to no more than 28% of your income.

When you start your search, check out recent sales in the area. It does not make sense to overpay the market, no matter how much you love a house. Make sure the house is inspected for environmental hazards, such as radon and asbestos, as well as for the standard structural defects, so you are not hit with huge bills for repairs and removal of toxins.

FIRST-TIME BUYERS ARE GETTING OLDER	
YEAR	AGE OF FIRST-TIME HOME BUYERS
1986	30.9
1987	29.6
1988	30.3
1989	29.6
1990	30.5
1991	30.7
1992	31.0
1993	31.6
1994	31.6
1995	32.1

SOURCE: Chicago Title and Trust Survey of Recent Home Buyers.

A RANGE OF MORTGAGE CHOICES

Financing your purchase requires sifting through a sometimes bewildering range of choices: 15-year, 20-year, and 30-year mortgages; fixed rates and adjustable rates. Initial interest rates usually are significantly lower on ARMs, as adjustable-rate mortgages are known, than on fixed-rate loans, to compensate the borrower for assuming some of the risk that interest rates will rise.

Financial advisers generally recommend a 30-year loan for younger home buyers because the monthly payments are lower. Although many people prefer the security of a fixed rate, ARMs can offer real cash-flow benefits with little risk for people who expect to move within a few years. Rate increases generally are capped at two percentage points a year and six percentage points over the life of the loan. The adjustments may be as frequent as every six months

20s–30s

- Weigh buying versus renting.

- Figure out what you can afford.

- Check recent sales in the area.

- Compare mortgage terms.

- See if Mom and Dad can help.

or not at all for the first seven years. Introductory rates typically are lowest on loans that adjust most frequently. (You can find more information on mortgages later in this chapter and in Chapter 6.)

If you cannot handle the whole thing yourself, Mom and Dad may be able to help. It can be in the form of a loan for the down payment, which is fairly straightforward, or a split-purchase arrangement, in which the parents wind up with an equity interest in the house and receive rent in proportion to their share. In either case, it is a good idea to consult a lawyer. Even a simple loan can have adverse tax consequences if interest is not charged at market rates.

Your 40s and 50s

Decisions about real estate become more complicated by the time you reach your 40s and 50s. Many people have outgrown their first, or even their second, homes by then. With more income than they had 10 or 20 years ago, and with significant equity in their existing homes, they can choose between trading up to something bigger and better or renovating and, perhaps, adding on to what they have. This is also the time when many people start thinking seriously about retirement. They may be considering a vacation home, perhaps a place to which they can eventually retire.

But having more opportunities also means there are more potential pitfalls. Do not let emotion overwhelm financial considerations. There may be steep transaction costs involved in selling your home, for instance. You will probably have to pay a real estate broker at least 6% of the sale price. There also may be origination fees on a new mortgage, lawyers' fees, deed-recording fees, and assorted other charges.

HOME IMPROVEMENTS

It may cost less to improve your current home and stay there. Keep in mind, however, that on average, homeowners recover only about 40% of the cost of renovations when they eventually sell. Real estate professionals say that such improvements as a new kitchen or new bathrooms typically add the most value in relation to their cost, while luxuries, such as an in-ground swimming pool, are the least cost-effective.

If you do renovate, keep receipts and other documentation. The cost of capital improvements to a home increases its tax basis and can reduce your capital-gains tax if you sell later. If you borrow to finance your home improvements, the interest is fully deductible for tax purposes, up to a combined total of all mortgage and home-improvement debt of $1.1 million, including home-equity debt.

There are other tax considerations. If you sell your home for a profit, you can delay paying any capital-gains taxes indefinitely, as long as you buy a replacement home within two years (before or after the sale) that is at least as expensive. If you buy a cheaper home and fix it up, those improvement costs count toward the purchase price for tax purposes, as long as you pay them by the two-year deadline.

A second home offers some of the same tax benefits as a primary residence, as long as you do not rent it out for more than 14 days a year. Mortgage interest and property taxes are usually fully deductible, although you cannot defer capital-gains taxes if you sell your vacation home for a profit. You can rent your vacation home out for up to two weeks a year and not pay any taxes at all on the income. But the tax consequences can become complicated if you decide to rent it for longer periods.

As for negatives, a vacation home is generally a riskier investment than a primary residence, since the vacation-home market is very sensitive to economic swings, and it can be even harder to get your money out in a hurry. Location and rental potential are important factors to consider. Maintenance and repairs can be expensive and a real headache to arrange from a distance. If you buy a vacation home with plans to rent it out when you are not there, you will have the additional headache of finding suitable tenants.

INVESTMENT REAL ESTATE

If you are interested in real estate as an investment, you might consider real estate investment trusts, or REITs, which are publicly traded and hold groups of properties. For most investors, though, REITs should not constitute more than 5% or 10% of a portfolio. Avoid real estate limited partnerships, which have generally proved

40s–50s

- Study costs and benefits of trading up.

- Delay capital-gains taxes on sale.

- Make capital improvements count.

- Get facts on vacation homes.

- Go easy on investment real estate.

to be awful investments—partly because returns have been poor or nonexistent and partly because it is next to impossible to get out of a limited partnership early if you decide you could find a better use for the money.

Indeed, if you own your home, you should not be concerned if you do not own any investment real estate. Considering both the need for diversification and liquidity in a portfolio, a home is probably all the real estate most people need. (Chapter 2 is filled with good ideas about building a solid investment portfolio.)

YOUR 60S AND BEYOND

By the time people are in their 60s, the mortgage is often paid off, and they have accumulated a significant amount of equity in their homes. The question is how and when to reap the benefits. The most direct way to cash out is to sell the property and trade down to a smaller place. That is a very hard thing for many older homeowners even to contemplate, because they have so much of themselves invested in their homes. But it may be the only practical solution. While there are mortgage products that enable homeowners to tap their equity for income, there can be hidden pitfalls.

Sentiment aside, selling your home and moving into a smaller place has much to be said for it. To begin with, buying a less expensive home, or maybe renting, frees up cash that you can put into income-producing investments and tap for living expenses. You also have the opportunity to move into a place that is more suitable for your current lifestyle—a home that requires less maintenance, for instance, or is arranged more conveniently, or is located in an area with a more congenial climate.

A TERRIFIC TAX BREAK

For homeowners age 55 or older who take this course, the tax collector can be unusually generous: You are exempt from paying taxes on the first $125,000 in capital gains on the sale of your home. But this tax holiday is a once-in-a-lifetime benefit. If two people own homes when they marry, which happens frequently with elderly widows and widowers, they can use the exclusion only once. Indeed, some financial professionals advise couples to sell both homes before they tie the knot so they can each use the benefit, sheltering a total of $250,000 from taxes.

If you do not move, you can still tap the equity in your home. One method is to take out a home-equity loan. This type of financing, which is secured by the equity in your home, comes in two basic flavors: loans and credit lines. The loans are a lot like normal mortgages, typically with fixed interest rates and regular monthly payments on interest and principal. The credit lines are revolving credit arrangements that charge interest only on amounts drawn, making them more like credit card debt; interest on credit lines usually is variable, meaning that payments can rise sharply if rates go up.

The interest you pay on home-equity loans is tax-deductible on up to $100,000 of borrowings, no matter how you spend the money. But if you do draw on your equity this way, you have to pay it back in monthly installments. As a result, a home-equity loan is probably of no use if what you really need is money to meet daily expenses.

A second alternative is a "reverse mortgage," which is just what its name implies. Instead of your sending the bank a fixed amount each month, the bank sends you a monthly check. You also can get a lump sum or a line of credit to draw on as needed. The amount is based on your age, the value of your home, and an interest rate that is embedded in the monthly payments. The loan usually is repaid by selling the house when you move or die. Because the payments you receive are usually based on life expectancy, the older you are, the more you get.

BEWARE OF THE RISKS

There are some very important caveats to embarking on a reverse mortgage. First, unless you can repay the reverse mortgage some way other than by the sale of your home, you will not have a house to leave to your heirs. Second, reverse mortgages are not cheap. Third, it can require some complicated arithmetic to make sure you are getting a decent deal, although lenders are now required to disclose how much you will actually get and the total annual cost of the mortgages they offer.

There are a number of different reverse mortgages available, so it is smart to consult with several lenders. Most homeowners should stick with "home-equity conversion" mortgages sponsored by the Federal Housing Administration or the mortgages backed by a new program from the Federal National Mortgage Association. The terms they offer are generally among the best available.

These loans can be a last resort for cash-strapped people who want to remain where they have lived for years and do not qualify for more conventional home-equity debt. Just knowing that such loans are available may keep you from worrying about whether you will outlive your money.

If you want the family homestead to pass to your heirs when you die, remember that your home could easily push the value of your estate over the limit for avoiding estate taxes. That makes it essential to get knowledgeable legal guidance on your options, including "qualified personal residence trusts." These trusts typically are set up so you keep the home for a specified period of time, but ownership eventually passes to your children or other beneficiaries. (You can find more information on qualified personal residence trusts and other aspects of estate planning in Chapter 5.)

60s +

- Think about trading down.

- Remember capital-gains exclusion for those over 55.

- Consider home-equity loans.

- Use care on reverse mortgages.

- Include home in estate planning.

THAT SPECIAL PLACE CALLED HOME

Whether it is a simple apartment or a fancy penthouse, a comfortable bungalow or a lavish estate, the place we call home is truly special. It provides shelter and warmth, comfort from the calamities of daily life, a private space in which to be ourselves and bring up our children, and often much, much more. For many of us, owning that home is one of our most important goals. Achieving that goal depends importantly on the financial planning lessons in earlier chapters, especially on our success in taking control of our spending and establishing a disciplined program of savings and investment.

Now it is time to examine some of the basics of real estate more closely. The following sections can help you decide just how much you can afford to pay when you are buying a home, minimize the hassle of finding the home you want, and figure out how to finance that home with a competitively priced mortgage. There are also tips on three subjects of great importance to many homeowners: home renovations, property taxes, and selling your home when you are ready to move on.

HOW MUCH CAN YOU REALLY AFFORD?

There are three questions to consider once you have made the decision to buy a home: what you want, what you need, and how much you can afford—and not necessarily in that order. Indeed, you should have at least a rough idea of what you can afford before you start shopping. It will help determine what kind of home you look for and the communities and neighborhoods in which you concentrate your search.

You can start with the rule of thumb that many lenders use: Mortgage payments, property tax, and insurance should not exceed 28% of your pretax income. Nonmortgage debt—such as outstanding student loans, car loans, and credit cards—is a factor, too. Most lenders do not want payments on all your debt, including the mortgage, to total more than 36% of your income. But individual circumstances can vary enormously; your own cash flow—what comes in, what goes out, and what is left over—is usually much more important. Spending more than a quarter of your monthly income on housing may be more than some people can handle comfortably.

THINK AFTER-TAX COST

The tax savings of home ownership will help. At the outset, because of the way mortgages are structured, most of your payment will be interest on the loan and, thus, tax-deductible, meaning that you can afford to pay more per month than you do in rent. If your monthly payment is $1,000, for instance, and you are in the 28% tax bracket, your after-tax cost will be a little more than $720 at the start. The tax deduction will shrink over time as the proportion of principal in the monthly payment rises. If your income increases over the same period, as is often the case for first-time home buyers, you should be able to handle the higher after-tax cost.

One way to figure out how much you can afford in mortgage payments is to take your current monthly rent and add the anticipated tax savings. Then, factor in other routine costs of home ownership, such as maintenance expenses and higher utility bills. When you know how much you can pay each month, your real estate agent or a potential lender can tell you how big a mortgage you can get at prevailing interest rates. If you know what interest rates are, you can calculate your monthly payments yourself by consulting financial tables in reference books available at most libraries. The lower the interest rate and the longer the term of the loan, the smaller the payment will be.

Since you are usually limited in how much you can borrow, you can afford more home if you can come up with a larger down payment. If you can put down as much as 20% of the purchase price, you will probably not have to buy private mortgage insurance. This insurance, which protects the lender in case you fail to make the payments you owe, tends to be costly. And the smaller the down payment, the higher the price you pay for mortgage insurance. Making a large down payment may also enable you to qualify for a lower interest rate on your mortgage.

Still, you should not use everything you have saved for this big purchase on the down payment. There usually are loan origination fees, or "points," to pay, as well as lawyers' fees and other costs of "closing" the transaction. You will probably need some new furniture, and repairs may be necessary before you can move into your new home. Cash for these expenses usually comes out of savings.

DOES IT MAKE SENSE TO STRETCH?

How much you stretch financially to buy a home depends on your individual circumstances and your tolerance for risk. If you are reasonably certain that your job is secure and that your income will increase over time, you might consider borrowing a little more than you really feel comfortable with now so that you will not have to move again in a couple of years. If your future income is less assured, or if you are approaching retirement, it would probably be smart to be more conservative.

QUALIFYING FOR A MORTGAGE

Estimate the purchase price of the home you would like to buy and the down payment you can afford. Fill in the blanks based on these assumptions and your personal financial situation; use the accompanying table to estimate your monthly payment. If your monthly housing cost does not exceed 28% of your pretax income and your total monthly costs do not exceed what is allowable, you will probably qualify for a mortgage.

1. MONTHLY GROSS INCOME

Total gross annual income of borrower and co-borrower $ _____
Divide total gross annual income by 12 _____ ÷ 12

Total Monthly Gross Income = $ _____

2. ALLOWABLE MONTHLY HOUSING COST

Total monthly gross income $ _____
Multiply by 28% _____ × 0.28

Allowable monthly housing cost = $ _____

3. MORTGAGE AMOUNT

Home purchase price $ _____
Down payment − $ _____

Mortgage loan amount $ _____

4. MONTHLY TAXES AND INSURANCE

Home purchase price $ _____
Multiply by 0.0025 (local requirements vary) _____ × 0.0025

Estimated monthly taxes and insurance $ _____

5. MONTHLY HOUSING COST

Monthly payment on 30-year loan (use accompanying chart) $ _____
Estimated monthly taxes and insurance + _____
Condo or homeowner's fee (if applicable) + _____

Total monthly housing cost $ _____

6. ALLOWABLE MONTHLY DEBT

Total monthly gross income $ _____
Multiply by 36% _____ × 0.36

Allowable total monthly debt payments $ _____

7. MONTHLY DEBT PAYMENTS OTHER THAN HOUSING

Car payment $ _____
Credit card(s) payments + _____
Student loan + _____
Other + _____

Total other monthly debt payments $ _____

8. TOTAL MONTHLY COSTS

Total monthly housing cost $ _____
Total other monthly debt + _____
Total Monthly Costs $ _____

FIGURING YOUR MONTHLY PAYMENT

Following are monthly principal and interest payments (in dollars) per $1,000 borrowed, according to length of loan.

INTEREST RATE	15 YEARS	20 YEARS	30 YEARS
6%	8.44	7.17	6.00
6.5%	8.72	7.46	6.33
7%	8.99	7.75	6.65
7.5%	9.27	8.06	6.99
8%	9.56	8.37	7.34
8.5%	9.85	8.68	7.69
9%	10.15	9.00	8.05
9.5%	10.45	9.33	8.41
10%	10.75	9.66	8.78

Reconsider your decision to buy if all you can afford is a home that you are going to outgrow in two or three years. It probably will not appreciate enough in such a short period to cover real estate commissions and other costs of selling, and you may find that you have lost money on your investment.

In fact, whatever your conclusion about how much you can afford to pay to buy a home, it is a good idea to take a little time to consider whether you might actually be better off renting. At the very least, running through the rent-versus-buy equation will help you to take a cool, analytical look at the costs involved in home ownership.

BUYING VERSUS RENTING: THE FINANCIAL EQUATION

Sure, owning a home is part of the American dream. But buying into that dream could prevent you from taking advantage of other, more attractive investment opportunities. And with all the extra headaches of maintenance, repairs, taxes, and a big mortgage, might you be better off renting instead? Take a little time to give yourself a reality check. The following analysis, based on calculations that real estate professionals use, can help you decide whether buying or renting is the way to go. Your own numbers will be different, but you will see how to do the math.

1. Start with a little comparison shopping.

Gauge how monthly rents relate to home prices in your area. These numbers vary widely; information gathered from relocation specialists and local real estate agencies can help. In the San Francisco area, for instance, a 2,000-square-foot, eight-room home cost about $380,000 in mid-1995, according to Runzheimer International, a management-consulting firm in Rochester, Wisconsin, that specializes in living costs. Annual rent for a similar home would have been $30,384. In the New York City area, the price tag was $261,245, with rent of $30,624 a year.

2. Total the cost of renting.

Multiply the annual rent by the number of years you would expect to stay in that home. If you rented for seven years, which is how often many in the mortgage business figure Americans move, the tab in New York would be $214,368.

Now deduct the amount of investment income you could expect to make from not using your nest egg as a down payment on a house. Be sure to adjust for what you would pay in taxes on that income. For the New York family, a 20% down payment on a $261,245 home would mean forking over $52,250 that otherwise could be generating interest. Assuming seven-year U.S. Treasury yields of about 6.5%, that would amount to an "opportunity cost" of some $28,950 in forgone compound interest over seven years—or about $19,700 if you paid federal income tax on each year's interest at a tax rate of 28%. (Treasury interest is exempt from state and local taxes.)

The bottom line is that the seven-year cost of renting the New York home would be roughly $194,650. The same calculation for the comparable San Francisco home, including interest on $76,000 of potential down payment, produces a total rent cost of $184,000.

3. Total the cost of buying.

Start by adding up all the tax-deductible costs, such as property taxes and interest on a mortgage for 80% of the purchase price. To figure the mortgage interest, you can ask any bank or consult reference books available at most libraries. You should be able to get at least a rough estimate of the property taxes from the local assessor's office.

Then figure what the total amounts to after tax. A difference in either the mortgage rate or property tax can substantially alter the calculations, so you may want to do the math more than once if you are looking at several homes. Property taxes, especially, can vary enormously from place to place, even in the same general area.

Assuming a 30-year mortgage rate of 8%, two points of interest up front, and property taxes of $8,000 a year, for example, the New York home buyer would pay more than $173,000 in interest and taxes over seven years—or $114,000 after tax at a 34% rate, including federal and state levies.

Add to that your estimates of what you would pay in homeowner's insurance, upkeep, and repairs. Include other expenses, such as heat or air conditioning, that would be paid by a landlord if you were renting. These numbers can vary widely depending on such factors as the age and condition of the home, the climate and cost of living in your area, and your lifestyle. Ask the seller or real estate agent for data and do a little research on your own.

Keeping the variables in mind, many financial experts say that it is reasonable to estimate that for most people these costs will average out to between 1% and 2% of the value of the home each year. Assuming the high end of that estimate, the total figure in the New York example comes to nearly $37,000 over seven years.

Adding up the two sums produces an estimated out-of-pocket cost of about $151,000 over seven years. Comparing this with the total cost of renting shows that in New York, buyers are ahead of renters to the tune of $43,650 after seven years—even assuming no appreciation in the value of the home. That is not a bad return on their $52,500 down payment.

By contrast, the same reckoning shows that the San Francisco home buyer would pay a total of roughly $203,000 over seven years for the privilege of owning—about $19,000 more than the total cost of renting. Owning looks like a losing proposition compared with renting, unless prices rise enough by the time the home is sold to make up the difference.

4. What about capital appreciation?

Calculate the price you would have to receive when selling the house to recover your extra costs, including paying 6% of the sale price to a real estate broker. To be conservative, you should also require that you end up with a decent return on investment. Some pros figure that you should reap an average return of 9% a year: four percentage points to compensate for your investment risk, three percentage points because the market is "illiquid," or difficult to trade in, and two percentage points for the time and hassle of managing your property. You might be willing to accept less, however.

In these examples, buying does not clear the 9% hurdle in New York unless the property increases in value. If the market did not budge for the whole time the house was owned, the buyers would be about $27,650 ahead, after paying a $16,000 broker's fee. (For simplicity, this assumes no other transaction costs.) That is equal to a compound return of nearly 6.25% a year on the $52,500 down payment.

In San Francisco, the case for buying is much more dependent on a rising market. Just to break even with renting for seven years, a family who bought a home would have to sell for almost $425,000, or $45,000 more than was paid. To recoup costs and also achieve a 9% annual return on the $76,000 down payment, they would have to sell the home for more than $490,000. They may decide that is a good bet, but at least they will go into it with their eyes open.

SHOPPING FOR A HOME

When you have figured out how much you can afford, the next step is deciding where you want to live. You will save many hours of valuable time by limiting your search to just a few neighborhoods or communities. It will be easier to find out about such things as property values, real estate taxes, and schools, for instance, and you will be a better negotiator if you have more information.

Think about your priorities. Besides the number of bedrooms and bathrooms, how important is it to be close to work, schools, or shopping? Do you want to have access to public transportation or recreational facilities? Make a list of what you want and what you need, and remember that there is a difference.

Although it is possible to find a home by reading newspaper advertisements and looking for For Sale signs, most buyers use real estate agents. Agents usually offer a larger selection, and now that listings are often computerized, they can match your wants and needs with available homes right in the office.

A BUILT-IN BIAS

Most real estate agents are engaged by the person selling a home and paid by commission, based on a percentage of the sale price. Everything else being equal, their first loyalty will be to the seller. This is not necessarily a problem if you are dealing with a thoroughly professional agent, but it is something you ought to keep in mind as your home search continues. It is possible to hire a "buyer's agent" to help you find the home you want at the lowest possible price. Although you will have to pay a negotiated fee, you could save time, money, and hassles in the end.

No matter how much you love a home, most people's wants and needs change over the years, so it is important to think about resale potential. The neighborhood is especially important because property values tend to rise and fall in tandem. Indeed, real estate professionals say it is usually better to buy the least expensive house in a good neighborhood than the most expensive home in a poor neighborhood. Even if you do not have children and do not plan to have any, good schools make it easier to attract buyers and you will probably get a better price. A swimming pool, on the other hand, may be a detriment, especially if it is the only one in the neighborhood. Maintenance can be costly and time-consuming and safety is an issue if there are young children around.

To make sure that you are not overpaying, find out what similar homes in the area sold for recently. Your real estate agent may have the information, or you can check documents on file in the county courthouse or city hall. If you are looking at condominiums and town houses, it is a good idea to visit at different times of day and talk with neighbors. You may learn all sorts of things about how the property is maintained and about noise levels.

CHECK THE FINE PRINT

If you are buying a condo, find out about the condominium association's rules and regulations. Perhaps you want to be able to rent out your apartment; or maybe you do not like the idea that the apartment next door might be owned by a company and used to house a continuing stream of visiting out-of-towners. Also review the condominium's financial statements to make sure there is cash available to pay for needed repairs. Otherwise, you could be stuck with a large special assessment to fix a leaky roof.

Once you have found a home you like, have a lawyer review the purchase agreement before you sign to make sure it is valid. Any agreement should be contingent on inspections for structural defects and environmental hazards, such as asbestos or radon. Finding problems does not have to preclude a purchase, as long as they can be remedied and you can negotiate a lower price to cover the costs.

FINDING A MORTGAGE

A home mortgage is the single biggest expense that most people face in their entire lives. Consider, for example, a $250,000 home purchased with a 30-year $200,000 mortgage at 8% interest. Over the life of the mortgage, the interest payments will total more than $328,000!

Because a mortgage is such a large and long-term transaction, even a minor improvement in the interest rate or other terms can make a meaningful difference in a family's budget. It is not unusual for a person to save tens of thousands of dollars by shopping actively for a mortgage and comparing the terms of various mortgages available.

But finding the best deal can take some real work. Sometimes it seems like there are more mortgages to choose from than there are houses. For example, you can select from fixed or adjustable rates. You may be offered loans that run 15, 20, or 30 years. If the rate is variable, it may adjust every six months, once a year, or after three, five, seven, or even ten years.

Still, mortgage shopping need not be intimidating. Though the details occasionally become complicated, the basic principles are simple. Start by gathering many competing quotes. Financial planners often recommend obtaining mortgage information from at least five potential lenders, with 10 to 20 being preferable.

How do you go about finding lenders to give you quotes? Several types of organizations make mortgage loans. They include savings and loan associations, mutual savings banks, commercial banks, some credit unions, and mortgage bankers. There are also mortgage brokers, which do not make the loans themselves but arrange them. Your real estate agent may know a few lenders in the area. Comparative information on mortgage rates and terms is available for a fairly low price from mortgage search services such as HSH Associates of Butler, New Jersey, and Gary S. Meyers & Associates in Chicago. Finally, do not overlook your telephone book. Look under mortgages in the Yellow Pages to find the names of lenders in addition to those you learn about from a real estate agent or a search service.

From each potential lender, seek information on interest rates, points, and lock-in provisions (more on these in a minute). Try to standardize the quotes as much as you can, getting information from each lender on a 20-year fixed-rate mortgage, for example, or a 15-year adjustable one. To winnow down your choices, select a few mortgages that have relatively low interest rates, then make your final decision based on an evaluation that includes points and lock-in provisions as well as the interest rate.

HOW LONG A LOAN?

One key decision you need to make is how long the term of the loan should be. The most common terms are 30, 15, and 20 years, though other terms can also be arranged by agreement between the lender and the borrower. The longer the loan, the lower your monthly payments—but the higher the amount of interest you pay over the years.

People with more disposable income at the start might do well to consider a 15-year mortgage. In return for higher monthly payments, the home is paid off in half the time. That makes 15-year loans a good choice for people nearing retirement. The interest rate usually is slightly lower than the 30-year rate, because it is less risky for the lender to lend for 15 years than for 30. On a $150,000 mort-

CHOOSING THE RIGHT MORTGAGE

How much you would pay per month varies with the type of mortgage, the amount financed, and the interest rate.

	MONTHLY PAYMENT (IN DOLLARS)		
LOAN AMOUNT ($)	1-YEAR ARM (5.39%)	15-YEAR FIXED RATE (6.80%)	30-YEAR FIXED RATE (7.29%)
50,000	280	444	342
100,000	561	888	685
150,000	841	1,332	1,027
200,000	1,122	1,775	1,370

NOTE: Based on average mortgage rates in early 1996; ARM rate is for first year only.
SOURCE: HSH Associates.

gage, for instance, homeowners would pay $1,101 a month on a 30-year mortgage at 8%. Assuming they could get 7.75% on a 15-year loan, the monthly payment would be $1,412. But with the 15-year mortgage, they would save about $142,000 in interest over the life of the loan.

Check a book of mortgage tables (which you can find in many libraries or at your local bank) to determine the shortest loan term you think you can comfortably handle.

Some lenders offer the option of biweekly payments for people who want to pay off their mortgages faster. The biweekly payments are half what a monthly payment would be, but they add up to the equivalent of one extra monthly payment a year, so equity builds up more quickly. The mortgage often can be paid off in 18 to 20 years, at a considerable savings of interest.

FIXED OR ADJUSTABLE?

One of the most important choices in selecting a mortgage is whether to go with a fixed rate or an adjustable one. Home buyers have to weigh the amount of risk they are willing to tolerate, where they are in their lives and careers, and how long before they plan to move.

Fixed-rate mortgages are generally considered a good choice for people who plan to remain in a home for the long term. They know what their payments will be and can therefore budget better for other expenses, such as children's education or a regular investment program. The 30-year fixed-rate mortgage is the stalwart of the industry, probably the kind your parents and maybe even your grandparents had. The payments are predictable, and equity builds up steadily. As time goes on, the payments typically become a smaller percentage of your income.

Adjustable-rate mortgages generally offer lower initial rates than fixed-rate loans. But the rate and the monthly payment move up and down, in tandem with an index (often tied to short-term interest rates). ARMs are particularly popular among young people who expect their incomes to grow enough to cover potential increases in monthly payments and among those who do not expect to remain in the same home more than a few years.

At the same time, ARMs can be risky. The monthly payment on

a 30-year $150,000 mortgage, for instance, would jump to $1,261 from $1,049 if the interest rate went to 9.5% from 7.5%. If rates marched all the way up to 12% (and they went higher than that in the 1970s), the monthly payment would be $1,543.

Your protection against backbreaking increases in your monthly mortgage payment comes from "caps." There are two kinds of caps. One limits how much your payments can rise each time the mortgage is recalculated. That is important, but even more crucial is the lifetime cap—the limit on how much the interest rate can rise over the entire life of the mortgage.

Many financial professionals say that for an ARM to be worth considering, the initial rate should be at least two percentage points lower than the fixed rate. Otherwise, you could find yourself paying more than the fixed rate by the end of the first adjustment period.

Typically, rates are lowest on ARMs that adjust every six months and only slightly lower than fixed rates on loans that adjust after seven or ten years. But a longer-term ARM may be just the thing for people who want the security of a fixed rate and know they are going to move in a few years.

Terms vary on loans that adjust less frequently. Interest rates on three-year and five-year ARMs, for instance, may adjust once every three or five years, or after the first three or five years and annually thereafter. Rates on seven-year and ten-year ARMs usually vary annually after the first adjustment, although it is possible to get a loan that adjusts once after seven years but remains fixed thereafter. Some adjustable-rate mortgages are convertible into fixed-rate loans during a specific period, usually between the second and fifth year.

On six-month and one-year ARMs, the interest rate typically can rise or fall a total of two percentage points a year, and five or six percentage points over the life of the loan. Lenders in the East and Midwest tend to link rates to an index based on Treasury securities, often the one-year T-bill, while the monthly cost-of-funds index issued by the Federal Home Loan Bank of San Francisco is more common in western states. A specified amount, called the margin, is added to the index to determine the mortgage rate. It is usually 2.75 to 3 percentage points, although interest rates often are discounted in the first year.

Which type of mortgage should you take if you are in doubt? Probably a fixed-rate mortgage. One advantage to a fixed-rate mortgage is that it has a certain "heads-you-win, tails-you-do-not really-lose" aspect. If interest rates rise substantially, the fixed-rate mortgage holder is protected, but the adjustable-rate mortgage holder may squirm, or in the worst case, even lose the home. If interest rates fall, the adjustable-mortgage holder benefits automatically. But fixed-rate mortgage holders are not shut out in the cold; they can take advantage of falling interest rates by refinancing—that is, taking out a new loan and paying off the old one. Refinancing does involve paying a new set of closing costs. However, these are usually somewhat smaller than the closing costs associated with the initial purchase of a home. (For more information on refinancing, refer to Chapter 6.)

Points and Other Closing Costs

When you buy a home, you encounter a cluster of costs in addition to the price of the home itself and the interest on your home mortgage. These extra costs are called closing costs because they are incurred at or near the "closing," the meeting at which you formalize your purchase. Closing costs typically run about 7% of the price of a home but can range from as little as perhaps 3% to as much as about 10%.

The most important closing cost is referred to as "points." Points are an amount paid to the lender, at the time of closing, above and beyond the regular interest payments you will be forking over monthly for the next 15 to 30 years. Each point equals 1% of the mortgage face amount. For example, if you have a $150,000 mortgage with three points, you pay $4,500 in points at the time of closing.

In shopping for a mortgage, a common problem is deciding between two mortgages, one of which boasts a lower interest rate and the other of which is saddled with fewer points. As a simple rule of thumb, you can take the number of points, divide it by the number of years you plan to stay in the house, and add the resulting fraction to the interest rate. Then you can compare mortgages on a reasonably uniform basis. If you want to make a more precise calculation, you can find point equivalency tables in some books about mortgages.

Some other closing costs include property taxes (prorated for the portion of the year you will be living in the home), homeowner's insurance, title search fees, title insurance, transfer tax, appraisal fees, attorneys' fees, and sometimes the cost of surveying the property.

Lock-In Provisions

Lenders vary considerably in when they "lock in" the interest rate that you will receive. Some lock in the rate fairly soon after you fill out a mortgage application. Others wait until the last minute before the closing. Some are in the middle, and still others give you a choice as to when the rate is locked in.

Obviously, a choice is preferable, since if rates are rising you will want to lock in as soon as possible to avoid a high rate, whereas if rates are falling you will want to delay the lock-in for as long as possible. Some lenders charge an additional fee for the privilege of locking in your rate when you want to. Others charge no separate lock-in fee. Ask about the lock-in provisions when you are shopping for a mortgage, and use it as a tiebreaking consideration between mortgages that have similar interest rates and points.

Using a Mortgage Broker

If the choices seem overwhelming, you could turn to a mortgage broker. A good mortgage broker can save you days of legwork and a lot of headaches, as well as thousands of dollars in interest costs, by shopping among several different lenders to find the best rates and terms and helping with the loan applications. But there are also mortgage brokers who can leave you in the lurch, waiting as the closing day approaches for a promised loan that just never materializes.

Clearly, you will still have to do some homework yourself. Many people may conclude that they would just as soon put the work into finding their own mortgages. For instance, unless you already know what loan rates and other terms are in your area, you will not be sure that you are getting a good deal from a mortgage broker unless you do some checking. You also have to check out the mortgage broker. Although most states now regulate mortgage brokers, in some places that consists merely of collecting a registration fee. Others have licensing requirements that may include a code of conduct. If mortgage brokers are licensed in your state, check with the licensing authority about whether any complaints or disciplinary actions have been filed.

Ask brokers how many lenders they work with; someone who represents just two or three lenders may not be able to find the best deal. Look for someone who has been in business at least a couple of years and ask what percentage of loan applications are actually funded. You want to be sure that the broker you choose can deliver on the great deal that has been promised. You should also be sure that the broker can handle the kind of loan you will need. Some brokers do not handle Federal Housing Administration or Veterans Administration loans, for instance, and some will not accept applications for loans above or below certain benchmark amounts. Some brokers charge an application fee, which many states limit to $300 or less. Lenders typically pay brokers between 1% and 1.5% of the value of the loan for bringing in the business and doing the paperwork, although that may vary in certain circumstances.

When you make your loan application, do not deposit any money with the broker before you receive a "good faith" estimate of all closing costs associated with the loan. It is federal law that you receive such an estimate within three days of making the application; it should include the broker's fees and how they will be paid.

WHICH RENOVATIONS PAY OFF?

At some point, almost every homeowner at least thinks about renovating. Maybe you would like to add a bath, expand the garage, or modernize the kitchen of a home you have owned for several years. Or maybe you want to overhaul a home you are buying before you even move in. Whatever the case, do not sink big bucks into the project until you have considered the payback: Will the renovations you want to make increase the value of your home in a way that will pay off when it is time to sell? Do not assume that the answer is always yes.

WHICH RENOVATIONS PAY OFF?

Some popular home-improvement projects are worth more than others when you sell your home.

PROJECT	AVERAGE COST ($)	PERCENTAGE RECOUPED
Minor kitchen remodeling	8,014	98
Bathroom addition	11,639	89
Two-story addition (family room, bedroom, and bath)	50,415	85
Major kitchen remodeling	23,243	85
Family-room addition	32,024	83
Master suite	35,560	82
Attic bedroom	21,795	82
Bathroom remodeling	8,365	81
Deck addition (pressure-treated pine)	6,528	71
New windows (sash, frames, and casings)	5,488	69
New vinyl or aluminum siding	5,211	68
Home-office addition	7,709	58

SOURCE: The October 1995 issue of *REMODELING* magazine. © Hanley-Wood, Inc.

Homeowners generally do best if they keep pace with the neighborhood. Just as you should not buy the most expensive house on the block, you should not create it. Houses generally sell for prices comparable to those around them, regardless of amenities. If you are putting in the first swimming pool in the neighborhood, for instance, do it because you like to swim. You are unlikely to recoup the cost unless you are lucky enough to find a buyer who is also an avid swimmer. Buyers who are looking in a neighborhood of three-bedroom, two-bath homes probably will not want to pay a big premium for a third bath with a Jacuzzi, either. But if everyone has three bathrooms and a Jacuzzi, someone buying a home with just two baths will expect to pay less.

Still, bathroom and kitchen renovations tend to be the most valuable you can make because these are the most heavily trafficked and visible rooms in a home. Indeed, minor remodeling of the kitchen, which could be as simple as replacing countertops and cabinets, can pay back more than its cost when you sell your home. A major kitchen remodeling, including new appliances, also generates a good return.

Most buyers these days want at least two bathrooms, so putting a second bath in a home with just one usually will pay off. Adding a family room or den also typically increases a home's value, because you are creating more living space. Basements, on the other hand, are probably the worst place to spend a lot of money because few people spend much time there. Adding a sun room rarely pays, perhaps because these additions often look like they are tacked on.

Some renovations have more value because of the tax consequences when you sell a home. The cost of anything considered a capital improvement, such as a new family room, for instance, or even a swimming pool, is added to your "basis" for purposes of calculating the capital gain subject to taxation. Painting the interior or exterior of a home usually is considered routine maintenance and does not carry a tax benefit. Landscaping, however, generally is treated as a capital improvement. Kitchen appliances generally qualify for capital-gains treatment if they are built in. Central air conditioning is a capital improvement, as is a new water heater or sprinkler system.

If you do make capital improvements, remember to save receipts so you can prove your case to the Internal Revenue Service. Homeowners commonly make the mistake of discarding such receipts with other records five or seven years after filing income tax returns, making it impossible to calculate their basis accurately when they sell their homes years later.

APPEALING A PROPERTY TAX ASSESSMENT

For many homeowners, property taxes are a significant part of the annual expense of maintaining a home. And with the rising cost of police and fire protection, schools, and the other local services that they finance, property taxes have become a growing burden for many homeowners. This tends to be especially true for older homeowners who are trying to make ends meet on fixed incomes. Yet few people do more than complain.

If your property tax bills seem to be getting out of hand, it may be worth at least thinking about appealing your tax assessment. The key is whether your assessment is out of line with the assessments of other, similar properties in your area. If property values in your area have fallen and your home has not been reassessed in recent years, for instance, you may have a case. If your neighbors with similar homes are paying less, it is probably worth checking further.

About half the homeowners who go through the process of appealing their assessments win at least a partial victory. The savings typically run between a few hundred dollars and $2,000 or so a year.

The first step should be to visit your local assessor's office to verify the information on file about your property. For instance, is the number of bedrooms and baths correctly recorded? Do the records show you have a finished basement when, in fact, your basement is unfinished? Are the recorded dimensions right? Simply fixing clerical errors often can reduce the assessed value of a property without the need for a formal appeal.

GET WHAT YOU DESERVE

There also may be tax breaks to which you are entitled, such as reduced rates for the elderly or disabled, that may not be properly entered in the files. Check the assessor's math, too.

Do not assume that you are getting a good deal because your home is assessed at just a fraction of its market value. Many jurisdictions use a percentage of the market value to calculate the tax bill. Local governments then can simply raise the tax rate when they need more funds.

While you are at the assessor's office, check the assessed value of properties comparable to your own. They should be homes on similar-sized lots in similar neighborhoods, but they do not have to be exactly the same. Assessors usually have a formula for calculating the value of an extra bathroom or a fireplace, for example, and you should be able to get that information.

If you decide to proceed with a formal appeal, the assessments of these comparable homes can be the basis for your case. You will need at least three properties, although five is better, and the assessments should all be as of the same date. If a comparable property has been sold recently, or if you have recently purchased your home, the sale price can often be used as the fair market value, but make sure you know the ratio used to determine the assessment.

A professional appraisal of your property may help your case. If you recently applied for a home-equity loan or refinanced your mortgage, you may already have one that you can use.

Forms necessary for filing a formal appeal usually are available at the assessor's office. Read the instructions carefully. There is usually a time limit, indicated on the assessment notice, and sometimes certain documents have to be submitted within a specific period before a hearing. Photographs may be required, and sometimes they must be mounted in a particular way.

WHAT TO EXPECT

Although specific procedures vary from state to state and sometimes from municipality to municipality, the basic process is generally the same. Typically, there is a hearing before a local agency, with further appeals possible to a state agency and finally the courts.

Some people hire an attorney or other experts who specialize in these appeals. However, their fees can total several hundred dollars, which cuts into any tax savings. Homeowners who represent themselves usually are just as successful as those represented by attorneys or other professionals. Free help with the paperwork and other requirements often is available at the local assessor's office or the appeals agency. If you do end up filing a lawsuit, however, you might want to hire a lawyer familiar with courtroom proceedings.

The evidence you present at the first hearing is crucial, so prepare yourself well. The National Taxpayers Union, a Washington lobbying group, publishes a brochure called *How to Fight Property Taxes.* It recommends attending someone else's appeals hearing to learn about procedures and to see what kinds of questions the appeals board asks.

For your own hearing, you should have

EIGHT STEPS TO A LOWER ASSESSMENT

Contesting your property tax assessment is apt to be more successful if you take an orderly approach.

1. Check the description of your property and other records, including mathematical calculations, in the assessor's files.

2. Make sure you have been granted all the exemptions and reductions you are entitled to.

3. Find out deadlines and other requirements for claiming deductions or filing an appeal.

4. Locate comparable properties.

5. Compare your assessment to the comparables, making adjustments for any differences in the properties.

6. Make an informal appeal first. If the assessor does not agree, file your appeal.

7. Attend an appeals board hearing to get a feel for the process.

8. Prepare a written summary of your case and rehearse your presentation.

SOURCE: National Taxpayers Union, *How to Fight Property Taxes* ($2), 108 N. Alfred Street, Alexandria, VA 22314.

copies of assessment records pertaining to your property. If your home is in need of major repairs, gather estimates of what those repairs would cost. Have enough copies for everyone on the appeals board. Make sure the information you have about comparable properties is correct. Keep your presentation short and to the point. You are not challenging your tax bill or how your local government spends its money. The only thing the appeals board can change is your assessment.

GETTING THE BEST PRICE
WHEN YOU SELL

Making a smart investment is not just a matter of buying at a good price. You also have to get a good price when you want to sell. That is as true when it comes to your home as it is with stocks and bonds. But while it is easy to discover the prices at which particular stocks and bonds are trading simply by checking the quotes in the newspaper, it can take a fair amount of effort to determine the price you can reasonably expect when you sell your home.

Finding out what similar homes are selling for in your area requires talking to neighbors, reading local newspapers, and consulting with real estate agents. Most agents have access to the Multiple Listing Service, a computerized listing of homes for sale and homes that have sold recently. It also can be a good idea to visit a few homes that are for sale to see how they compare with yours.

You can set the price a little higher—say, 3% to 5%—than what you expect to get, to leave some room for negotiations. But do not set it too high unless the housing market is really tight. If you set the asking price too high, you risk driving away potential buyers. Indeed, real estate professionals say the biggest mistake homeowners make when they sell is overestimating the value of their homes. Sure, you paid a lot when you bought it, and you have poured more money into fixing it up since then. But the bottom line is that you can sell your home for only what a buyer is willing to pay. In general, the best advice is to follow neighborhood practice: Find out what the difference was between closing price and asking price on homes that have sold recently, and price your home accordingly.

NEGOTIATE THE COMMISSION

One way to increase your proceeds from the sale without increasing the price is to negotiate the commission you pay the real estate agent. The standard is 7% of the sale price, but many agents will accept 6% or even less, especially on an expensive house. On a $300,000 home, for instance, even a one percentage point discount would save you $3,000, and an agent getting a 6% commission would still be paid a tidy $18,000. The time to negotiate the commission is before signing on with an agent. You might consider offering the agent a little extra if the selling price is above a certain level.

Of course, you could save the full commission by selling your home yourself. But selling your own home is a lot of hard work. You have to arrange and pay for advertising, screen potential buyers, and be available to show the home, sometimes on short notice. Your property is generally not included on the Multiple Listing Service, which many buyers use to locate homes. When the time comes, you also have to do all the negotiating—probably with a cheapskate potential buyer who expects to pay less than if you were using a broker. When all is said and done, there is no guarantee that you will come out ahead financially by doing it yourself.

So using a broker is probably the reasonable thing to do. But make certain you get your money's worth. Interview two or three agents before you hire one. Ask them each to make a "selling presentation"— that is, to describe how they propose to sell your home and where they would set the price. Listen not only to what they would do but also to why. You are going to pay this person several thousand dollars, so you should feel comfortable that you will be well represented.

Whether you use an agent or not, this is the time to get the clutter out of the living room,

A CHECKLIST FOR HOME SELLERS

Here are five steps that can help you sell your home faster and get a better price.

1. Verify selling prices of similar homes in your neighborhood.
2. Interview at least three real estate agents.
3. Set a reasonable price.
4. Make minor repairs and cosmetic improvements.
5. Get rid of clutter.

fix up the yard, and make the minor repairs that you have been talking about for years. A fresh coat of paint or newly refinished floors make any home more attractive. Old doorknobs and stained carpet can turn off potential buyers. You might even consider asking your neighbors if you can help clean up their yards.

If you are painting, choose neutral colors; your buyer may not like orange walls in the bathroom. Do not spend money on major renovations, however. You are usually better off asking a few thousand dollars less for a home with an old kitchen than spending tens of thousands on something that may not suit your buyer's taste.

SOME IMPORTANT TAX CONSIDERATIONS

You may have to share the proceeds of the sale of your home with Uncle Sam, but you can keep the tax bill to a minimum. In principle, you are obligated to pay tax on any gain on the sale of your home in the year you sell it. But in most cases, you can postpone the payment, perhaps indefinitely, if you buy a new home of equal or greater value within two years. Both the old and new homes must be a "principal residence," that is, the place where you live most of the time.

If you have two or more homes, only one of them can qualify for this tax deferral. If you rent part of your home, or use part of it as an office, only that portion of the sale price allocated to your principal residence is considered eligible for deferral, and you will pay tax on the remainder. You generally cannot deduct a loss on the sale of a home.

Calculating the gain is more complicated than subtracting the price you paid from the price you received. Under the tax law, it is the difference between the "amount realized" and the "adjusted basis." You generally can deduct expenses related to the sale—the real estate commission, legal fees, and advertising costs—from the sale price when calculating the amount realized. Your adjusted basis includes not only the price you paid when you bought your home but also the cost of most capital improvements.

The Internal Revenue Service generally classifies as capital improvements work that adds value to your home and that will remain part of the home after you sell, such as a new kitchen or bathroom, central air conditioning, wall-to-wall carpeting, and insulation. Although maintenance and repairs generally do not qualify, such things as a new roof, storm windows and doors, and landscaping do. IRS Publication 523, *Selling Your Home,* has a more complete list. You have to be able to prove how much you spent on capital improvements, so keep all receipts and canceled checks in a safe place.

FOR THOSE AGE 55 AND OVER

Homeowners age 55 and older receive a special tax break. They can exclude $125,000 of the gain from the sale of their principal residence from taxation. This is an important benefit for people trading down to a smaller home after retirement or those who want to sell their home and rent afterward. Without the exclusion, they could pay as much as $35,000 in federal tax alone.

It works like this: Say you bought your home for $50,000 in 1970. Over the years you spent another $50,000 on renovating the kitchen, adding a half-bath downstairs, and insulating the attic. You sell the house for $225,000 and move to a retirement community, where you rent a condominium. As long as you have owned and lived in the home for three of the five years preceding the sale, the entire $125,000 gain is tax-free.

Unlike the tax deferment for all sellers who buy a home of equal or greater value, the $125,000 exclusion protects the gain from taxation forever. You can take advantage of it only once in a lifetime, however, so use it carefully. For example, say an older man who owns his home and an older woman who owns hers decide to marry. If they both sell before they tie the knot, they can exclude up to $250,000 in gains—$125,000 each. But a married couple can take only one $125,000 exclusion between them. And if one spouse has already used the exclusion before the wedding, the couple will not be able to use it again if they sell a home during their marriage.

Think carefully about using the exclusion if your gain is less than $125,000, because you will forfeit the remainder. If you are buying another home that you reasonably expect to sell at some later date, you might want to wait. But be realistic about the size of the gain you anticipate; you may not be in the new home long enough for the exclusion to be worthwhile.

VACATION HOMES

It happens thousands of times a year. A happy vacationer, relishing the fresh air and relaxed pace of some seaside resort or mountain retreat, falls in love with this idyllic spot and decides it would be great to own a place of his or her own. Maybe a cottage or a condo, or just a time share. After all, the rationalization goes, it must be a great investment.

Not necessarily. Generally, you should buy a vacation home only if you are going to use it and enjoy it. Sure, you may be able to rent out that cottage, interest on the mortgage is usually tax-deductible, and there are other possible tax breaks. But despite all that, few people make real money on a second home.

In addition to monthly mortgage payments, there usually are real estate taxes, maintenance costs, and heating and utility bills. If you want to cover some of those costs by renting the home out, you have the hassle of finding tenants or the expense of paying a rental agent. The cost of maintenance and repairs likely will go up, too, if you rent, and you will probably have to make the arrangements over the phone by long distance. If and when you want to sell, you may not be able to find a buyer. The vacation-home market is much more sensitive to changes in the economy and tax laws than is the market for primary residences.

If You Decide to Buy

When shopping for a vacation home, follow the same general guidelines as you would for a primary residence. Consider how much you can afford, what you want and what you need in a home, and where you want to be located. Location is more than a question of whether you prefer the mountains or the seashore. If you buy far from your primary residence, it will take you longer, and may cost you more, to get there. Do you want to be near shopping and cultural activities? You may long for someplace remote, but if you plan to rent to others, accessibility and amenities usually are important.

There is also the resale value to consider; as much as you love the place now, you may eventually want or need to sell it. Homes in areas that can be used during three or four seasons of the year tend to sell faster and garner higher prices. Property near the beach is more expensive, but when times are tough, it typically does not fall as fast or as much as other vacation real estate.

Before buying you might want to rent in the area for a while to see how you like it. Especially if you are buying a vacation home with the intention of retiring there eventually, try renting first for all the seasons you plan to live there. Vacation homes typically take longer to sell than primary residences, and you would not want to be stuck in a place you hate.

If you do not want the hassles of owning a house, or you plan to use a vacation place for only limited periods, condominiums or "time shares" may be an alternative. There is someone to do the maintenance and maybe to help with renting during the time you are not using it. But these types of homes have pitfalls of their own and may be even harder to sell when the time comes.

CHECK IT OUT YOURSELF

Do not depend on what the real estate agent tells you about possible rental income; check with other owners and local rental companies. If you are considering a condo, talk to owners of neighboring units about such things as noise levels and maintenance, just as if you were buying a primary residence. Review the financial reports of the homeowners' association to make sure there are adequate reserves for repairs and improvements.

Find out who owns and operates the common facilities, such as the golf course or the swimming pool, and what your rights are. If you are buying a place overlooking the golf course, for instance, you do not want it to be sold to a shopping center developer or turned into a parking lot. Even if the facility is not sold, a new operator could change hours and accessibility.

If you are buying directly from the developer, which usually entails discounted financing and a smaller down payment, remember that anyone who buys from you is unlikely to get a similar deal from the bank. That will affect future prices. If only a few units have been sold, and the developer is going to be around for a while, you will be competing both for renters and for prospective buyers.

Time shares offer annual occupancy rights at a resort, usually in weekly segments. Financing typically is provided by the developer, which can make these rights hard to sell and may have tax consequences. There usually are maintenance fees to pay whether or not you actually use the property, and because there are so many units available, they often are hard to rent. Time shares generally work best for people who really are going to use the property every year— in a ski resort, for instance—or for those who plan to trade their rights in order to use property elsewhere. It may be difficult, however, to get the weeks you want in the places you want to be.

Maybe You Would Rather Have a Boat?

Boats are expensive to buy, expensive to use, and expensive to maintain. Indeed, it has often been said that the two happiest days in a boat owner's life are the day he buys a boat and the day he sells it.

That aside, if you like living on the water and have time and money, a boat can make a dandy vacation home. After all, if you do not like the neighbors you can simply leave, and if your boat is big enough, you can go anywhere in the world. When you dock, you will be with people of similar interests, or you can go off by yourself. Assuming that the boat costs more than $25,000 or so, you can finance it for 15 or 20 years, just as you would a house. And as long as the boat has sleeping quarters, a kitchen (the "galley" in boatspeak), and bathroom facilities (the "head"), interest on the loan usually is deductible on your income tax return.

But buying a boat is a more complicated decision than buying any other kind of vacation home. To begin with, it really is a lifestyle choice. You have to know how to navigate and understand the rules of the waterways. Unless you can pay someone else to do the work, you also must have the skill, temperament, and time to maintain the boat and its equipment. Before buying, you might rent a few times from a charter operator to gain experience with different kinds of boats. When figuring out how much you can afford to pay, remember that the interest rate on the loan is likely to be higher than on a house and insurance will cost more, because of the greater risk. You will probably have to pay for a place to put the boat, and there are various state and local licensing and registration fees.

It is usually a good idea to work with a broker who knows the market for the kind of boat you want. A professional also can find out if a boat has ever been severely damaged and who did the repairs. Be prepared to travel. Unlike a home, the boat you want can be anywhere in the world. To find a broker, get references and read the advertisements in boating magazines. If there is something that looks interesting, call and ask about it. But the questions a broker asks you may be more important than the answers to the questions you ask. Is the broker paying attention to what you want, the price you can afford to pay, and your ability to use what you are buying?

Unless you must have everything brand new, or you want a boat with custom features, you will generally do better with a used boat. Prices can be half what you would pay for something new, the boat will be tested, and someone already will have equipped it with all the gadgets you need. Such things as radios, radar, and electronic navigational systems can cost thousands of dollars. Do not buy anything before it is inspected by a qualified surveyor. A good surveyor can make any boat look like it is on the verge of sinking, which may help you negotiate a lower price. More important, your life may depend on the condition of the boat.

The Tax Rules on Second Homes

A second residence usually is much like your first as far as the Internal Revenue Service is concerned. Property taxes and mortgage interest are generally tax-deductible. (Mortgage interest is not deductible on more than two homes unless they are rental property.) And if you rent out a second home for 14 days or less, the income is tax-free; you do not even have to declare it on your income tax return.

The tax consequences become complicated, however, if you rent out a vacation home for more than two weeks each year. It is generally treated as a second residence if you rent it out for fewer than 15 days, as rental property if you use it yourself for fewer than 15 days, or as a hybrid, or combination of both, which requires you to allocate costs according to a specific formula. The following paragraphs give an overview. In many situations, you should consult a tax professional.

IF YOU WANT TO RENT IT OUT

If your house or condo is rental property, you can deduct operating expenses—such as utilities, maintenance, and insurance—as well as advertising and commissions and depreciation, in addition to property taxes and mortgage interest. But in most cases, you can use those deductions only to offset rental income or income from other "passive" investments, such as limited partnerships. You also can carry forward those losses to offset rental income in future years or to reduce your gain when you sell the property.

There is a special tax break for people who actively participate in managing their rental property and whose adjusted gross income is under $150,000. To qualify as an active participant in the management, the IRS expects you to make decisions on matters such as new tenants, rents, and expenditures. Assuming they qualify, a couple filing jointly whose adjusted gross income is no more than $100,000 may be able to deduct rental losses of up to $25,000 from salary and other income. Those with higher adjusted gross income may be able to take a smaller deduction, but this benefit is phased out completely when a couple's adjusted gross income reaches $150,000.

Real estate professionals, such as brokers and developers, are also free of the passive-loss constraints if they meet certain tests. This can be a real boon for some couples. A surgeon, for instance, could deduct rental losses incurred by her developer husband from her earned income on their joint return.

You can use a rental house yourself for fewer than 15 days or 10% of the number of days that it is rented, whichever is greater, and you can spend time there to do repairs and maintenance. If the home is rental property, the portion of your mortgage interest allocated to your personal use is considered personal interest, and it is not tax-deductible.

The calculations grow more difficult if your property is part vacation home and part rental property, which is usually the case if you rent it out more than two weeks a year and spend more than two weeks there yourself. A portion of your expenses can be used to offset your rental income, and the portion of your mortgage interest allocated to personal use is deductible. Property taxes are fully deductible.

But the IRS requires that you take the deductions in a certain order, and there is disagreement between the IRS and the Tax Court over how to calculate the percentage of real estate taxes, mortgage interest, and other expenses allocated to rental property. IRS Publication 527, *Residential Rental Property (Including Rental of Vacation Homes)*, explains the rules and has worksheets, but you still will want to consult a tax professional. If you use the Tax Court's method, you may risk an audit.

Finally, you should know that if your principal residence is in one state and you have a vacation home in another, when you die, your will is going to be subject to probate in both states, unless the properties are owned by a trust or other entity.

INVESTMENT REAL ESTATE

From an investment point of view, the only real estate most people need is their own home. Typically, the family home represents about half the household's net worth—a lot to have in a single asset class, not to mention in a single asset. Moreover, this asset is "illiquid," meaning that it can be difficult to get your money out when you need it.

Still, many investors do buy real estate for a variety of reasons. Perhaps they are renting a home and want real estate to comprise some portion of their investments. Sometimes, investors think they can score a really big gain on a particular piece of property. They may simply look at it as a good buy.

Owning real estate also has psychic rewards that do not come with stocks or bonds or mutual funds. Some people just like to be able to point to a building or a piece of land and say, "That's mine."

If you do want to invest in real estate, there are several ways to do it, depending on your individual situation and your goals. But keep in mind that if it is truly to be an investment, financial considerations should outweigh emotional ones. Most investors should stick with real estate investment trusts (REITs) and mutual funds that invest in real estate, rather than buying individual properties that might require you to put up tens of thousands of dollars. While your gains could be bigger if you happen to have a big chunk of your money in a single property that soars in value, you could sustain a huge loss if the market goes the other way.

REITs and real estate mutual funds provide much more diversified investments for much smaller initial outlays. REITs are packaged like mutual funds and sold like stocks. They own pools of property or mortgages and pass at least 95% of an untaxed stream of earnings to shareholders. These days most are equity REITs, which usually own 20 to 100 properties each. Mortgage REITs own mortgages rather than the actual real estate.

THE RECORD ON REITS

Returns on real estate investment trusts have trailed the stock market in recent years.

	1-Year	3-Year	5-Year	10-Year
REITs	18.31%	12.24%	16.56%	7.55%
S&P 500*	37.57%	15.30%	16.59%	14.86%

*Standard & Poor's 500-stock index.
Note: Total returns, including dividends and price changes, for periods ending December 31, 1995.
Source: National Association of Real Estate Investment Trusts.

It is usually better to own equity than to own debt because of the appreciation potential. An investor should evaluate the merits of the type of property a particular REIT owns, as well as regional and local economics. As with any other investment, you should also consider the REIT's debt and other balance-sheet issues. The handful of mutual funds that invest in real estate generally hold REITs. The advantage for the individual investor is that they are selected by a professional. Find a low-cost fund and check out the reputation and track record of the manager before investing.

SAVE YOURSELF SOME GRIEF

Limited partnerships declined in popularity after most of the tax benefits disappeared with the Tax Reform Act of 1986. As a result, there are some apparent bargains. But use caution: Partnership units are difficult if not impossible to sell because there is not an active secondary market. The loss of tax benefits made it clear that many partnerships were overpriced and poorly managed. The few new partnerships may be somewhat better, but they still are not very liquid and there can be stiff up-front costs related to the acquisition of property.

You also can invest in rental real estate either by yourself or as part of a small group. If you work hard at fixing it up, maintaining it, and finding tenants, you may have a reasonable chance of making a profit. You will not have much diversification, however. The neighborhood could change, or the property could be damaged by flood, hurricane, or earthquake, and your investment could be worthless. You generally should not put your money in a single property unless you are prepared to lose it all. If you buy more than one property, do what you can to mitigate the risks. Do not own two lots on the same block, for instance, or four condominiums in the same development.

8

CUTTING YOUR TAXES AND SAVING YOUR SANITY

$

"The income tax has made more liars out of the American people than golf has," Will Rogers once said. "Even when you make a tax form out on the level, you don't know when it is through if you are a crook or a martyr."

Amen.

If Will Rogers were still alive, he would probably say that his observation is even more apt today than 50 or 60 years ago. For many Americans, our complex tax code resembles what Winston Churchill once said of Russia: "A riddle wrapped in a mystery inside an enigma."

No wonder many well-educated people simply throw up their hands and turn over the job of filling out their tax returns to professionals. About half of the approximately 118 million individual income tax returns filed each year are done by paid preparers, and for many affluent Americans with complicated situations, that may be the only sane move. John Young, former chief executive of Hewlett-Packard, spoke for many upper-income Americans when he told *The Wall Street Journal* that he would like to be able to prepare his own return but did not even dare do so because the subject "got beyond my competence long ago."

Still, even taxpayers who turn the dirty work over to accountants and other specialists should not simply wash their hands of the matter. Leaving taxes entirely to the experts can be hazardous to your wealth.

PLANNING AND ORGANIZING

Taxes represent by far the largest single component in the average American family's budget, according to a study by the Washington, D.C.–based Tax Foundation, a nonprofit research group. Families typically pay more in federal, state, and local taxes each year than they spend on housing, food, and clothing combined.

But many people could cut the financial burden significantly by devoting a little more time and energy to planning and organizing their taxes. While the tax laws change constantly—and probably are in the midst of change once again as you read these words—many basic concepts remain essentially the same. Master them, and you will be way ahead. Then, make it a point to consider the tax consequences of any major decision:

- Want to increase your savings? Make full use of your employer's tax-advantaged 401(k) plan.
- Need a loan for a new car? Think about a tax-favored home-equity loan.
- Want to ease the strain of child-care expenses or medical costs? Take advantage of reimbursement plans at work that allow you to pay such expenses with pretax dollars.
- Pruning your stock or mutual fund portfolio? Be careful which shares you sell. The difference in taxes may be large.

This chapter is not intended to be an all-inclusive tax manual or a replacement for Internal Revenue Service instructions. That would require a separate book, or perhaps even a fat encyclopedia. Besides, IRS Publication 17, *Your Federal Income Tax,* which is free, provides comprehensive and generally reliable advice. So do many of the telephone book–sized tax guides published by major accounting firms and other tax specialists.

Instead, what follows is designed to outline major tax considerations, advice, strategies, and often overlooked opportunities, based on interviews with some of the nation's leading tax lawyers, accountants, and financial advisers. It also should help readers steer clear of several major tax potholes and help those who want to dig more deeply find the additional information they need.

A FEW CAVEATS

As you look for answers to your tax problems, keep a couple of caveats clearly in mind. First, never make any decisions based solely on taxes. Although that may sound obvious, the sad fact is that many investors shoot themselves in the foot by obsessing endlessly about taxes and focusing solely on how to avoid the tax collector's grasp. It is easy to become overly concerned about taxes, to structure one's life around ways to cut taxes at all costs—even if that means, say, passing up a golden investment opportunity that might involve paying some taxes.

Second, do not assume that even intensive study will automatically lead to sharply lower taxes, or that you can somehow take steps to guarantee that you will never have to undergo the anguish and pain of an IRS audit. Over the past few decades, Congress has eliminated or whittled away many of the best-known and most widely used shelters. Our tax laws have proliferated so rapidly and grown so breathtakingly complex that even the most sophisticated software programs cannot handle all the questions that arise.

Even some former IRS officials say the only solution is to rip the tax law up and start from scratch. "I would repeal the entire Internal Revenue Code and start over," says Shirley Peterson, a former IRS Commissioner and former Justice Department official. The system's "inordinate complexity" is so confusing and intimidating, she says, that it "contributes mightily" to discouraging people from complying.

WHO GETS AUDITED?

Your chances of being audited by the Internal Revenue Service increase significantly if your income is $100,000 or more or if you file Schedule C for income from self-employment.

TYPE OF RETURN	PERCENTAGE AUDITED
1040, 1040A, 1040EZ	
With income	
Under $25,000	1.00%
$25,000 to less than $50,000	0.53%
$50,000 to less than $100,000	0.72%
$100,000 and over	2.94%
SCHEDULE C	
(Sole Proprietorships) with gross receipts	
Under $25,000	4.39%
$25,000 to under $100,000	3.01%
$100,000 and over	3.57%
SCHEDULE F	
(Farms) with receipts	
Under $100,000	1.16%
$100,000 and over	1.74%
Total	1.08%

NOTE: Data are for fiscal year 1994; income on individual returns is before deductions, losses, and other adjustments.
SOURCE: Internal Revenue Service.

SMART TAX MOVES THROUGH THE AGES

Taxpayers searching for ways to cut their tax bills should always beware of easy generalizations. A seemingly bulletproof tax strategy that may save your neighbor large amounts of money may be exactly the wrong strategy for you.

The following sections highlight some of the major tax issues for people in various age groups. You will find opportunities to reduce your tax bite and to make the tax laws work for you in boosting your savings and investment returns. But before you try anything complicated, ask a competent tax adviser how it would work in your individual circumstances.

Your 20s and 30s

Many young people just starting out in their careers do not give much thought to taxes because they assume there is not much they can do except pay them. But even people with very simple finances can benefit by taking a little time to acquaint themselves with the basics. Simple steps—such as keeping good records, making sure your withholding is properly adjusted, and taking advantage of the tax breaks that are available through your employer—can cut your tax bills and allow you to skip some headaches.

Get in the habit of keeping your financial records organized as you go through the year. This will help you know where you stand and prevent you from wasting time when you prepare your tax returns. And if you hire someone to do your taxes for you, good records can lower the fee you will have to pay. In particular, put check stubs and receipts for charitable contributions and other deductible expenses in a file folder so you do not forget them. Also keep together the year-end tax information statements you receive from banks, mutual funds, brokerage firms, and others showing income they have reported to the Internal Revenue Service. If you have a new baby, be sure to get a Social Security number for him or her as soon as possible—you will need to list it on your return.

IRAS, 401(K)S, AND KEOGHS

One of the smartest moves at any age is to take the fullest possible advantage of tax-advantaged retirement-savings plans, such as Individual Retirement Accounts, employer-sponsored 401(k)s, and Keogh plans for the self-employed. For example, the money you elect to have taken out of your pay and contributed to a 401(k) plan at work is not subject to federal income taxes. It also escapes state income tax in almost all states that have an income tax. And your nest egg will likely grow faster than other investment accounts you might have since it is boosted by tax-deferred compounding.

If neither you nor your spouse is covered by an employer-provided retirement plan, such as a pension, 401(k), or profit-sharing plan, you can put up to $2,000 of taxable compensation into an IRA each year and deduct the sum from your taxable income. Your spouse is also eligible to make a deductible contribution—up to $2,000 a year if he or she is employed. (If your spouse is not employed, beginning in 1997, the two of you together can contribute up to $4,000.) The money grows tax-deferred until it is withdrawn.

Even if either you or your spouse qualifies for a workplace plan, you still may be able to deduct the maximum IRA contribution if your income is less than certain amounts. For singles, the amount is $25,000; for married couples, the joint amount is $40,000. Beyond those levels, singles who make up to $35,000 and couples with combined income of up to $50,000 may qualify for a lesser deduction.

Make up your mind not to touch the money you put into retirement plans until you retire. Leaving the money alone will help you to build a handsome nest egg, and it will save you from paying a significant tax penalty. Money withdrawn from a tax-advantaged retirement plan before you turn 59½ generally is subject to income taxes, plus a 10% penalty. Thus, if you withdraw $10,000 to pay your credit card bills, you will owe income taxes on that amount—plus, typically, a $1,000 penalty. There are a few exceptions, such as if you take out the money for huge medical expenses, but for the most part you should consider the money untouchable until you reach 59½.

Another significant tax saver for young people is the so-called flexible spending account offered by many employers. This account allows you to have pretax dollars withheld from your wages to pay unreimbursed medical costs—such as insurance deductibles, co-payments, and medical expenses that are not covered by your health plan—and eligible child-care and elder-care expenses. There is no set maximum for employee contributions to medical-spending accounts, but most employers usually limit them to $2,000 or $3,000 per year. The tax law allows contributions of up to $5,000 a year to child-care spending accounts, but employers sometimes impose lower limits.

There is another tax break that can help some parents with child-care expenses. This is a child-care credit that allows you to subtract a limited amount of eligible costs right from your tax bill. The exact amount depends on your expenses and how much you earn, but the most you can claim for one child is $720, and the maximum is $1,440 for two or more children. If your employer offers a child-care spending account and you earn more than about $25,000 a year, go with the employer's plan—it will be a better deal for you. You cannot claim a federal tax credit for expenses paid through a spending account, and the maximum amount of expenses you can apply toward the credit is $4,800 for two or more children, $2,400 for one. (You can find out more about flexible spending accounts and other company benefits in Chapter 4.)

TAX SAVINGS ON DOCTORS AND DAY CARE

If you put away a couple of thousand dollars in a flexible spending account to pay for unreimbursed medical expenses or eligible child-care costs, you will not reduce your take-home pay by as much as you might think. The tax savings can make an important difference.

IF YOU PUT AWAY:	AND YOUR ANNUAL EARNINGS ARE:	YOU WILL PROBABLY SAVE THIS MUCH IN TAXES:	
		SINGLE	FAMILY OF FOUR
$2,500 ($48.08/week)	$25,000	$566.25	$566.25
	$40,000	$891.25	$566.25
	$60,000	$891.25	$891.25
	$80,000	$811.25	$736.25
	$100,000	$811.25	$736.25

NOTE: Reflects savings on federal income tax and Social Security and Medicare taxes based on 1995 rates. Depending on your state, you may save additional amounts in state taxes.

SOURCE: © 1995 Buck Consultants, Inc.

If you are planning to adopt a child, a new tax break may be a big help. Under a provision of a law enacted in 1996, many people who adopt children can claim a tax credit for qualified adoption expenses, such as attorney fees and court costs, of up to $5,000 for each child (or up to $6,000 for a U.S. child with "special needs"). The provision also allows some employees to exclude from gross income certain amounts of adoption expenses paid by their employers. But these credits and exclusions are available only to parents whose income is less than $115,000, and are phased out for parents with income above $75,000. Also, parts of the provision were scheduled to expire after a few years, so be sure to consult the latest IRS instructions or an accountant.

STANDARD OR ITEMIZED DEDUCTION?

Once you buy a home or start paying steep state taxes, your deductible expenses may top the standard deduction everyone gets. (In 1996, the standard deduction was $4,000 for single people, $6,700 for joint filers.) Homeowners, for example, can deduct property taxes and mortgage interest. Also, do not forget about "points," or prepaid interest that many lenders charge when you take out a mortgage. (A point equals 1% of the mortgage; thus, one point on a $100,000 mortgage would be $1,000.) For the year in which you take out a mortgage to buy or improve your main home, the points you pay to the lender are fully deductible. (For a fuller discussion of points, see the Home, Sweet Tax Shelter section later in this chapter.)

To see if you should itemize, add up all such home expenses, any state and local income taxes you paid during the year, plus your charitable contributions. Make sure you have proper receipts from the charities for any donations of $250 or more. And if you gave any group more than $75 and got something, such as a meal, in return, you generally need a written statement from the organization showing how much of your gift is deductible. A glance down Schedule A may remind you of other costs, such as job-hunting expenses, that could push you into the itemizing zone.

Industrious workers who take on more than one job should make sure they do not have too much withheld from their multiple paychecks for Social Security and Medicare taxes. This shows up on

20s–30s

- Keep good records.
- Contribute to retirement plan.
- Use flexible spending account.
- Get Social Security card for baby.
- Adjust withholding.

your pay stub as FICA (Federal Insurance Contributions Act). Your total FICA withholding should not exceed 7.65% of your combined pay up to a certain amount ($62,700 in 1996). Once you make that much, from one job or a combination of jobs, any extra earnings should have only 1.45% withheld for the Medicare portion of FICA. If necessary, ask your payroll office to adjust your withholding.

THE PRICE OF MARITAL BLISS

Thanks to a bizarre tax-law quirk, many two-income married couples wind up paying much more in combined taxes than they would have owed if they had remained single and merely moved in together. The extra tax can easily amount to several thousand dollars. Talk about "family values"!

Treasury officials, tax experts, and lawmakers have roundly criticized this "marriage penalty" for many years. But it persists, mainly because government officials fear it would be too costly to fix.

The penalty does not catch all married couples. In fact, some couples may benefit. For example, when one spouse is employed and earns much more than the other, the couple's combined income tax may actually be lower than what they would pay as two single individuals.

But those who are hurt outnumber those who benefit, according to some economists. The penalty is especially harsh on two-income couples whose incomes are relatively similar.

Even so, some other aspects of the tax law are stacked strongly in favor of marriage. For instance, for estate-tax purposes, if both you and your spouse are U.S. citizens there is generally an unlimited marital deduction—which means you can leave each other an unlimited amount of money. Because estate taxes can be extraordinarily high, the saving can be enormous.

Here is one suggestion: If you are planning to get married late in the year and would be hit by this penalty, consider postponing the official ceremony until the following year. That way, you can each file as single for one more year and use the tax savings to pay for your honeymoon.

YOUR 40s AND 50s

As people move into their peak earning years during their 40s and 50s, their tax situations often become much more complex, increasing the importance of tax planning and organization.

Tax advisers say many people in this age group would benefit by paying more attention to the benefits of tax-advantaged investments. Even many people who do not consider themselves wealthy will benefit from more time and attention to this area.

Start by focusing on tax-exempt municipal bonds. These bonds, better known as "munis," are issued by state and local governments. Issuers range from major states, such as New York, Illinois, and California, to tiny municipalities and school districts around the nation. Contrary to their reputation, these bonds are not just for the super-rich. A 7% tax-free bond for someone in the 28% federal tax bracket is equivalent to a fully taxable bond yielding more than 9.7%. These bonds make even more sense for someone in higher tax brackets. That same 7% tax-free bond for someone in the 39.6% federal tax bracket is equivalent to a fully taxable bond yielding more than 11.5%.

The case for buying munis becomes even more compelling if you live in a high-tax area, such as New York City or California. In such places, investors often prefer to buy bonds issued only within the state's borders. That is because New York, California, and most other states do not tax income on bonds issued by the state itself or municipalities within the state's borders. Thus, a New York tax-exempt bond yielding 7% is equivalent to a fully taxable bond yielding more than 13% for a New York City resident in the top tax bracket. (For New York City residents, that top tax bracket, after including federal, state, and local taxes, can exceed 50%.)

Only 4.7 million individual income tax returns reported tax-exempt interest in 1993, according to the IRS. That is only about 4% of all individual returns received by the IRS each year, and it is a small fraction of the number of people financial advisers say could benefit from owning munis.

But do not go overboard merely to avoid paying taxes. Many people in low-tax states may come out ahead by buying out-of-state bonds with higher yields and paying the state tax. Moreover, some states have no income tax. And in any event, it may be wise not to put all of your eggs in the basket of one state. Diversifying may help you avoid being hurt in case the state or one large county runs into unexpected turbulence. Another idea is to buy bonds insured by private insurers. An insured bond typically sports a triple-A rating, the highest available.

Keep taxes in mind when picking stocks as well as bonds. Some upper-income people may find it advantageous to put a greater emphasis on stocks that pay little or no dividends. Dividends are taxable as ordinary income, where the top federal rate is 39.6%. But the maximum rate on long-term capital gains, which is any profit you re-alize when you sell an investment held more than a year, is only 28%.

Tax advisers also urge people in this age group to be sure they are taking full advantage of employer retirement plans as well as other tax-deferred retirement plans. This is one of the most easily overlooked areas. For most people, the best advice is to set aside as much as possible in an employer-sponsored 401(k). Be sure to see if your plan allows employees to set aside after-tax contributions, which—like the rest of the money in your retirement-savings plan—can grow tax-deferred until withdrawn. Also consider putting money into an Individual Retirement Account, especially if you are not cov-ered by a retirement plan at work and are eligible to make tax-deductible IRA contributions.

Thinking of adopting a child? See if you can take advantage of a new tax break that may mean significant savings. Beginning in 1997, many people who adopt children can claim a tax credit for quali-fied adoption expenses, such as attorney fees and court costs, of up to $5,000 for each child (or up to $6,000 for a U.S. child with "spe-cial needs"). But the rules are tricky, and parts of this tax break were scheduled to expire after a few years. For further details, see the sum-mary in this chapter's section for people in their 20s and 30s, and be sure to study the IRS instructions or consult an accountant.

Many people who work for a company also have other jobs, such as consulting, freelance writing, or public speaking. Some of the out-side income they earn may be sheltered in a special tax-deferred re-tirement plan, such as a Keogh or Simplified Employee Pension for self-employed individuals.

Have you switched jobs recently? If so, make sure that you have not accidentally overpaid Social Security taxes. There is a relatively easy way to recover that money, but it is up to you to find out and take the initiative. IRS Publication 17 explains how to calculate a tax credit for excess Social Security taxes paid and includes a handy worksheet.

In some companies, big or small, executives at the upper eche-lons may find it advantageous to defer some of their pay until after they retire, rather than taking it all now when they are in the top tax bracket. Many executives also will need to acquaint themselves with the rules on stock options.

40s–50s

- Consider tax-exempt municipal bonds.

- Be a tax-smart stock market investor.

- Take advantage of tax-deferred savings options.

- Do not overpay Social Security if you change jobs.

- Beware of early-retirement tax traps.

EARLY-RETIREMENT TAX TRAPS

More and more people in this age group are taking early retirement. Some are doing so voluntarily. Others are doing so involuntarily through layoffs or buyouts. If you are among this group, watch out for some painful tax traps.

For example, be especially careful about the 10% tax penalty that can result from cashing in special retirement plans, such as an IRA, before you turn 59½. The rules here can be remarkably complex, and it probably will help to consult a tax specialist.

Upper-income taxpayers may want to consider buying a retirement home now and renting it out until they are ready to stop working—or are told by their employer to leave. That can produce valuable additional mortgage deductions. It can also produce peace of mind in knowing where your retirement years will be spent. But do not purchase a retirement home with the idea that you are making an investment that will generate lucrative rental income. Few people make real money renting out a vacation home, and the tax rules can be very complicated.

Many employees who go into business for themselves will need to master a new set of tax rules or find someone trained in that field. One point to consider: If you are self-employed or work for a small, closely held company, figuring out how much to pay yourself and other top executives can be difficult and can sometimes lead to thorny tax questions. The IRS often challenges owners of small businesses, arguing that executive pay is overly lavish and thus should not all be deductible as a business expense. But tax advisers say it is not necessary for you to panic and cave in merely because the IRS disallows deductions. Several businesses recently have gone to the U.S. Tax Court on this issue and won. When in doubt, consult a tax specialist on executive pay who is familiar with the details of these cases.

TIMING CAN BE IMPORTANT

Many people in their 40s and 50s have some degree of control over when they get paid and when they can take deductions. That can lead to valuable tax savings.

In general, tax advisers urge clients to accelerate deductions and defer income. That means taking as many deductions around the end of each year as possible and deferring income until next year. This explains why many schools and charities receive the bulk of their contributions in December of each year.

But in some cases, the reverse strategy may work best. For example, suppose you were unemployed most of this year and, thus, had very little income, but you just started a lucrative business. You might want to accelerate as much income as possible into this year, when your tax bracket is lower, and defer deductions until next year, when you will have more income and those deductions will be worth considerably more.

Timing can also be important if you run a business where you can control when you get paid. Deciding when to send out a bill can save a bundle in taxes.

Your 60s and Beyond

Retirement and old age bring special tax challenges as well as a few unique opportunities that many younger taxpayers may wish they had.

Do not overlook at least one big, once-in-a-lifetime break: The tax laws allow those age 55 or older to sell their homes and exclude up to $125,000 of the gain from taxes. (For a married couple filing separately, the limit is $62,500 per person.) This provision could save a homeowner $35,000 in capital-gains taxes. But pay close attention to the details. For example, the law makes it clear that this is something you can do only once. And if you are married, neither you nor your spouse may take advantage of the exclusion if either of you took it previously.

That can call for some planning. Suppose two 55-year-olds who are planning to marry want to sell their separate homes and buy a new one together. Assuming that neither has taken advantage of this special break, they should consider selling their homes before getting married so that each can claim a $125,000 exclusion. If they wait until after they are married, their total combined exclusion will be $125,000. Or suppose a 60-year-old man decides to marry a woman who already has used the exclusion. He should consider selling his home before getting married so that he can use the exclusion. That tax break will disappear once he is married.

TRICKY WITHDRAWALS

One of the trickiest issues for many people in this age group is how to withdraw money from retirement-savings plans. It may seem tempting to grab all your hard-earned money in one lump sum, and in some cases that may be a smart move. There may, however, be better strategies. You will find more information on this subject in the Guide to Retirement Planning, Appendix D. But this area can be so complex that you should consider seeking professional advice from your tax adviser, your company, or both.

While income taxes may seem painful, estate and gift taxes can be even more so. There are many ways, though, to ease the sting.

Accountants urge many upper-income people who can afford to do so to consider making more gifts each year to other family members. The tax laws allow you to give anyone $10,000 a year free of taxes. The donor does not have to pay any gift tax, and the recipient does not owe any income tax. You can make this gift to as many people as you like, and a married couple can give $20,000 a year to each recipient.

There is a way to give even more: Pay someone else's school tuition or medical bills. That does not count toward the $10,000-a-year limit. But be sure to pay those bills directly, rather than giving the money to someone else to pay the school or doctor.

Remember that the tax law generally allows one spouse to leave an unlimited amount of money directly to the other spouse (assuming that spouse is a U.S. citizen) without having to worry about estate taxes. It is also possible to donate securities or other property to your favorite charity and retain some income for life. There are special types of trusts that you can form to help ease the tax burden.

ESTATE-TAX AUDITS

The larger the estate you leave, the more likely it will be audited by the Internal Revenue Service.

TYPE OF RETURN	PERCENTAGE AUDITED
Gross estate of	
Less than $1 million	8.20%
$1 million to	
less than $5 million	22.78%
$5 million and over	48.00%
Total	15.17%

NOTE: Data are for fiscal year 1994.
SOURCE: Internal Revenue Service.

THE REWARDS OF GENEROSITY

Consider donating stock, bonds, art, and collectibles that have risen in value to your favorite museums, schools, and other qualified non-profit groups. If you sold such appreciated property, you would have to pay capital-gains tax on the difference between what you received for the item and your cost basis. But if you donate it to a qualified recipient, you can deduct full market value.

Many people in this age group move from the frigid Northeast or Midwest to the Sun Belt. If you move, you need to be sure to cut enough of your old ties so that you are not subjected to taxes in two states. New York has a reputation for being especially aggressive in going after people who have moved out of state while maintaining ties, such as a house, an apartment, country-club membership, or

---

60s +

- Take 55+ home-sale break.

- Plan 401(k), IRA withdrawals.

- Check estate-tax strategies.

- Donate appreciated property.

- Cut tax ties if moving.

other affiliation. Some experts recommend that to avoid needless hassles from state tax officials, you should sever any significant tie with your previous state. Because this can be such a complex issue, check with a state tax specialist before moving.

TAX-EXEMPT HEADACHES

Tax-exempt bonds can be great for high-bracket taxpayers. But they can sometimes lead to surprising tax headaches.

Suppose a widow paid an investment manager $10,000 a year to manage her money. Investment-management fees typically are deductible as a "miscellaneous" deduction. But if the widow's money is invested entirely in tax-free bonds, she cannot deduct any of that $10,000. The rule is that you may deduct investment, custodial, and trust administration fees and other expenses you paid for managing investments that produce taxable income.

Similarly, suppose the widow paid $100 for a safe-deposit box and used it to keep only her tax-free bonds. That $100 is not deductible as a miscellaneous expense. For the fee to be deductible, the safe-deposit box would have to be used for storing investments that produce taxable income.

EASING THE HASSLE OF TAX TIME

Sorry, but there is no way to make paying taxes fun. It is possible, however, to make the annual exercise of filing your return a bit less taxing—on your sanity and on your bank account.

The trick is not to allow yourself to be overwhelmed by anxiety about tax compliance or lust for deductions. Fear and loathing often lead people to throw up their hands and do nothing; obsessive tax avoidance frequently leads even smart people to do foolish things, from making bad investments to pursuing unnecessarily complicated tax strategies. As with other aspects of personal finance, keep it simple and get it done.

Making tax planning a year-round issue will help. Too many people put off even thinking about taxes until just before the filing deadline, when it is too late to do much about their tax situation. The real tax savings are realized over the course of the year by considering the tax consequences before you make important financial decisions.

SPOTTING DEDUCTION OPPORTUNITIES

Keeping your records in order will reduce tax headaches and save you money, too. If you get in the habit of staying organized as you go along, you will eliminate the desperate, last-minute search through desk drawers, filing cabinets, and shoe boxes for the brokerage statement or the charity receipts you need to figure your tax bill. Good record keeping makes it easier to spot itemized deductions, to estimate your future tax liability, and to figure out ways to avoid overpaying.

Mutual fund investors, for instance, can easily make costly mistakes without good records of how much they paid for their fund shares. Home buyers can save hundreds of dollars by keeping track of things like points, the additional interest that buyers typically pay up front at the closing. People who give money to charity must have receipts for any gifts of $250 or more; it no longer is enough just to have a canceled check.

Keeping organized tax records can make it much easier for your spouse or other family members to take over in case something happens to you. And organized records are a must in case the IRS summons you for an audit. Failure to keep good records has torpedoed many a taxpayer's case in the U.S. Tax Court, the special court where taxpayers may go to argue their case without first having to pay their tax tab. Perhaps even more important, you may be able to avoid a costly battle with the IRS merely by showing that you have good records.

Tidying up your records will also lower your bill if you hire someone to handle the chore of preparing your return. One of the classic blunders many people make is to dump mountains of unorganized tax records, bills, and receipts into a big box or shopping bag, then drop the mess on the preparer's desk. Accountants and other tax preparers generally charge extra to dig through this sort of hodgepodge.

But no matter how much you may trust your accountant, never turn over the only copy of your records. Make copies of all important documents. If your accountant loses your records, the IRS is not likely to show you much sympathy. There may be some documents and tax forms that you will need many years from now that should be photocopied and placed in a separate file. These include any papers relating to a home purchase or sale, as well as details of nondeductible contributions to an Individual Retirement Account.

AVOIDING BAD ADVICE

You can also save yourself a lot of grief if you avoid bad tax advice and do not waste money and time pursuing complicated strategies that generate little if any real savings. There is simply no reason to let yourself be led astray by inexperienced preparers or know-it-all relatives. Commission-driven salespeople pushing municipal bonds, annuities, life insurance, and other tax-advantaged investments are also not a good source of tax advice. Although some or all of those products might have a place in your financial inventory, the risk is that the seller's principal motivation may be making a sale, not solving your problem. Even if he or she has the facts right, the salesperson could encourage you to put taxes ahead of other, more important considerations.

Comprehensive tax-preparation guides that are updated annually are available from several major publishers and accounting firms, and the IRS itself will let you have one of the best for free—its Publication 17, *Your Federal Income Tax*. If you are handy with a computer, low-cost tax-preparation software can often help speed the search for the right answer.

Finally, you really do not have to do it all yourself. In fact, for many people with complex tax situations, it would be foolish even to try mastering all the tax-law provisions that apply. The rules can be counterintuitive, and the penalties for making honest mistakes can be hefty. Knowing when to surrender and seek experienced professional help is important.

HOW LONG SHOULD YOU SAVE OLD TAX RECORDS?

Some pack rats retain tax returns forever. But that is probably excessive.

You very well may need records pertaining to home improvements, purchases, and sales decades from now. The same is true with nondeductible contributions to Individual Retirement Accounts. So it is only prudent to stash such records in a safe place.

Otherwise, there is little reason to hold on to most tax returns after six years. The IRS generally has about three years in which to examine your return, six if there is substantial underreporting of income. But there is no time limit for matters involving fraud.

READY, SET, GO

Dig out the calculator, dust off the PC, and pour yourself a cup of coffee: It is time to sit down and do your taxes—or, at least, get the information off to the accountant.

While much of the advice taxpayers receive deals with the dreary details of filling out tax forms, at least half the battle is sorting out the year-end statements that show how much you earned from your employer, bank accounts, stocks, and other investments, and how much you paid out for deductible items, such as home-mortgage interest, state and local taxes, and charitable contributions.

Breaking the task into two parts—getting the paperwork together, then filling out the return—can make the job much less daunting. And it can reduce errors, lower your taxes, and cut tax-preparation fees. Here is a look at the tasks to tackle first.

• **Sort the mail.** Start by hauling out last year's federal, state, and local returns to remind yourself what you will need to pull together this year. Then collect all that mail you have been getting since January: those forms from banks, brokerage firms, mutual fund companies, and mortgage lenders, as well as the W-2 from your employer. Also gather records of any income from self-employment or other sources, such as jury-duty fees or lottery winnings.

Next, match the statements to items reported on last year's return. You may find it helpful to staple envelopes to the old return, then file documents for wages, interest, dividends, and other income and for itemized deductions in the appropriate envelopes.

Looking at last year's returns can remind you of income sources you may have overlooked, such as interest on a checking account or a mortgage-escrow account. It will also reveal whether a document has not arrived. If it is later than early February and you do not have an information statement, contact the issuer and get it. Partnership statements, however, may take longer. Also check that the information squares with your own records. If it does not, ask for a corrected statement. The IRS relies heavily on the information on these forms to flag returns that omit taxable income or claim excessive deductions.

KNOW YOUR TAX BRACKET

Your federal income tax bracket depends on your filing status and your taxable income. Just how much income it takes to put you in a specific bracket is adjusted each year for inflation. These are the federal tax brackets for the 1996 tax year.

TAX RATE	TAXABLE INCOME			
	SINGLE	MARRIED FILING JOINTLY	HEAD OF HOUSEHOLD	MARRIED FILING SEPARATELY
15%	Up to $24,000	Up to $40,100	Up to $32,150	Up to $20,050
28%	Over $24,000 to $58,150	Over $40,100 to $96,900	Over $32,150 to $83,050	Over $20,050 to $48,450
31%	Over $58,150 to $121,300	Over $96,900 to $147,700	Over $83,050 to $134,500	Over $48,450 to $73,850
36%	Over $121,300 to $263,750	Over $147,700 to $263,750	Over $134,500 to $263,750	Over $73,850 to $131,875
39.6%	Over $263,750	Over $263,750	Over $263,750	Over $131,875

SOURCE: Internal Revenue Service.

If you plan to do your return yourself, this is also a good time to check whether you have all the necessary tax forms. If you do not, you can get copies at post offices, libraries, some banks, and the IRS. If you have a child, be sure to get him or her a Social Security number. The IRS now requires you to list the Social Security numbers of all dependents claimed on your return. (If your baby was born in December 1996, you do not have to list a Social Security number until you file your return for the 1997 tax year.)

• **List income and losses.** Make a list of income from all sources. Taxpayers who want to go further, or who plan to prepare their own returns, might want to break their income sources into separate piles corresponding to the forms and schedules on which the income will be reported:

Form 1040: Wages; salaries; bonuses; alimony received; Social Security benefits; distributions from pensions, annuities, profit sharing, or other retirement plans; prizes

Schedule B: Interest and dividend income

Schedule C: Income from self-employment or sideline jobs

Schedule D: Capital gains and losses

Schedule E: Supplemental income and losses (rents, royalties, partnerships, estates, trusts)

• **List adjustments and deductible expenses.** Adjustments to income reduce a taxpayer's adjusted gross income. The adjustments, which are reported on the front of Form 1040, include deductible contributions to Individual Retirement Accounts, alimony paid, Keogh contributions, and self-employed health insurance premiums.

Itemized deductions, which are reported on Schedule A, are subtracted from adjusted gross income to determine your taxable income. Since various types of deductions are treated differently, they should be listed separately.

• **List expenses that qualify for credits**. Credits for expenses such as child care or dependent care can reduce the amount you owe Uncle Sam. List the amounts you paid as well as any reimbursements you received from your employer so you—or your accountant—will be able to calculate the credits later.

• **List tax payments.** Do not forget amounts withheld from wages and estimated payments.

• **Decide on your filing status.** Most married couples will benefit by filing a joint return. But there are cases where it may pay for a married couple to file separate returns. For example, suppose the spouse with the lower income has large amounts of deductions, such as medical costs. That spouse might be able to use all those deductions by filing separately,

GETTING A FILING EXTENSION

What if you simply cannot collect all your records in time to file by the mid-April deadline? Apply for an automatic four-month extension by filing Form 4868 before the April deadline. More than 5.7 million people did just that in 1994.

This does not give you any extra time to pay your taxes. You are supposed to estimate how much you owe and pay any amount due when filing for the extension. You can still receive an extension if you do not pay, but you will be liable for interest and perhaps penalties.

Need even more time? The IRS does grant additional extensions until mid-October, but these are not automatic. You must have a good reason. Examples include a medical emergency or not having important records you need to complete your return. To request an additional two months, fill out Form 2688.

rather than jointly, because it would be easier to meet the threshold tests: For example, medical expenses are deductible only to the extent they exceed 7.5% of a taxpayer's adjusted gross income.

Making the Most of Your Deductions

These days, finding tax deductions is like striking oil.

With top-bracket filers running into federal rates of around 40%, every dollar of deductions they dig up can save roughly 40 cents in federal taxes. Including state and local income taxes, a deductible dollar can save some people 50 cents or more.

If you have itemized deductions in the past, start with a quick glance down your old Form 1040s and Schedule As. That should jog your memory for the obvious, perennial write-offs: mortgage and home-equity interest you pay on up to $1.1 million in debt for a primary home and a second home; charitable donations of cash and property; and state taxes you pay.

But in addition to those popular write-offs, taxpayers should also investigate some of the following easily overlooked deductions.

• **Retirement accounts.** You may be able to lower your taxes and benefit from tax-deferred compounding by contributing to an Individual Retirement Account. If neither you nor your spouse is covered by an employer-provided retirement plan, such as a pension, 401(k), or profit-sharing plan, you may be eligible to put up to $2,000 of taxable compensation a year into an IRA and deduct the sum from your taxable income. Your spouse is also eligible to make a deductible contribution—up to $2,000 a year if he or she is employed. If your spouse is not employed, beginning in 1997, the two of you can contribute up to $4,000, split between two accounts. The money grows tax-deferred until it is withdrawn, typically years later after you retire.

You may be able to make a deductible IRA contribution even if you or your spouse is covered by an employer-sponsored plan—as long as your income falls under certain thresholds. For singles, the most you can earn and still deduct the maximum contribution is

$25,000; for married couples, the combined amount is $40,000. Singles who make up to $35,000 and married couples who make up to $50,000 may get a lesser deduction.

Just because your employer offers a retirement plan, it does not necessarily mean that you are covered for purposes of the IRA rules. That hinges on whether you or your spouse is an "active participant" in such a plan. Perhaps you have not been on the job long enough to qualify. Or maybe your employer did not make a contribution for the year into the company's profit-sharing plan. If you are not sure, check the W-2 form employers send out around the end of January: If you are considered an active participant in the company retirement plan, it should be indicated on the form.

You can set up your IRA and make your contribution for the year as late as the day you file your return for that year, not including any extensions you get. If, say, you make a contribution for 1996 before April 15, 1997, you can deduct the sum from your 1996 taxable income.

Self-employed people—or even those with regular jobs who have qualified self-employment income, such as director's fees in some cases or freelance writing income—have other options. They can stash about 13% of their self-employment earnings up to a certain dollar amount ($22,500 in 1996) in special accounts called Keoghs or Simplified Employee Pensions. With special types of retirement plans called "money-purchase" Keoghs, you may even be able to deduct up to 20% of your income (up to $30,000 in 1996). You have until your filing due date, including any extensions, to make your contribution for the prior tax year. But Keoghs have to be set up by December 31 of the year in which you want the deduction. Otherwise your contribution can reduce only your current year's tax bill.

• **State taxes.** As many people know, you can deduct the income taxes you have paid to the state during the year. But sometimes taxpayers deduct only the amount of state taxes withheld from their pay, forgetting about that check they wrote out to the state last April when they filed their return for the previous year. That money is deductible on your return for the year you wrote the check. Local real estate taxes are also deductible. And you can deduct automobile property tax, too, if your state assesses the tax based on the car's value.

• **Investment interest.** Interest on loans you took out in order to invest is generally deductible, as long as you have offsetting investment income and you did not use the loan to buy tax-exempt securities. If you do not have enough offsetting investment income in one year, you can carry the deduction over into subsequent years. But if you are using investment interest to offset long-term capital gains, you may wish to let the deduction ride another year. Reason: If you are in the 31%, 36%, or 39.6% federal tax brackets, you already receive a break on long-term capital gains, which are taxed at a maximum rate of 28%. You might want to forgo the interest deduction, pay the capital-gains tax, and save the investment-interest deduction for a later year when it might shelter income, such as dividends and interest, that would otherwise be taxed at your highest rates.

• **Charitable gifts.** If you itemize deductions on your tax return, you can generally deduct money and property you contribute to churches, hospitals, and other qualified charities. Charitable deductions can equal up to 50% of your adjusted gross income. There is a lower ceiling if you are giving property that has appreciated in value or you make donations to charities such as veteran's organizations, public cemeteries, or fraternal organizations. But you can carry forward any excess for five years.

You must have a receipt for any donation valued at $250 or more. You also generally need a statement showing how much of your gift is deductible if you give more than $75 to an organization and get something in return, such as theater tickets.

• **Moving deductions.** Job-related moving expenses are deductible even if you take the standard deduction. But you can deduct only the moving expenses that were not reimbursed by your employer. To qualify, the move has to be related to a new job or new job location. In addition, the IRS wants to see that the new job would add at least 50 miles to your current commute. For instance, say you now live 20 miles from work, and you get a new job. The new job has to be at least 70 miles from where you live now if you want to deduct the costs of moving to a more convenient home. There is also a "time test" for employees and self-employed workers. For example, employees generally have to work at least 39 weeks at the new job site for the deduction to hold up. If you leave the area before having worked there 39 weeks, you may have to declare the value of the deduction as income. Such expenses as meals, temporary lodging, and pre-move house-hunting costs are not deductible.

• **Liquidated investments.** People who owned limited partnerships or trusts that were liquidated or sold during the year may have left-over deductions from those investments.

For instance, losses from limited partnerships over the years may have been nondeductible because they were "passive" and could only offset income from similar passive investments. In the year the investment is sold or otherwise disposed of, however, you can usually deduct all those carried-over passive losses against capital gains or ordinary income, such as your salary.

The beneficiary of a trust also might earn a deduction the year the trust is terminated for carried-over capital losses or net operating losses.

A tax adviser should review such deductions, since they can be tricky.

• **Miscellaneous deductions.** Some of the best deductions are off-limits unless, taken together, they add up to more than 2% of your adjusted gross income. Someone making $50,000, then, can deduct only miscellaneous expenses that exceed $1,000. But what is deductible may surprise you. Here is a sampling:

- Unreimbursed business expenses of an employee
- Union dues and expenses
- Employment-related education
- Job search expenses
- Subscriptions to professional publications
- Depreciation of home computer required by an employer
- Dues to professional societies
- Medical exams required by an employer
- Passport for business trip
- Protective work clothing

- Research expenses of a college professor

- Tools and supplies used in your work

- Appraisal fees to figure a casualty loss

- Clerical help connected to collecting investment income

- Legal fees to keep your job

- Safe-deposit box rental

- Service charges on dividend reinvestment plans

- Tax advice and preparation fees

- IRA trustee fees, if separately billed and paid

These are just a few of the possible deductions. Keep in mind that any expense reimbursed by your employer is generally not deductible. For more information, see IRS Publication 529, *Miscellaneous Deductions*.

MEDICAL DEDUCTIONS

Medical deductions are hard to come by. Once you add up all allowable medical costs, you must subtract 7.5% of your adjusted gross income from the total. Only excess medical costs are deductible on your Schedule A. Someone earning $50,000, then, could deduct only medical expenses that topped $3,750.

Still, it is not impossible to reach that level, and some of the qualifying expenses may surprise you:

- Insurance premiums

- Insurance deductibles and co-payments

- Prescription drugs

- Contraceptives and abortions

- Psychologist or psychiatrist visits

- Travel to the doctor, dentist, or other medical professional, including parking and tolls

- Part of the cost of installing a pool for medical therapy, provided the costs are reasonable and you exclude any value that is permanently added to your home from the deduction

To the extent costs are reimbursed by an insurance company, they are not deductible. For more information, see IRS Publication 502, *Medical and Dental Expenses*.

Easy Ways to Attract Unwanted Attention

Most people like to keep a low profile when it comes to taxes. But you cannot always avoid attracting the Internal Revenue Service's attention. Sometimes, it is because of entirely legitimate deductions that nonetheless raise questions. And sometimes it is for things that no one reading this book would ever do.

• **Deduct part of your home expenses as an office.** A Supreme Court ruling has made it very tough for many salespeople, teachers, consultants, and other self-employed workers to deduct any of the costs of a home office. So even if you are convinced that you are entitled to do so, remember that your chances of being audited rise sharply.

• **Report a loss on Schedule C.** Schedule C is the form for people with income from self-employment. It allows you to deduct legitimate business expenses, and if those expenses are high enough, you will end up with a loss. Be ready to defend yourself.

• **Do not sign your return.** Neglecting to sign your return is an open invitation to the IRS to reject it.

• **Neglect to report taxable income.** Your employer sends forms each year to the IRS reporting your income; companies that pay you dividends and interest also report those payments to the IRS. Guess what? The IRS looks to see if you have reported an equal amount on your return.

• **Cross out the statement above your signature swearing that you are filing a truthful return.** Some tax protesters have tried altering this statement, but the IRS typically refuses to accept such a return. The courts typically refuse to accept protesters' arguments.

• **Do not file a return because you fervently believe the United States has no right to impose an income tax.** Forget it. The IRS routinely hits tax protesters with hefty penalties for this kind of flaky excuse.

The Alternative Minimum Tax

If you think doing your taxes is a pain in the neck, pity the poor folks who get caught by the alternative minimum tax (AMT), a special tax that hits some upper-income taxpayers. People who are subject to the AMT are prime candidates for really good professional tax help.

Basically, the AMT is intended to blunt the benefit some taxpayers receive from various deductions or excluded income. For instance, some senior executives get incentive stock options from their employers. If they follow the rules, these lucky folks can use the options to buy their employers' stock at a below-market price and not have to worry about taxes until they sell the shares. That is, they can do so under the regular tax rules. For AMT purposes, the difference between the fair-market value of the stock and the special, lower price they pay for it is taxable in the year the incentive stock options are exercised.

People who stand a good chance of being subject to the AMT first have to figure their tax liability under the regular tax rules, then recompute it using the AMT rules. If the AMT rules result in higher tax, that is what the taxpayer must pay.

An experienced tax pro can often help people who run the risk of being caught by the AMT navigate their way around it by planning the timing of deductions and income. In other cases where there is no escape, they can help taxpayers make the best of it.

Fortunately, most of the people affected by the AMT can afford the kind of tax help they need. The vast majority of taxpayers can only wish we were fortunate enough to have such problems.

What If You Cannot Afford to Pay?

It happens to many people for many different reasons: a serious injury; the loss of a job; a disastrous investment; a lawsuit. Whatever the reasons, many people in financial distress find that they simply cannot pay the IRS the full amount they owe. And, believe it or not, the IRS can actually be understanding.

One option is to ask for permission to pay in installments. How do you do that? If you owe less than $10,000 and you really do not have the cash, attach Form 9465 to the front of your tax return. If you owe more than that, you have to fill out a financial statement and provide more documentation of your finances. You should receive a reply from the IRS within 30 days, the IRS says. There is a $43 user fee for signing up for an installment agreement, and there is a $24 fee for restructuring or reinstating an agreement.

Another option is to ask the government to accept less than the full amount of taxes you owe, taking advantage of an increasingly popular IRS program called Offers in Compromise. The latest statistics show sharp increases in the number of offers that the IRS receives and accepts.

But do not expect the IRS to compromise for less than you owe unless you can prove that there is absolutely no way for you to pay the full amount. IRS officials routinely demand extensive proof before they will agree to compromise. Be prepared for an avalanche of questions and demands for documentation.

DOING BATTLE WITH THE IRS

Suppose you are hit with a big tax bill that you do not agree with, and you have exhausted all your appeals within the Internal Revenue Service. You can fight the IRS in court without first having to pay a penny of the tax due—but only if you go to the U.S. Tax Court, which hears cases around the nation.

Many taxpayers who appeal to this court represent themselves, without relying on a lawyer. But because the tax law can be so extraordinarily complex, it may be wise to consult a lawyer about the nature of your case and for advice on which court to choose.

For details on filing requirements and other rules, write:

Clerk's Office
United States Tax Court
Washington, DC 20217-0002

There are other options. Suppose you already have paid the disputed tax in full, filed a claim for a refund, and had no luck. Then you may try filing your case in a federal district court or the U.S. Claims Court.

TRY THE ADVOCATE

When all seems lost, consider turning for help to the IRS Taxpaper Advocate. That is the name for the IRS's problem-resolution program, which has staffers around the country to rescue stricken taxpayers from the jaws of bureaucratic bunglers.

It will not help everybody, but some people who have used it say it can be of great assistance. For example, it does not intercede in audits, because there is an IRS appeals process for that. But these officials can handle more routine snafus, such as stalled refunds and erroneous penalties.

In most areas, you can attempt to reach IRS problem-resolution officers by telephoning

800-829-1040. However, as with most IRS phone numbers, it may be difficult and frustrating getting through to the right person. Be persistent—although you may need to invest in a phone that automatically redials.

For voice-recorded information about the program, you may call IRS Tele-Tax; in most areas, the number is 800-829-4477. You also may call 800-829-3676 and ask for IRS Publication 1546, *How to Use the Problem Resolution Program of the IRS.* Also ask for Publication 1, *Your Rights as a Taxpayer,* and Publication 594, *Understanding the Collection Process.*

Estimated Taxes and Withholding

Uncle Sam is not like a genial bartender. You cannot simply run a tab of your annual tax bill and then come clean once a year on April 15. That is why your employer must withhold from your paycheck throughout the year. And that is why, four times a year, many taxpayers have to pay estimated taxes.

If you wait to write a check for any shortfall when filing your return, the IRS could hit you with penalties. Generally, the rules require that you pay at least 90% of your ultimate tax bill during the year, through withholding or estimated taxes. If your withholding plus estimated tax payments will not cover 90% of your tax bill, then you may owe penalties on the shortfall—whether or not you write a check April 15.

There is a safety net. If you have managed, through withholding or estimated payments, to pay 100% of what you owed last year (or 110% if you made more than $150,000 last year), you can usually escape a penalty. It is smart, therefore, to check your withholding to make sure it will total enough over the course of the year to at least keep you from having to pay a penalty.

Adjusting withholding is also a good way to avoid having to make estimated tax payments on income from investments, self-employment, and other sources not subject to withholding. In fact, all things being equal, withholding is frequently a better way to pay such taxes. The reason is that you can meet your tax obligation through withholding any time during the year. Generally speaking, quarterly payments cover only tax owed on income you received in the same quarter or later in the year.

Say you received a $5,000 capital gain in January 1996 and decided at the end of that year to pay the $1,400 capital-gains tax through a quarterly payment, which you send in by January 15, 1997. In all likelihood, you have made the wrong move. Under IRS rules, the first payment should have been made by the April 15 after you earned the gain—in this case, April 15, 1996. You could be penalized for underpaying.

If, instead, you ask your employer to withhold an extra $1,400 from your December 1996 pay, the IRS would treat the money as though it had been paid in evenly over the course of the year.

Many people withhold heavily from their year-end bonuses to cover just this kind of tax shortfall. Withholding from bonuses is also considered paid in pro-rata over the year. But you have to receive the money before the end of the year. And you have to tell your company's payroll department ahead of time to boost the withholding. Otherwise the amount withheld is apt to be a flat 28%, plus any state withholding.

But those who owe too much to use withholding or who are not employees of a company that withholds for them must face the complex world of estimated tax payments.

To figure what your quarterly check should be, the IRS provides a form called 1040-ES. Any quarter in which you receive sizable sums of income from which taxes have not been withheld, you should run through the form. It includes a worksheet that will help you project your tax bill, including self-employment tax.

Self-employment tax is the entrepreneur's version of the Social Security and Medicare taxes that are withheld from employees' paychecks, at a rate of 7.65%. Self-employed people must pay the employer and employee share of such taxes, however, which comes to 15.3% of their first $60,000 or so of earnings, and 2.9% on all self-employment income above that. (The exact amount is subject to adjustment annually.) If you have a salary, you may have paid in enough Social Security tax through your job, however, so you may owe only the 2.9% portion.

Those who pay estimated taxes usually have to do so ratably throughout the year. That means the IRS expects you to pay one-fourth of your bill each quarter equally, due April 15, June 15, September 15, and January 15 of the next year. (If a due date falls on a weekend, the deadline becomes the following Monday.)

If, however, you receive a windfall in, say, the third quarter and suddenly realize that means you must pay estimated taxes, then you need only start paying by the due date for that quarter. You can pay what you will owe on the windfall all at once or over the remaining two quarterly periods for the year.

If you earn most of your income in one or two quarters late in the year, fill out the worksheet for those with "annualized income" in IRS Publication 505, *Tax Withholding and Estimated Tax.*

A FOUR-STEP WITHHOLDING PLAN

Getting your withholding to more closely match your tax liability is sometimes frustratingly difficult, especially for two-income couples. But if you have patience, it is possible to achieve at least a rough approximation.

1. Fill out an updated Form W-4.

Your payroll department may be able to help. Working couples should fill out the Two-Earner/Two-Job Worksheet on the back. In most cases, advisers say, both spouses will have to take zero withholding allowances and maybe ask that an additional amount be withheld. File the new W-4 with your employer.

2. Check your new withholding.

When your new withholding shows up in your paycheck, multiply it by the number of pay periods left in the year. Do this for your paycheck and your spouse's. Add that amount to the amount that was withheld earlier in the year, before you amended your W-4s.

3. Estimate your tax liability.

Use Internal Revenue Service Publication 919, which is updated annually, to figure out what your tax tab for the year is likely to be.

4. Adjust your withholding.

If you find that the amount being withheld is not enough, ask your payroll department to withhold an additional amount equal to the projected shortfall. For example, if you see that you will come up $1,000 short for the year and you expect to receive 17 more semimonthly checks, you can fill out another new W-4 that instructs your company to withhold an extra $59 per paycheck.

If you find that too much is being withheld, ask your payroll department how many additional allowances you should take to decrease your withholding by the projected overpayment. And yes, file another new W-4.

HOME, SWEET TAX SHELTER

Many people earn their best tax breaks from their homes.

They often receive their first sizable tax deductions by writing off mortgage interest and property taxes. Once they have built up some equity in their home, it becomes a vehicle for tax-favored borrowing, since they can take out a home-equity loan of up to $100,000 and deduct the interest on it, virtually regardless of how they spend the money.

Here is a look at the major tax considerations of home ownership.

• **When you buy.** When you take out a mortgage to buy your principal residence, you can deduct any points you pay to the lender. Points, which are typically paid at the closing, are additional interest collected by mortgage lenders. Each point is equal to 1% of the mortgage amount, so two points on a $100,000 mortgage would be $2,000—far from small change. Fortunately, you can deduct the points in full for the year you pay them, provided that they are not out of line for your area and that they represent prepaid interest, which points typically do.

If the seller pays the points, you can still deduct them if you are the buyer. But when you later sell the house, you must subtract the full amount of the points in figuring your cost basis on IRS Form 2119, Sale of Your Home.

• **Once you own.** When you own your home, you can deduct all of the mortgage interest you pay, plus the property taxes your state or city imposes, provided such deductions and any other itemized deductions you have for the year add up to more than the standard deduction.

You will find how much interest you have paid on your Form 1098 from the mortgage lender. That form is sent to both homeowners and the IRS. A word of caution, though: Sometimes the 1098 you receive may be wrong. For example, it may not reflect a check mailed in late December for payments due January 1. If that happens, you should go ahead and deduct the full interest you paid for the year, including the December amount, but attach a statement to your return explaining why your deduction does not match what the bank has reported. Or if you have enough time, ask your bank to issue a corrected form before you file.

• **When you refinance.** If you refinance your loan and have to pay more points, you generally cannot deduct them all in one year. Typically, you have to deduct them pro-rata over the life of the loan.

• **When you sell.** Selling a home, even at a big profit, often does not trigger immediate capital-gains taxes. You postpone the tax on the profit as long as you buy a replacement home that costs at least as much as the one you sold. (By the way, if you qualify, this postponement of tax is mandatory, not optional. Who says the tax collector never gives you a break?)

Taxpayers qualify to roll over their profits from a sale into a new home if they purchased the new home either two years before or two years after the date of sale. The date of sale is listed on your Form 1099-S, Proceeds from Real Estate Transactions. If you did not receive the form, the date of sale is either the date the title is transferred or the date "the economic burdens and benefits of ownership are transferred to the buyer," whichever is earlier, says the IRS.

A word of warning, though. If you replace your home more than once in two years, you may face tax on any profit you realize on any sales after the first one. This rule does not apply if you move for work-related reasons that would qualify you to deduct your moving expenses.

Homeowners keep track of their postponed profits on Form 2119, which they must file with the IRS. Although people typically roll over capital gains untaxed from house to house, chances are someday they will face taxes on the cumulative deferred sum. So, if you have not been in the unfortunate position of selling at a loss each time you sell one home and buy another, it is important to minimize the profits you report on Form 2119.

One way to do so is to increase the amount you report that you pay for each new house, known as its "adjusted basis." You subtract the adjusted basis from the sale price to come up with your capital gain. You can add the cost of significant home improvements over the years, such as a new roof or remodeling, to the home's adjusted

HOME IMPROVEMENTS THAT CAN HAVE A TAX ADVANTAGE

Improvements that permanently and substantially enhance the value of your home can be added to its "basis," reducing the taxable gain when you sell.

PERMANENT INSIDE IMPROVEMENTS

Sinks	Counters	Garbage disposals	Tubs
Cabinets	Jacuzzi	Towel racks	Track lighting
Alarm systems	Built-in bookcases and furniture	Fireplaces	Flooring
Heating and air conditioning	Water heaters	Attic and ceiling fans	Telephone jacks

MOVABLE ITEMS, IF LEFT BEHIND

Appliances (washers, microwaves, etc.)	Mirrors	Fireplace equipment
Game-room equipment	Exercise equipment	Garden tools

OUTSIDE ADDITIONS AND IMPROVEMENTS

Porches	Decks	Garages	Septic tanks
Cesspools	Sheds	Patios	Terraces
Barbecue pits	Tennis courts	Swimming pools	Hot tubs
Pathways	Driveways	Fences	Swing sets
Dog houses	Screen doors	Mailboxes	Gutters
Drainpipes	Additional acreage	Landscaping	Trees and shrubs

SOURCE: Coopers & Lybrand L.L.P.

basis. You can also lower your stated profits by the amount you spend on such selling costs as commissions, advertising, and legal fees.

If you sell for less than you paid, watch out. While you may think your misfortune gives you a deductible loss, you are probably wrong for two reasons.

First, losses on the sale of a home are almost never deductible. If you move out of your home and then rent it out for longer than a temporary stretch of time, you may be able to deduct a subsequent loss in value as a business loss. But the tax law is not clear on how long you have to use your home as a rental property before it qualifies as a business.

Second, selling your home for less than you paid does not necessarily mean that you actually have a loss. You may have previously rolled over untaxed profit from an earlier home that exceeds the decline in the value of your latest home. Say ten years ago you sold a home for a $50,000 profit, deferring taxes on that amount by buying a new, $150,000 home. This year you sell the second home for $125,000—a $25,000 "loss." If you replace the last home within two years, you will roll over $25,000 of gain, rather than $50,000. Retirees or others who trade down by buying a new home that costs less than the adjusted price of their old home may owe a tax on the price difference.

Rather than paying the tax, some taxpayers may elect on Form 2119 to exclude up to $125,000 of home-sale profits. You must be age 55 or older to do so, and you should be aware that once you use it, you cannot use it again. So you may want to go ahead and pay the tax on a $25,000 gain, for example, if you think years from now you might realize an even greater home-sale profit.

• **When you have a second home.** A second residence, say a vacation house, is treated essentially like your first for tax purposes. Property taxes and interest on up to $1 million in mortgage debt on the two homes, plus $100,000 of home-equity debt, generally are deductible. If you rent out your second home for 14 days or less, you do not have to declare the income on your income tax return. But the tax consequences can become complicated if you rent it out for 15 days or more. There is more information on this later in this chapter and in Chapter 7.

TAXES AND INVESTING

One of the biggest mistakes many investors make is neglecting to focus on taxes. What may look like a brilliant investment decision may actually turn out to be a poorly timed major blunder after factoring in taxes. Or what may look like a highly conservative, uninspired investment decision may seem to be a brainstorm after considering taxes.

THE BASICS

When it comes to income taxes, it is not just whether your investments made money or lost it that counts. How you played the game can be vitally important to the Internal Revenue Service. Reporting interest and dividends is pretty straightforward. It becomes more complicated if you had offsetting capital gains and losses from investment sales, extensive mutual fund transactions, or income from rental real estate. Start with the easy stuff first.

• **Interest income.** Interest from bank accounts, most types of bonds, and other sources generally is taxable at ordinary income tax rates. Interest from U.S. Treasury bonds, bills, and notes is subject to federal tax, although not to state and local taxes. How much you have to report to the IRS on your tax return is shown on forms you should receive from financial institutions in January.

Interest income from municipal bonds is generally exempt from federal income tax—and from state income tax for residents of the state where the municipal bond was issued. Note that the IRS requires you to report tax-exempt interest anyway.

• **Dividend income.** Dividends paid on corporate stock and mutual funds are taxable at ordinary income tax rates. Again, how much you have to report to the IRS on your tax return is shown on forms you should receive in January. Check those statements carefully for any distribution that is a partial return of capital. Such distributions are not taxable, but you must reduce the basis, or cost, of that investment by the distribution amount. This will increase your gain (or reduce your loss) when you eventually sell the investment.

Foreign income taxes are often withheld from foreign dividends paid to U.S. taxpayers and mutual funds, and investors frequently are entitled to a credit for that withholding against U.S. taxes. But claiming a credit is so much work that many people are happy to settle for an alternative: taking a deduction. Tax credits reduce the tax you have to pay dollar-for-dollar; deductions reduce your taxable income and, thus, are less valuable.

• **Capital gains.** Gains from sales of investments held for more than a year are long-term gains and are taxed at a top stated rate of 28%. That is way below the maximum 39.6% federal income tax rate for ordinary income such as salary, interest, and dividends.

On Schedule D, you list short-term gains and losses on assets held for a year or less and combine them to produce a net short-term gain or loss. You figure your net long-term gain or loss the same way. Then you combine those two numbers to arrive at your overall net gain or loss.

If you have both a long-term net gain and an overall net gain, you turn to the Capital Gain Tax Worksheet in the 1040 instructions. You use this worksheet to figure your total income tax.

If you have an overall net loss, you may deduct as much as $3,000 of it from your ordinary income in any one year (or $1,500 each for a married couple filing separate returns). Then, in effect, you store any excess loss to offset capital gains or ordinary income in future years.

Mutual Fund Tax Tips

Mutual fund investors may be able to save especially large amounts of taxes by focusing on the details. With a little study, some investors may discover they can transform what would have been a huge capital-gains tax into little or no tax, simply by choosing one of the various methods that are available when shares are sold. Fund experts say many investors wind up overpaying in this area because of some remarkably simple errors or because they did not realize they had several options available to report gains or losses on sales of fund shares.

Consider this example: You invested $1,000 in a mutual fund several years ago and told the fund to reinvest all your subsequent dividends automatically in new shares. Over the years, you save all your statements and have a total of reinvested regular and capital-gains distributions of $1,000. This year, you sell all your holdings for $5,000. What is your taxable gain?

The answer may seem to be $4,000. Wrong. The right answer is

$3,000. That is because your cost is your purchase price ($1,000) plus all those reinvested dividends (another $1,000), on which you have already paid taxes. Subtract $2,000 from $5,000, and that is your gain. Thus, it is especially important to save any documents showing how much you have received in reinvested dividends. Good record keeping can be the difference between a big tax bill and a small one. Otherwise, you may wind up paying tax twice on all those reinvested dividends.

Figuring your gain or loss becomes more complicated if you sell some, but not all, of the fund shares that you purchased at various times and prices. There are three basic ways to do it. Which one produces the lowest tax bite will depend on the circumstances.

• **First in, first out.** One method is to assume that the fund shares you sold were the first ones you bought. This method may work best for investors whose fund shares have dropped sharply in value. It is also the method the IRS assumes unless you specify otherwise. Be careful: In a rapidly rising market, this method can be a very costly one to choose.

• **Average cost.** You simply calculate the average cost of all the shares you purchased and use that figure as your cost in calculating gains or losses on shares you sell. This method has grown popular because many funds now provide this information to their shareholders. Another version of the average-cost method involves separating your shares into short- and long-term holding and getting averages for each. But relying on either version of the average-cost method may not be as advantageous as the third general method.

• **Specific identification.** With this method, you pick out and sell specific shares in order to produce the lowest possible tax bill. As you might expect, though, the IRS has set up some tough obstacles. You have to specify in writing at the time of the sale which shares you are selling and obtain written confirmation of this selection from the fund. Unfortunately many funds say they simply are not equipped to do this.

See IRS Publication 564 for further details on the tax treatment of gains and losses on mutual fund sales.

SOME OTHER FUND ADVICE

Many mutual funds offer check-writing privileges, which means shareholders can take money out of the fund merely by writing a check. That is very convenient. But do not forget that every time you write a check, you may have a taxable transaction, with a gain or loss that needs to be reported. That is even true if you are switching money from one mutual fund to another fund in the same fund group.

Remember that you have to report capital gains and losses even on mutual funds that invest in tax-exempt state and local government bonds.

Be especially careful about investing in mutual funds around the end of each year. Mutual funds typically distribute income and capital gains to their shareholders late each year, usually during November or December. If you receive a distribution, you will generally have to pay taxes on it—unless you bought the shares for a tax-deferred account, such as an Individual Retirement Account. You will be stung with a tax bill even if you invested in the fund just a few days earlier. You can encounter the same problem at other times of the year if you invest shortly before a distribution is made, although the biggest fund payouts usually occur late in the year. Take this tip from mutual fund professionals: Before you invest in a fund, call the fund and ask if it plans any distributions and if so, when, and how much. Then consider waiting until just after the record date for any payment.

Another caution: Suppose a mutual fund says it will pay a distribution to shareholders of record in late December of 1997 and you do not receive the distribution until the following January? The distribution is taxable for 1997.

THE DEVIL IS IN THE DETAILS

Where taxes are concerned, you always have to focus on the details if you want to avoid paying too much or running afoul of the Internal Revenue Service. Here are five areas to watch:

• **Investment losses–investment gains.** Losing money is never pleasant, but a loss may seem a little less painful if you can use it to cut your tax bill. Say you bought a hot stock several years ago and sold it this year for $25,000 more than you paid for it. Terrific—only now you are facing having to pay a big capital-gains tax. But suppose that you are $25,000 in the hole on another not-so-hot stock you bought two years ago. It may be worthwhile to swallow your pride and dump that loser this year. The $25,000 loss could be used to offset the $25,000 gain, saving you from having to pay any capital-gains taxes.

• **Investment losses–ordinary income.** Selling an investment at a loss can save you money even if you have no investment gains. Up to $3,000 of investment losses may be used to reduce your taxable income from salary and other sources—assuming your taxable income is at least equivalent to the amount of the deduction. If your net capital loss is greater than $3,000, or if it exceeds your income, you can carry over the unused portion of the loss into subsequent years.

• **"Wash sales."** No, this has nothing to do with laundry. A wash sale is what the IRS calls it when an investor sells a bond or some other security and buys substantially the same security within 30 days before or after the sale. Do that, and you are not able to deduct a loss on the security you sold.

So if you buy a new stock or bond right away to replace the one you have sold, make sure the new one differs in some significant way from the old one. For example, if you sell a bond and decide to buy a new one, make sure the new bond has a different interest rate or maturity date, or perhaps buy a bond of a different issuer.

• **Municipal bonds.** Buying tax-exempt bonds issued by the state in which you live, or municipal-bond funds that invest only in those bonds, can be a smart move, especially for investors in such states as California, Massachusetts, and New York that have high tax rates. With such in-state bonds, you escape federal and state income tax on the interest.

But it makes little or no sense to take this approach in states with no state income tax or with very low taxes. Large numbers of people in Texas (which has no state income tax) and Florida (which also has no state income tax but does have a small tax on "intangibles," such as out-of-state bonds) do just that. Many of these investors could be earning higher returns—and diversifying their portfolios—by buying out-of-state bonds.

Another common mistake involving tax-exempt bonds is forgetting that they are not exempt from capital-gains taxes. Any gains or losses on municipal bonds that you sell are treated the same as gains or losses on your other investments. Thus, if you buy a municipal bond for $10,000 and sell it several years later for $20,000, you have a long-term capital gain of $10,000. You cannot exclude that gain by arguing it is a tax-exempt bond.

Figuring out taxes on sales of tax-free bonds can be tricky. The rules can be enormously complex, especially for bonds you purchased for less than their face amount after a certain date. What may seem like a simple capital gain may be ordinary income, or a mixture of capital gains and ordinary income. Common sense is not always a good guide. Consult an expert.

• **Rental real estate.** This is another area where it can easily pay to see a tax specialist. Rental income is shackled to the forbidding passive-loss rules, and people who rent out a vacation home part-time may find they are sinking fast if they try to do their own calculations.

Usage of a part-time rental property may be classified for taxes as "personal," "rental," or "mixed," depending on the number of days of each kind of use. Things can become really complicated in cases of mixed usage, which is when you use your vacation home for more than 14 days or 10% of the total number of days it was rented out, whichever is greater. If you did, you must deduct expenses according to complicated rules, and the deductions cannot exceed your rental income. You may wind up with a passive loss that you can use only to offset the next year's rental income from the same property.

Give yourself a real tax break: Call an accountant before you invest in rental property.

TAX TIPS FOR THE SELF-EMPLOYED

Face it. Being in business for yourself is no bowl of cherries. And not the least of it is the mountain of tax requirements.

Even if you are just a sole proprietor, there is that special Schedule C you must file with your individual tax return, the record keeping, and those quarterly estimated payments. And how about having to pay both the employer's and the employee's portions of the Social Security and Medicare taxes!

Still, there are also plenty of nice things about being self-employed—even some of the tax rules. Being self-employed opens up a wide range of tax deductions and tax-saving opportunities that most people who work for large companies just do not have.

Keeping More of What You Earn

Many self-employed people pay lots of unnecessary tax each year because they do not take time to learn how to make the most of the special deductions available to them. If you are self-employed, you very well may have overlooked some of these tax-saving ideas. Keep in mind that people who are self-employed are always wise to seek professional tax advice. Certainly, you should not try any of the following without getting professional guidance about whether it is applicable in your individual situation.

• **Buying equipment.** The general rule when you buy such things as computers, office furniture, and other equipment is that you must depreciate it over the number of years the IRS figures you will benefit from the property. But thanks to a special provision in the tax law known as Section 179, you can deduct up to a certain amount for many such items in the year you put them to use.

But be careful: You generally cannot choose this speeded-up depreciation for so-called listed property that you do not use more than 50% of the time for business. Listed property includes cellular phones, computers, and property that is otherwise considered entertainment-related, like a VCR. You usually have to depreciate those items over a number of years. You also cannot use Section 179 for cars, real estate, or property held for investment.

There are also a number of qualifications. Among other things, you typically cannot bring your business income below zero with this election. And years after you elect to deduct an item all in one year, the Section 179 election can come back to haunt you. If you go out of business before you would have finished depreciating a piece of property under the normal rules, you may have to repay some of the tax benefit you got from choosing Section 179 treatment.

• **Deducting health care costs.** Self-employed individuals may deduct a portion of their health insurance premiums, a tax break that takes at least some of the sting out of being responsible for your own health coverage. But you can get an even better deal if you hire your spouse.

You read that right. Self-employed people can pay for family health insurance for employees and deduct the premium payments as a business cost—even if the employee is the business owner's spouse and the plan covers the business owner as a dependent. You may even be able to deduct your family's other medical costs as a business expense by setting up a medical-reimbursement plan, in which you agree to reimburse your spouse-employee for things like dental or vision care or other out-of-pocket medical costs.

Caution: If you later hire other employees, you will have to reimburse your other workers to the same extent you do your spouse. Also remember that when you hire employees, including your spouse, you have payroll-tax obligations and other administrative responsibilities.

• **Tax-advantaged retirement plans.** One of the biggest breaks available to self-employed people is the ability to shunt hefty chunks of deductible dollars into special retirement plans, such as Keoghs or Simplified Employee Pensions (SEPs). Each year, you may be able to sock away as much as 20% of self-employment earnings (up to $30,000 in 1996). Both Keoghs and SEPs are tax-deferred retirement plans available through banks, brokerage firms, and mutual fund companies that allow you to put your money in a variety of stock and fixed-income investments. The contributions are deducted from your taxable income, and taxes on the earnings are deferred until the money is withdrawn.

SEPs are generally easier to administer than Keoghs. But only Keoghs offer the chance to shelter up to 20% of your pay. With SEPs alone, the limit is about 13% of pay (to a maximum of $22,500 in 1996). You can reach 20% by setting up both a profit-sharing plan and a money-purchase Keogh. With a profit-sharing plan, you contribute a percentage of compensation to a SEP or a Keogh. But you also have some discretion to forgo contributions if you choose. With a money-purchase Keogh, you are generally obligated to fund the plan every year.

Self-employed people who have employees generally cannot contribute to Keoghs or SEPs unless they also fund plans for their employees. See an accountant before tackling this.

• **Home offices.** When you use part of your home exclusively for business, you may be able to write off a pro rata portion of the utility, mortgage-interest, and homeowner's insurance expenses.

A tip: You may be able to choose the most preferential way of determining what percentage of such expenses you attribute to your home office. If all the rooms in your house are of roughly equal size, you could just take one-fifth, say, of the expenses in a five-room house. If not, then you would divide the square footage of your home office by the total square footage of your house.

But before you start tallying it all up, make sure you will pass the tough IRS tests that determine who can write off any home-office expense. It is especially tough if you spread your work between many job sites.

You must, for instance, make sure your home office is used "exclusively" and "regularly" as your "principal place of business" for the business you perform there. Or use it regularly and exclusively to meet with clients, customers, or patients as a regular part of your business.

Each word of these limitations for deducting the home office has been extensively dissected and argued over by the IRS and taxpayers. For instance, whether your home office is your "principal place of business" is a very tricky question, with the answer turning on how important your duties are there and the amount of time spent there compared with other business places.

In an eight-page explanatory revenue ruling issued by the IRS, there is an example of a woman who sells jewelry through mail order and at craft shows. She spends 25 hours a week at home filling mail orders and about 15 hours a week peddling her wares at craft shows or consignment shops. Because she performs the principal moneymaking chores of her business at more than one place, the IRS focused on where she spent the most hours. That was home, and she got the deduction.

But a teacher who spent more hours at home than in the classroom lost the deduction, since his job's primary focus was teaching, which he does not do at home. Thus, his home cannot be his principal place of business.

It is a little easier if your home office is in a separate structure, such as a garage. In that case, while you still must use the space exclusively for business, it does not matter how much time you spend there or whether clients visit you there. Costs like rent and upkeep are usually deductible.

Make sure you can show your business is conducted with an intention to make a profit and that it is not merely a hobby. And be aware that people who have depreciated part of their home can have major headaches figuring out their taxes when they sell that home years later.

You should also be aware that taking the deduction, no matter how legitimate, makes you more susceptible to being audited by the IRS.

• **Car expenses.** When you use your car for business trips, you may be able to deduct an array of related costs.

There are some restrictions. Driving from

HELPFUL INFORMATION FROM THE IRS

These Internal Revenue Service Publications contain information that will be of great help to many people who are self-employed:

- Publication 505: *Tax Withholding and Estimated Tax*
- Publication 535: *Business Expenses*
- Publication 560: *Retirement Plans for the Self-Employed*
- Publication 587: *Business Use of Your Home*
- Publication 590: *Individual Retirement Arrangements (IRAs)*
- Publication 917: *Business Use of a Car*

STRATEGIC DEDUCTING

Self-employed people often have expenses they could take either on their personal tax return or on their Schedule C business return. Examples of expenses that can go either way include home-equity interest if proceeds of the loan were spent on the business; property taxes on a car used largely for business; business-related tax advice; or state or local business-profit taxes.

When there is a choice, it is almost always preferable to deduct such expenses on your business return. You not only reduce your income taxes that way but also trim the level of income hit by the 15.3% self-employment tax. In addition, you can deduct the full amount of certain expenses, such as tax advice; if you claim such miscellaneous expenses as itemized deductions on your regular return, you can deduct only amounts in excess of 2% of your adjusted gross income.

home to a regular workplace is deemed to be commuting, so the associated costs are not deductible. Also, all car expenses must be prorated if you use your car partially for personal travel.

Generally speaking, though, you can deduct the cost of gas, repairs, oil, registration and license fees, supplies, and car-club dues on Schedule C. You may also be able to depreciate the car, usually over six years but sometimes even longer. In lieu of actual operating costs, you can deduct a specified amount per mile. Either way, you can also deduct parking fees, tolls, property taxes based on your car's value, and interest you pay on a car loan.

• **Hiring your kids.** Hiring your kids can be a big tax saver, too. Anything you pay them as bona fide employees is tax-deductible for the business. And your kids may not owe much tax on the income, either.

For instance, you can pay Junior up to the amount of the standard deduction, and he will not owe any income tax on it. (The standard deduction is adjusted each year; in 1996, it was $4,000 for singles.) The next $23,000 or so you pay him will be taxed at only a 15% rate. (Again, the exact amount is adjusted each year.) And if your child is under 18, you do not have to pay Social Security taxes on his or her salary.

WHEN IT IS TIME TO CALL FOR HELP

It does not pay to be brave.

For many people with complex tax situations, it would be foolish even to try mastering all the tax-law provisions that could apply. The tax rules can be so counterintuitive, you can easily drive yourself crazy. And the penalties for making honest mistakes can be hefty.

Those who undoubtedly should seek professional counsel include couples going through divorce, entrepreneurs who have purchased or sold their own businesses, and anyone facing the alternative minimum tax, a separate tax system that forces many upper-income Americans to pay tax on sums that are not taxable for regular income tax purposes. Investors who have sold bonds, especially municipal bonds they originally purchased at a discount, and people who own rental property would also be well advised to ask for help. So would people who have moved overseas or have just returned to the United States from a foreign posting.

Tax professionals can help you deal with the complex filing requirements in such situations. Even more important, they can also give advice on longer-term tax planning that may save you far more than the price of their help.

Finally, even if you do not feel your tax situation is all that complicated, you may still want to pay someone to do the dirty work for you. There are, after all, many more interesting things to do than struggle over a tax return. Little wonder that paid preparers handle two out of three long-form 1040 federal returns and nearly 1 in 10 of the supposedly simple 1040EZs.

HIRING A PRO

Once you have decided to get professional help, where do you find someone you trust at a price you can afford? After all, even though a preparer signs your return, you are the one who is on the hook for interest and penalties if the IRS finds something wrong.

Qualifications and fees vary enormously. Anyone can claim to be a tax expert without getting a license or being cleared by the IRS, and there are many preparers who have simply hung out a shingle with no discernible training.

Among the choices are big chains, such as H&R Block, and Jackson Hewitt Tax Service. Preparers at these chains must pass tests each year to prove at least a basic proficiency in tax preparation. Then there are certified public accountants (CPAs) and "enrolled agents." CPAs are tested and certified by their states to do a range of accounting work, including taxes. Enrolled agents have either passed

ADVICE FROM THE IRS

It is free—if you can get it.

Each year, the IRS is flooded with phone calls from taxpayers seeking help on their returns. Tax specialists say the quality of IRS advice generally is good, especially on relatively straightforward questions such as on what line to put what type of income.

But getting through by phone can be nearly impossible, especially around mid-April. Indeed, reports from the General Accounting Office, Congress's watchdog agency, indicate that it is much tougher than it once was to reach the IRS by phone.

Even if you can get through, the IRS is probably not the place to go if you have a tricky question or are unsure about a gray area of the law. The IRS says its toll-free helpers had an impressive accuracy rate of 89.5% in 1994. That was up from 89.1% the prior year. But that still means they were wrong more than 10% of the time. Unless your question is simple, save yourself time and aggravation: See a private specialist.

a tough IRS tax exam or have spent at least five years working for the IRS in certain job classifications. Some preparers have qualified to use the designation Accredited Tax Preparer by taking courses and a national test through the College for Financial Planning in Denver.

CONTINUING EDUCATION

Most tax preparers, especially if they belong to a professional society, are forced to undergo some degree of continuing education—an absolute necessity in the ever-changing world of taxes. If you find that a preparer you are considering has lagged educationally, you might want to keep looking.

Be prepared to pay a CPA anywhere from $75 to $250 an hour. Fees of enrolled agents may be slightly lower. Chains like H&R Block and Jackson Hewitt often charge the least, but many of their clients tend to use simpler returns like the 1040A or 1040EZ.

Simply picking the most accredited or most expensive preparer will not guarantee quality help. While most of H&R Block's clientele file ultrasimple returns, for instance, many branches have enrolled agents with years of experience doing more complex tax returns. Tax lawyers often do not prepare returns at all. And some CPAs who specialize in auditing, for instance, do very little tax work except maybe around filing time.

To find a good preparer, you must ask some questions. Find out how many years a candidate has been preparing returns and how often he or she does returns with your particular tax problem. If you have many passive activity losses and some rental properties, for in-

CHECKING UP ON PROFESSIONAL PREPARERS

The following professional associations can tell you if a preparer has taken the classes necessary to be a member in good standing.

ENROLLED AGENTS
- National Association of Enrolled Agents (301) 212-9608

CERTIFIED PUBLIC ACCOUNTANTS
- American Institute of Certified Public Accountants (201) 938-3100

stance, you would want to steer clear of somebody who is unfamiliar with Form 8582 or Schedule E.

Ask who will represent you in case of an audit and how you will be charged in such an instance. In some of the storefront chains, the person who prepared your return may not be the one handling an audit. You should find out what happens if you are penalized for a preparer's mistakes. You could also ask to speak to clients with tax situations similar to yours or clients who have gone through an audit with the preparer.

If your tax life is especially complex, you might do well to consider a tax firm that has many partners or associates. Frequently, such firms have a policy that more than one person reviews your return before it goes out the door. Each member of such a multiprofessional firm often has unique strengths the others can tap, too. Taxes have become so complex that there is no one who knows everything.

CYBERHELP FOR DO-IT-YOURSELFERS

If you have a home computer and a relatively uncomplicated tax life, you might consider tax software as a backstop to filing your return solo. These programs often cost no more than $40 and come both in early-bird versions to help you get started on your return before the end of the year and in final versions for preparing the return you actually send to the IRS. Two top sellers are TaxCut by Block Financial and TurboTax by Intuit.

The programs guide you through your return, either by asking questions and slotting the numbers for you on the right lines on the return, or by letting you use the computer as a souped-up calculator, where you input the numbers yourself. The programs' strengths are the tax tips that pop up as you go along that can help keep you from running afoul of tax laws or alert you to deductions you might not have known you could take. They also do the math, a nice plus for those whose checkbooks seem to be constantly off-kilter.

But as good as some of the programs have become, using them is not like having an accountant in a box. Only a savvy tax professional can guide you through more complex situations and advise you about the alternatives if you enter a gray area.

9

STEERING CLEAR OF MISTAKES AND SCAMS

"Experience," as Oscar Wilde once noted wryly, "is the name everyone gives to their mistakes."

When it comes to finances, most of us have plenty of experience. We certainly make enough mistakes.

Some blunders may be clear only with perfect 20/20 hindsight. For example, you may still be kicking yourself about that stock you sold at $69 a share that soared shortly thereafter to $175. Or perhaps you missed a great opportunity to save money by refinancing your home mortgage. While you sat biding your time, convinced that interest rates would continue to fall, rates suddenly lurched back up again.

Although painful, these kinds of mistakes are not usually fatal—and they often are unavoidable, even for the best and brightest on Wall Street. But some other mistakes—the ones you really want to avoid—can easily endanger your family's financial security or undermine the quality of your life. Here are just a few examples:

• Neglecting to buy enough liability insurance could subject you and your family to a devastating loss if someone is injured on your property and takes you to court.

- Sinking your severance pay into a "business opportunity" you saw advertised on television or in your local newspaper, or entrusting your savings to a crooked investment adviser, could mean the difference between retiring to that condo in Arizona and moving in with one of your kids.

- Not buying life insurance with a big enough death benefit could condemn your family to years of struggle if you were to die unexpectedly tomorrow.

- Failing to make out a will, or to update an old will, could mean that some of your relatives and friends you would like to leave something to would get nothing.

- Failing to begin putting money aside early enough could leave you unable to afford the college education you want for your children.

Fortunately, many mistakes like these can often be averted by taking some simple precautionary steps. Indeed, steering clear of many of the biggest financial potholes is merely a matter of educating yourself about the basics of personal finance, making certain that you have a secure financial safety net, and taking advantage of valuable opportunities, such as a tax-deferred retirement-savings plan at work.

You also should heed a few simple, old-fashioned rules that may sound stunningly obvious but all too often are ignored: Investigate thoroughly before you invest. Know the people you are dealing with, especially people to whom you have entrusted large amounts of money. And do not sign anything unless you have read it and understand it thoroughly.

These words of caution, as well as other advice in this section, may sound overly harsh and suspicious. After all, most people are accustomed to trusting others, especially when it comes to arcane issues involving investments and finances. Doing homework on investments and finances also may sound boring and overly cautious. Yet, as many victims will tell you, even small doses of knowledge in this area can save large amounts of headaches and financial suffering later.

Above all, do not be ashamed to ask questions—lots of questions. The only truly dumb questions are the ones we are afraid to ask.

DO NOT BE SMUG

Beware also of overconfidence. Even some of Wall Street's smartest and most successful executives and money managers have been badly burned by con artists, swindlers, and professional scamsters. Others have lost fortunes chasing seemingly surefire investment opportunities that went bust. Wealthy people often are no better than the rest of us when it comes to picking the right time to buy or sell an investment. As John Kenneth Galbraith, the author and economist once observed: "The association of intelligence with money is deeply suspect. This should be everyone's guiding rule."

Consider the experience of John Whitehead, a former co-chairman of Goldman Sachs, one of the country's most prestigious and most powerful investment firms. He was one of many wealthy individuals who handed over large amounts of money to the Foundation for New Era Philanthropy, which promised to double the money of hundreds of nonprofit institutions. The foundation later collapsed, filing for bankruptcy protection in 1995.

Mr. Whitehead was a true believer in New Era right up to the end. Not long before the foundation's collapse, he told a reporter for *The Wall Street Journal:* "It's remarkable. It's absolutely aboveboard, thoroughly honest. It may sound a little bit too good to be true, but it's absolutely wonderful." Later, he was dismayed: "Oh, my God, I cannot believe it. I'm normally very skeptical about these kinds of things, and it is hard for me to believe that I was played for a sucker."

Or take Warren Buffett, the billionaire investment wizard. He readily admits to having made some king-sized mistakes. Looking back on some of his biggest errors, he wrote the following in the 1994 annual report of Berkshire Hathaway, the company he long has headed: "Top honors go to a mistake I made five years ago that fully ripened in 1994: Our $358 million purchase of USAir preferred stock, on which the dividend was suspended in September. In the 1990 Annual Report I correctly described this deal as an 'unforced error,' meaning that I was neither pushed into the investment nor misled by anyone when making it. Rather, this was a case of sloppy analysis, a lapse that may have been caused by the fact that we were buying a senior security or by hubris. Whatever the reason, the mistake was large."

There is little reason to be concerned about the long-term financial health of Mr. Buffett or Mr. Whitehead. But most of the rest of us are of more modest means, and we have much less room to maneuver.

THE HIGH PRICE OF CRIME

Scams, swindles, cons, rip-offs. Call them what you will, investment frauds cost Americans $10 billion a year, according to the Federal Bureau of Investigation. People often lose money to crooks because they do not check up on the professionals upon whom they rely. This applies not only to investment advisers but also to lawyers, accountants, and tax preparers. Many people depend too heavily on their innate ability to sort out trustworthy professionals from charlatans. Con artists often are highly gifted salespeople, with ever-changing schemes, who excel at appealing to investors' fear and greed.

As Securities and Exchange Commission officials emphasize repeatedly, there is no substitute for checking public records for clues that could tip you off to a possible fraud. Those records can be tremendously helpful in warning you about potential problems. Moreover, powerful new computers are making it easier than ever to search through valuable public records.

Still, while investment frauds and other scams grab the headlines, more people probably lose far more money in perfectly legal dealings. They follow bad advice either from inexperienced financial advisers or from advisers who put their own interests ahead of their clients' affairs. They pay large commissions and management fees when less expensive products and services would fit their needs just as well. They do not take advantage of easy opportunities, such as retirement-savings plans at work, that can cut their current income taxes while helping them achieve their long-term goals.

Finally, too many people fail to take that last step. They may go to great lengths to do financial planning but never finish the job. Some create complicated trusts but never put any assets in them. Some develop smart investment programs but never get around to revising their portfolios. Succumbing to inertia is one of the easiest mistakes to make. As you learned in Chapter 1, just keep it simple and get it done.

AVOIDING THE BIG MISTAKES THROUGH THE AGES

Most people do dumb things with money from time to time. Some people make it a bad habit. But if you pay attention to the financial fundamentals, keep your eyes open for opportunity, and watch out for those who see you as their opportunity, you should be able to avoid the most painful mistakes.

The following sections highlight some of the major errors of commission and omission made by people in their 20s and 30s who are just getting started, individuals grappling with the conflicting demands of middle age, and older men and women trying to preserve their financial security and the quality of their lives through a long and well-deserved retirement.

YOUR 20S AND 30S

When you are fresh out of college and just starting in your career, it is easy to assume that you cannot make costly mistakes because you earn so little and have accumulated so little. That is Mistake Number 1. Even at this early age, it is remarkably easy to make mistakes that can haunt you for years.

Financial planners agree that one of the biggest mistakes younger people make is piling up too much debt, especially on credit cards. It is easy to run up large credit card balances these days, as lenders compete vigorously to attract customers. But credit cards are among the most expensive ways to borrow. Moreover, many recent graduates may already owe tens of thousands of dollars on college loans. Add the rent, car payments, and the minimum monthly payments on a number of credit cards, and the total can be staggering.

Another common mistake is failing to take advantage of all tax-deferred retirement-savings opportunities, especially those offered by your employer. Some people do not participate because they are making so little money that they think they need it all for everyday living expenses. Others may be trying to collect enough for a down payment on a car or home. Still others may assume they do not need to start thinking about retirement at such a young age, or they may simply be confused because the retirement plan sounds complicated.

DO NOT PASS UP FREE MONEY

Contributing to a 401(k) plan or similar savings plan at work will make a significant improvement in the quality of your retirement, and it will lower the taxes you pay today. In addition, many employers match all or part of whatever you contribute, up to a certain amount—in effect, giving you free money. And if you need some of the money quickly, such as to buy a car or make a down payment on a home, you can borrow from the plan at most companies and pay it back later. In short, this is something you cannot afford to pass up.

Also, do not neglect to consider participating in a stock-purchase plan if your employer offers one. Some employers offer employees the right to buy stock in the company at a below-market price with no brokerage commission. Employees often have a choice of buying shares on a lump-sum basis or spreading out the purchase over a specified period, such as one year, through payroll deduction. Some of these plans can be convenient and easy ways to build savings. But do not make your employer's stock your sole investment. Diversification is crucial for long-term investment success.

It is sometimes easy for young people to fall into what financial planners refer to as the "invincibility trap." This is the mind-set that makes you feel as though you will outlive Methuselah and remain forever healthy and accident-free. Thus, many young people, even those with families, often fail to buy enough insurance, especially liability insurance and disability coverage. Those with families are making an especially big mistake if they fail to buy adequate life insurance. Term life insurance typically is very inexpensive for people in their 20s and 30s. It also is worth buying disability insurance if you are not covered at work or if your employer offers only minor coverage.

When just starting out, most people rent, rather than own, their homes, and hand-me-down furniture is common. Thus, it may be easy to forget about property insurance. But such coverage typically is relatively cheap. It really does not make sense to go without it. Consider buying "replacement-cost" coverage, which pays the cost to replace or repair your possessions, up to the policy's set maximum, rather than the much lower actual cash value of that old living room set.

PAY ATTENTION TO TAXES

Taxes are another area where young people can slip up. After all, many young people have relatively simple returns, with few if any deductions, exemptions, or exclusions. What could possibly go wrong?

Plenty.

One classic mistake made by many newly married couples is signing a joint income tax return without fully understanding everything on it. That seemingly innocent and trusting act can lead to years of trouble, frustration, and even financial ruin. Remember that when you sign a joint tax return, you typically are jointly liable for all tax debts. If your marriage later breaks up, you may find yourself saddled with the tax debts of your former spouse—even if that person is the one with the money. About the only way out could be proving that you were an "innocent spouse," something that is very tough to do, no matter how innocent you may be. This problem crops up frequently, tax accountants and lawyers warn. Thus, if your spouse refuses to explain something that looks questionable to you, be persistent. In some cases, it may even make sense to file separately, even though doing so usually means paying more in taxes.

Another error is not taking enough time to read your company's benefit plan booklet, especially the section about insurance payouts on high-cost medical conditions. Make sure you follow the requirements laid out by your employer, or you may not be covered for some expensive services and procedures. At the same time, check for useful benefits you may have overlooked. Many employers offer flexible spending accounts that let you have pretax dollars withheld from your salary to pay for medical expenses that are not covered by your health plan and for dependent-care expenses, such as babysitting or elder-care fees.

Finally, do not think that you are too young or that you have too little to be of interest to crooks. In fact, inexperience and youthfulness could make you an easy mark. For instance, are you buying a car? Beware of lenders offering seemingly attractive interest rates well below current market rates. If a loan sounds too good to be true, it probably is. For example, be on guard if someone offers you a loan at a "simple interest" rate. This may initially seem highly appealing, but simple interest is financial jargon for a rate that is based on the original principal amount of the loan. On a loan where the principal declines, the true interest rate can be much, much higher.

Many years ago, a New Yorker was offered a simple interest rate of 11% on a car loan at a time when such loans generally went for several percentage points above that level. When he showed up to sign the final papers, he noticed that the documents showed the "annual percentage rate," which is the real borrowing cost, was about 20%. Since he wanted the car, he went ahead with the transaction anyway, but he quickly arranged to refinance the loan with a bank at a much lower rate.

Your 40s and 50s

Many people in this age group are so busy earning a living and balancing the conflicting demands of life that they neglect to take even the basic steps to protect what they already have. One of the biggest blunders is failing to buy enough liability insurance coverage for your home, car, and other property. Waiting until after an accident occurs is the wrong way to discover your mistakes. Besides, a little extra liability coverage typically is not that expensive and can help you sleep more soundly at night. Consider an "umbrella" liability policy of $1 million or more.

Making sure you have enough life insurance can be critically important for families with dependents, such as young children. If your budget is tight, do not scrimp on the amount of coverage you need by purchasing a "cash-value" policy that includes a savings component. Get a less expensive "term" policy so that you can afford the death benefit you need. At the same time, if you have no dependents, you may be wasting money by buying any life insurance.

Another big blunder is failing to make out a will or forgetting to update an out-of-date will. Although these steps may sound obvious, lawyers say a remarkably large number of very successful men and women simply do not want to think about such grim matters, or they cannot be bothered with the intricacies of estate planning. Even people with wills often neglect to do some basic contingency planning. For example, if you have chosen a guardian for your child, be sure to name a backup guardian, just in case the person you chose declines the honor or cannot handle the responsibilities.

Your 40s and 50s are often peak earnings years, and that can make you an attractive target for a variety of illegitimate financial advisers and pitchmen. Take time to investigate thoroughly before trusting your financial well-being to anyone. Computer databases, law-enforcement authorities, reference books, and other public sources can tell you if the person you are considering has ever been disciplined or involved in litigation.

A top-notch adviser should be delighted to provide you with proof of credentials as well as details of how his or her firm has done over the years. Do not settle for investment results only during bull markets; ask for longer-term numbers that show how that firm has done in bearish markets, too. In general, the rule is simple: trust, but verify. Investors should also consider using several different investment firms to avoid placing a big bet solely on one hot hand.

VEILED SALES PITCHES

Beware of making snap decisions after going to a financial planning or investment seminar. Often, these seminars are thinly veiled sales pitches from brokers, insurance agents, and financial planners. While they may be sincere, they may also fail to mention alternatives offered by other firms that could be far more beneficial to you.

Be careful in monitoring what a broker does with your account. Never forget that brokers are paid commissions for buying and selling. Thus, be on guard against what is known as "churning," or making needlessly large numbers of trades designed primarily or exclusively to generate commissions for the broker. Be sure to tell the broker in writing what your investment goals are and how much risk you are comfortable in taking. Never hesitate to ask how much the broker receives for whatever investments are recommended. Many types of investments carry much higher rewards for the broker than others. There is a strong temptation for an unscrupulous broker to push those that pay the most, rather than what would benefit the investor the most.

Do yourself a big favor and just hang up on cold calls from people pitching stocks, bonds, commodities, or other investments. Often, such solicitations are scams or involve investments that are simply inappropriate. Many Americans willingly hand over large amounts of money to untrained brokers reading from carefully prepared scripts promising lavish returns.

Never be afraid to ask how much financial advice will cost. That is true not only when you are looking for an investment counselor but also when you are choosing a mutual fund. It is equally true when picking an estate planner, an accountant, or a lawyer. If you receive a bill that seems outrageously high, do not hesitate to challenge it. Such bills often turn out to be highly inflated—and highly negotiable. A husband and wife once were astonished to receive a lawyer's bill for $1,000 for what they considered to be relatively simple wills. With some reluctance, the husband phoned the lawyer and asked if there had been some mistake. No, the lawyer said, the $1,000 was correct. But, he quickly added: "What do you think is fair?" They settled for $500.

SHORTCHANGING YOUR RETIREMENT

If you have been conscientiously putting away money in an employer's retirement-savings plan, be careful about pulling out that money if you are, say, changing jobs or facing a financial hardship. To begin with, money you withdraw and spend today will shortchange your retirement. If that longer-term wisdom is not enough to dissuade you, consider this: Withdrawals are subject to income tax and, generally, a 10% federal penalty for people under age 59½. If you are switching jobs, you can avoid the taxes and penalties by having your retirement savings transferred directly to an Individual Retirement Account or to your new employer's "qualified" plan. If you face a financial emergency, consider taking a loan from

40s–50s

- Write a will or update an old one.

- Update insurance coverage.

- Investigate advisers carefully.

- Hang up on "cold calls."

- Avoid retirement-fund withdrawals.

your plan. Many employers allow you to borrow as much as half of the money in your account, up to $50,000.

After working in the United States for many years, you may be interested in an overseas job. If so, beware of the many con artists promising high-paying foreign jobs. Often, you are asked to pay an up-front fee to help get you to the promised land. Unfortunately, some of these companies fail to deliver. When checking out one of these advertisements, ask for examples of people who have actually gotten jobs overseas and take the trouble to check out what you have been told before putting down any money.

Be careful about structuring ownership of property. In some cases, joint ownership may be advantageous. But in other cases, it may create more headaches than it is worth. This area can be highly complex and may warrant a visit to a professional adviser.

Your 60s and Beyond

Welcome to the Golden Years—and watch your wallet. This can easily turn into the Dark Ages, thanks to armies of smooth-talking financial vultures and con artists who specialize in fleecing the elderly.

Even sophisticated investors can fall prey to high-pressure sales tactics from telemarketing scamsters or those who peddle their wares on television and radio and at free seminars. They zero in on the elderly because, as robber Willy Sutton once said about banks, that is where the money is. Con artists often peg their schemes to the latest headlines. For example, when interest rates are low and falling, you may hear pitches about a variety of "guaranteed safe" investments offering high returns. Among other ideas in this genre are interests in wireless cable licenses, rare coins, gasoline futures, oil leases, vending machines, and second mortgages—all of which are anything but safe, much less guaranteed.

Never send money to anyone purely on the basis of a telephone investment sales call, no matter how friendly and smooth the salesperson sounds. Similarly, never give out your Social Security, checking account or credit card numbers, or any other personal information to people over the telephone unless you are completely confident that you know the other person, that you have checked that person out carefully, and that the person has a legitimate need for the information.

MUNDANE MISTAKES CAN BE SERIOUS

While scams may be especially painful for their victims, people over 60 often fall prey to other, much more mundane money mistakes. Perhaps the biggest of these is putting too much money in supposedly ultrasafe investments, such as Treasury bills, bank certificates of deposit, money market funds, short-term municipal bonds, and bond funds. All of these may seem prudent, and it probably is wise to keep a sizable portion of your retirement money in fixed-income investments. But it can be dangerous to keep everything locked up in the fixed-income markets, which can be extremely volatile and highly sensitive to changes in inflation, both perceived and actual. Treasury bills and money funds may seem totally safe, but they typically provide little or no protection against inflation. The risk is that by playing it too safe, the investor might run out of money much earlier than expected.

Many elderly investors also make the mistake of looking only at an investment's yield, regardless of risk or other factors. This can result in purchasing much riskier bonds than they had intended. Or they may buy very long-term bonds, without realizing that these types of bonds will be hammered the hardest if interest rates surge. Pay attention to an investment's "total return," a measure that takes into account not only interest or dividend payments but also price changes. When tempted to grab the highest-yielding bond you can find, heed the words of Raymond F. DeVoe Jr., a New York–based investment analyst. Among "DeVoe's Unprovable but Highly Probable Theories" is this one: "More money has been lost reaching for yield than in all the stock speculations, scams, and frauds of all time."

If you are still employed and trying to decide when to retire, at least consider the merits of working a few extra years. Paying for a lengthy retirement will be expensive. Working a few extra years reduces the number of years you will have to depend on your savings, and it gives you more time to build up that savings. If your employer has a traditional pension plan—which promises a certain amount a month for life based on your age, length of service, and salary—staying on the job a few more years may boost your pension check by 25%, 50%, or even 100%.

Beware of buying health insurance that duplicates what you already have. Insurance regulators say many seniors, terrified of soaring medical bills, buy the same coverage from multiple companies, only to discover too late that they have wasted their money. Also beware of falling for sales pitches that focus on insurance for a single disease, such as cancer. It is usually smarter and much more cost-effective to buy broader insurance coverage. Focus closely on details of any exclusions.

One of the most painful mistakes that many seniors make is missing out on a once-in-a-lifetime opportunity to save taxes on a home sale. In essence, this provision allows many people who are age 55 or older to sell their home and exclude capital gains up to $125,000. It sounds simple, but taking maximum advantage of this offer may require careful thought and planning.

For example, suppose a 60-year-old man and a 59-year-old woman are planning to get married. They each own their home, and neither has taken advantage of the $125,000 exclusion. They would be well advised to consider selling their homes separately before getting married so that each of them can take advantage of the full exclusion. Once they are married, they have only one $125,000 exclusion between them.

Be sure to read the fine print on this important exclusion. For example, during the five-year period ending on the sale date, you must have owned your own home—and lived in it—for at least three years.

AVOIDING UNPLEASANT SURPRISES

Thinking about moving to a warmer climate? Before making the move, analyze the financial implications, or you may be in for some unpleasant surprises. Some people mistakenly assume they will be able to enjoy a much better lifestyle in a new state because it has a lower income tax rate than their old home state. Or perhaps it has no state income tax at all. But there may be other levies, such as higher property taxes, sales tax rates, or local fees, that more than

60s +

- Beware of telemarketing scams.

- Do not give out Social Security or credit card numbers.

- Take advantage of special home-sale tax break.

- Check tax consequences of moving.

- Put records in order.

offset this seeming advantage. There may also be tricky estate-tax problems.

Many people fail to put their records in order. Even the best-laid financial plans can go awry if important documents and records are missing. Take the time to compile a financial inventory, such as the one in Appendix B, and update it regularly. A neatly organized set of records can save you and your family large amounts of money in legal and accounting fees.

SCAMS, CONS, SWINDLES, AND FRAUD

Many people assume they are much too smart and much too sophisticated to fall victim to con artists and swindlers. When they read about someone losing thousands of dollars buying worthless securities or entrusting a retirement nest egg to an investment adviser who uses the money to feather his or her own nest, the common response is disbelief: How could anyone have been so stupid and so careless?

But the sad truth is that the financial world can be a vicious jungle, filled with sophisticated crooks determined to part you from your hard-earned savings. Although scams may seem obvious when you read about them, they are often hard to detect when they are happening to you. "Boiler-room" operators—those slick salespeople working out of high-pressure telemarketing offices in Southern California, Texas, Las Vegas, and south Florida—ought to be easy to spot. But even experienced investors fall prey to their tactics. It is difficult to appreciate just how persuasive con artists can be until you are actually on the receiving end of their sales pitches.

So stifle that instinct to assume it could never happen to you. No matter how sophisticated or cautious you think you are, you could be a target, especially if you have large amounts of money. The elderly tend to be particularly vulnerable. Scamsters love to pick on senior citizens, who often are too polite, too lonely, or too eager for help with their finances to run the other way. But do not let down your guard just because you have yet to get your first gray hair. Swindlers strike victims of all ages, both rich and poor.

Many victims fail to learn from their mistakes and, thus, fall prey to other scams. "It's like the guy who goes to Vegas to the 21 or craps tables," a rehabilitated boiler-room salesman explained to a *Wall Street Journal* reporter several years ago. "He's losing, but he keeps playing because he thinks there's a chance of winning it back." The former salesman said he sometimes took customer lists from one job to the next, soliciting clients he had already scammed. Some con artists try to disarm potential victims by feigning sympathy for a previous loss.

THE CROOK YOU KNOW

Less obvious than boiler-room operators—and hence potentially much more dangerous—are the many con artists who stack the odds in their favor by infiltrating religious, educational, and social organizations. By tailoring their sales pitches to the weaknesses and worries frequently shared by group members, these crooks often are able to sway individuals who usually are far from gullible. "Affinity frauds" have included investments in silver, gold, foreign currencies, second mortgages, mortgage-backed securities, promissory notes, and real estate. Victims have included doctors in Utah, political conservatives in San Diego, wealthy Polish and Indian immigrants in New York, and well-to-do Chinese-American business owners in San Francisco.

Scamsters are quick to pick up on the latest social and political trends, using come-ons that sometimes sound like they came right out of the morning's news headlines. Regulators have reported a growing number of rip-offs aimed at political conservatives. Among these are chain letters appealing to the recipients' presumed desire to get the government off the backs of the people and asking them to send money to individuals named in the letter. Recipients are then supposed to send letters to additional recipients, who will send them money—and so on, and so on, in a supposedly never-ending chain. This is essentially a "pyramid" scheme, a classic scam in which money from new participants is used to pay off people who got in at an earlier stage. Regulators say these scams typically collapse in the end, leaving a trail of anger, frustration, and often big financial losses.

Today's con artists also receive a big boost from technology. Thanks to on-line computer services and investment talk shows on radio and television, cold calls are not the only way they can get their message into your home. Computer services have proved especially attractive outlets for unscrupulous promoters pumping up prices of thinly traded penny stocks.

DO NOT FALL FOR IT

Con artists will assume virtually any guise if they think it will help them get you to part with your money. Law-enforcement authorities say there are cases each year of taxpayers handing over cash to people posing as Internal Revenue Service agents. In California, unsuspecting people at dozens of businesses throughout the state fell for a scam in which a person posing as a Federal Express deliveryman showed up with what he claimed was a cash-on-delivery (COD) package from state tax officials. After the phony courier left, the victims found that they had handed over good money for an envelope of state tax forms—which, of course, are available for free. California officials have tried to counter this scheme by announcing to anyone who will listen that they never, ever send anything COD to taxpayers. But the nervousness most people feel when they deal with tax authorities makes such gullibility at least partly understandable.

Some of the most effective scams have been pulled off by lawyers, accountants, and money managers who initially were honest but later proved unable to resist temptation. In such cases, many of the usual warning flags, such as a lack of credentials, simply were not flying.

But while con artists keep growing more and more sophisticated, and their scams are constantly mutating, law-enforcement officials say there are many steps you can take to minimize the chances of being plundered. Some of the best advice is so obvious when you read it that it hardly seems worth repeating—except that so many people so often ignore it:

• Never give a stranger any personal information, such as your Social Security number or a credit card number.

- Never be bashful about asking for proof of someone's identity. And do not just examine a shiny badge. Take down the name and number of the person and verify it.

- Just hang up if you get a cold call from a stranger trying to sell you commodities, stocks, bonds, or other securities over the phone.

- Always investigate before you invest or give someone money— even if the person offering that terrific deal is a member of your church or synagogue, country club, or bowling league.

- Beware of someone who offers to pick up your check by private overnight-express service. Regulators say that can often be a sign of trouble. Not only does it indicate undue haste, but also it could be that the person making the suggestion does not want to be open to mail-fraud charges.

Keep in mind that there is a wealth of help available to assist you in screening for potential scams. You will find phone numbers or addresses of state securities regulators and others who can help listed in Appendix A.

THE PERILS OF FAILING TO CHECK CREDENTIALS

Clever con artists are keenly aware that Americans often are much too trusting and polite to question the credentials of someone who is well dressed and well spoken. Scamsters also understand the average person's eagerness to help people in trouble and to cooperate with law-enforcement authorities to catch crooks. They have capitalized on these generous impulses with several cruel scams that often succeed masterfully in robbing people of large amounts of their savings.

Among the oldest and most popular is the "bank-examiner hoax," a fraud often perpetrated on the elderly. There are various versions of it, but here is one basic way in which it unfolds: You get a call from someone claiming to be a bank official or examiner who is investigating a teller suspected of theft from your account or others in the bank. The caller asks your help. Would you please go to your bank, withdraw several thousand dollars, and meet a "police officer" or "investigator" outside the bank? Do not tell anyone.

So, you cast aside your skepticism and agree to help. Outside the bank, you hand over the cash as "evidence" to someone who flashes a badge or credentials that certainly look official. Sometimes, that person calls back several hours later to thank you and to say that while the investigation is proceeding smoothly, more withdrawals are needed. Needless to say, once you hand over more money, you never see or hear from the con artist again.

Compounding the problem, victims often are too embarrassed to report to the bank or law-enforcement authorities that they have been fleeced. They would rather suffer in silence than face questions about how they could be so gullible.

The moral is simple: Take the time and effort required to make sure you know with whom you are dealing. A single phone call could save you a tremendous amount of embarrassment and financial pain.

Guarding against Investment Fraud

For many victims of investment scams, the culprit is not some faceless stranger but a trusted financial adviser. How on earth can you protect yourself from such betrayal?

Start by taking a close look at your finances and asking some hard questions. Is there anyone you rely upon so heavily that you would be destitute if that person turned out to be unreliable or crooked? For example, if you use a money manager, does that person have complete authority to make investment decisions without consulting you? Does that person also keep all of your investments at his or her office?

Even if this individual appears totally trustworthy, consider using the same principle that so many advisers recommend with investments in general: Diversify. Separate the money manager from the money, perhaps by keeping your money and securities in a bank custody account or some other safe place.

MORE THAN ONE PERSON

You might also spread your assets among several different advisers or money managers. Admittedly, it may cost more in fees than if you gave everything to one person. But it can be a smart move. Regulators say some victims of crooked money managers could have minimized the damage if they had not turned over all their personal investments, corporate investments, life insurance, stock brokerage investments, pension investments, and money market funds to one person.

If you have not already done so, give yourself a thorough financial audit. Make sure you have seen all the original documents relating to your most important investments. Regulators say some swindles could have been prevented if investors had demanded to see original documents for the investments their money managers claimed to be making. Examples to ask for are the originals of all certificates of deposit, stock and bond certificates, and mutual fund confirmation statements. At the very least, meet regularly with your adviser and ask to see the original investments to confirm that what your adviser tells you has been done for you has actually occurred.

WATCH THOSE ZEROS

Be especially careful about salespeople peddling what are known as zero-coupon municipal bonds. A zero-coupon bond is a bond that pays no interest each year, as regular bonds do. Instead, the investor buys the bond at a hefty discount from its face value. The difference between what investors pay for such a bond and what they receive when the bond comes due or is sold in the resale markets is their return. Make sure, though, that the bond you have bought really is legitimate. Because a zero-coupon bond does not pay any interest until it matures, it is a tempting vehicle for con artists to sell to unsuspecting investors.

Verify that anyone you do business with in the securities industry has a license. Ignore anyone who says he or she does not need one. If the person is selling a security, there has to be a license.

Often, money managers will send you a letter saying that they are required by Securities and Exchange Commission rules to offer to send you certain forms but they will do so only if you request them. Request them.

Buying real estate requires special care. In general, be sure to use a lawyer or professional adviser who fully understands the intricacies of real estate and tax law. Never agree to skip a title search, even

> ### SCREEN OUT CYBERSCAMS!
>
> With the increasing popularity of on-line computer services, the information superhighway has become the haunt of a growing band of digital-age bandits. Although a savvy investor can glean a lot of useful information while zipping through cyberspace, you should use the information you pick up from bulletin boards and discussion groups at your own peril. The seemingly generous person posting those terrific investment tips may be paid by someone to help solicit your business or investment.
>
> Be especially leery of any messages with such loaded expressions as "hot," or "high, government-guaranteed returns," or "double your money in six months." Also watch out for messages involving thinly traded stocks, or stocks that trade for pennies, or those listed on regional or foreign stock exchanges. Never hesitate to ask for the name and background of anyone offering stock tips.

though it may be tempting to do so to save money. Insist on seeing and verifying all original documents. Make sure an experienced lawyer examines them for you. Skimping on legal fees in such a complex area can be an invitation to disaster. This is a highly popular area for fraud.

STEERING CLEAR OF BOGUS "BUSINESS OPPORTUNITIES"

The advertisements sound appealing, especially if you are looking for a second job, are unemployed, or are bored with retirement and eager to get back to work.

"Business-opportunity" ads in newspapers and elsewhere often offer tantalizing visions of buying into established organizations with solid financial performances. In many cases, regulators say, the come-on sounds something like this: "We are not just selling you a business, we put you *in* business." Or an ad will say you can earn in only one week what it takes most people to earn in an entire year.

Tragically, the truth can be much different. State and federal regulators estimate that well over $100 million a year vanishes into a black hole of worthless business-opportunity rip-offs. Growing numbers of fast-buck operators are pushing worthless schemes involving vending machines, amusement games, pay telephones, and display racks for greeting cards, CD-ROM computer software, and other items.

Most of these swindles are not new. But they are claiming more and more victims, regulators say, for several reasons. One is the use of high-pressure telemarketing. Another is the large number of early retirements, buyouts, and corporate downsizings that are leaving

---

INVESTIGATE, INVESTIGATE, INVESTIGATE

For more details on business-opportunity fraud, check with securities regulators in your state or with your state attorney general's office. Also write for a free copy of a publication on the subject by the Federal Trade Commission and the North American Securities Administrators Association.

Business Opportunities
NASAA
One Massachusetts Avenue, Suite 310
Washington, DC 20001

• Additional information is available from the following:

Federal Trade Commission, Division of Marketing Practices
Washington, DC 20580
202-326-2222

International Franchise Association
1350 New York Avenue NW, Suite 900
Washington, DC 20005

many people in their 40s, 50s, and early 60s vulnerable to offers of alternative sources of income.

There is no foolproof way to avoid being swindled. But there are steps you can take to minimize the risk of disaster. For example, be sure to demand and carefully check out all required disclosure documents. Show them to an expert in the field as well as to your lawyer and financial advisers. Never jump into a new field without checking what you have been told with veterans in the business. If a business claims to have been profitable, be sure to check all the accounting techniques with an expert. Be sure the business has complied with all applicable state registration laws. As regulators point out, this is not a guarantee that you will make money. But it can be a way to help detect crooks. Check references carefully and watch out for what regulators refer to as "singers," people who provide phony testimonials to a business's bright future.

MISTAKES THAT CAN REALLY HURT

Smart people often do some pretty dumb things with money. They shop all over town to get the best price on a household appliance or new sporting gear, but they invest thousands of dollars without taking time to investigate. People with bulging savings accounts carry large unpaid credit card balances month after month. People with kids worry about chicken pox and braces, but they just do not get around to writing a will or updating their life insurance.

Some people learn just enough to be dangerous to themselves. Take the New Yorker who knew he was supposed to diversify his investments but also wanted an ultraconservative portfolio. Thus, he "diversified" by sprinkling large amounts of his money among utility stocks, bank stocks, and fixed-income securities. He felt highly secure—until interest rates suddenly surged, driving down the market value of all those investments at once. As he later recalled with a wince, that was an expensive way to learn that diversification means more than just buying a batch of different securities. Diversification means making sure that your investments do not all march in the same direction in reaction to some unexpected news bulletin or financial trend.

Many people hurt themselves by failing to take advantage of valuable opportunities in company benefit plans, such as retirement-savings programs, that not only can make a huge difference in the quality of their lives in retirement but also generate immediate tax savings. Many employers offer medical-spending accounts and child-care reimbursement accounts that cut the cost of doctors and babysitters by getting Uncle Sam to foot part of the bill.

To help you avoid as many of these mistakes as possible, the following pages summarize some of the biggest blunders people make in key areas of personal finance. Some are errors of commission—things that people do that just are not smart. But many are errors of omission—things people should do but too often fail to do.

INSURANCE MISTAKES

Many people skimp on life insurance coverage needed to protect their dependents; they do so not because they are lazy or could not afford to buy the amount of coverage they should have. Instead, people all too often skimp on the size of the death benefit so that they can buy an expensive cash-value policy that includes a tax-deferred savings component. For the same amount of money or even less, they could buy a much larger term life insurance policy, which does not have any savings feature. If they had money left over to invest, they could plow it into low-cost mutual funds.

Failing to obtain proper auto and home insurance is another serious mistake. Some people who rent fail to buy a renter's policy to protect themselves in case their belongings are stolen or lost in a fire. Many people select policies with small deductibles—the amount you have to pay before the insurance kicks in—but do not buy enough coverage to protect themselves from a really serious loss. For instance, the minimum auto liability insurance coverage required by many states is simply not enough. Make sure you have liability coverage of at least $100,000 per person and $300,000 per accident. Adding an umbrella liability policy of $1 million or more to your auto and home policies can be a smart move. Similarly, it is wise to pay a little extra to insure your home and possessions for their replacement cost rather than their much lower "actual cash value." You can help pay for this better protection by raising your deductible to, say, $500 from $100 or $200.

Do not forget to update your policies regularly. Your needs may change, your dependents may change, and so should your insurance coverage. Also, watch out for needless duplication. One of the easiest ways to waste money is to buy health insurance or disability insurance that duplicates existing coverage.

Never buy insurance solely on the basis of price. Although cost is obviously a consideration, you should be sure to take into account the insurer's reputation for dealing with customers and claims and check its financial strength with independent analysts, such as A. M. Best or Weiss Ratings.

FLATTERY GOES ONLY SO FAR

Never agree to serve on the board of directors or trustees of any organization without thoroughly investigating its insurance coverage. It may be a big honor to be selected. But remember that you and your fellow directors or trustees may be held responsible for some calamity, such as the treasurer running off to Brazil with large amounts of the institution's money.

How much coverage is enough?

One easy way to find out is to call directors and trustees of other institutions and ask them for advice. For example, if you are named a trustee of a private school, ask trustees or heads of other schools how much insurance protection those schools have purchased for their trustees and what, if any, problems they have run into in this area.

Volunteer work can be tremendously enjoyable and can make a difference in the lives of other people. But it may also lead to horrendous legal problems. Be sure you are adequately protected in case disaster strikes.

BENEFITS MISTAKES

Many people fail to take the time and effort to understand what benefits their employers offer and how to make maximum use of them. Perhaps the biggest blunder is failing to take advantage of tax-deferred savings opportunities at work, such as 401(k) plans. These plans may be the only retirement savings many workers have, so it is essential to participate. Contributions cut your current income taxes, and employers frequently match contributions up to a certain limit. This is free money, and it is foolish to pass it up.

Too many employees also fail to take advantage of medical-reimbursement accounts, which allow you to have pretax dollars withheld from your salary to pay for such expenses as the deductible portion of medical bills and services that are not covered by health insurance. The savings can be significant. Dependent-care accounts give working parents a similar break on such expenses as day care, summer camp, preschool, and after-school care for children under age 13. These accounts can also be used to cover eligible expenses in caring for a dependent elder.

If you want to ask for trouble, do not bother to review your employer's medical plan until after you are in the hospital. To save on medical expenses, employers are tightening eligibility requirements, excluding more pre-existing conditions, adding more caps on treatment, and denying claims of employees who fail to follow the procedures spelled out in the fine print.

One of the most serious blunders people make with company benefits occurs when they change jobs. Instead of rolling over the money in their 401(k) or similar retirement plan into an Individual Retirement Account or a new employer's retirement plan, they take a lump-sum distribution and spend it on a new house,

> **MOTHERHOOD AND THE COMPANY HEALTH PLAN**
>
> If you are planning to start a family, failing to review your health coverage before pregnancy can lead to some costly surprises. Health plans at some small companies do not pay for routine pregnancy care. Even where pregnancy care is covered, preapproval is often required for certain procedures, such as ultrasound and amniocentesis tests. Also, without prior approval, most plans now pay for only one or two days in the hospital after a vaginal delivery, or three to four days after a Caesarean section. And definitions of what constitutes a "day" vary.

boat, or vacation. Obviously, that can leave them short when it is time to retire. But less obviously, it can also trigger a nightmarish series of more immediate problems. To begin with, 20% of it will be withheld for income taxes. Also, if you are not yet 59½, you will owe income taxes on the rest of the money—and, generally, a penalty, too. Thus, before going on a spending spree in such cases, consider checking with a tax adviser.

INVESTMENT MISTAKES

One of the biggest investment mistakes is failing to start early enough. If you begin putting aside just $3,900 a year when you are 25, for instance, you can accumulate a $1 million retirement nest egg by the time you turn 65, assuming your investments earn 8% a year. But if you wait to begin saving until you are 45, you will have to sock away some $21,900 a year. That is clearly an impossible amount for most people, so those who delay will have to get by on a much smaller retirement fund, or put off retirement, or keep working, at least part-time.

Once you have begun a regular investment program, not paying attention to your asset allocation can torpedo your plans. Academic studies suggest that over 90% of a portfolio's return is determined by how the money is allocated among stocks, bonds, and supersafe cash investments. In particular, too many people keep too big a share of their investments in certificates of deposit and other fixed-income securities that barely keep pace with inflation. Instead, these investors should consider increasing their holdings of common stocks, which historically have provided superior protection against inflation. This goes for retirees, too, since you could easily have to make your money last until you are 85 or 90 years old.

Failing to diversify your investments adequately is another potentially fatal error. It is not enough to spread your money among a number of stocks if many of those stocks are from companies in the same industry or are affected similarly by economic factors and market conditions.

Many investors go astray because they try to dart in and out of the financial markets at just the right moment to obtain the highest possible returns. Such "market timing" almost never works over the longer run. Instead, consider a much less bold but more reliable strategy known as "dollar-cost averaging," which involves investing a fixed amount each month or so, regardless of what the latest Wall Street mood may be.

If you buy individual stocks, beware of placing heavy emphasis on a brokerage firm's research report recommending a stock. Although many reports can be valuable in helping you form an opinion about a stock, brokerage-house analysts often face heavy pressure to see a bright and sunny outlook even when dark clouds may be rolling in rapidly. Sometimes, analysts keep a "buy" recommendation on a stock long after they privately have turned negative but are afraid to say so for fear of offending some powerful people or companies. Negative reports in print are relatively rare. Analysts often try to avoid issuing grim reports saying "sell," relying instead on softer-sounding advice such as "hold." One firm used to rate poorly performing stocks of its investment-banking clients as "long-term attractive."

Bond shoppers need to resist the temptation to reach for yield. Putting yield above all else when buying fixed-income investments is one of the easiest ways to lose money in the bond market. At any given time, a yield that is higher than yields on other, similar investments, is typically a sign of high risk. Many people who invest in bonds also get burned because they do not understand an eccentricity known as the "call" provision, a bit of legalese that allows many corporate and municipal bond issuers to redeem their bonds long before the final maturity date. This usually happens when interest rates are significantly lower than what the issuer has been paying. By selling new bonds with lower yields, bond issuers are able to pay off some of the bonds outstanding and save a bundle. But the investors who are paid off early typically must reinvest at lower rates. Investors who do not want to be burdened with details of call features should stick with Treasury bonds: No newly issued Treasury bond may be called prior to its maturity date.

Failing to invest in tax-exempt municipal bonds can be a serious mistake for people in higher tax brackets. But beware of a few pitfalls. Because prices often vary sharply from one dealer to another, it is important to gather competing prices from numerous dealers. The same rule applies when you sell.

Also, do not become so focused on beating the tax collector that you really do something dumb, such as buying municipal bonds for an Individual Retirement Account or other tax-deferred savings plan. Putting tax-exempt bonds in an IRA does not double-up the tax exemption, and tax-exempt bonds typically offer yields well below those of taxable bonds. Some investors buy only municipal bonds issued by their home states because income from such bonds is exempt from state as well as federal income taxes. But you could end up with a very undiversified portfolio. Besides, some states do not even have a state income tax.

TAX MISTAKES

Because the tax code is enormously complex, it is remarkably easy to make costly mistakes without even realizing it. Tax lawyers often remark that it is not what you do not know that hurts you; it is what you think you know that just is not so.

Some people mistakenly assume that it does not matter whether they file an income tax return on time as long as they are entitled to a refund. After all, they say, why should the government care if you are late filing for a refund? That certainly sounds reasonable. But it may turn out to be a huge blunder. Suppose, for example, that you have miscalculated and it turns out that you actually owe the government money? Or suppose the Internal Revenue Service later disagrees with some of your deductions? Then you may be hit with massive penalties plus interest. Take a tip from tax lawyers: Filing on time can save a lot of headaches.

Failing to file a tax return because you do not have enough money to pay is asking for trouble. If you do not have the money, file anyway and ask the IRS to settle for payment in installments or to settle for less than you owe. (That is called an "offer in compromise.") Whatever you do, do not make the mistake of waiting to file until the tax collector comes knocking on your door. The IRS vows to be much tougher on those who wait to be caught than on those who turn themselves in voluntarily.

Do not assume that just because you can get an automatic four-month filing extension until mid-August you do not have to pay your taxes until then. The extension applies only to when you must file your return. Any taxes must be paid by mid-April. Otherwise, be prepared to pay interest and possibly nasty penalties as well. And do not assume you can always get an automatic extension beyond mid-August. It is true that the IRS does grant an additional two-month extension to some taxpayers—but only to those who can present a convincing excuse, such as a medical problem or loss of important records.

When it comes time to write out a check for what you owe, never make it payable to "IRS." Instead, write out "Internal Revenue Service." If your check falls into the wrong hands, "IRS" can be changed to "MRS," followed by someone's name.

When mailing an important document or tax return to the IRS or to a court, consider taking special precautions. Suppose you need to be able to prove that you mailed something on a certain date. Take the trouble to get a record, such as a receipt for certified mail. Or deliver it in person to the nearest IRS office and get a copy of whatever you are filing date-stamped by an IRS representative.

IRS officials and postal workers may try telling you that this is unnecessary and that most people do just fine by dropping their return in the mailbox. The IRS also has argued that a registered or certified letter proves only that you mailed a letter, not what was in it. Even so, if you get into a dispute with the IRS over precisely when you sent something, having a dated record can be critical to your case.

REMEMBER THE NANNY TAX

Many people who employ someone to look after the kids or clean the house do not bother with the employment taxes that are due in most cases when you pay household help $1,000 or more a year. Sometimes, it is because it just seems like too much trouble. Other times, the housekeeper begs them not to do so. Ignore such requests. And do not forget about state and local tax requirements. Although the federal law now requires you to file only once a year, many states still require quarterly filings.

ESTATE-PLANNING MISTAKES

Many people, even those who should know better, fail to write a will. It may be tempting to postpone this unpleasant task because you are too busy or because you have too few assets to justify the time and expense. Think again. Dying without a will can create enormous headaches for your family and friends. It can be an especially tragic mistake for married couples with young children. If you die without a will, you generally are leaving your family's fate in the hands of a court-appointed administrator, who may not handle your affairs in the manner you would want. A carefully drawn will can save enormous amounts of time and anguish for your heirs.

When choosing an executor, trustee, or guardian, be sure to check with that person to see if he or she is willing to serve and shares your values and interests. Also remember to choose a backup guardian in case your first choice cannot serve if and when the time comes, or at least provide a mechanism for this to be done at a later date. The same advice holds true when choosing executors and trustees; it can be a tragic error to neglect to pick backups.

Failing to pay attention to details is asking for trouble. For example, when selecting a charity as a beneficiary, make sure you have the full and correct name of that charity. Lawyers say failure to give a correct name can lead to lengthy court battles. It is also important to be sure you have the proper number of witnesses for your will and that the act of witnessing was done correctly.

GIVE SOME OF IT AWAY

If you have a large estate and can afford to make gifts to your children, consider making use of the $10,000-a-year gift exclusion. That means you and your spouse can each give $10,000 to your son, daughter, another relative, or any other person without having to pay any gift or estate taxes. The recipient does not owe any income tax on your gift, either.

Do not make the mistake of assuming you can make changes in your will unilaterally without proper documentation. Any changes must be made carefully in the presence of witnesses. If the changes are big enough, consider redoing the entire will. Make sure your heirs know where to find your latest will, and leave copies of it with your lawyer or someone else you trust completely.

USING FINANCIAL SEMINARS WITHOUT BEING USED

Educational seminars conducted by brokers, insurance agents, and financial planners are becoming commonplace at major corporations and at many small companies, too. Financial seminars are also all the rage at federal, state, and local government offices and at non-profit employers, including school districts and hospitals.

Attending these seminars may be very useful and may give you ideas on how to help yourself. But they may also lead to investment blunders. It is worth remembering that the information presented at these seminars sometimes may be slanted or misleading. Brokers and others may have subtle biases in favor of the investments they sell, and they may fail to mention important options available to employees.

Typically, workplace financial seminars may include at least a superficial discussion of the company's 401(k) or other retirement plan. The seminars also are commonly given when the company is downsizing and offering early-retirement packages. Many brokers and other financial professionals see the seminars as an opportunity to meet and impress potential customers. If they are successful, people conducting the seminars may be able to sell an employee a mutual fund or an insurance policy. Or they may be able to persuade a departing employee to roll the money in a 401(k) plan into an Individual Retirement Account managed by their firm.

Employees usually fail to realize that a seminar speaker may have a personal financial agenda. While some brokers, insurance agents, and financial planners adhere to ethical standards when speaking at company-sanctioned seminars, others do not. Although employers invariably insist that the broker or agent refrain from recommending specific products or actually selling in the classroom, this does not prevent biases from occurring.

SOME QUESTIONS TO CONSIDER

Asking the following questions can save you a lot of grief—and protect your hard-earned savings—if you attend financial seminars.

- **How is the speaker compensated?** While some employers hire professional lecturers to help employees understand their retirement plans better, most rely on brokers, insurance agents, and financial planners who often view employee seminars as a way to gain new customers.

- **Is the information slanted?** For example, does the speaker dwell on mutual funds, annuities, life insurance, and other investments sold by the speaker's firm? Does the speaker recommend only investments with the highest commissions?

- **Is the information confusing?** Sometimes brokers and others giving workplace seminars may make the material more confusing than it is in order to gain employees as clients.

- **Is the advice oversimplified?** Seminar speakers may also fail to tell employees about all their options when making decisions, such as whether to accept an early-retirement package or how to deal with money accumulated in an employer-sponsored retirement plan. Beware if the speaker subtly discourages employees from seeking advice from other sources, including their plan sponsor, lawyers, accountants, and fee-only advisers.

TIPS ON CHOOSING A FINANCIAL EXPERT

Picking the right financial team—brokers, planners, lawyers, and accountants—can make all the difference. Often, the best way to find reliable advisers is to ask trusted friends and relatives for suggestions.

Sometimes, that is all it takes. But more often than not, you need to do some elementary detective work and ask tough questions in order to be reasonably certain that you are dealing with someone who is reliable and trustworthy, who understands thoroughly what your goals are, and who has the knowledge and resources to handle your affairs successfully.

Failing to ask tough questions is one of the biggest mistakes many people make. Not only do you deprive yourself of valuable information, but you also risk sending the wrong message. Ask securities regulators, and they will tell you: Beware of sounding passive. All too often, one regulator says, an investor walks into the office of a broker or financial planner, throws up his hands, and candidly admits: "Look, I really am confused. I just do not know what to do. I do not understand this stuff. I trust you. Please take care of everything for me." Even if that is exactly how you feel, regulators advise you to resist the temptation to say so. Such a naive approach may be the green light for some unscrupulous brokers and other advisers to take advantage of you.

Law-enforcement authorities and securities regulators say you should interview your financial experts with the same care and attention you would if you were talking to a doctor who was preparing to perform major surgery on you. Never be ashamed of asking tough but polite questions. The people you are questioning typically will have more respect for you, not less. If they refuse to give you answers, leave in a hurry. If you do not understand their answers, ask for clarification.

No matter how distinguished a broker, financial planner, accountant, or lawyer may be, consider checking that person's background. Start by calling your state securities regulators to see if any complaints have been filed. Nearly all states require licensing of investment advisers and the salespeople who work for them. Then tap into the Central Registration Depository, operated as a joint venture of the National Association of Securities Dealers and the North American Securities Administrators Association (800-289-9999), and ask for any information about your broker. Many people are unaware that this service exists. It can turn up valuable information about past problems.

When considering a financial adviser, be sure to get any documents about the adviser's firm that are on file with the Securities and Exchange Commission. These can provide valuable background information on the people who work for the firm you are considering, as well as such other items as the basic fee structure. They can also warn you of disciplinary actions.

When looking for someone to help with your taxes, do not assume that all accountants and other tax specialists are essentially the same. There are many different types, with a wide range of training and experience. Do not make the mistake of assuming that someone labeled an "accountant" or a "public accountant" is automatically a "certified public accountant," or CPA. There are strict state licensing requirements for CPAs. Ask for proof of credentials.

When looking for a broker, be especially careful if you are asked to sign a statement giving "discretionary authority" over your account. That means the person is asking you for the right to make investment decisions without consulting you first. Some people do, at some point, give this authority to trusted financial advisers. But giving such authority to someone you do not know well can be a huge mistake.

Make it clear from the outset what your basic financial objectives are and how much risk you are comfortable with taking. If your primary goal is preservation of capital, say so. Even better, put it in writing and hand it to the broker, keeping a copy for yourself. Beware of brokers who try to sell you something without even asking you what your investment objectives are.

Consult professional trade associations to find out whether the person you are considering hiring has been involved in any wrongdoing. Also consider searching through various computer databases that monitor major publications to see if there have been any articles, flattering or unflattering, about that person. Major newspapers, including *The Wall Street Journal,* run stories about "disciplinary actions" by securities exchanges. While some disciplinary actions may be for technical violations, others are far more serious. Even though a disciplinary action by itself may not be reason enough to disqualify someone from being a good broker, it can often be a highly important warning signal.

Whenever you receive a sales pitch for any investment, call securities regulators and ask if that product is registered. Also ask if the person who called you with that sales pitch is licensed.

SOME QUESTIONS YOU OUGHT TO ASK

When you interview a financial professional you are thinking about hiring to manage your money, plan your estate, prepare your taxes, or advise you on general financial matters, here are some questions you owe it to yourself to ask.

- What are your credentials? What is your educational background? How long have you been working in your field? How many firms have you worked for? If you are a job-hopper, please explain why.

- Have you ever been disciplined or punished by anyone in the securities industry? If so, please provide details and let me know how I can verify what you are telling me.

- If you are a securities broker, what is your "CRD" number? That stands for Central Registration Depository. It can help you verify whether that broker has been the target of complaints. If any broker refuses to divulge that information, leave in a hurry.

- How are you paid? Do you receive a commission? Do you get a basic fee unrelated to how much trading you do? Is your pay based at all on your performance? Is your fee based on how much money you manage? Is your fee based on an hourly rate? How does that rate compare with other advisers in your area? Even if the fee is based on an hourly rate, ask whether there is a minimum.

- If the person manages money, ask how his or her performance has been over several different periods and how that record compares with broad market indexes during those periods. (Try to pick long enough periods of time so that you include down markets as well as up markets.) If the person you are interviewing has consistently failed to beat a broad market index, such as the Standard & Poor's 500-stock index, ask why. Perhaps that is a sign that you should be looking elsewhere—or turning to "index" funds, mutual funds that are designed to match broad market indexes.

- What research services, if any, do you offer me in addition to handling my investments?

- How much do you expect your services to cost me? If you cannot tell me with great precision, at least give me a range of what it might cost.

- Can you provide me with the names of other clients I can call as references?

- How old is your firm, who are its top officers, and what financial information can you give me?

- Have you given me copies of all the documents that you have filed with government regulators or professional associations?

TWENTY WAYS TO SHOOT YOURSELF IN THE FOOT

1. Placing too much faith in cash.

Sure, the stock market may seem like a giant casino and bonds may sound both boring and complex. Even so, too many people make the mistake of keeping overly large amounts of their savings in checking accounts that pay little or no interest. Or their Individual Retirement Accounts are heavily invested in money market funds, barely keeping pace with inflation. Often, these people are simply too confused or intimidated to make any decision, or too fearful of making a costly mistake. But keeping too much of your money in cash is an easy way to miss out on much more lucrative investment opportunities.

2. Investing based on a cold call.

It may seem hard to believe, but every day highly intelligent people refuse to hang up on salespeople they do not know who call around dinnertime, pitching some seemingly surefire investment idea. In many cases, those otherwise highly intelligent people wind up sending money. Take some advice from securities regulators: When you get a cold call, just hang up.

3. Buying last year's hot investment.

The fact that a mutual fund or other investment did really well last year says nothing about how it will do next year and in years to come. Moreover, because investments tend to go in and out of fashion, last year's dazzling star could well turn out to be this year's dog. Focus on longer-term results.

4. Neglecting to update your investments.

While buying and holding is often smart, holding without watching can leave an investor riding a stock all the way to the top and all the way down again.

5. Getting bonds backward.

When interest rates go up, bond prices head down. This may sound elementary. Yet many people have trouble grasping this inverse relationship. Failing to understand it thoroughly can be hazardous to your wealth.

6. Thinking "fixed-income" is "fixed-value."

Perhaps because bonds are called fixed-income investments, many people seem unprepared for losing money when bond prices fall. A lot of people assume a $10,000 bond will be worth $10,000 from the time it is issued until it matures. But the market value changes whenever interest rates rise or fall. People apply the same faulty logic to bond mutual funds, not realizing that they can lose money in a bond fund if interest rates rise enough.

7. Equating high yields with high returns.

Many investors shop for bond funds based solely on yield. But yield is only part of the picture. Investors need to find out answers to such questions as what types of bonds a fund holds, how risky those bonds are, and what their credit ratings are. They also need to know such things as the maturity of the bonds, who the investment managers are, and what their long-term track record has been.

8. Believing a guarantee is always a guarantee.

Even guaranteed investments lose money. For instance, insured bonds protect you in case of a default, but market conditions that cause resale prices to fall can cause a significant loss in the value of your portfolio.

9. Assuming that anything sold in a bank is insured.

Bank deposits are insured by the federal government. But mutual funds and other investment products that are increasingly being sold in banks are not deposits, and they are not guaranteed.

10. Buying mutual fund shares late in the year.

Investors who purchase mutual funds in November or early December risk buying just before the funds pay out annual capital-gains distributions. Do this, and you will be getting back some of the money you just paid in—and you will have to pay income tax on it.

11. Accepting a mutual fund at its face value.

Mutual fund names are often misleading. A fund that has the word "value" in its name may actually be a "growth-stock" fund. Funds can use "government" in their name even if they have only a small portion of their assets invested in securities other than government bonds.

12. Writing checks on bond funds.

Many people do not realize that every time they write a check against a bond fund, it triggers a sale of fund shares. This is a taxable transaction that requires you to compute the capital gain or loss on the share sold. It can be a nightmare—or a big accounting bill—at tax time.

13. Getting the taxes wrong on "market-discount" municipal bonds.

The tax rules on these bonds can be mind-numbingly complex, especially if you purchased them in the resale market at a discount from their face value after April 30, 1993. Under a provision of the 1993 Tax Act, part or all of any gain you make from buying these bonds in the secondary market and later selling them or holding them to redemption may be taxed as ordinary income. Thus, consider handing over the job to a qualified tax specialist, and be sure to remind that person that you may be subject to the "market-discount bond" rules stemming from the 1993 Tax Act.

14. Violating the "wash-sale rule."

Suppose you have lost money on a stock but still think its long-term outlook is favorable. It may pay to sell the stock now, creating a loss that can be used to cut your total tax bill. But if you do so, be sure to wait at least 31 days before buying back the same stock. Failing to wait that long will keep you from using the loss for tax purposes. The general rule to remember is: Do not buy back substantially the same security within 30 days before or after the sale.

15. Relying on credit ratings as though they are carved in stone.

Ratings can and do change overnight. What you thought was a triple-A bond can quickly become a junk bond. Be sure to ask your broker or advisers for updates on your bonds, just as you would on stocks.

16. Falling for coins, baseball cards, and other collectibles.

Buy these "collectibles" only if you truly enjoy owning and collecting them. Do not rely on them as investments that will put your child through college or fund your retirement.

17. Assuming that all tax-free bonds are tax-free.

Most states tax interest income received on out-of-state bonds. For example, if a New York City resident buys Connecticut bonds, the interest on those Connecticut bonds is fully taxable in New York State and New York City. Also, capital gains on municipal bonds are taxable.

18. Neglecting to complete a "durable power of attorney."

Okay, you have seen a lawyer and signed a will. If you die tomorrow, your family and friends will be protected. But suppose you do not die tomorrow. Suppose, instead, that you are seriously injured and unable to manage your affairs. In such cases, it can be critical to have a carefully thought out durable power of attorney, which basically is a document that gives someone else the legal authority to make and execute decisions on your behalf should you become incapacitated.

19. Putting it in the wrong name.

Elaborate estate planning is often undone by this common mistake. An example: If property is held in joint name with rights of survivorship, the property will go to the survivor automatically, regardless of what your will says. Similarly, people who buy huge life insurance policies and keep them in their own names make the death benefit part of their estates and thus subject to estate tax upon death. The problem can be avoided by creating an irrevocable insurance trust to own the policy.

20. Neglecting the final step.

Many people go to great lengths to do financial planning but never finish the job. For instance, some people consult lawyers about drafting their wills but never get around to completing the process. Others always intend to move some more money out of money market funds or bank CDs but become paralyzed by confusion. Whatever it is that you need to do, make up your mind to get it done.

10

PUTTING THE PIECES TOGETHER WHEN YOU DO NOT FIT THE MOLD

$

For many people, personal finances simply do not follow a well-worn pattern. Some have delayed marriage and children, whereas others have opted for the single life. The rise of second marriages and second families has created a crazy quilt of overlapping family groups. Even well-established categories have myriad variations. Singles, for example, are not always "single." Some have lifetime partners; others are raising children. People with children may have two or more sets, and those children may be of vastly different ages.

Whatever their individual circumstances, these people often feel lost when it comes to dealing with money because many of the conventional assumptions that go into financial planning just do not apply. If you are one of those people, you may find help here. The earlier chapters in this book focused on life's major financial issues from the perspective of people in their 20s and 30s, those in their 40s and 50s, and those in their 60s and beyond. This chapter is for people whose lives do not fit the mold.

It is not possible to cover every special case, of course, but the ones discussed here are among the most common. They include situations created by lifestyle choices, by happenstance, and even by economic conditions. This chapter is not intended to provide all the answers but rather to start you in the right direction. Perhaps the most important lesson you can learn from these pages is that the basic rules of personal finance covered in the earlier chapters of this book remain the same. It is only the manner in which they are applied that may require alteration to develop a workable financial plan.

SO MUCH FOR TRADITION

People who do not live traditional lives have lots of company. The conventional definition of a family—mother and father living with their children under the age of 18—applies to only about one out of four households these days. Married couples continue to decline as a percentage of the 96.4 million American households, dropping to only about 55% from 74% in 1960. Longer life spans and corporate restructuring are changing traditional career patterns, too. People now commonly have two or more careers over a lifetime. Often, they are forced to retool their work lives just when they would normally be in their peak earning years.

All this can take a psychological toll. For some, not fitting the mold can carry a feeling of failure. Single parents, for example, may have a hard time making ends meet because they are carrying the cost of housing, food, child care, and other necessities by themselves. While they may intellectually understand why they cannot ever seem to get ahead, emotionally they may end up wondering what they have done wrong.

Others can be frustrated by rules that make them pay a price for being different. A couple may save thousands of dollars a year in income tax by not being married. Still, that savings may be a pittance compared with the estate taxes they will owe if they stick to their decision to remain together unmarried. The traditional assumptions embodied in U.S. tax and

---

HOW WE LIVE TODAY

For a growing number of Americans, traditional stereotypes no longer apply.

Of the 96.4 million households in the United States in 1993:

- Only 55% were married couples, compared with 61% in 1980 and 74% in 1960.

- Only about one in four met the "traditional" family definition of Mom and Dad living at home with children under the age of 18.

- A full 12% of family householders were headed by a woman, and more than two out of three of those homes included children under age 18.

- The number of men heading households with children under the age of 18 with no spouse present has more than doubled since 1980, accounting for 1.5 million households.

- Almost 25% of all households are people who live alone, the majority of them women.

SOURCE: U.S. Bureau of the Census data, cited in *The Official Guide to the American Marketplace*, New Strategist Publications Inc., Ithaca, N.Y.

property laws may eventually push them toward a marriage they would otherwise forgo.

Still others can find the complexity of their situations overwhelming. What may be a straightforward decision in traditional families can turn into a convoluted tangle for those who do not fit the mold. In a second marriage, for example, Mom and Dad cannot simply leave everything to each other, with the understanding the survivor will eventually leave it all to the kids. That is because the kids may be his, not hers. If he leaves all his money to her, his kids may never see a penny. The only way to make sure the kids are provided for is to make specific provisions, usually through a series of trusts. But to craft these trusts properly, people need to confront some very uncomfortable issues, including death, divorce, and remarriage—issues people usually prefer to avoid.

GOING BACK TO BASICS

The most difficult financial planning situations may be those created by happenstance. In these cases—the loss of a spouse, for example, or the diagnosis of a terminal illness—people are often overwhelmed by their new circumstances. Having thought they were on one track, they suddenly find themselves overtaken by a financial and emotional tidal wave. But, like others who find themselves in special circumstances, these people can find answers by going back to the basics. They need to look at their cash flow and calculate their net worth. Then they can take the next steps, by reallocating their investments appropriately and making any necessary lifestyle changes.

Going back to the basics is a smart move for anyone navigating uncharted terrain. Regardless of your circumstances, the challenge is to balance current lifestyle against future needs—such as the down payment on a home, college tuition, or retirement. You have to invest to accomplish those goals, you need to protect yourself against emergencies, and you need to figure out what you want to leave behind. The crucial difference when you do not fit the mold is that some of the questions that you must ask are very different.

SINGLE PEOPLE, MULTIPLE PROBLEMS

Singles cannot all be lumped together. Young singles may be awash with debt but light on responsibilities, with their biggest concerns housing and job stability. Older singles may have more assets, but own a house and be responsible for aging parents. Others are raising children. Indeed, some singles are single only in the eyes of the law; they are members of heterosexual or gay couples living with people they consider partners for life.

But the bottom line for many singles is that they have no one to count on but themselves. Even those with long-term partners will find that the law deprives them of basic supports in times of illness or disability. That is why singles need to create their own safety nets, and they cannot afford to think in the short term.

If you are single, the first thing you need to do is make sure that you will be taken care of in the way you would like should you become ill or incompetent. You need a health care proxy to name someone to speak for you in case you are no longer able to make medical decisions. You also need a durable power of attorney authorizing someone to act on your behalf, or even a revocable living trust, in case you are unable to run your own affairs. (You will find details about this in Chapters 1 and 5.)

SOMEONE TO MAKE DECISIONS

The documents are simple to prepare with the help of a good lawyer—except for one thing. Who do you pick to make such major decisions on your behalf? Your only sister may live in Singapore, your parents may be getting on in years, and your best friend may be a lousy manager.

One answer is to set up a revocable living trust to handle your affairs should you become unable to manage them. Then name an institution, such as a bank or trust company, to share the trustee responsibilities with a friend or relative. This reduces the burden on the friends or family, and it also protects you if your friend or family member turns out to be a bum choice.

Finding the right professional, though, will take some home-work. Interview prospective trustees until you find a firm that is a good match. Make sure you are comfortable with the institution's philosophy and that you understand how it will operate as your representative. Remember that it is the firm you are hiring and that the individuals administering your affairs may change from time to time.

Insurance is an essential part of any safety net, although life insurance may be unnecessary if you have no one depending on you who would be hurt or put at risk because of your death. Adequate health insurance and disability coverage are essential. This insurance usually comes through the workplace, but do not just assume your coverage is sufficient. Take a close look at your policies. If what you have is not enough, get supplemental coverage. Remember, this kind of insurance can be bought only before you actually need it.

Providing for long-term care in old age is something else to consider. You need to take a closer look at your options, starting as early as age 55. Long-term-care insurance policies are one possibility, but they tend to be very expensive. Many people decide against them, preferring to "self-insure" by maintaining adequate savings. Nonetheless, the exercise of reviewing long-term-care needs is helpful, forcing people to come up with alternatives. (For more information about long-term-care insurance, refer to Chapter 3.)

Retirement planning is particularly important for singles who have only themselves to rely on. Yet, the fact that you are responsible for all of your own household expenses can make it difficult to maintain a disciplined savings program. Many singles, for example, spend a lot of money on entertainment—and some view that expense as an investment in finding a mate. But as a single, you do need to pay special attention to building a comfortable nest egg. The way you go about that task is the same as everyone else: Invest for the long term, which means using stocks or stock mutual funds as a major part of your retirement portfolio.

BRINGING FOCUS TO ESTATE PLANNING

Estate planning poses some special problems for singles. Without children or a spouse depending on you, you may have no clear idea where you want those assets to go after your death. Some singles find that without a clearly defined need, estate planning can be a nebulous and frustrating experience. But freedom from family obligations also provides the opportunity to explore a variety of creative options.

Some singles may decide that the best plan is simply to spend all their money while alive. Others may decide to use their money to help family members—for example, paying for the college education of nieces and nephews. Or they may look to establish some sort of personal memorial, such as a scholarship fund that may bear their name. Many singles strike a philanthropic note with their estate planning, often establishing a meaningful connection with a specific cause or group during their lifetime. The relationship continues after death, with the organization named either in the will or as beneficiary of a trust. Such funds can even be earmarked for a program of specific interest to the individual donor, be it youth basketball or immigrant literacy.

COPING WITH THE CONFLICTS OF SINGLE PARENTS

Single parents are a distinct subset of singles, but even here there are many variations. People become single parents by choice, by accident, due to divorce, or because their spouse has died. And just as the types of single parents vary, so do their resources.

Single parents by divorce may have had their family finances wiped out by legal fees and the cost of setting up a new household. Those who are single parents by choice have no one who will share the cost of raising the kids. Those who are recent widows or widowers may have lots of insurance money but be struggling with the emotional toll of having their lives turned upside down.

Still, single parents share some basic concerns. Not only do they face all the problems of singles, but they also must deal singlehandedly with the issues of parenthood. The combination typically leaves them short on time, short on money, and very short on support. The conflict between time and money is a big one. As the sole wage earner of the household, single parents want to provide for their families, but they also feel the need to spend more time with their kids. That pits work commitments directly against family commitments—and leaves single parents juggling.

There is no easy answer. Single parents usually find they must make compromises. Some scale back on professional aspirations to spend time with their families; others find they can squeeze in extra on-the-job hours by bringing their work home to the family. Still others may actually change careers in order to create a more flexible work schedule.

But while you are busy juggling, make sure you take full advantage of the breaks available to you. Many employers have a dependent-care reimbursement program, which can let you pay up to $5,000 of your child-care expenses with pretax dollars. And when preparing your taxes, remember that you may be able to file using the more favorable "head of household" rates. You qualify if at the end of the year you are unmarried—or, if you are married, you have not lived with your spouse for at least six months—and pay more than half the cost of keeping a home for yourself and at least one dependent.

PLANNING FOR ALL CONTINGENCIES

Estate planning is a special worry for single parents. Here the safety net must be designed to take the children into account. That is likely to mean purchasing life insurance. But even more important is the question of who takes care of the children if something happens to you. Since you have no backup, you need to take extra care in crafting an estate plan that considers all contingencies.

Of course, the general rules of estate planning discussed in Chapter 5 still apply. You want to make sure that any assets to be inherited by minor children will go into a trust. This approach keeps the children from gaining control of all their inheritance outright when they reach the age of 18 or 21. Moreover, it gives you a say in how the money should be spent by making specific provisions in the trust documents.

To a greater extent than married parents, single parents may want to build a team approach into their estate plans, thus creating a broader support system for the children. The team should include a guardian who will bring up the children and one or more other people who will handle the children's money. While the guardian can also serve as trustee, most financial advisers recommend at least one trustee be someone other than the children's guardian, preferably a banker or other professional trustee.

Once you have crafted this team, make sure the people you have named are willing to take the job. And do not forget to name backups in case your first choices are unable to serve.

MONEY MATTERS FOR UNMARRIED COUPLES

In a world where law and custom favor conventional husband-and-wife pairings, unmarried couples face some unique personal finance problems. That is because unmarried couples operate without the safety net that tax and property laws have traditionally provided those who are married. They may have been together for decades or even raised children together. But without some very careful planning, unmarried couples will find they can neither inherit each other's property nor speak for each other during a crisis.

For some couples, the questions center on who gets the joint property—be it the beach house or the television—if the relationship goes bust. Although uncomfortable, such issues are best dealt with up front, before major purchases are made. A signed contract governing shared property saves couples ugly bickering if things do not work out.

But for many unmarried partners, the question is not who gets the house, but rather how to make sure their other half does inherit, while paying as little estate tax as possible. This problem is particularly acute for gay couples who might eagerly embrace matrimony if same-sex marriage were legally recognized.

A LOOK AT UNMARRIED COUPLES

Some 5 million U.S. households are headed by unmarried couples. Of these:

- 70% are heterosexual couples.
- 30% are same-sex couples.
- Almost 40% are between the ages of 25 and 34.
- A full 5% are over the age of 65.

SOURCE: U.S. Bureau of the Census data, cited in *The Official Guide to the American Marketplace*, New Strategist Publications Inc., Ithaca, N.Y.

THE SIMPLICITY OF JOINT OWNERSHIP

Perhaps the simplest approach to the problem is to have ownership papers of property bought together list the couple as joint owners with rights of survivorship. Upon one partner's death, the property—be it house, car, stocks, or bonds—belongs to the survivor. This is not the same as being "tenants in common," another form of shared ownership under which the property passes not to the survivor but through the decedent's estate.

If both partners did not originally pay for the property, the buyer can still switch to joint ownership with rights of survivorship by simply adding the partner's name. But before doing that, take into account the fact that the buyer may then owe federal gift tax of 37% to 55% on the value of any transferred ownership that exceeds $10,000 a year.

Property that is not jointly owned typically passes to your heirs by will or through a trust. A will, which is the document that names your executor and tells how to distribute your assets, is particularly important for unmarried couples. Without one, the state will distribute estate assets according to a formula that is not likely to include the surviving partner. Unmarried couples need to take special care in drafting their wills to make sure they are not open to challenges by disgruntled relatives. Each partner, for example, should have his or her own lawyer, so that family members cannot claim that one partner or the other was not properly represented. Someone who draws up a will while ill may also want to take some additional steps. An AIDS patient, for example, may want to obtain a medical opinion from one or two doctors so that family members cannot later claim lack of mental competence at the time the will was written.

Putting property into a revocable living trust is another way to avoid challenges to a will. That is because property in trust typically bypasses probate, the legal process of certifying that a will is genuine. This works particularly well for people who are concerned about becoming ill or incapacitated, since a trust provides for management under those circumstances. Once the trust is created, the co-trustee—typically the partner—can manage trust affairs without seeking any further legal approval. Upon death, the assets are subject to estate tax but pass directly to the beneficiaries named in the trust document.

NOW THE BAD NEWS

All this maneuvering may establish legal rights, but it will do very little to reduce the estate taxes that will eat up anywhere from 37% to 55% of any amount in the estate above $600,000. That is because unmarried couples cannot take advantage of the unlimited marital deduction that allows someone to leave everything to a surviving spouse without paying any estate taxes.

Unmarried couples also need to consider drafting documents that give one partner the right to speak for the other under a variety of emergency circumstances. The first is a durable power of attorney, which, among other things, allows someone else to handle financial chores—paying taxes, applying for benefits, paying bills, or borrowing money—if you are unable to do so yourself. Without such a document, permission must be granted by the court, which often chooses to give these powers to members of the immediate family.

In circumstances where you cannot make your own medical decisions, a health care proxy will allow your partner to speak for you. A living will, recognized in most states, spells out your wishes about whether resuscitation, artificial feeding, or other "heroic measures" should be undertaken to keep you alive in extreme circumstances.

OLDER PARENTS OF YOUNG CHILDREN

After waiting to have children, many parents in their 40s or 50s find themselves out of step with traditional financial planning. Sure, it is great to be in your peak earning years when you have your first child. That means diapers and child care are not such a shock to the budget. But what about college? And what about retirement and estate planning? The basic rules may still apply, but the timing is all wrong.

Your child will still be in college when you are in your 60s. Instead of enjoying a carefree retirement, you may be watching big chunks of your nest egg going to tuition. This can create a real conflict, since most people do not have enough money both to provide their children with a good education and to fund a comfortable retirement for themselves without making some serious compromises.

Looked at from this perspective, education planning actually becomes a retirement decision. The nuts and bolts of dealing with it depend largely on family resources. Those with sufficient resources may want to set aside enough money to pay for college while the kids are very young. This settles the question of whether the money will be there when needed. Those with less may set up a disciplined savings program for both college and retirement. Or they may decide to delay their planned retirement. In some families, a spouse without a paying job may opt to get one.

SEGREGATE THE MONEY

When putting that money aside, make sure you segregate it. Keep retirement money in retirement accounts and education money in an education account in your own name. That not only makes it clear what the money is for, but it keeps the money out of your kids' hands when they turn 18 or 21, depending on the state in which you live. Then invest for the long term, weighting your portfolio more heavily toward stocks and stock mutual funds than you otherwise might.

Keep in mind, however, that your circumstances may change dramatically by the time you actually get around to using these funds. For example, people who use Series EE savings bonds to pay for their kids' college education get a tax break on the interest if they do not make too much money. That amount— $95,250 in 1996 for couples filing jointly—is indexed to inflation. You may be well above that limit today, but 15 years from now your income could be substantially lower. Thus, you might avoid paying some or all of the tax on those bonds when you cash them in to pay tuition bills. (You can find more on saving for college in Chapter 5.)

MORE BABIES HAVE OLDER MOMS

The number of women age 40–44 who have given birth has gone up steadily since 1976, as have the number of women giving birth between the ages of 35 and 39.

| YEAR | NUMBER OF WOMEN GIVING BIRTH (IN THOUSANDS) | |
	AGE 40–44	AGE 35–39
1976	5,685	6,064
1980	5,983	7,144
1985	7,226	8,859
1990	8,905	10,111
1994	9,972	11,093

SOURCE: U.S. Bureau of the Census.

Not all of the solutions are financial. You might want to consider some lifestyle changes, too. You can avoid private school fees by moving to a town with a good public school system. You may even want to consider moving the family to another state to take advantage of a high-quality state university system.

Other concerns for older parents with young children include estate planning, which must take into account the fact that your children could still be relatively young when you die. Using trusts can guarantee that children come into any inheritance gradually, rather than receiving it all at once when they are as young as 18.

THINK CREATIVELY

The choice of a guardian who will raise your children and a trustee who will handle your children's inheritance can be critical, too. While younger parents often choose their siblings, age becomes a major factor with those who start their families later in life. Your brother and sister may have grown children and be preparing for retirement. That means you would be asking them to start over just as they are embarking on a new lifestyle. Consider some creative alternatives. If your children have a 25-year-old stepbrother, he might be a reasonable choice for guardian. Then, a more experienced family member could take on the money-management responsibilities, perhaps with the help of a professional trustee.

Life insurance may also present a quandary. At your age, there is no real low-cost option, whether you are talking about term insurance, which provides only a death benefit, or cash-value policies, which also include an investment component. But while the numbers may be a shock, the basic decision-making process remains the same. Ask the key questions: How much insurance do you need and how long will you need it? For many, buying term life will be the only way to afford the coverage they need. But if you have enough discretionary income and want insurance to cover your entire life expectancy, you need to look at cash-value policies. One option is a term life policy that allows you to convert to a cash-value policy later without taking a physical. (For some useful tips on buying the life insurance you need, refer to Chapter 3 and try the worksheet in the Buyer's Guide to Life Insurance, Appendix C.)

SEAMLESS SOLUTIONS FOR BLENDED FAMILIES

The patchwork of family groups that often comes with divorce and remarriage can create real dilemmas. While balancing the needs of one family member against another is tough enough in a traditional family, what happens if Mom has one set of kids, Dad has another, and they have a third set together? With children of varying ages, often in different households, such blended families can easily find that the orderly pattern of long-term savings gets seriously out of whack. It does not help that the "his, hers, and theirs" categories apply not just to the kids but also to the family assets.

Blended families need to take a close look at family resources as well as the demands headed their way. The basic questions are when do you want to spend your money, and who is going to spend it? Start by figuring out what you are willing to pay for. Both spouses may agree that college is important, but what if Dad has most of the assets? Does that mean his kids get to go to Harvard, but hers have to go to a community college?

DOING WHAT IS REQUIRED

The questions about who gets what do not stop with the college tuition. What happens when children from a previous marriage want help with graduate school, a down payment on a house, or a business investment? Sexist as it may sound, financial advisers say the answer typically lies with the new wife, who tends to have a profound effect on the way the husband deals with children from a previous marriage. In most cases, financial advisers say, that means Dad does what is required and nothing more. But just doing what is required can be a big stretch—particularly for those paying child support and alimony at the same time they are providing for their current families. Big expenses are probably funded on a pay-as-you-go basis, and there simply may not be much left over for discretionary spending.

Taking a long-term view, however, can help blended families stay on track. Once you decide what you are willing to pay for, you can start investing to meet those goals. Near-term expenses, such as your teenage daughter's college tuition, may require conservative Treasury bills. But longer-term investments should be structured for growth, typically in the stock market. (Refer to Chapter 2 for more information.)

When estate planning enters the picture, the headaches of blended families are compounded. That is because the traditional lines of inheritance do not necessarily apply. Without some no-nonsense planning, one spouse or the other may find that his or her children are effectively disinherited.

A major goal of estate planning is avoiding taxes, which can take from 37% to 55% of anything over $600,000 in an estate. The natural aversion to paying taxes makes people want to defer them as long as possible. But people with multiple families often find tax avoidance in direct conflict with the desire to provide for their children. Take, for example, the "unlimited marital deduction." This allows people to leave everything to their spouses, deferring the payment of estate taxes until they both are dead. But use this approach in a blended family, and it is possible that your house and business will end up with your spouse's kids, not yours.

THE Q-TIP SOLUTION

One common strategy is to put your assets into a qualified terminable interest property trust, or Q-TIP trust, for the benefit of your spouse. This will give your spouse access to all of the income for life, but upon his or her death, the assets will pass to the intended beneficiaries, usually your children. But Q-TIPs are not for every blended family situation. Consider what happens if the new spouse and the kids are close to the same age. Under this scenario, the children are going to be so old by the time they inherit that using a Q-TIP may defeat your original intent. You would do better in such a case to leave a portion of the estate to the kids at your death, with the rest going into a Q-TIP. Or you could buy insurance on your life through an irrevocable trust that benefits the children to make up for the share of the estate that goes into the Q-TIP for your spouse.

One final note: Estate planning is something that should always be done only with experienced professional help. For blended families, that is doubly true.

DEALING WITH THE FINANCIAL PAINS OF DIVORCE

Marriage may not be forever, but the tax and financial complications of getting divorced can often seem to last that long. Too many people do not think about taxes and financial planning until after the ink on the settlement has dried. Sure, they hire a good divorce lawyer. But when they are spending thousands of dollars in legal fees, they are often reluctant to pay another professional's bill.

Yet predivorce planning with a tax lawyer or accountant—and in many cases a financial planner—can save a divorcing spouse from making irrevocable mistakes. For example, a tax attorney or accountant can help figure out which settlement structures are most advantageous from a tax standpoint. He or she will be able to steer you clear of some common pitfalls—continuing to file joint returns when divorce is imminent, for example, or failing to pay alimony for a long enough time—that could increase tax liability in the future.

Similarly, a financial planner can help develop realistic projections of living expenses, providing needed perspective on both the size and the structure of any settlement. Such help can be invaluable to people whose spouses always handled family finances. The planner can also help you decide which assets—be they the family home, the stock portfolio, or the beach house—are really worth hanging on to and which are not.

A good adviser can also help you figure out how to invest your settlement money and adjust your lifestyle to your new circumstances. One thing is certain: Both partners in a divorce will have to get by on less than they were used to. That is especially true for homemakers in their 50s and 60s who may never match the wage-earning power of their former spouses. Unless a couple is extraordinarily wealthy, the two are unlikely to be able to maintain anything near their old lifestyle.

Every divorce is different, and there is no one right way to hammer out a divorce settlement. Still, there are some common issues that divorcing couples face, and understanding the rules can prevent some big mistakes.

ALIMONY AND CHILD SUPPORT

Alimony generally is tax-deductible for the person who pays it and taxable income for the person who receives it. Child support is neither tax-deductible for the payer nor taxable income for the recipient. As a payer, you would prefer the sum to be alimony; as a recipient, you would prefer child support. Thus, it is important to consider the after-tax cost and benefit to each spouse before setting alimony as part of the division of marital assets.

To qualify as alimony, payments must usually be in cash. They must end when the recipient dies, and they cannot be disguised child-support payments. The rules of alimony also contain some significant tax traps for the unwary. People who structure their settlements improperly may find the tax collector at the door, often years later, with a very large bill. If the size of alimony payments drops significantly during the three years immediately after a divorce, for example, a portion of the payments could be "recaptured" by the Internal Revenue Service. That means the tax status of the payments would be reversed, becoming taxable to the payer and deductible by the recipient.

Say a divorcing couple decides that the husband will deduct as alimony the payments he makes when he buys out his wife's half of a $400,000 home. Instead of simply paying her $200,000 in a tax-free lump-sum settlement, he gives her $300,000 to cover both her share and the taxes she will owe on the alimony, and he deducts the $300,000 on his tax return for the year he makes the payment. But years later, he faces the prospect of being forced by the IRS to pay recapture tax on $285,000 of that alimony—the $300,000 minus $15,000 that the IRS considers exempt from recapture. And since his wife was previously taxed on that disallowed alimony, she would then be allowed a $285,000 deduction.

You can avoid being snagged by the recapture rules fairly easily if you know what to do. In this example, the husband would have avoided the steep drop-off on payments that triggered recapture taxes if he had simply paid the $300,000 in three equal annual installments.

Some people are tempted to disguise child-support payments—which are not deductible—as alimony, thus boosting their tax deductions. But they run the risk of being caught by the IRS, and it is easy to get tripped up. The dodge is often caught when the person receiving child-support payments—which are not taxable—reports less taxable alimony than the paying spouse deducts.

Timing can also be crucial. If alimony payments from one former spouse to another stop within six months of a key event in their child's life—a 21st birthday, perhaps—the IRS could link the events and disallow all or part of such payments as child support.

THE FAMILY HOME

To many people, the family home represents familiarity and security. So they keep the house as part of their divorce settlement, letting their spouse hang onto some other valuable asset, such as the pension plan. Yet many who make this decision end up regretting it. Unlike other assets, a house yields no income but can cost a bundle. Even if the mortgage has been paid off, there can be thousands of dollars in annual property tax, not to mention continuing maintenance expenses.

Many who keep the house discover not only that it is too big, but also that it costs far more than they can afford. The expenses become untenable, and they are forced to sell. Then, as they trade down to a less expensive home, they are hit with a whopping capital-gains tax because the house has appreciated so much in value.

Many financial planners recommend that spouses sell the house as part of the settlement, sharing both the proceeds and the tax liabilities. Even then, such a division of property can be fraught with tax consequences. Timing becomes critical, and failure to pay attention to the rules can result in some very big tax bills. If you move out of your home before a divorce, for example, you may lose the ability to claim the home as your primary residence when it is later sold. That could cost you the ability to defer taxes on your portion of gain on the sale.

Another risk is that people who are 55 years old or older may be unable to take the special tax exemption on up to $125,000 of capital gains from the sale of their home. That could happen if they move out for too long and lose the right to claim the home as their primary residence. A knowledgeable tax professional may be able to find ways to preserve such tax breaks.

TAX RETURNS

Divorcing couples should carefully consider the income tax filing status they select in the years just before a divorce. While filing jointly often saves taxes, it can be perilous for those looking to untangle their finances from their future ex. If it later turns out that your former spouse never paid Uncle Sam for the tax due, you could be responsible and owe the full amount.

This shared liability can hit particularly hard if you sell a home right before a divorce. Say a couple who always filed joint returns sold a home last year for $200,000—$100,000 more than their adjusted cost basis. Because the two planned to divorce this year and roll over their individual shares of the proceeds into new principal residences within two years of the sale, they elected to defer taxes on the gain. No problem here, as long as they both actually do so.

But there can be big trouble if one or the other has a change of heart. Say the husband rolls over his $50,000 gain by buying a $100,000 home by next year, and the wife spends her $50,000 to get a master's degree, without ever paying the capital-gains tax. Years later, the husband could get a tax bill for $14,000—plus, perhaps, interest and penalties. In such cases, many may find there is little recourse but to pay the bill.

One solution is to file separately. This means you report and pay taxes based solely on your own income and deductions. The taxes that the two of you will owe will often be higher than if you had filed jointly, but the IRS cannot later dun you for shortfalls on your spouse's return. Another possibility for a divorcing parent may be to file using the more favorable "head of household" rates. To qual-ify, you must live apart from your spouse for at least six months of the year and provide the main home for the kids for more than half the year.

PENSION PLANS

Retirement plans can be an important part of any settlement, but you need to understand both the tax ramifications and your own financial situation to make a wise choice. Pensions, 401(k)s, and In-dividual Retirement Accounts can be particularly valuable to home-maker spouses, who may have no retirement plans of their own and will probably be hard-pressed to save for retirement in the years fol-lowing divorce.

In order to get a piece of your spouse's "qualified" plan—such as a 401(k) or a profit-sharing plan—you need a court-issued Qual-ified Domestic Relations Order (QDRO). Such an order is not necessary for nonqualified plans, such as Individual Retirement Ac-counts or many deferred-compensation plans and annuities. The QDRO, which must be approved by the plan administrator to be valid, will act as a lien to stop your former spouse from cleaning out a pension plan that was awarded in part to you. It can also make sure that a husband, say, who receives funds from his former wife's company plan pays tax on the money. Otherwise, the plan would notify the IRS that the wife withdrew part of the pension, and she would owe the tax.

If your spouse has a traditional pension plan, which promises a specified benefit after retirement, you would be entitled to pay-ments once your ex hits his or her earliest retirement age. If, how-ever, your spouse is covered by a defined-contribution plan—such as a profit-sharing plan—you could get your share distributed to you as a lump sum at any time without having to pay an early-withdrawal penalty. But you would owe ordinary income tax on the entire amount if you took it in cash. A better solution, if you do not need the money to live on, is to have it rolled over directly into an IRA. A direct rollover would allow you to defer taxes until the money is actually withdrawn.

INVESTMENTS

Your spouse may offer to split the investment portfolio, or even give you more than half, but that does not mean it is a good offer. To paraphrase George Orwell, some investments are more equal than others. In general, the best investments in a divorce settlement are the ones that are most liquid. Cash is king, but stocks, bonds, and mutual funds are also usually easily valued and easily sold. Remember, however, that you are not likely to walk away from the divorce table with a balanced portfolio. You may get all the AT&T stock, while your ex gets the mutual funds. That means you will need to reshape your investments to make sure you are properly diversified.

Which investments should be avoided? Topping the list are limited partnerships. Not only are these complex investments difficult to value accurately, but they are also hard to sell. Moreover, they are often saddled with tax liabilities and many are nearly worthless. Real estate is another tricky investment. Although rental property can produce valuable income, it may be subject to some stiff taxes in the event you need to sell. Before you accept real estate as part of any settlement, get an outside appraisal and have your CPA or financial planner check out tax issues. Also, make sure you are ready to assume the responsibilities that go with managing any property.

If you have a stake in a spouse's business, it is usually smart to negotiate for a cash buyout. Why? Ask yourself one question: Would you rather have the money in hand or have to rely on your ex's good faith and business savvy in running a concern over which you have no control? Be sure to get the business appraised independently. An outside appraiser will be better at spotting any legerdemain in the business financial statements. That will keep you from finding out years later that your former spouse managed to greatly understate the value of the company.

INSURANCE

In general, a lump-sum divorce settlement is preferable to alimony because you do not have to rely on your ex for continued payments.

But few people have the financial resources to provide for an equitable settlement in one lump-sum payment. Since your payments are likely to be spread out over time, make sure your spouse has a life insurance policy that will cover your part of the settlement in case of death.

If you are covered by your spouse's company health plan and the company has 20 or more employees, you should be able to continue to buy that coverage for 36 months under COBRA, the federal Consolidated Omnibus Budget Reconciliation Act of 1985. You can try to get your spouse to cover those costs, since the premiums can be expensive. Even if you have to pick up the tab yourself, your spouse's health plan may be better than anything you can find on the open market, particularly if you have any pre-existing health problems. (Chapter 4 tells you more about COBRA, while Chapter 3 has a useful section on buying your own health care coverage.)

ESTATE PLANNING AND NONCITIZEN SPOUSES

Many lawyers do not ask, and many clients forget to mention it. But when it comes to estate planning, the citizenship of your spouse is a critical factor. That is because the unlimited marital deduction—which allows you to leave everything to your husband or wife without paying any estate tax—does not apply to spouses who are not U.S. citizens. If you write a standard U.S. will without taking that fact into account, Uncle Sam may collect a bundle when you die.

The intent of the law, passed in 1988, is to keep surviving spouses from returning to their home countries with their untaxed inheritance money. But the law is so restrictive that many noncitizen spouses opt to become U.S. citizens rather than comply with its onerous requirements.

Keep in mind that unlike many other countries, the United States levies estate taxes on the worldwide assets of the deceased, be they U.S. citizens or simply U.S. residents. Moreover, if the surviving spouse is a noncitizen, assets held jointly by the couple are considered to be 100% in the first-to-die spouse's estate, unless the noncitizen spouse can prove that he or she contributed.

Folks with less than $600,000 in assets need take no special steps. Any U.S. resident can pass that amount tax-free to anyone they want, no matter what their citizenship. But anything over $600,000 passed to a spouse who is not a citizen is subject to estate taxes unless it is put into a qualified domestic trust, or QDOT.

But even that does not solve the estate-tax problem if the surviving spouse needs to get at the principal. The reason is that any principal taken out of the trust is taxed as if it had been part of the estate of the first-to-die spouse. Moreover, the estate-tax rate is calculated to include all prior distributions, thus potentially pushing successive withdrawals into higher estate-tax brackets.

That is a big penalty to pay. A husband with a $1 million estate could leave his noncitizen wife $600,000 tax-free and put the remaining $400,000 into a QDOT. But as she withdrew that QDOT principal, the government would collect $153,000 in taxes on money that a citizen spouse would have inherited tax-free.

There are also restrictions on the management of a QDOT. At least one of the trustees must be either a U.S. citizen or corporation. QDOTs may also be restricted in the amount of assets invested in real property located outside of the United States.

TRANSFERRING ASSETS

To avoid the constraints of a QDOT, many couples opt to transfer assets to the noncitizen spouse. For couples with assets of up to $1.2 million, simply dividing the assets equally between the two partners can effectively solve the problem since each can leave the other up to $600,000 free of estate taxes. Couples with more than $1.2 million may want to shift most of the assets to the noncitizen spouse, since the unlimited marital deduction remains intact when it is the U.S. citizen who inherits. But such transfers can be yet another trap for the unwary: Any gifts above $100,000 a year to a noncitizen spouse trigger the gift tax.

Becoming a citizen is the easiest answer for many. In fact, estate attorneys typically recommend documents be worded in such a way that a QDOT is effective only if the spouse remains a noncitizen.

Timing of that citizenship, however, is important. If it is obtained before or within nine months of the spouse's death—the deadline for filing estate taxes—there is no need for the QDOT at all. After that time, estate taxes become due unless a QDOT is established. Even then, the surviving spouse can avoid paying QDOT taxes by remaining a resident and leaving all trust principal untouched until obtaining U.S. citizenship.

If your spouse was oblivious to the problem and never took any estate-planning steps, there is still a way to avoid estate taxes if you are not a U.S. citizen. If you initiate proceedings within nine months of your spouse's death, you can ask the court for permission to

ESTATE-TAX TRAPS FOR NONCITIZENS

- U.S. residents, whether citizens or not, pay estate taxes on their worldwide assets, not just those in the United States.
- Assets held jointly are considered to be 100% in the estate of the first-to-die spouse unless the noncitizen spouse can prove that he or she contributed.
- Any gifts above $100,000 a year from a spouse to a noncitizen spouse trigger the gift tax.
- Do not forget pension plans and Individual Retirement Accounts, which typically pass outside the will and thus are not subject to QDOT provisions unless specific action is taken.

set up your own QDOT. This limits estate taxes to any principal money withdrawn from the trust. Then, if you wish, you can begin the process of becoming a citizen to avoid estate taxes altogether.

AFTER THE DEATH OF A SPOUSE

While some things have to be decided fairly quickly after the death of a spouse, the best approach is to take it slow. No matter how competent or intelligent you are, the death of a spouse will turn your life upside down. The adjustment to single life can be an emotional roller coaster ride. Decisions made during this period are often ones that people regret.

A few things, unfortunately, cannot be put off. You may, for example, be executor and responsible for initiating probate proceedings. Or you may have to decide how you want to receive life insurance benefits. Make the decisions that just cannot wait, but build in as much future flexibility as possible.

Consider your late spouse's life insurance. Insurers may push you to use the death benefit to buy an annuity that can provide you guaranteed income for the rest of your life. But annuitizing the death benefit will lock your money into a single investment at a time when making decisions will be difficult. Many people would be better off taking a lump-sum payment and parking it in Treasury bills or some other safe place for at least six months. That will give them time to adjust, to consider their new financial realities, and to plot a savings and investment course calculated to help them afford their current needs and longer-term goals.

The same is true for the deceased's retirement plans, which in many cases can also be annuitized. To maintain future flexibility, the entire plan can be rolled over directly into an Individual Retirement Account set up for that purpose in your own name. But make sure the rollover goes directly from one plan trustee to another; if the money passes through your hands, 20% of the amount will be withheld for taxes.

DISCLAIMING ASSETS

If your spouse fell a little short on estate planning, you may want to take a close look at what you inherit. You have nine months from the date of death to disclaim property left to you, thus potentially reducing the estate taxes due upon your own death. This technique takes advantage of the "unified credit," which allows $600,000 in every estate to pass free of federal estate taxes.

Here is how it works. A widower who finds himself with about $1.5 million in assets when his wife dies will pay no federal estate taxes because the unlimited marital deduction allows spouses to leave everything to each other tax-free. But when the widower dies, everything in his estate over $600,000 will be subject to estate taxes at rates ranging from 37% to 55%. By disclaiming up to $600,000 of his wife's estate, the widower could take advantage of his wife's unused unified credit. Once disclaimed, the assets would pass tax-free to the succeeding beneficiaries, usually the children. And that will significantly reduce the taxes eventually paid on his estate.

Still, many people do not want to disclaim anything. They do not want to give up control of a major asset, and for good reason. Once money passes to the children, there is nothing obligating the kids to return it should Mom or Dad find themselves in financial difficulties.

Timing is another factor, since you can disclaim only assets that you have not yet laid claim to. That means the decision to disclaim may have to be made at a time of great turmoil when the surviving spouse is feeling uncertain about the future.

WATCH OUT FOR VULTURES

The feeling of uncertainty can play a major role in the financial affairs of recent widows and widowers. It can make them easy targets for brokers, insurance agents, and others who want to sell them things. Knowing this, these salespeople often follow the obituaries and pitch their calls to the surviving spouse. Some of these salespeople are honest but greedy. Many are probably incompetent. And at least a few may well be crooks.

One way to deflect these assaults is to put together a team of trusted advisers, including a lawyer, accountant, and financial planner. This team can then provide a good sounding board while the surviving spouse starts to take hold of the financial reins. Having a good team can not only help with the learning process but also make it easier to resist the impulse to let any other individual take control.

Many people, however, will need a financial education before they can really take control. A good starting place can be the inventory of assets required by probate. Once you know what you have, you can start to figure out what you need. Then you can begin slowly to allocate those assets to achieve your long-term objectives.

Learning how to handle investment risk is perhaps the most difficult part of any financial education. Recent widows, never having handled the family finances, can become fearful that they will end up alone, penniless, and homeless. Some turn ultraconservative, stashing all their money in certificates of deposit. But many widows are far too young to take such a conservative investment approach. A widow in her mid-50s, for example, can easily live another 30 years. That is a long time. If she does not take some moderate risk by buying stocks or stock mutual funds, her investments will have a hard time keeping pace with the rate of inflation.

PROVIDING FOR A DISABLED CHILD

Estate planning when you have a disabled child is like trying to construct a safety net while gazing into a crystal ball. Will your child be able to function as a fully independent adult or need some form of continuing care? Will he or she be eligible for government funding? Hold a job? And where will your child live when you are no longer there?

The difficulty of answering those questions with any degree of certainty means your estate plans have to be flexible enough to handle a variety of possibilities. Perhaps the best way to start is to work backward. Begin with your destination in mind. Decide where you would like your children to be if you died tomorrow, and work from there.

As with more traditional families, you need to make a will. But in deciding how to divide your assets, it is important to consider one factor other parents do not even have to think about: government funding. Government programs are important for many disabled persons, since care is expensive and can rapidly deplete a family's finances. But there are many things the government does not cover, such as over-the-counter medicines, trips to visit family members, reading material, and even soap. Typically, it is the parents who fill the gap and pay for these items.

Upon their deaths, however, parents cannot simply leave money to their disabled child as a way of continuing to provide these extras. Inheriting as little as a few thousand dollars can cut a child off from needed programs. That means parents must find a way to pay for these items without actually giving money to the child. The answer, for most, is a "special needs trust." Properly crafted, such a trust will protect access to government funding. Just as important, it also creates an entire management system to support the child when you are no longer there.

HOW YOU SAY IT IS CRUCIAL

The wording of these trusts is critical, as is the careful assignment of authority. The beneficiary, for example, can have no power over the trust or its assets. Moreover, the trust must be specifically created to be supplemental, providing only extras for the child. If improperly drawn, the government may insist that trust funds be spent before the child receives any other assistance. To protect against possible rule changes in years to come, the document should also include an escape clause. This would terminate the trust and distribute the assets if there should be any serious attempt by the government to break the trust.

Before creating such a trust, the family must thrash out some important issues. The first is deciding who will assume responsibility for the child after the parents' deaths. Family members are often the best option, and advisers say it is important to name plenty of backups. Allocating responsibility according to the strengths of individual family members is also a good idea. One person may be better at managing trust investments; another may be better at evaluating programs and deciding how the money will best benefit the child. This division of labor also keeps individual family members from becoming overwhelmed and burning out.

In some cases, there are no family members who can take on the responsibility for a disabled child. Here, parents may turn to professional trustees, such as banks. Those most suited to the task are likely to have social workers and private-care managers on staff. Another alternative is use of a master trust or pooled trust, typically created by a nonprofit group to provide a management umbrella for funds from a group of individuals.

Some parents opt to create their own alternatives. In many places, parents join together to establish group residences for their children; others agree to serve as trustees for each others' children. Whatever option the parents choose, they should make sure the trustee is flexible enough to deal with changing circumstances.

The second important issue is how to allocate family resources. The problem here is that what is fair is not always equal. In many cases, the disabled child may simply need more. Parents have to be realistic about what their child's needs will be, then have a frank discussion with other members of the family.

FUNDING A TRUST

How much is enough? That depends on both the severity and the type of disability. Start by looking at current costs, figure out what extras will be needed once the parents are gone, then factor in inflation. A $250,000 trust could generate about $1,000 a month without ever tapping the principal, assuming the trust earned 5% after taxes and expenses. If the parents decided to let the trustee tap the principal, the available monthly funds could be higher, but the trust would no longer be self-sustaining.

Money to fund such a trust often comes from life insurance. Last-to-die policies, which are cheaper than other types because benefits are not paid until the second parent dies, can work well here. And since death benefits are usually paid expeditiously, funds would be available when needed for the child.

Having carefully crafted and funded a trust, you must still make sure that the money is properly spent. If not, your child may lose government benefits anyway. For example, under Supplemental Security Income, a federal assistance program for the disabled, a recipient can receive only $60 of unearned income in any calendar quarter. That is just $20 a month. Anything above that will reduce benefits dollar-for-dollar. Trustees can minimize the problem by keeping money out of the hands of the beneficiary. That means making payments directly to providers. Even large, salable items, such as furniture, should be owned by the trustee, who then allows the beneficiary to use them.

Trustees and others who assume responsibility for a disabled child need a wealth of information to avoid such traps. That is one reason why advisers recommend that parents write a "letter of intent," clearly outlining the child's history, setting priorities for care and services, and even discussing their own hopes and expectations. Details about past treatment, for instance, can help the trustees and guardians make better decisions about future programs, living arrangements, and other matters. Even little things—such as the child's special fondness for, say, train trips—can make a big difference in the child's future happiness. And that can make such a letter the most important part of any plan.

FINANCES FOR THE TERMINALLY ILL

Financial matters are probably the last thing on the minds of people who have just been diagnosed with a terminal illness. But after anger and denial have passed, it is the financial concerns that can become daunting. How will you pay those escalating medical bills? How will you take care of yourself and family members who depend on you? How will they manage after you are gone?

These questions are best addressed with brutal honesty. So temporarily shelve that positive mental attitude so important to fighting your illness and direct some of your energies toward money matters. Yes, you may be able to beat your illness. But it is important to revise your financial plans for the real possibility that you will not.

For many, the first step may be to make sure that their estate plans are in order. That means having a will, a durable power of attorney, a health care power of attorney, and any of a variety of trusts. But while some tax planning techniques benefit the dying, the basics here are virtually the same as for healthy folks.

Far more dramatic are the changes that take place in the other aspects of financial planning. Take cash flow, for example. People who go on disability will find they typically receive only 60% of their base pay. But unreimbursed medical expenses, the need for more professional services, increased living costs, and the need to assume medical and life insurance premiums can mean an increase in expenses of 40% or more.

This means people diagnosed with a terminal illness will need to find some new sources of cash. Typically, there are six places to look: government entitlement programs such as Social Security and Medicare, medical insurance, life insurance, disability insurance, employee benefits, and credit.

Insurance and company benefits, often overlooked by the healthy, become significant assets when you are seriously ill or dying. A medical insurance policy that will pay $1 million of your medical bills is suddenly worth more than most people's investment portfolios, more than their homes. As possibly your most valuable asset, it requires your attention.

Start by reading all your insurance policies and your employee-benefit handbook as well. Sure this is tedious, but it is essential that you understand your benefits, particularly those that are likely to become important as your disease progresses. Armed with this knowledge, you can make intelligent choices about how to make the best use of your benefits. You may, for example, discover that your company plan allows you to buy additional life and disability coverage without meeting any special medical criteria.

Cast the same analytical eye on your other benefits. Retirement plans may no longer be the vehicle for your golden years, but that does not mean you should stop funding them. Such plans can be a good way for people to pay for a serious illness. Not only do employers provide matching funds for many retirement plans, but also the 10% penalty for early withdrawals is typically waived for someone who is disabled.

Credit can provide another important source of funds for the terminally ill when paperwork snarls and insurance delays wreak havoc with their cash flow. When applying for new credit cards and lines of credit, remember to get credit life insurance that will pay off these debts upon death. The peace of mind that comes with this coverage more than offsets the increased cost.

Investment priorities will also change when you have a terminal illness. Long-term growth must take a backseat to liquidity. You want to have a portfolio of short-term or limited-maturity bond funds and money market investments. Only people with substantial wealth should continue investing for growth.

Of course, some decisions will depend on whether you are single or have a family to worry about. Someone who has a family and dependents is going to face issues a single person will not. Family considerations, for example, are likely to be a major concern in deciding how best to use life insurance. Many insurance companies let people accelerate death benefits if their life expectancy is less than six months or a year. Other firms called "viatical" settlement companies will buy your death benefits for 50% to 85% of their value, assume the premiums, and collect the benefits when you die.

But such steps are often taken as a last resort. For one thing, either approach will deplete the benefit intended to support your family. Moreover, these funds may deprive you of Medicaid and other government benefits reserved for low-income people.

Still, such arrangements can be an important source of funds for those who have few other assets. One man used a viatical settlement to move his family from New York and buy a home in Atlanta. Although death benefits might have left the family with more money, this approach allowed him to settle his family into a new life before he died.

Such difficult decision making is only part of the planning process for those who are terminally ill. They must also deal with the everyday business of being sick, which typically includes a mountain of paperwork. Even the transition from full employment to disability generally involves so much paperwork that completing the necessary forms for both your employer and the government can take nearly two months. Do not slough it off. Failure to file a needed form in timely fashion can mean losing a benefit. And it may be up to you to know that you are supposed to file that form. Employers, for example, typically provide no special notice that group life insurance needs to be converted to an individual policy within 31 days. It is in the employee handbook you received when you were hired.

This is one area where many people can benefit from using professionals. Often disease-specific support groups or medical institutions provide access to social workers and other counselors who can help. Many people opt to hire someone to make sure that insurance claims are properly filed and that premiums are paid on time. Such claims-assistance professionals can become critically important if there is a possibility of incompetency, since a missed insurance premium at this point is a real crisis.

TAX PLANNING FOR THE TERMINALLY ILL

Only death and taxes are certain. But when death is imminent, those with a thorough knowledge of estate-planning basics can often save their heirs a bundle. Such tactics are not for everyone. It is hard enough to deal with issues of mortality when death is a remote possibility, but it is much harder to deal with them when it is actually happening.

Still, those who are willing to talk taxes as they near their deathbed may be able to make a significant dent in their estate taxes. Here are some areas that the terminally ill can consider:

• **Gifting.** Since everyone can make annual gifts of up to $10,000 to an unlimited number of individuals tax-free, people with terminal illnesses may want to make full use of this exclusion. Some people take the technique so far that they make out deathbed checks to children and grandchildren, but the checks must be cashed before death to qualify for the annual exclusion.

• **Avoiding capital gains.** Do not sell stocks that have big capital gains. Remember that your heirs will inherit your stock at its current value, not the much lower price that you paid. Recognizing the gains before you die will subject you to needless taxes.

• **Taking capital losses.** This is the flip side of the capital-gains issue. Since all securities are marked to market at the time of death, you lose any capital losses not used before your death.

• **Using your IRAs and 401(k)s.** If you withdraw money from these retirement plans, you will incur income taxes. But someone will eventually have to pay those taxes. If you pay them, your estate will be smaller and that may mean lower estate taxes. But if you leave the plans intact for, say, your children or grandchildren, the entire pretax amount will be included in your estate.

• **Making charitable gifts.** If you make a charitable gift before you die, you will get an income tax deduction in addition to reducing the size of your estate. But if the gift is made as part of your will, there will be no income tax deduction.

• **Consider a conservation easement.** If you own valuable real estate that you plan to pass to your kids, they may find that estate taxes are so high that they cannot afford to keep the property. But if you put a conservation restriction on the property, the value of the land will drop dramatically, often reducing the estate taxes owed to an affordable level.

IN LINE FOR A BIG INHERITANCE?

Your daddy is rich, and so is your mom. One day, they say, it will all be yours.

You are not alone. More than $10 trillion is expected to pass to baby boomers by the year 2040, according to a study by Cornell University researchers. That is roughly $90,000 for each and every baby boomer. Of course, averages lie. Most baby boomers will receive little or nothing. The wealth is so unevenly held that only a quarter of all baby boomers will actually inherit more than $50,000.

If you are one of the lucky ones, though, how do you factor all that future money into your current plans? That is a tough question because no one really knows how and when that money will change hands. Unless the money is already in trust, potential heirs have no way to calculate the actual size of their inheritance. Dad may remarry, spend a large portion on medical care, or give most of it to charity.

Equally problematic is when baby boomers will take charge of that money. With more people living in good health into their 90s, junior may find that he does not come into his inheritance until he is in his 60s or 70s. That is too late to help buy the big family house, pay for the kids' college education, or even fund the first years of retirement.

Some in this situation might decide the best thing to do is simply plan as though they are getting nothing. But it is hard to ignore the possibility of such an inheritance. Better, perhaps, to put a conservative valuation on family money and assume it will not pass to you until Mom and Dad are well into their 90s.

WHAT IT TAKES TO BE PREPARED

Take the time to put your own financial house in order. Ask the basic questions and start sorting out your feelings about money. How much money does your family really need? What are your long-term financial goals? How will you accomplish them?

A basic understanding of investing is also important. You do not have to become an expert, even if you will be inheriting a small fortune. You can rely on a money manager. But you need enough understanding to make sure your money manager is competent and trustworthy.

This is also a good time to develop personal priorities. People who inherit large amounts of money have the potential to have a big impact through their charitable giving. Look for issues you think are important and places where you would like to put your time and money. If large enough, your inheritance may allow you great creativity.

All this preparation should go a long way toward reducing the personal conflicts that come from a large inheritance. These conflicts can be particularly acute if the person inheriting is relatively young and has not found his or her way in either the professional world or in personal relationships. Large inheritances, for example, commonly create rifts between husband and wife as the couple tries to figure out who the money really belongs to and what an appropriate lifestyle is now. If the two have different money styles, the arrival of so much money often heightens these differences.

Family expectations can weigh heavily, and people who inherit may feel that they are not really free to do what they wish with their inherited money. The need to work can also become moot, giving people with large inheritances more freedom to choose what they want to do. That sounds like a dream come true to many, but society is not tolerant of the idle rich. Those who flounder in finding their life's work may find that their self-esteem suffers, too.

INFLATED EXPECTATIONS

The flip side of these problems are the ones caused by inflated inheritance expectations. Your parents may have $1 million or $10 million today, but that does not mean that is what you will inherit. One reason for this is that folks today are living well past 75, the age when most people stop accumulating money and start to spend down their wealth. Typically, the most expensive years are the ones right before death.

It is possible for Mom and Dad to spend all of their money, even if they have $1 million. If both end up in a nursing home, the bills in many parts of the country can run $160,000 a year, thus rapidly depleting family resources. Then there are the taxes. The trillions of dollars to be inherited in the next 50 years are, in fact, a pretax amount. The figure does not take into account the huge amount that will be lost to estate taxes and sometimes even income taxes.

A retirement plan with $500,000 in it, for example, gets hit by both federal and state income taxes as the money is withdrawn. That money would push most heirs into a high enough bracket that they would lose 40% of that inheritance money. Upper-bracket people would lose closer to 50%. Then there are estate taxes, which kick in on estates of over $600,000 and can be as high as 55%. That means the original $500,000 could be down to as little as $125,000 by the time Uncle Sam and his state relatives are done taking their shares.

Much of the touted wealth transfer is also tied up in family homes and family businesses. Thus property can change hands, but the new owner may not feel any richer. Or worse, people may find themselves facing huge estate taxes for an asset they do not want but cannot find a buyer for.

All these problems are compounded by the fact that families rarely feel comfortable discussing money issues. Ignorance here, however, can do real damage. Folks whose inheritance is not what they expect can become hurt and angry. Even worse, people who do not coordinate their planning with other family members can find themselves working at cross purposes.

WHAT WOULD YOU DO WITH A WINDFALL?

More than a quarter of baby boomers responding to a survey said they would use a $50,000 inheritance to pay off debts, while another 25% would use the money for their children's education. The remainder would use the windfall for retirement and other purposes.

Pay off debts	26%
Fund children's education	25%
Save for retirement	20%
Put toward home purchase	14%
Buy personal items	4%
Give to charity	2%

SOURCE: First Interstate Bank Trust and Private Client Services Group.

SURVIVAL GUIDE FOR THE NEWLY UNEMPLOYED

If you have just become a statistic in the world of corporate re-engineering, downsizing, restructuring, or whatever the boss called it, take a deep breath: Your trip to the exit door will set the tone for your financial health over the next several months. In today's tough job market, you need to make sure you are taking advantage of all the possibilities presented by your departure.

That means not only understanding the fine points of your severance package and making sure you get good references, but also looking for opportunities for work within your company after the ax falls. It pays to put aside the hurt feelings and think strategically. You may be able to stay on the payroll for another six months or even a year by offering to help handle the transition. Or you may be able to land a consulting position in some area where the company is now shorthanded.

Such maneuvering, of course, is only a temporary solution. All you have done is bought yourself time. But that can be worth a lot when the future is uncertain. Staying on the job, for example, may let you keep not only your office and secretary but also your health insurance and other benefits.

It can also give you the opportunity to reorganize your finances while you are still receiving a paycheck. People faced with imminent job loss have to take a hard look at their money needs, but making smart decisions in the midst of emotional upheaval is difficult. The general rule is that in the face of uncertainty, people should gravitate toward liquidity and flexibility. But that does not mean selling investments willy-nilly to raise cash.

You may have a visceral urge to sell, but resist it. Rather, put together a cash-flow analysis that provides a reasonable idea of how long existing funds will hold out. Having the numbers in black and white will allow you to take a more calm and orderly approach to making the necessary financial decisions. The results of the analysis may actually be comforting, showing that you have more time than you thought to make your next career move.

Of course, some decisions need to be made in short order. Here is a look at a few things you should consider as you choreograph your departure:

• **Severance pay.** Depending on your company, your position there, and your length of service, severance can range from nothing to over two years of salary. Usually there is little room to negotiate the amount. But many companies do give you the choice of taking a lump sum or a continuation of salary.

Which is better? The lump sum provides you with greater flexibility, and it protects you from the potential financial misfortunes of your employer. But before you decide, find out if salary continuation will prolong your benefits, such as health insurance and funding of your retirement plan. If so, salary continuation may be a far better deal. However it is paid, severance money should be kept liquid. This is the money you will use to pay living expenses until you find another job, so do not simply make it part of your investment portfolio.

• **Unemployment insurance.** Every little bit helps, so apply for unemployment benefits at the earliest date possible. But do not expect unemployment to carry you. Benefit calculations vary from state to state, but middle managers and executives will find unemployment replaces only a small fraction of their former salaries. The benefit is further diminished come tax time, since unemployment benefits are considered taxable income.

• **Health insurance.** Under COBRA, the Consolidated Omnibus Budget Reconciliation Act of 1985, companies must offer employees who are losing their group health coverage the right to buy that coverage, typically for 18 months. Many people probably will not be able to do better on the open market. Unless you can get health care benefits through your spouse's employer, the smart move is to pick up COBRA, remembering that COBRA is only a short-term answer. You should start shopping for replacement coverage early, particularly if you have health problems.

• **Life and disability insurance.** You may be able to hold onto that group term life insurance policy that your company purchased for you. In some cases, you can simply assume the premiums; in others, you have to convert to a higher-priced cash-value policy. In either case, the main attraction is that you do not have to take a qualifying physical. Some corporate disability plans are also convertible to individual policies, providing a newly unemployed person a benefit that no insurer will sell them once they no longer have an income. But many companies either do not mention or simply do not realize these options are available. Employees facing unemployment need to do their own homework in these areas. Often they can greatly improve their benefits if they know what to ask for.

REALITY CHECK FOR THE SELF-EMPLOYED

For many people, the loss of a job is the start of self-employment. If you are thinking of striking out on your own, you need to give your personal finances as much scrutiny as your business plan. That is because when you are building a business—be it a consulting firm, day-care center, or small manufacturing plant—the business becomes your most important investment. If successful, it will end up funding all your personal goals, ranging from the kids' college tuition to your own retirement nest egg. But while it is growing, that business can dictate everything from where you put your extra cash to the health insurance you carry.

That is why it is important to know where you stop and where the business begins. To make self-employment work, you need to conduct your business as a business. At the most basic level, that means having separate checking accounts, separate telephones, and separate bookkeeping. It also means setting a reasonable salary for yourself based on what the business can afford and taking it on a regular basis.

Keeping these clear lines between the business and the personal serves two purposes. First, it can prevent you from taking too much money out of your business, increasing the likelihood that there will be enough cash not only to cover expenses but also to let the business grow. Equally important, separating personal and business financial matters can give you some financial stability in the midst of the likely fluctuations in your business cash flow.

Having drawn the lines, it is important to recognize that your personal balance sheet will nonetheless affect your business. Lenders will take your personal financial strength into account when making loans to your business. You cannot afford to plow all your money directly back into the business. You need to accumulate enough capital so that you become a good lending risk. You also can help make yourself "bankable" by establishing a working relationship with a banker early on.

IT REQUIRES DISCIPLINE

The need for personal liquidity probably means cutting back on stock investments, at least in the beginning. It also probably means scaling down your lifestyle as well. Living beneath your means will help maintain personal liquidity, allowing you to focus on building the business.

That takes discipline. There is, for example, the temptation to overdo tax write-offs. Some self-employed people focus on the fact that equipment, such as a car or a computer, can be written off by the business. Instead, figure out if the business really needs and can afford to make such a purchase. The same restraint is needed when it comes to benefits, such as insurance and retirement plans. These are attractive perks in a thriving business, but they are usually too expensive for a young and growing one. That means the self-employed should look elsewhere for these benefits until the business is profitable enough to afford them.

What kind of benefits should you buy yourself? Buy the ones that will protect you, your family, and your business in case of an emergency. That means health insurance comes first, followed by disability and then life insurance. Retirement is at the bottom of the list. Membership in professional associations or the Chamber of Commerce can help cut costs when buying life, health, and disability insurance. This gives you a chance to obtain group rates until the business is financially healthy enough to buy its own group coverage.

WATCH THE TAX CONSEQUENCES

If you opted for a corporate structure in launching your business, you also need to be careful about how your benefits are purchased and owned. Disability and life insurance benefits, if triggered, may turn out to be taxable income for you if your company paid the premiums. A good rule of thumb: Pay the premiums yourself unless you have thoroughly researched the tax consequences.

On the retirement front, a self-employed person has several options, ranging from starting a new plan to simply opening an Individual Retirement Account. (You can find more information in Chapter 4.) To decide among them, the first question to ask is how much money you can afford to put into a tax-deferred retirement plan. For those who are just starting out, an answer of $4,000 or less for a married couple may lead to an IRA. Here is why.

With one option—a Simplified Employee Pension, or SEP—you can salt away as much as about 13% of your pretax self-employment earnings up to a certain dollar limit ($22,500 in 1996). But if your business is barely in the black, that 13% does not add up to much. The same is true if you opt for a Keogh plan, another option that can have similar limits. And if you have any employees, both of these types of plans require that you contribute for these employees as you do for yourself.

As such, you may actually be able to put away a much higher amount by simply opening an IRA for the yearly maximum of $2,000 ($4,000 for a married couple). Your IRA contributions may be tax-deductible.

GLOSSARY

WATCHWORDS OF WEALTH

Stockbrokers, insurance agents, and other financial specialists can make you feel as though you have just landed on another planet. They even have their own special language. But it is your money they are after, so you had better speak the lingo. The phrases explained in the following glossary should help you cut through the jargon.

Accidental-death-and-dismemberment insurance. A type of insurance that pays if you are killed or maimed in an accident but provides no benefit in the event of illness or illness-related death.

Actual-cash-value coverage. In home insurance, the type of policy that pays only the current, depreciated value of furniture and other household possessions when they are damaged or destroyed. Provides less protection than replacement-cost coverage.

Adjusted gross income. A step in arriving at how much of your income is taxable by Uncle Sam. Adjusted gross income, or AGI, consists of your gross income from taxable sources minus certain items, such as payments to a Keogh plan or a deductible Individual Retirement Account. AGI minus deductions and personal exemptions equals your taxable income.

Alimony. A type of payment from one former spouse to another that is agreed to as part of a divorce settlement. Alimony is tax-deductible for the person who pays it and taxable income for the person who receives it.

Alternative minimum tax. A special, highly complex tax measure designed to ensure that most high-income individual taxpayers and companies do not escape taxation because of certain deductions and exclusions.

American Depositary Receipt. ADRs stand in for a foreign company's shares to facilitate trading in the United States. The shares themselves remain in the custody of a responsible third party, typically a bank. Through ADRs, Americans can invest directly in a foreign company while avoiding currency conversions, intimidating fees, and other obstacles to investing abroad.

Annual percentage rate. The interest rate borrowers pay on a loan. Most of a loan's up-front fees are factored into the APR.

Annual-renewable-term life. Term life insurance that is renewed each year, with premiums going up each time.

Annuity. A stream of payments that continue for the recipient's life, or some other period. Also, a tax-deferred investment account sold by insurers, banks, brokerage firms, and mutual fund companies, and a common investment option in certain retirement plans. With an "immediate" annuity, the buyer hands over a lump sum and receives payments that begin immediately. The purchase is usually irrevocable, and payments are usually fixed for life. With a "deferred" annuity, the money remains in the annuity to accumulate without being taxed until taken out, usually years later. "Fixed annuities" provide a rate of return that is fixed for a year or so but that then can move up and down. "Variable annuities" allow investors to allocate their money among a basket of mutual fund–like "subaccounts"; the return depends on the performance of the funds selected. Watch out for high fees and penalties for early withdrawals.

ARMs. Not parts of your body, but adjustable-rate mortgages. Home mortgages with interest rates that move up and down over time, based on changes in market interest rates.

Asset allocation. How your money is divided among various types of investments. If you decide to put 50% of your money in stocks, 30% in bonds, and 20% in a money market fund, you have just made an asset-allocation decision.

Asset-management accounts. All-in-one accounts that allow customers of brokerage firms to buy and sell securities and store cash in one or more money market mutual funds. Asset-management accounts generally offer check-writing privileges, credit or debit cards, and automatic transfers from one account to another. They often come with an annual fee of up to $100.

Assets. Things you own, including real estate, investments, and personal property.

Balance sheet. A listing of assets, liabilities, and net worth as of a particular date. "Balance" refers to the fact that assets equal liabilities plus net worth.

Balanced funds. Mutual funds that invest in a combination of stocks and bonds. A typical mix is 60% stocks and 40% bonds. Balanced funds are especially suitable for retirees and nervous stock market investors. But you may be able to save some money on fund-management fees—and, thus, boost your returns—if you create your own balanced portfolio by purchasing a good, low-cost stock fund and a good, low-cost bond fund.

Bear market. When the bears are growling on Wall Street, it means stock or bond prices are falling. Nervous Wall Streeters also talk about market "corrections" and "crashes" and stock prices "heading south."

Beneficiary. A person you name in your will, life insurance policy, retirement plan, or other financial arrangement to receive a benefit at your death.

Bodily injury liability coverage. As part of an auto policy, the liability insurance that pays if someone is hurt or killed in an accident that is your fault.

Bond Buyer Municipal Bond Index. An index based on 40 long-term municipal bonds that is often used to track the performance of tax-free municipal bonds. The index is compiled by *The Bond Buyer,* a trade publication that also has several other closely watched municipal bond indexes.

Bond rating (debt rating). An assessment of the likelihood that investors will receive the promised interest and principal payments on time. Bond ratings are assigned by independent agencies, such as Moody's Investors Service and Standard & Poor's.

Bonds. IOUs issued by governments and corporations to finance their operations. When you buy a bond, you lend money to the issuer with the understanding that you will be repaid on or by a set maturity date. In the meantime, the borrower agrees to pay you interest at a specified rate. Because of that promise, bonds are often called fixed-income securities. Investors who buy bonds and hold them until maturity can count on getting their principal back with interest, assuming the borrower does not default. But those who sell before maturity may receive more or less than they paid. That is because market prices of bonds fluctuate with changes in interest rates: When interest rates fall, bond prices rise; when interest rates rise, bond prices fall. Although many investors have been brought up to believe that investing in bonds protects them from the market gyrations associated with stocks, bond prices are sometimes quite volatile and many investors have lost a lot of money.

Book value. The difference between a company's assets and its liabilities, often expressed on a per-share basis. A company's book value, which is also known as stockholder's equity, can be found in the company's annual report.

Break the buck. When a money market fund's share price falls below the $1-a-share value it is intended to maintain, the fund is said to "break the buck." Money funds are supposed to be safe investments and easily convertible into cash; thus the stable $1 share price. Cases of breaking the buck have been rare.

Brokerage firm. When you buy or sell a security, you generally do so through a brokerage firm. Brokerage firms fall into two main camps, full-service brokers and discount brokers. Discount brokers charge far lower commissions than full-service brokers, and a growing number of deep discounters charge especially low commissions. But there is a trade-off. If you use a discount broker, you will get little or no investment advice, so you must be willing to make your own buy and sell decisions. A full-service broker, on the other hand, will help you pick investments and devise a financial plan.

Bull market. In the Wall Street menagerie, bulls are optimists, and thus a bull market is when prices are rising.

Cafeteria plan. A flexible-benefit plan offered by many employers that gives workers a certain number of credits and a menu of bene-fit options on which to spend them. The list may include medical coverage, life insurance, disability coverage, vacation days, and den-tal care. Employees who do not want a particular benefit can spend more on another, or receive the difference in cash.

Capital gain. Money you make when you sell stocks, bonds, and cer-tain other types of investments at a profit. If you lose money, it is called a capital loss.

Cash-value life. Life insurance coverage that incorporates a tax-deferred savings component in addition to providing a certain death benefit. Types include whole life, universal life, and variable life.

Cash. Yes, that is the money in your wallet. But for Wall Streeters, cash also consists of supersafe investments, such as money market funds and Treasury bills. Because there is little or no chance that you will lose money, such investments are sometimes called "cash equivalents."

Certified Financial Planner (CFP). The best-known financial plan-ning designation, given to qualifying planners by the CFP Board of Standards, Denver.

Charitable lead trust. A trust that pays a charity income from a do-nated asset for a set number of years, after which time the principal goes to the donor's beneficiaries with reduced estate or gift taxes.

Charitable remainder trust. This trust lets people leave assets to a favored charity and receive a tax break but still retain income for life. This works best for people with a large appreciated asset, which, if sold, would generate large capital-gains taxes.

Chartered Financial Consultant (ChFC). Financial planning designation given to qualifying planners by the American College, Bryn Mawr, Pennsylvania.

Chartered Life Underwriter (CLU). A professional designation given to qualifying life insurance agents by the American College, Bryn Mawr, Pennsylvania.

Child support. Money paid by one former spouse to another to cover the cost of raising children. These payments are neither tax-deductible for the person who pays them nor taxable income for the one who receives them.

Closed-end funds. Mutual funds that sell a limited number of shares, after which they are closed and the shares are listed on a stock exchange. Thereafter, the only way new investors can get in is to buy some of the exchange-traded shares. A closed-end fund's shares may trade for more or less than the per-share value of the fund's portfolio holdings. When a fund is trading at a discount to its portfolio value, it is often considered a bargain. These funds are also known as publicly traded funds and exchange-traded funds.

Closing costs. A variety of costs paid in conjunction with purchasing a home or taking on a new mortgage. Closing costs often include points, which typically are a form of additional interest. Other closing costs may include property taxes, title insurance, transfer tax, and attorneys' fees.

COBRA. The Consolidated Omnibus Budget Reconciliation Act of 1985 provides people the right to buy continuing health insurance through their former employers for a minimum of 18 months. COBRA offers up to 36 months of continuing coverage for those people insured through a spouse's work plan who lose that coverage due to divorce, separation, or death of the spouse.

Collision coverage. The part of an auto insurance policy that covers damage to your car in an accident.

Compounding. Financial advisers love to talk about the magic of compounding. What magic? If your investments make 10% a year for five years, you earn not 50%, but 61.1%. Here is the reason: As time goes on, you make money not only on your original investment but also on your accumulated gains from earlier years.

Comprehensive coverage. The part of an auto insurance policy that pays if your car is stolen or vandalized or otherwise damaged by something other than a collision.

Conservation easement. A restriction placed on real estate that limits or prohibits development and, thus, lowers the property's value. Conservation easements are often used to lower estate taxes on family real estate, thus allowing family members to retain ownership of the family farm or beach retreat when they might otherwise be forced to sell to cover the tax bill.

Convertible bonds. Interest-paying bonds that can be converted into a fixed amount of a company's common shares. These hybrid securities—sometimes described as T-bills with lottery tickets attached—derive part of their value from the interest payments and part from the potential for stock appreciation. Investing in convertibles is always tricky because they are difficult to evaluate. Careful diversification and assessment of both credit quality and appreciation potential are essential. Many market professionals say individuals are better off going with mutual funds than trying to buy convertibles on their own.

Credit-shelter or bypass trust. A trust that allows a married person—who can leave everything to his or her spouse tax-free—to preserve the exemption that allows $600,000 in every estate to pass to nonspouses free of federal estate taxes. By putting money into such a trust, you in effect "bypass" your spouse's estate while still giving him or her access to the assets.

Deductible. Under an insurance policy, the amount of loss or expense that you must shoulder yourself before the insurance company begins paying.

Defined-benefit plan. A traditional pension plan, which pays retirees a fixed monthly check based on their age, salary, and length of service.

Derivatives. Financial instruments with returns that move in response to some underlying asset or index.

DIF score. A rating, arrived at with a secret formula, used by the Internal Revenue Service to help figure out which returns to select for audits. DIF stands for "discriminant function."

Disability insurance. Insurance that can replace part of your income if illness or injury leaves you unable to work for an extended period.

Disability-waiver-of-premium rider. In life insurance, an added policy provision that continues coverage, without requiring premium payments, if the policyholder becomes disabled.

Disclaimer trust. A trust designed for couples who do not yet have enough assets to need a credit-shelter trust. A disclaimer trust allows the surviving spouse to disclaim up to $600,000 of the estate and have those assets put into a credit-shelter trust.

Diversification. When you diversify, you spread your money among a slew of different securities, thereby avoiding the risk that your portfolio will be badly bloodied because a single security or a particular market sector turns sour.

Dividend yield. A company's annual dividend expressed as a percentage of its current stock price.

Dividends. Payments made to stockholders by many, although far from all, companies. Payouts generally are made in quarterly installments.

Dollar-cost averaging. This popular investing technique involves investing a fixed amount at set intervals, regardless of what is happening to stock prices. When share prices are down, your investment buys more shares, while the reverse is true when share prices are buoyant. Stocks tend to rise over time, so those who use dollar-cost averaging should end up owning shares that are worth significantly more than the price they paid. Mutual funds, which typically demand minimum subsequent investments of just $50 or $100, are especially good for dollar-cost averaging.

Dow Jones averages. The Dow Jones Industrial, Transportation, Utilities, and Composite Averages are widely used indicators of stock market performance. The industrial average is based on 30 major industrial issues. It was created by Charles H. Dow, a founder of *The Wall Street Journal*, and first published in 1896. The transportation average tracks 20 stocks, the utilities average, 15. The Dow Jones Composite Average comprises the 65 stocks that together constitute the industrial, transportation, and utilities averages.

Dow Jones Global Indexes. Some 2,700 companies' stocks in 29 countries worldwide are tracked by geographic region and by 120 industry groups. Collectively, they represent more than 80% of the equity capital on stock markets around the world. All of the indexes are weighted by market capitalization, which is the product of price times shares outstanding. Thus, each country carries a weight proportionate to the relative value of its equities to all those in the world. The U.S. market is the world's biggest, and the U.S. component of the global indexes has the most stocks, more than 700.

Durable power of attorney. This document allows someone to conduct your personal and financial affairs even if you become legally incompetent. A power of attorney expires upon the giver's death.

Earnings yield. A company's per-share earnings expressed as a percentage of its stock price. This provides a yardstick for comparing stocks with bonds, as well as with other stocks.

Endorsement. In some forms of insurance, a provision added to a policy to add to or alter the coverage.

Estate taxes. Taxes levied by the federal and state governments on the transfer of your assets after you die. Uncle Sam levies estate taxes on the worldwide assets of both U.S. citizens and U.S. residents.

Executor. The person named in your will to handle the settlement of your estate.

Expense ratio. This figure tells you how much a mutual fund charges each year as a percentage of total fund assets. A fund with a 1.55% expense ratio, for instance, levies $1.55 for every $100 it has under management. Included in this figure are the fund's management fee, shareholder servicing costs, and any annual 12b-1 fee. A 12b-1 fee, which is named after the applicable Securities and Exchange Commission regulation, is levied to pay for the cost of attracting new investors to the fund. The fee may be used to buy advertising or to compensate brokers who sell the fund.

Federal funds rate. The interest rate that banks charge each other on loans for very short periods, usually overnight. This rate, which long has been closely controlled by the Federal Reserve, has a big impact on other short-term interest rates. *See also* **Federal Reserve System.**

Federal Open Market Committee. A 12-member group within the Federal Reserve that sets the nation's monetary policy. *See also* **Federal Reserve System.**

Federal Reserve System. The nation's central bank. Often referred to simply as the "Fed," it was designed by Congress to help provide the United States with a safe and stable monetary and financial system. The Fed's actions are monitored closely by investors and traders around the world, mainly because the Fed has the power to influence key short-term interest rates and control the amount of money and credit flowing through the U.S. economy. The Chairman of the Federal Reserve Board, a seven-member group based in Washington, is often referred to as the second most powerful person in the nation's capital.

FICA. The letters stand for Federal Insurance Contributions Act, but for most employees, they are simply the notation on their pay stubs showing how much was withheld for Social Security and Medicare.

Financial planner. A type of financial adviser, ideally with broad knowledge of all areas of personal finance. But no particular training or credentials are required, and many incompetents and even some outright crooks call themselves planners. Fee-only planners are paid solely by their clients—that is, they do not receive sales commissions or other compensation from other sources. Fee-plus-commission planners charge fees for advice and other services and also receive commissions on the sale of investment and insurance products.

Flexible spending account. An employee benefit offered by many companies that allows employees to have pretax dollars withheld from their salaries to pay for unreimbursed medical expenses and dependent-care expenses, such as babysitting or elder-care fees.

Floater. An insurance policy that covers specific items of personal property, such as jewelry.

401(k) plan. An employer-sponsored retirement-savings plan funded by employees with contributions that are deducted from pretax pay. Employers frequently add matching contributions up to a set limit. Employees are responsible for managing the money themselves, allocating the funds among a selection of stock, bond, and cash investment funds. Investment gains are not taxed until the money is withdrawn.

403(b) plan. A retirement-savings plan for employees of colleges, hospitals, school districts, and nonprofit organizations. The plan, which is similar to the 401(k) plan offered by many corporate employees, is funded by employees with contributions that are deducted from pretax pay. Employees manage the money themselves, selecting from fixed and variable annuities and mutual funds. Investment gains are not taxed until the money is withdrawn.

Futures contract. An agreement to buy or sell an asset—such as pork bellies or U.S. Treasury bonds—at a set time in the future at an agreed-upon price.

General-obligation bond. A municipal bond, typically one issued by a state or local government, that is backed by the issuer's "full faith and credit." That generally means the repayment of principal and the payment of interest on the bond are backed by the issuer's power to tax. These bonds, often referred to simply as "GOs," are very different from bonds backed by the revenue from a specific project, such as an airport. *See also* **revenue bond.** GOs typically offer lower yields than revenue bonds with the same rating and maturity.

Generation-skipping trust. A trust used to help the very wealthy leave money to their grandchildren's generation without paying the 55% generation-skipping tax.

Gift tax. Federal taxes owed on gifts if they exceed both the annual limit of $10,000 per recipient and the $600,000 lifetime unified credit.

Growth. This label is applied both to a type of mutual fund and to a style of investing. Growth funds invest for capital gains, the profit that you make when you sell an investment for more than your cost. But these funds do not necessarily use the growth-stock investment style, which involves buying stocks that may have little or nothing in the way of current earnings but have the potential for rapid earnings growth.

Guaranteed investment contracts. Investments offered by insurance companies that promise preservation of principal and a fixed rate of return. Individuals invest in GICs through 401(k)s and other retirement plans.

Guaranteed-replacement-cost coverage. Home insurance coverage that may pay some rebuilding or replacement expenses even in excess of the policy's stated amount.

Guardian. The person designated responsible for minor children or others needing special care.

Hard assets. Also known as tangible assets, these investments tend to perform well when the inflation rate is picking up. Gold and other precious metals are among the best-known hard assets.

Health care power of attorney. Document authorizing someone to make medical decisions for you in the event you are temporarily or permanently unable to do so. This document, also called a health care proxy, is often coupled with a living will.

Hedge. An investment strategy designed to limit the risk of loss. For instance, someone who owns airline stocks might buy an oil stock to hedge against the damage to airlines of rising oil prices.

Hedge fund. A little-regulated, private investment partnership that may invest huge sums in currencies, bonds, and stocks worldwide. Despite the name, many hedge funds do not necessarily hedge. Indeed, the spectacular returns and mighty tumbles for which they are known often result from mammoth market bets using borrowed money. Hedge funds typically require minimum investments that start in the hundreds of thousands of dollars.

Home-equity debt. Borrowing secured by a homeowner's equity in a home. Home-equity loans allow you to borrow a certain amount and pay it back over a specified term, and they generally carry fixed interest rates. Home-equity lines of credit allow you to draw upon them as needed, and they usually carry adjustable rates. Interest payments on up to $100,000 of home-equity debt are generally tax-deductible. (That is on top of the interest write-off you get on mortgage loans of up to $1 million.)

Index funds. Most mutual funds are run by money managers who actively buy and sell securities in an effort to outpace both competing funds and a benchmark index. Index funds have more modest aspirations. They try to mimic the performance of a stock market or bond market index by buying all or many of the securities that comprise the index. Because they typically charge very low expenses, index funds tend to outpace many of the higher-cost funds that are run by active managers.

Individual Retirement Account. A tax-deferred plan that can help you build a retirement nest egg. Individuals whose income is less than certain amounts or who are not active participants in an employer's retirement plan generally can deduct some or all of their annual IRA contributions when figuring their income tax. Others can make nondeductible IRA contributions.

Initial public offering (IPO). Closely held companies use IPOs to sell shares to the general public. Although some IPOs have turned out to be fabulous long-run performers, many languish following the hoopla that surrounds an inaugural stock issue.

Itemized deductions. When you figure your income tax, these are the items that may be subtracted from your adjusted gross income if you do not take the standard deduction. Examples of itemized deductions include state and local tax payments, gifts to charity, and certain amounts of home-mortgage interest.

Junk bonds. Bonds issued by companies whose financial condition is considered sufficiently precarious that they might default on their interest payments. Because of that risk, junk bonds typically offer higher yields than bonds with superior credit ratings. That is why junk bonds are referred to less pejoratively as high-yield bonds.

Keogh plan. A tax-deferred retirement plan for small-business owners or self-employed people who have earned income from their trade or business. Contributions to a Keogh plan are tax-deductible.

Kiddie tax. Special tax treatment for investment earnings of children under age 14.

Level-premium term insurance. Term life insurance on which premiums are projected or guaranteed level for a certain period, typically 5, 10, 15, or 20 years.

Liabilities. Amounts you owe.

Liability insurance. Insurance that pays if you are sued or legally responsible for a loss. Liability coverage, which also covers legal-defense costs, is typically included in auto and home insurance policies.

Life insurance illustration. A computer projection of how a policy might perform in future years. One prepared for an existing policy is called an in-force illustration.

Life insurance trust. A trust set up to buy life insurance coverage or to become the owner of an existing policy. When a policy is owned by a trust, the death benefit is not counted as part of the insured person's estate for estate-tax purposes.

Liquidity. A measure of how quickly and easily investors can cash in a security. Treasury bills and money market mutual funds are highly liquid because they can be converted to cash at any time. Real estate and art are relatively illiquid because they are difficult to sell quickly.

Living trust. A revocable trust formed while you are alive, it is often used to avoid probate or to provide for the orderly management of assets if you should become disabled or incompetent.

Living will. A document indicating the type of care and degree of medical intervention you would want in the event of a life-threatening medical condition. It is often coupled with a health care power of attorney.

Load funds. Mutual funds that charge a sales commission, as opposed to no-load funds, which do not levy a fee when you buy or sell. Some fund groups that sell directly to the public offer low-load funds, which charge an up-front fee of 2% or 3%. But most load funds are sold by brokers. To compensate brokers, load funds usually charge either a front-end sales commission when you buy the fund or a back-end sales commission when you sell. In addition, many broker-sold funds charge an annual 12b-1 fee, which is also used to compensate brokers. The 12b-1 fee is included in the fund's expense ratio.

Loan-to-value ratio. The ratio of the principal balance of a home loan to the estimated market value. A $100,000 home with a $75,000 mortgage, for example, has a loan-to-value ratio of 75%. Few lenders will make a loan for the full value of a home; most have a maximum loan-to-value ratio of 75% to 95%.

Long-term-care insurance. Insurance that provides some coverage for nursing-home stays and home health care for people with disabling conditions.

Managed care. Medical plans in which access to health care services is managed to hold down unnecessary costs. The most common form of managed care is the health maintenance organization, or HMO, which restricts patients to the HMO's own stable of doctors. Premiums are lower than for traditional fee-for-service health care plans, and the charge for each doctor visit is generally only $5 to $15. Some newer arrangements are the point-of-service and preferred-provider plans, which may charge the low per-visit price of an HMO for treatment by doctors in the plan's network and allow out-of-network treatment with reimbursement at about 70% or so of eligible costs.

Margin debt. Debt incurred when you borrow against the securities in your brokerage account. Investors can generally borrow up to 50% of the value of stocks owned or up to 90% of the value of bonds, depending on the type of bond and its maturity.

Marginal tax rate. The tax rate you would owe on your next dollar of taxable income. This can be highly valuable information when you are making investment decisions.

Marital-deduction trust. A trust set up to receive money left to a spouse under the unlimited marital deduction and to impose some restrictions on those funds. The terms of the trust may require use of certain financial advisers, for example, or may protect assets from possible claims should the surviving spouse remarry.

Market timing. Shifting money in and out of investment markets, in an effort to take advantage of rising prices and avoid being stung by downturns. Few if any investors manage to be consistently successful in timing markets.

Market-value coverage. Home insurance that pays only the current value of a home, not the possibly higher replacement cost.

Medicaid. The government program that provides health care assistance for the poor.

Medicare. The government program that provides health care assistance for older and disabled people.

Money market account. A federally insured account available at many banks, credit unions, and savings and loan associations. Not to be confused with a money market mutual fund, which is not insured.

Money market fund. A type of mutual fund that invests in stable, short-term securities. Money funds are designed to be easily convertible into cash and are structured to maintain an unchanging value of $1 a share. Only the yield is supposed to fluctuate.

Municipal bonds. Bonds issued by state or local government authorities that usually pay interest that is exempt from federal income taxes. Also, most states do not tax interest on bonds issued by municipalities within that state's borders. For example, a New York City resident who buys a New York municipal bond would not owe any federal, state, or city income taxes. Because of their tax advantage, municipal bonds often are highly popular among people in higher tax brackets.

Mutual funds. Investment companies that provide a way for small investors to pool their money so that together they can afford to hire a professional money manager. Shareholders usually can buy or sell mutual fund shares on any day that the securities markets are open. Though a fund is technically owned by its shareholders, it is usually set up, managed, and distributed by the fund's investment adviser and its affiliated companies.

Nasdaq Composite. A widely watched stock market index that includes virtually all issues traded on the Nasdaq Stock Market.

Nasdaq Stock Market. A system set up for the trading of so-called over-the-counter stocks, those not listed on major exchanges. Nasdaq began as an acronym for National Association of Securities Dealers Automated Quotations, but now does not stand for anything but itself, Nasdaq insists. The system is operated by the National Association of Securities Dealers.

National Association of Securities Dealers (NASD). A membership organization for securities-brokerage firms and underwriters in the United States that promise to abide by association rules. It sets guidelines for ethics and standardized industry practices and has a disciplinary structure for looking into allegations of rules violations. The NASD also operates the Nasdaq Stock Market.

Net asset value (NAV). For a mutual fund, the NAV is the value of all investments held by the fund, usually expressed in per-share terms. The NAV is calculated daily at the close of markets.

Net worth. One's total assets minus total liabilities—the amount of money you would have if you sold all your possessions and paid off all your debts.

No-fault laws. Laws in a number of states that provide for injuries incurred in an auto accident to be covered by your own auto insurance policy, regardless of who was at fault. Intended to reduce the cost of auto insurance, the laws also limit the right to sue after an accident.

No-load funds. Unlike load funds, these funds do not charge a front-end or back-end sales commission. In addition, to be classified as no-load, a fund cannot charge an annual 12b-1 marketing and distribution fee equal to more than 0.25% of fund assets.

Option. In the financial world, an option is an agreement allowing an investor to buy or sell something—such as shares of stock—within a specified period and at a set price. Options that give the holder the right to buy are "calls," whereas those that give holders the right to sell are "puts."

Penny stocks. Many penny stocks do indeed have a share price of less than $1, but this informal designation now often includes stocks that are priced at $5 and below. While many legitimate companies have share prices that low, the term "penny stocks" usually refers to speculative companies with little or no real business that are heavily promoted by unscrupulous, hard-selling brokerage firms.

Pension maximization. A controversial strategy, often espoused by life insurance agents, of using insurance to augment a company pension benefit. Under this arrangement, a retiree takes pension payments for his or her own life only and buys life insurance to provide for a surviving spouse. Also called pension max.

Personal Financial Specialist (PFS). Financial planning designation given to qualifying accountants by the American Institute of Certified Public Accountants, based in New York.

Points. An amount paid to a mortgage lender, at the time of closing, above and beyond the regular interest payments. Each point equals 1% of the mortgage face amount. When you are buying a home, points are tax-deductible in full for the year you pay them, provided that they are not out of line for your area and that they represent prepaid interest, which they usually do. If you pay points when you refinance, however, you must amortize the tax deduction over the life of your loan.

Power of attorney. *See* **durable power of attorney.**

Price-to-book ratio (P/B). A company's stock price divided by its per-share book value. If a company's stock is trading below book value, that may mean the shares are undervalued.

Price-to-earnings ratio (P/E). A company's stock price divided by its per-share earnings over a 12-month period. This is possibly the most popular way of valuing stocks, and P/E information is published daily in the stock tables of many major newspapers. Dividing by a company's earnings over the past 12 months produces a trailing P/E ratio, while estimated earnings are used to calculate a forward P/E.

Prime rate. The interest rate banks use as a base for a wide range of loans to medium and small businesses and to individuals.

Private mortgage insurance (PMI). PMI is generally required by lenders if your down payment is less than 20% of a home's purchase price.

Probate. The procedure in each state required to validate a will.

Profit-sharing plan. A retirement plan funded by employer contributions that are based on a share of the company's profits. Employees are frequently responsible for managing the money themselves, selecting from such investments as mutual funds, company stock, and guaranteed investment contracts. Investment gains are not taxed until the money is withdrawn.

Qualified domestic trust (QDOT). A type of trust that allows non-U.S. citizens to inherit from their spouses without immediately owing estate taxes.

Qualified personal residence trust (QPRT). A complicated trust that can be used to remove your home or vacation home from your estate.

Qualified terminable interest property trust (Q-TIP). A type of marital trust often used in a second marriage, a Q-TIP gives a surviving spouse rights to all trust income and, in some cases, access to principal, as well. But when that surviving spouse dies, the assets go to beneficiaries named by the trust grantor.

Real estate investment trusts. Publicly traded securities commonly knows as REITs. REITs come in two varieties, equity REITs and mortgage REITs. Mortgage REITs, which are more akin to a bond market investment, lend money to real estate owners and then pass on the interest they earn to shareholders. Equity REITs purchase real estate. Their shareholders' profit or loss depends on their income (usually from rent) and their gains or losses from selling properties.

Replacement-cost coverage. Home insurance that pays the cost to replace or repair the home or possessions, up to the policy's set maximum. Provides more protection than market-value coverage on the home or actual-cash-value coverage on contents.

Revenue bond. A bond that is backed by revenue from a specific project, such as an airport or turnpike. This differs from a general-obligation bond, which is backed by an issuer's full faith and credit. *See also* **general-obligation bond.**

Reverse mortgage. A loan against a home that can be paid to the homeowner as a lump sum, a cash advance, or a line of credit. Used by some homeowners as a source of income in retirement.

Rider. In life insurance, a provision added to a policy to add or alter the coverage.

Risk. Like beauty, risk is in the eye of the beholder. Investments typically are deemed risky if there is a high chance of losing money, either because the issuer gets into financial trouble or because the entire market collapses. But investors face other risks, most notably the risk from inflation. Stocks, for instance, are widely considered to be risky, meaning they are prone to dramatic short-term losses. But if your chief concern is outpacing inflation over the long haul, then stocks are far less risky than bonds or money market investments, because stocks generate far higher long-run returns.

Russell 2000. A widely watched index of small-company stocks.

Second-to-die insurance. A type of life insurance that covers two individuals in one policy and pays a death benefit only at the second death. Most commonly purchased by affluent older couples to pay estate taxes at death.

Sector funds. Mutual funds that invest in a single-industry sector, such as biotechnology, gold, or regional banks. Sector funds tend to generate erratic performance, and they often dominate both the top and the bottom of the annual mutual fund performance charts.

Securities and Exchange Commission. The SEC is the federal agency responsible for enforcing securities laws and setting standards for disclosure about publicly traded securities, including mutual funds.

Short sale. A short sale is a bet that the price of a stock will fall. A short seller borrows stock he or she thinks is overvalued, then sells it—hoping that before long other investors will see the same thing and sell their shares, driving down the price. The short seller will then cover the short—or buy back shares to replace the borrowed ones—pocketing the difference between the higher selling price and the lower repurchase price.

Simplified Employee Pension (SEP). A retirement plan for the self-employed that is also referred to as a SEP-IRA.

Special needs trust. A trust used to provide supplemental funds for a disabled person without jeopardizing access to government programs.

Standard & Poor's 500 index. The S&P 500 is a very widely followed stock market index made up of large-capitalization stocks and leading companies within major industries in the U.S. economy.

Standard deduction. When you figure your income tax, this is how much you can deduct from your taxable income if you decide not to itemize your deductions. About 70% of all individual income tax returns use the standard deduction.

Stocks. By buying stocks, you become a part owner of a company. Stockholders are rewarded in two ways. A company's shares will tend to rise over time, as the company's earnings improve. In addition, shareholders often receive quarterly dividends, and those dividends may also rise over time. Stocks are sometimes known as equities. Among the three major financial assets, stocks are the best long-term performers, easily outpacing both bonds and cash.

Surrender value. The amount of money a policyholder would receive upon dropping, or surrendering, a cash-value life insurance policy. This amount may be far less than the accumulated cash value because of surrender charges.

Tenancy in common. A way in which two people can own property together with no rights of survivorship. Should either die, the deceased's share of the property will pass through his or her estate, not to the survivor.

Term life. The simplest form of life insurance, in which an insurer promises to pay a certain death benefit if you die during the term for which the policy is in effect. Types include annual-renewable and level-premium term.

Total return. A security's total return reflects not only the income that it pays out from interest or dividends but also any change in its share price or principal value. In the case of mutual funds, you have to reinvest the income and capital-gains distributions to match the fund's published total return.

Treasury bills, notes, and bonds. U.S. government securities, backed by the government's full faith and credit. Treasury bills are short-term securities, available in maturities of 3, 6, and 12 months. Newly issued Treasury notes mature in two to ten years; Treasury bonds mature in ten years or more.

Umbrella liability coverage. Supplemental liability insurance, providing increased protection against lawsuits or other losses for which you are legally responsible.

Unified credit. For estate- and gift-tax purposes, a tax credit that allows every taxpayer to exclude up to $600,000 in assets.

Uniform Gifts to Minors Act and Uniform Transfers to Minors Act. Accounts governed by these acts allow a minor child to own property. The account is managed by a custodian until the child reaches the age of majority. State law determines both the type of account and the age when the child gains control of the assets.

Uninsured-motorist coverage. The part of an auto insurance policy that pays your losses in an accident caused by a hit-and-run driver or one who is not insured.

Unit investment trust. A fixed portfolio of bonds or stocks with a specific maturity date. Generally sold by brokers.

Universal life. A type of cash-value life insurance that gives policyholders considerable flexibility to skip payments or vary the amounts they pay.

Unlimited marital deduction. This allows most married couples to leave everything to each other free of estate taxes when they die.

U.S. savings bonds. Series EE savings bonds are issued by the federal government and sold by most banks, credit unions, and savings and loan associations. They are also available through payroll deduction plans offered by many employers. Interest is exempt from state and local income taxes.

Value investing. Value investors are the stock market's bargain hunters. They often lean toward beaten-down companies whose shares appear cheap compared to current earnings or corporate assets. Value investors typically buy stocks with high dividend yields or that trade at a low price/earnings ratio or a low price-to-book value. The value investment style is often contrasted with the growth style. The two styles tend to take turns being popular on Wall Street. One year growth stocks will be all the rage; the next year value stocks may dominate.

Variable life. A type of cash-value life insurance in which policyholders can allocate their accumulated cash value among several stock and bond investment accounts. Many variable policies are technically of the variable universal variety, meaning they also offer the payment flexibility of universal life insurance.

Viatical settlements. Arrangements by which a company will buy the life insurance policy of a terminally ill person for a percentage of the death benefit, pay the premiums, and collect the benefits upon death.

Whole life. The most widely purchased type of cash-value life insurance. If premiums continue to be paid, coverage is usually guaranteed for the whole of life.

Will. A legal document that specifies how assets are to be distributed at your death and names guardians for minor children.

Wilshire 5000 index. A broad-based stock market performance measure.

Wrap account. An investment plan that wraps together money management and brokerage services. Wrap plans are popular for their simplicity. For one all-inclusive annual fee, an investment firm provides the services of a professional money manager, who creates a portfolio of stocks and bonds or mutual funds and takes care of all the trading.

Yield. An investment's yield is the amount of income that it generates during the course of a year, expressed as a percentage of either the investment's market value or its original value. With money market funds, certificates of deposit, and other supersafe investments, your entire investment gain is reflected in the yield. But with stocks and bonds, which fluctuate in value, yield is only one component of your total return.

Zero-coupon bond. A zero-coupon bond does not make periodic interest payments. An investor buys a zero at a hefty discount from its face value and receives a much larger sum when the bond matures. The return is the difference between what the investor paid for the bond and what that person gets when the bond matures or is sold. Prices of zero-coupon bonds react far more violently to changes in interest rates than ordinary bonds: When rates fall, zeros post sharp short-term gains. But when rates surge, prices of zeros fall especially sharply.

APPENDIX A

HELP!

$

*M*aybe you need additional information, or you are trying to find a particular kind of financial specialist. Maybe you want to check up on an insurance company or a stockbroker. Or maybe you want to complain. Sometimes, all you really need is to get in touch with the right person. The addresses and phone numbers on the following pages should point you in the right direction.

BANKING AND CREDIT

FINDING A GOOD DEAL ON A CREDIT CARD

- **Bankcard Holders of America**
A national nonprofit consumer organization that publishes guides on the wise use of credit. BHA also offers lists of the best low-rate, no-fee, secured, and rebate/frequent flier cards.

524 Branch Drive
Salem, VA 24153
540-389-5445

• **RAM Research**
Publishes CardTrak, a monthly report listing the best Visa and MasterCard credit cards. Each issue covers low-rate cards, no-fee cards, gold cards, rebate cards, and secured cards.

P.O. Box 1700
Frederick, MD 21702
800-344-7714

CHECKING MORTGAGE RATES

• **HSH Associates**
Publishes mortgage information. For $20, HSH will send a mortgage-shopping kit that includes a list of dozens of lenders' rate quotes.

1200 Route 23
Butler, NJ 07405
800-873-2837

CAR LEASING

• **Reality Checklist**
The Reality Checklist, developed by a coalition of state attorneys general, plaintiff's attorneys, and consumer groups, breaks down the financial parts of an auto-lease deal. Write for a copy of the Reality Checklist and a tips sheet on auto leasing ($1.50 and a stamped, self-addressed envelope).

Reality Checklist
P.O. Box 7648
Atlanta, GA 30357-0648

TO CHECK A BANK'S SAFETY

A few private firms rate the safety of individual banks, savings and loan associations, and credit unions for a small fee.

• **Bauer Financial Reports**
P.O. Box 145510
Coral Gables, FL 33114-5510
800-388-6686

• Veribanc Inc.

P.O. Box 461
Wakefield, MA 01880-0461
800-442-2657

CREDIT REPORTS

To get a copy of your credit report, call or write one of the three
biggest bureaus.

• Equifax

800-685-1111

• Experian (formerly TRW)

800-682-7654

• Trans Union

National Consumer Relations Disclosure Center
P.O. Box 390
Springfield, PA 19064-0390
610-690-4909

WHERE TO COMPLAIN

• **For complaints about nationally chartered banks, call the office of the Comptroller of the Currency's Consumer Complaint Hotline (800-613-6743) or contact the agency's nearest regional office:**

Northeastern District Consumer Affairs Specialist
1114 Avenue of the Americas, Suite 3900
New York, NY 10036
212-819-9860

Midwestern District Consumer Affairs Specialist
2345 Grand Boulevard, Suite 700
Kansas City, MO 64108
816-556-1800

Southeastern District Consumer Affairs Specialist
245 Peachtree Center Avenue, Suite 600
Atlanta, GA 30303
404-659-8855

Southwestern District Consumer Affairs Specialist
500 North Akard, Suite 1600
Dallas, TX 75201-3394
214-720-0656

Central District Consumer Affairs Specialist
One Financial Place, Suite 2700
440 South LaSalle Street
Chicago, IL 60605
312-360-8800

Western District Consumer Affairs Specialist
50 Fremont Street, Suite 3900
San Francisco, CA 94105
415-545-5900

• **Complaints about FDIC-insured state-chartered banks that are members of the Federal Reserve System:**

Federal Reserve Board
Offices of the Ombudsman
20th and C Streets NW
Washington, DC 20551
800-337-0429

• **Problems with FDIC-insured state banks that are not members of the Federal Reserve System:**

Federal Deposit Insurance Corporation
Office of Consumer Affairs
550 17th Street NW
Washington, DC 20429
800-934-3342

• **Complaints about federally chartered or insured savings and loan associations:**

Office of Thrift Supervision
Consumer Affairs
1700 G Street NW
Washington, DC 20552
800-842-6929

• **Complaints about credit discrimination, improper disclosure or calculation of credit charges, inaccurate credit reports, unauthorized use of credit or debit cards, and problems with debt collectors:**

Federal Trade Commission
Division of Credit Practices
6th Street and Pennsylvania Avenue NW
Washington, DC 20580
202-326-2222

• **Complaints about federally chartered credit unions:**

National Credit Union Administration
1775 Duke Street
Alexandria, VA 22314-3428
703-518-6330

EMPLOYEE BENEFITS

• **Employee Benefit Research Institute**
Nonprofit research group publishes primer on employee benefits, *Fundamentals of Employee Benefit Programs,* that covers life insurance, health insurance, retirement plans, and other benefits ($24.95 plus $4.95 shipping and handling).
2121 K Street NW, Suite 600
Washington, DC 20037
202-659-0670

• **Pension Rights Center**
Nonprofit advocacy group publishes fact sheets and pamphlets on pension issues including pension problems, divorce, and survivor ben-

efits. Publications range from $2 to $24. Write to request a free publications list (send stamped, self-addressed envelope).

918 16th Street NW, Suite 704
Washington, DC 20006-2902
202-296-3776

FINANCIAL PLANNING

You can contact the following organizations for names of member planners in your area.

- **American Institute of Certified Public Accountants**
  For a list of CPAs with the Personal Financial Specialist (PFS) designation, request product G00616.
  AICPA Order Department
  P.O. Box 2209
  Jersey City, NJ 07303-2209
  800-862-4272

- **American Society of CLU and ChFC**
  Insurance agents and planners who hold the Chartered Life Underwriter and Chartered Financial Consultant designations.
  800-392-6900

- **Institute of Certified Financial Planners**
  Planners with the CFP designation.
  800-282-7526

- **International Association for Financial Planning**
  Planners who have a designation or academic degree in planning and who meet certain other qualifications.
  800-945-4237

- **National Association of Personal Financial Advisors**
  Fee-only planners and a useful form for when you are interviewing planners.
  800-366-2732

INSURANCE

INSURANCE-COMPANY RATING AGENCIES

Checking to see how an insurance company has been rated by one or more professional rating agencies is a smart move before buying any kind of policy. Here are the names and phone numbers you need to call for an insurer's ratings. You can also check your local library or ask an agent to supply ratings reports.

- **A. M. Best Co.,** Oldwick, N.J.
  800-424-2378 or 900-555-2378

  Cost is $2.95 plus $4.95 for each rating.

- **Duff & Phelps Credit Rating Co.,** Chicago
  312-368-3198 (no charge)

  Written reports cost $25 per insurer.

- **Moody's Investors Service,** New York
  212-553-0377 (no charge)

- **Standard & Poor's Ratings Group,** New York
  212-208-1527 (no charge)

- **Weiss Ratings Inc.,** Palm Beach Gardens, Fla.
  800-289-9222

  Charges per insurer: oral rating, $15; brief report, $25; detailed report, $45.

STATE INSURANCE DEPARTMENTS

State insurance departments are a trove of useful information when you are in the market for insurance. Many publish shopper's guides and surveys that show what different insurers charge for similar coverage. These regulatory agencies also keep track of consumer complaints. (The 800 numbers listed here may be for in-state use only.)

《

- **Alabama**
  Insurance Department
  P.O. Box 303351
  Montgomery, AL 36130-3351
  334-269-3550

- **Alaska**
  Division of Insurance
  3601 C Street, Suite 1324
  Anchorage, AK 99503-5948
  907-269-7900

- **Arizona**
  Department of Insurance
  Consumer Affairs and Investigation Division
  2910 N. 44th Street, Suite 210
  Phoenix, AZ 85018
  602-912-8444

- **Arkansas**
  Insurance Department
  1123 South University Avenue
  400 University Tower Building
  Little Rock, AR 72204-1699
  501-371-2600
  800-852-5494

- **California**
  Insurance Department
  Consumer Services Division
  Ronald Reagan Building
  300 S. Spring Street
  Los Angeles, CA 90013
  213-897-8921

- **Colorado**
  Division of Insurance
  1560 Broadway, Suite 850
  Denver, CO 80202
  303-894-7499

• **Connecticut**
Insurance Department
P.O. Box 816
Hartford, CT 06142-0816
860-297-3800

• **Delaware**
Insurance Department
Rodney Building
841 Silver Lake Boulevard
Dover, DE 19903
302-739-4251
800-282-8611

• **District of Columbia**
Insurance Administration
P.O. Box 37422
Washington, DC 20013
202-727-8009

• **Florida**
Department of Insurance
200 E. Gaines Street
Tallahassee, FL 32399-0300
800-342-2762
904-922-3100

• **Georgia**
Insurance Department
2 Martin Luther King Jr. Drive
716 West Tower
Atlanta, GA 30334
404-656-2056

• **Hawaii**
Department of Commerce and Consumer Affairs
Insurance Division
P.O. Box 3614
Honolulu, HI 96811
808-586-2790

《

• **Idaho**
Insurance Department
Public Service Department
700 W. State Street, 3rd Floor
Boise, ID 83720
208-334-4250

• **Illinois**
Department of Insurance
320 W. Washington Street, 4th Floor
Springfield, IL 62767
217-782-4515

• **Indiana**
Department of Insurance
311 W. Washington Street, Suite 300
Indianapolis, IN 46204-2787
800-622-4461
317-232-2395

• **Iowa**
Insurance Division
Lucas State Office Building
E. 12th & Grand Streets, 6th Floor
Des Moines, IA 50319
515-281-5705

• **Kansas**
Insurance Department
420 SW Ninth Street
Topeka, KS 66612
913-296-3071
800-432-2484

• **Kentucky**
Insurance Department
P.O. Box 517
Frankfort, KY 40602
502-564-3630

• Louisiana
Insurance Department
P.O. Box 94214
Baton Rouge, LA 70804-9214
504-342-5900
800-259-5301

• Maine
Bureau of Insurance
Consumer Division
State House Station 34
Augusta, ME 04333
207-624-8475

• Maryland
Insurance Administration
Complaints & Investigation Unit
501 St. Paul Place
Baltimore, MD 21202
410-333-6300

• Massachusetts
Division of Insurance
Consumer Services Section
470 Atlantic Avenue
Boston, MA 02210
617-521-7777

• Michigan
Insurance Bureau
P.O. Box 30220
Lansing, MI 48909
517-373-0220

• Minnesota
Insurance Department
Department of Commerce
133 E. 7th Street
St. Paul, MN 55101
612-296-4026

• **Mississippi**
Insurance Department
Consumer Assistance Division
P.O. Box 79
Jackson, MS 39205
601-359-3569

• **Missouri**
Department of Insurance
Consumer Services Section
P.O. Box 690
Jefferson City, MO 65102-0690
800-726-7390
573-751-2640

• **Montana**
Insurance Department
P.O. Box 4009
Mitchell Building, Room 270
Helena, MT 59604-4009
406-444-2040

• **Nebraska**
Insurance Department
Terminal Building
941 "O" Street, Suite 400
Lincoln, NE 68508
402-471-2201

• **Nevada**
Division of Insurance
Consumer Services
1665 Hot Springs Road, Suite 152
Carson City, NV 89710
702-687-4270
800-992-0900

• **New Hampshire**
Insurance Department
Life and Health Division
169 Manchester Street
Concord, NH 03301
603-271-2261
800-852-3416

• **New Jersey**
Department of Insurance
20 West State Street
Roebling Building, CN325
Trenton, NJ 08625
609-292-5360

• **New Mexico**
Insurance Department
P.O. Drawer 1269
Santa Fe, NM 87504-1269
505-827-4500

• **New York**
Department of Insurance
160 West Broadway
New York, NY 10013
212-602-0429
Outside of New York City:
800-342-3736

• **North Carolina**
Department of Insurance
P.O. Box 26387
Raleigh, NC 27611
919-733-7343
800-662-7777

• **North Dakota**
Insurance Department
Capital Bldg., 5th Floor
600 E Boulevard
Bismark, ND 58505-0320
800-247-0560
701-328-2440

- **Ohio**
  Department of Insurance
  Consumer Services Division
  2100 Stella Court
  Columbus, OH 43215-1067
  800-686-1526
  614-644-2673

- **Oklahoma**
  Insurance Department
  P.O. Box 53408
  Oklahoma City, OK 73152-3408
  405-521-2828

- **Oregon**
  Department of Consumer and Business Services
  Insurance Division
  350 Winter Street NE, Room 440-1
  Salem, OR 97310
  503-378-4484

- **Pennsylvania**
  Insurance Department
  Consumer Services Bureau
  1321 Strawberry Square
  Harrisburg, PA 17120
  717-787-2317

- **Rhode Island**
  Insurance Division
  233 Richmond Street, Suite 233
  Providence, RI 02903-4233
  401-277-2223

- **South Carolina**
  Insurance Department
  Consumer Services Division
  P.O. Box 100105
  Columbia, SC 29202-3105
  803-737-6160
  800-768-3467

· **South Dakota**
Division of Insurance
500 East Capitol Avenue
Pierre, SD 57501-5070
605-773-3563

· **Tennessee**
Department of Commerce & Insurance
Insurance Assistance Office
500 James Robertson Parkway
Volunteer Plaza, 4th Floor
Nashville, TN 37243
615-741-4955
800-525-2816

· **Texas**
Department of Insurance
Complaints Resolution, MC 111-1A
333 Guadalupe Street
P.O. Box 149091
Austin, TX 78714-9091
512-463-6515
800-252-3439

· **Utah**
Insurance Department
Consumer Services
3110 State Office Building
Salt Lake City, UT 84114
800-439-3805
801-538-3805

· **Vermont**
Department of Banking, Insurance, and Securities
Consumer Complaint Division
89 Main Street
Drawer 20
Montpelier, VT 05620-3101
802-828-3301

• **Virginia**
Bureau of Insurance
Consumer Services Division
P.O. Box 1157
Richmond, VA 23218
804-371-9741

• **Washington**
Insurance Department
Office of the Commissioner
P.O. Box 40255
Olympia, WA 98504-0255
800-562-6900
360-753-7300

• **West Virginia**
Insurance Department
P.O. Box 50540
Charleston, WV 25305-0540
800-642-9004
304-558-3386

• **Wisconsin**
Insurance Department
Complaints Department
P.O. Box 7873
Madison, WI 53707-7873
800-236-8517
608-266-0103

• **Wyoming**
Insurance Department
Herschler Building, 3rd Floor East
122 W. 25th Street
Cheyenne, WY 82002-0440
800-438-5768
307-777-7401

SOURCE: National Association of Insurance Commissioners.

INVESTING

INVESTOR EDUCATION AND INFORMATION

• **American Association of Individual Investors**
In addition to hosting conferences, the AAII publishes a monthly journal on investing topics and an annual guide to low-load mutual funds.

625 North Michigan Avenue, Suite 1900
Chicago, IL 60611
312-280-0170

• **Investment Company Institute**
A trade association of fund companies; the ICI publishes an annual directory of mutual funds ($8.50).

1401 H Street NW, Suite 1100
Washington, DC 20005
202-326-5800

• **Mutual Fund Education Alliance**
Puts out information on no-load and low-load mutual funds, including its semiannual *Investor's Guide to Low-Cost Mutual Funds* ($15).

1900 Erie Street, Suite 120
Kansas City, MO 64116
816-471-1454

• **National Association of Investors Corp.**
A national, not-for-profit organization of investment clubs and individual investors.

P.O. Box 220
Royal Oak, MI 48068-0220
810-583-6242

• **The Savings Bond Informer Inc.**
A fee-based service that provides savings bond owners with a written detailed analysis of individual bond holdings. Also sells *U.S. Savings Bonds: A Comprehensive Guide for Bond Owners and Financial Professionals* ($24.95).

800-927-1901

BUYING TREASURY SECURITIES DIRECT

You can buy Treasury securities without a broker through the government's Treasury Direct program. For more information, contact the Treasury Department's Bureau of the Public Debt (202-874-4000) or your nearest Federal Reserve Bank or branch.

FEDERAL RESERVE BANKS AND BRANCHES

Atlanta
104 Marietta Street NW
Atlanta, GA 30303
404-521-8653

Baltimore
P.O. Box 1378
Baltimore, MD 21203–1378
410-576-3300

Birmingham
P.O. Box 830447
Birmingham, AL 35283-0447
205-731-8708

Boston
P.O. Box 2076
Boston, MA 02106–2076
617-973-3810

Buffalo
P.O. Box 961
Buffalo, NY 14240-0961
716-849-5000

Charlotte
P.O. Box 30248
Charlotte, NC 28230
704-358-2100

Chicago
P.O. Box 834
Chicago, IL 60690
312-322-5369

Cincinnati
P.O. Box 999
Cincinnati, OH 45201
513-721-4787, Ext. 334

Cleveland
P.O. Box 6387
Cleveland, OH 44101
216-579-2000

Dallas
P.O. Box 655906
Dallas, TX 75265-5906
214-922-6770

Denver
P.O. Box 5228
Denver, CO 80217-5228
303-572-2470 or 2473

Detroit
P.O. Box 1059
Detroit, MI 48231
313-964-6157

El Paso
P.O. Box 100
El Paso, TX 79999
915-521-8272

Houston
P.O. Box 2578
Houston, TX 77252
713-659-4433

Jacksonville
P.O. Box 2499
Jacksonville, FL 32231-2499
904-632-1179

Kansas City
P.O. Box 419033
Kansas City, MO 64141–6033
816-881-2883

Little Rock
P.O. Box 1261
Little Rock, AR 72203
501-324-8272

Los Angeles
Attn: Marketable Securities
P.O. Box 2077
Los Angeles, CA 90051
213-624-7398

Louisville
P.O. Box 32710
Louisville, KY 40232
502-568-9236 or 9238

Memphis
P.O. Box 407
Memphis, TN 38101-0407
901-523-7171, Ext. 423

Miami
Attn: Treasury Direct Unit
P.O. Box 520847
Miami, FL 33152–0847
305-471-6497

Minneapolis
250 Marquette Avenue
Minneapolis, MN 55480
612-340-2075

Nashville
301 Eighth Avenue, North
Nashville, TN 37203-4407
615-251-7100

New Orleans
P.O. Box 61630
New Orleans, LA 70161
504-593-3200

New York
Federal Reserve—P.O. Station
New York, NY 10045
212-720-6619

Oklahoma City
P.O. Box 25129
Oklahoma City, OK 73125
405-270-8652

Omaha
2201 Farnam Street
Omaha, NE 68102
402-221-5636

Philadelphia
P.O. Box 90
Philadelphia, PA 19105
215-574-6680

Pittsburgh
P.O. Box 867
Pittsburgh, PA 15230-0867
412-261-7802

Portland
P.O. Box 3436
Portland, OR 97208-3436
503-221-5932

Richmond
P.O. Box 27622
Richmond, VA 23261
804-697-8372

Salt Lake City
P.O. Box 30780
Salt Lake City, UT 84130-0780
801-322-7882

San Antonio
P.O. Box 1471
San Antonio, TX 78295
210-978-1303 or 1305

San Francisco
P.O. Box 7702
San Francisco, CA 94120
415-974-2330

Seattle
P.O. Box 3567
Seattle, WA 98124
206-343-3605

St. Louis
P.O. Box 14915
St. Louis, MO 63178
314-444-8703

Washington, D.C.
Capital Area Servicing Center
1300 C Street SW
Washington, DC 20239-0001
202-874-4000

Device for the hearing-impaired (TDD)
202-874-4026

STATE SECURITIES DEPARTMENTS

If you want to check on whether a broker and his or her employer
are licensed to sell securities or have been the subject of investor complaints or disciplinary actions, consider contacting your state's securities department. For most states, a telephone number is listed
below. (The 800 numbers may be for in-state use only.) But if an
address is shown instead, that means your state will accept only written requests for information.

• **Alabama**
Securities Commission
334-242-2984

• **Alaska**
Department of Commerce and Economic Development
907-465-2521

· **Arizona**
  Corporation Commission
  602-542-4242

· **Arkansas**
  Securities Department
  501-324-9260

· **California**
  Department of Corporations
  213-736-2495

· **Colorado**
  Division of Securities
  303-894-2320

· **Connecticut**
  Department of Banking
  203-240-8230 or 800-831-7225

· **Delaware**
  Department of Justice
  302-577-2515

· **District of Columbia**
  Public Services Commission
  202-626-5105

· **Florida**
  Office of the Comptroller
  904-488-9805 or 800-848-3792

· **Georgia**
  Office of the Secretary of State
  404-656-2895

· **Hawaii**
  Department of Commerce and Consumer Affairs
  808-586-2730

• **Idaho**
Department of Finance
208-334-3684

• **Illinois**
Office of the Secretary of State
217-782-2256 or 800-628-7937

• **Indiana**
Office of the Secretary of State
317-232-6681 or 800-223-8791

• **Iowa**
Department of Commerce
515-281-4441

• **Kansas**
Securities Commission
913-296-3307

• **Kentucky**
Department of Financial Institutions
477 Versailles Road
Frankfort, KY 40601

• **Louisiana**
Securities Commission
Energy Centre
1100 Poydras Street, Suite 2250
New Orleans, LA 70163

• **Maine**
Department of Professional and Financial Regulation
207-624-8551

• **Maryland**
Attorney General's Office
410-576-6360

• **Massachusetts**
Secretary of the Commonwealth
617-727-3548

• **Michigan**
Department of Commerce
517-334-6200

• **Minnesota**
Department of Commerce
612-296-2283

• **Mississippi**
Office of the Secretary of State
601-359-6364 or 800-804-6364

• **Missouri**
Office of the Secretary of State
573-751-4136 or 800-721-7996

• **Montana**
Office of the State Auditor
406-444-2040 or 800-332-6148

• **Nebraska**
Department of Banking and Finance
402-471-3445

• **Nevada**
Office of the Secretary of State
702-486-2440 or 800-758-6440

• **New Hampshire**
Bureau of Securities Regulation
603-271-1463

• **New Jersey**
Department of Law and Public Safety
201-504-3600

• **New Mexico**

Regulation and Licensing Department

505-827-7140 or 800-704-5533

• **New York**

Department of Law

Bureau of Investor Protection and Securities

120 Broadway, 23rd Floor

New York, NY 10271

212-416-8222

• **North Carolina**

Office of the Secretary of State

919-733-3924

• **North Dakota**

Office of the Securities Commissioner

701-328-2910 or 800-297-5124

• **Ohio**

Division of Securities

614-644-7381

• **Oklahoma**

Department of Securities

405-235-0230

• **Oregon**

Department of Consumer and Business Services

503-378-4387

• **Pennsylvania**

Securities Commission

717-787-8061

• **Rhode Island**

Department of Business Regulation

401-277-3048

- **South Carolina**
  Securities Division
  803-734-1087

- **South Dakota**
  Division of Securities
  605-773-4823

- **Tennessee**
  Department of Commerce and Insurance
  615-741-3187

- **Texas**
  State Securities Board
  512-305-8300

- **Utah**
  Department of Commerce
  801-530-6600 or 800-721-7233

- **Vermont**
  Department of Banking, Insurance, and Securities
  802-828-3420

- **Virginia**
  State Corporation Commission
  804-371-9051

- **Washington**
  Department of Financial Institutions
  360-902-8760

- **West Virginia**
  State Auditor's Office
  304-558-2257

- **Wisconsin**
  Office of the Commissioner of Securities
  608-266-3431 or 800-472-4325

- **Wyoming**
  Secretary of State
  307-777-7370

SOURCE: North American Securities Administrators Association.

OTHER USEFUL NAMES AND NUMBERS

- **Securities and Exchange Commission**
  Office of Investor Education and Assistance
  450 Fifth Street NW
  Washington DC 20549
  202-942-7040

- **American Stock Exchange**
  Inquiries Analysis Department
  86 Trinity Place
  New York, NY 10006-1881
  212-306-1452

- **Municipal Securities Rulemaking Board**
  Legal Department
  1150 18th Street NW, Suite 400
  Washington, DC 20036
  202-223-9347

- **National Association of Securities Dealers Inc.**
  1735 K Street NW
  Washington, DC 20006-1500
  301-590-6500

- **New York Stock Exchange**
  11 Wall Street
  New York, NY 10005
  212-656-3000

RETIREMENT AND ESTATE PLANNING

SOCIAL SECURITY AND MEDICARE

- **Social Security Administration**

800-772-1213

The Social Security Administration is the "horse's mouth" when it comes to information about the Social Security program. To check that your income is being correctly recorded or to get an estimate of the retirement benefit to which you will ultimately be entitled, ask for Form SA-7004-SM, "Request for Earnings and Benefit Estimate Statement."

- **U.S. Health Care Financing Administration**

800-772-1213 (for publications)

800-638-6833 (Medicare Hotline)

This is the agency that administers the Medicare program. It offers two excellent free resources: *The Medicare Handbook* and *Guide to Health Insurance for People with Medicare.* Supplies tend to dwindle late in the year.

ELDER CARE

- **National Academy of Elder Law Attorneys**

Professional association whose members deal with Medicaid, trusts, estates, and other senior issues. Publishes a registry of attorneys ($25) and a free brochure of tips on choosing an elder law attorney.

1604 North Country Club Road

Tucson, AZ 85716

520-881-4005

- **American Association of Homes and Services for the Aging**

Trade association that represents nonprofit nursing homes, continuing-care retirement communities, assisted-living facilities, independent senior housing, and community services for the aging. Offers free list of accredited continuing-care retirement communities; sells other publications.

901 E Street NW, Suite 500
Washington, DC 20004-2037
202-783-2242

• American Health Care Association

A federation of 51 affiliated associations representing nonprofit and for-profit nursing and assisted-living facilities. Publishes free brochures and consumer guides on nursing homes, assisted-living facilities, and other long-term-care topics.

1201 L Street NW
Washington, DC 20005
202-842-4444

• United Seniors Health Cooperative

A nonprofit consumer organization that publishes information on various health care issues affecting seniors, including private long-term-care insurance and continuing-care retirement communities.

1331 H Street NW, Suite 500
Washington, DC 20005-4706
202-393-6222

• National Council on the Aging

Nonprofit educational group publishes a free list of recommended books, videos, and other resources for the elderly and their caregivers.

409 Third Street SW
Washington, DC 20024
202-479-1200

• National Association of Area Agencies on Aging

Membership organization of area agencies on aging offers Eldercare Locator (800-677-1116) that directs callers to state and community-based agencies or other service providers for the elderly or their caregivers.

1112 16th Street NW, Suite 100
Washington, DC 20036-4823

• **Children of Aging Parents**

Nonprofit group provides information and referral services for care-givers of the elderly.

1609 Woodbourne Road, Suite 302A

Levittown, PA 19057-1511

800-227-7294

APPENDIX B

YOUR PERSONAL
FINANCIAL
INVENTORY

$

PULLING IT ALL TOGETHER

A personal financial inventory is simply a list of the people and things that are important in your financial life. It includes your accountant, lawyer, and other financial and legal advisers. It lists your savings, investments, and other assets. It shows the money you owe and to whom you owe it. And it tells where you keep your will and other essential financial documents.

An up-to-date inventory can be an invaluable road map for family members in the event of your disability or death. For couples, an inventory can pull together the basic information about the separate financial matters that each routinely handles. Otherwise, one person's sudden death or disability could leave the other in the dark about the location or even the existence of valuable assets. A personal financial inventory is also a smart way for aging parents to ensure that their wishes are carried out and their interests are protected in the event of disability. It will also make it easier after their death for their grown children to handle the necessary details.

Do not be put off by the length of the following list of items to include. Some may not apply to you. And in each case, you need only jot down a few key facts. Couples should be sure to indicate, though, whether an item applies to one or the other or to both. To make life a bit easier, you may want to photocopy the following pages and fill in the items that apply. Or you can make your own customized list. Doing your inventory on a home computer—just make a list using any word-processing program—will facilitate periodic updating. Store the inventory in your home files and put a photocopy in your safe-deposit box.

FINANCIAL INVENTORY FOR _____

DATE _____

PERSONAL INFORMATION

Family Members	Birth Date	Social Security Number	Location of Birth Certificate

(Continued)

FINANCIAL AND LEGAL ADVISERS

ADVISERS	NAME	ADDRESS	PHONE NUMBER
Accountant			
Attorney			
Employee Benefits or Personnel Manager			
Person Given Power of Attorney			
Financial Planner			

(Continued)

SAVINGS AND INVESTMENTS

	Institution	Account Number	Phone Number	Location of Key Records
Bank Accounts				
Mutual Funds				
Brokerage Accounts (and names of brokers)				
Other Investments (and names of other investment advisers)				

(Continued)

RETIREMENT PLANS

	Company Contact or Financial Institution (phone number)	Type of Plan (pension, profit-sharing, 401(k), 403(b), IRA, Keogh SEP, deferred annuity, deferred compensation)	Location of Key Documents
Current Employer			
Former Employers			
Other			

REAL ESTATE

Properties Owned (addresses)	Outstanding Mortgages and Home-Equity Loans (account number, name of lender, phone number)	Location of Deeds and Other Records

(Continued)

INSURANCE

Type of Coverage	Insurer	Policy Number	Agent (name, address, phone number)	Policy Location
Life				
Home				
Auto				
Umbrella Liability				
Medical				
Disability				
Long-Term Care				

(Continued)

DEBT (MONEY I/WE OWE)

NON-MORTGAGE LOANS OUTSTANDING	LENDER (NAME, ADDRESS, PHONE NUMBER)	ACCOUNT NUMBER	AMOUNT OWED
Credit Cards			
Car Loans			
College Loans			
Investment Debt			
Other			

(Continued)

RECEIVABLES (MONEY OWED TO ME/US)

Names	Address and Phone Number	Amount Due

(Continued)

WILL AND OTHER ESSENTIAL DOCUMENTS

	Where Kept	Attorney Who Prepared (name, address, phone number)
Will (date and name, address, phone number of executor)		
Durable Power of Attorney		
Health Care Power of Attorney		
Living Will		
Trust Documents		

(Continued)

SAFE-DEPOSIT BOX

SAFE-DEPOSIT BOX NUMBER AND LOCATION
(AND WHERE ANY EXTRA KEY IS KEPT)

Contents	Description

(Continued)

ANY OTHER IMPORTANT DOCUMENTS

Other Documents	Where Kept

APPENDIX C
BUYER'S GUIDE TO LIFE INSURANCE

$

HOW MUCH LIFE INSURANCE DO YOU NEED?

The first step in buying life insurance or evaluating your current coverage is to decide how much you should have. The following worksheet can help you make a reasonable estimate of your need.

FOUR EASY STEPS

Begin by identifying sums you would want your beneficiaries to have immediately at your death. For instance, you might want a certain lump sum to provide for your children's college costs. You might want to earmark money to pay off the mortgage on the family home. That is an important goal for many insurance buyers, although it often does not make sense to retire a mortgage early.

Step two is to estimate how much income you want to provide for your survivors' future living expenses. Consider such factors as your family's current annual expenses and the income your survivors would collect from a spouse's wages and Social Security. Multiply the amount of income needed by the number of years for which the need will last. Add that total to the sums your survivors would need immediately to figure your total insurance need.

Got a big number? You do not necessarily need to rush out and buy insurance for that full amount. You may already have some insurance provided by your employer or purchased in past years. Step three is to subtract that existing coverage from your total insurance need.

Finally, you may want to subtract all or part of your savings and investments. Your family will need less insurance if there is a large investment portfolio generating income.

You may be able to run through all of this in five minutes flat. After all, part of the idea was to keep the worksheet simple so you would have one less reason to procrastinate on getting needed coverage in place.

PLAY WITH THE NUMBERS

Still, to do the job right, give it a little more time and thought. If you are married, work through the numbers with your spouse. The amount of life insurance you need depends on some very subjective assumptions about how your loved ones would live after your death.

If a woman with young children currently works part-time, for example, would she continue that work schedule if her husband died tomorrow? Might she return to full-time work to boost her income? Or might she take off a few years to spend more time with her children as they adjust to a tragic change in their lives?

Some people want enough insurance to assure income for the surviving spouse's entire life. Others might buy insurance to provide for a spouse until retirement age, at which time Social Security and other retirement plans would come into play. (Financial planners say some men assume—inappropriately—that their wives would remarry within several years. They buy too little insurance to provide for a nonworking wife because they do not want to "feather the nest" for husband number two.)

You should try out various assumptions to see the often dramatic effect on the bottom-line insurance need. Then pick a number with which you feel comfortable.

A LIFE INSURANCE WORKSHEET

Completing this worksheet, based on one by Boston financial and insurance adviser Virginia Applegarth, can help in estimating how much life insurance you need. Use current dollar amounts, and for guidance on specific items, see the accompanying instructions.

The example is for a 45-year-old man who earns $75,000 a year. His wife, age 42, earns $25,000 working part-time. Their two children are ages 15 and 12.

FUNDS TO COVER SPECIAL NEEDS

	YOU	EXAMPLE
1. Funeral and other final expenses	$ _____	$10,000
2. Estate taxes	+ _____	+ _____
3. Paying off mortgage (optional)	+ _____	+ 250,000
4. Paying off other family debts (optional)	+ _____	+ 10,000
5. College fund	+ _____	+ 120,000
6. Other special needs	+ _____	+ _____
7. Subtotal	= _____	= 390,000

FUNDS FOR SURVIVORS' LIVING EXPENSES

	YOU	EXAMPLE
8. Current household expenses	_____	51,500
9. Target percentage	× _____	× 67%
10. Survivors' annual expenses	= _____	= 34,505
11. Social Security benefits	− _____	− _____
12. Spouse's take-home pay	− _____	− 20,000
13. Annual need	= _____	= 14,505
14. Number of years needed	× _____	× 38
15. Subtotal	= _____	= 551,190

GETTING TO THE BOTTOM LINE

	YOU	EXAMPLE
16. Total amount needed (lines 7+15)	_____	941,190
17. Existing insurance	− _____	− 150,000
18. Income-producing assets (optional)	− _____	− 65,000
19. Additional Insurance Needed	= _____	= **$726,190**

INSTRUCTIONS AND EXPLANATIONS

1. Insurance specialists suggest figures between $5,000 and $20,000.

2. Federal estate taxes are imposed on estates of $600,000 or more, but sums left to a spouse are not subject to the levy. State taxes vary. If applicable, seek legal advice.

5. For the 1995–96 academic year, average costs for college tuition, fees, room, board, and other expenses were $9,285 at public schools and $19,763 at private schools, according to the College Board.

6. This might be a lump sum for one's elderly parents or for a favorite charity.

8. Family's annual employment income, minus taxes and money set aside as savings. (If you completed Worksheet 1.3 in Chapter 1, you can use the result here.) Also subtract mortgage principal-and-interest

(Continued)

payments if part of the insurance proceeds would be used to retire the mortgage. In the example, the couple's $100,000 of wages is reduced by $25,000 of tax, $7,000 in savings, $16,500 of mortgage payments.

9 and 11. You might use a target percentage of 80% to reflect the likelihood that some expenses would drop in your absence. But a higher figure, perhaps 100%, might make sense if the family would have added costs for child care or other services. You can call the Social Security Administration to get a personal estimate of your Social Security benefits. As a shortcut, if there are minor children and the calculation is simplified by not including Social Security benefits as income, use a target of two-thirds (67%).

14. The example assumes the wife will live to age 80 and the husband wants to provide for her until then.

17. The example assumes the husband has group insurance at work of two times his pay.

18. Savings and investments plus any sums that would be paid at death from retirement plans. You might leave your accumulated savings out of the calculation if you want insurance to provide for your spouse until retirement age and the assets to take over after that.

TIPS ON SHOPPING FOR TERM LIFE

Here are five steps that can help you find decent term life insurance with minimal stress.

• **Pick your products.** The number of years for which you need coverage determines the specific types of term insurance for which you should get quotes. To beef up coverage for only a year or two, look at annual-renewable term. If the need is longer—but has a pre-

MATCHING A LIFE INSURANCE POLICY TO YOUR NEEDS

The length of time for which you need life insurance protection is a major consideration in selecting the right type of policy.

Length of Need (in years)	Some Products to Consider
1–2	Term: annual renewable
3–5	Term: 5-year level premium; annual renewable
6–10	Term: 10-year level premium; annual renewable
11–15	Term: 15-year level premium; annual renewable
16–20	Term: 20-year level premium; annual renewable
	Cash Value: various types
More than 20	Term: emphasis on convertibility
	Cash Value: various types

dictable end, such as your child's college graduation—a cheaper choice may be a level-premium term plan whose annual cost will stay the same for 5, 10, 15, or even 20 years. The initial level-premium period should be at least as long as the period for which you need coverage.

• **Care to convert?** If your budget dictates term insurance, but you may need coverage for more than 20 years, select a term policy with the thought of converting to cash-value later on. Most term policies give holders the right to switch to a cash-value plan at the same insurer, regardless of health. But while most policies are convertible at least to age 60, some of the cheaper term policies restrict conversion to the first several years. There may also be restrictions on the types of cash-value plans you can pick.

Consider how attractive a particular insurer's cash-value products might be. Two companies that are known for highly regarded cash-value products and decent, although not bargain-basement, annual term are USAA Life Insurance in San Antonio, Texas, and Northwestern Mutual Life Insurance in Milwaukee, Wisconsin.

• **Gather some quotes.** Just a few phone calls will send a number of term insurance proposals headed your way. Here are four good sources:

> Quotesmith, a Darien, Illinois, firm that maintains an extensive database of term products and acts as an agent (800-556-9393). At no cost, Quotesmith will supply a long list of prices and rank policies by their guaranteed cost over periods of 1, 5, 10, 15, or 20 years.
>
> Northwestern Mutual: Contact a local agent.
>
> USAA, which sells direct by phone and mail (800-531-8000).
>
> Wholesale Insurance Network, which represents several insurers other than USAA that sell direct to consumers (800-808-5810). The absence of agent commissions does not affect term prices much, but it can boost policy performance if you later convert to a cash-value plan.

• **Rather meet face-to-face?** In addition to contacting a Northwestern Mutual representative, who sells primarily for that company, you can look for an agent who sells term from multiple insurers. Keep in mind, though, that agents usually make far more selling a cash-value policy than a term policy. To locate an agent active in term, consider calling Quotesmith (800-556-9393) or Compulife Software, Amherst, New York (800-567-8376), for the names of local agents who use those companies' term-comparison software.

• **Add it all up.** Do not put too much weight on the first-year cost of term coverage. Rather, add up the likely cost of each policy over the number of years for which you expect to keep the plan in force. For a more refined calculation, you can use a calculator or computer to figure the value of those payments in today's dollars.

Also consider what the costs might be if you decide to keep the coverage longer. That is particularly important if you are looking at level-premium plans. Most of those policies let healthy policyholders reenter—that is, qualify for attractively priced new coverage—after the initial level-premium period. Make sure you look at the much higher premiums the insurer expects to charge if you cannot qualify to reenter.

Weigh price against other features, such as conversion rights and insurers' financial strength ratings.

• **Explore other options.** Compare the proposals you have received with any supplemental group coverage offered by an employer. Also consider term plans offered to members of professional associations or other groups. Such plans are occasionally a good deal, although not often. If a group plan has a single rate for everyone, that is probably a good deal for older workers and smokers but a lousy choice for young nonsmokers.

Another possibility for people in New York, Connecticut, and Massachusetts is the reasonably priced Savings Bank Life Insurance available at local savings bank offices.

TIPS ON SHOPPING FOR CASH-VALUE LIFE

To avoid unnecessary aggravation in buying cash-value insurance, there is one thing you must recognize up front: You cannot comparison shop for these protection-plus-savings combinations in the same way you would for other types of insurance. You cannot identify the best of a handful of policies by looking at the annual charge or by adding up some column of numbers on an agent's proposal.

A policy with a low price tag, for instance, may not be a bargain. There is a chance your coverage will expire years earlier than you want. And you will not necessarily get the best value from the policy that is projected to provide the beefiest cash value and death benefit 20 years from now. The computer-generated projections, or illustrations, used to sell insurance are easily manipulated by insurers and agents. They definitely do not tell you which of a handful of cash-value policies will really deliver the best value over the next 20 years or so.

All this means you will not do yourself a favor if you gather cash-value insurance proposals from many different agents. What you probably will do that way is drive yourself crazy.

What should you do? Most cash-value buyers should focus on just one or two carefully selected insurers. Narrowing down the field to a couple of good candidates does not have to be as difficult as you might fear.

CONSIDER BUYING DIRECT

If you are inclined to buy through a local insurance agent, you will find some suggestions on how best to do that in a few more paragraphs. But first, consider an alternative: buying your coverage from one of the handful of insurers that bypass the agent route and sell direct.

The reason to consider such a direct-marketed policy is simple. The insurer does not have to pay a large sum to the agent for bringing in your business—and it can pass that savings along to you. The so-called low-load policies these direct marketers sell allow you to build up a substantial cash value in the very first year. That is money you could walk away with if your circumstances changed and you decided to drop the coverage after a short time. In contrast, an agent-sold policy might have hardly any surrender value after even three or four years. Drop that coverage, and you could well take a financial bath.

Moreover, the advantage of low-load coverage is not just temporary. All other things being equal, a low-load policy will deliver higher cash values and death benefits over time. In essence, the higher early-year cash values give you a head start on long-term performance.

For low-load whole life or universal life, you might start with USAA Life Insurance, San Antonio, Texas (800-531-8000). USAA's products look very good in historical performance data compiled by insurance rating firm A. M. Best. (Unlike USAA's auto and home policies, which are available only to current and former military officers and their families, the life products do not require a military connection.)

Another good source is Ameritas Life Insurance, Lincoln, Nebraska (800-552-3553). Ameritas sells well-regarded cash-value coverage direct, while also selling traditional commissioned products through agents.

Low-load buyers can also contact Wholesale Insurance Network, which represents Ameritas and several other insurers that sell direct (800-808-5810). And discount securities broker Charles Schwab in 1996 began selling low-cost universal policies from highly rated insurer Great-West Capital Life & Annuity Insurance (800-684-3922).

PICK A COMPANY FIRST, AN AGENT SECOND

If you would rather sit down with a local agent, seek out representatives of one or two companies whose policies have performed well in the past. Among whole-life insurers, for instance, Northwestern Mutual Life Insurance of Milwaukee, Wisconsin, is widely praised for solid performance and good customer service. A few other companies that win plaudits from some insurance specialists are Guardian Life Insurance, New York; Massachusetts Mutual Life Insurance, Springfield; and State Farm Life Insurance, part of the big State Farm group in Bloomington, Illinois.

One of the frustrations of buying whole or universal life insurance is a paltry supply of historical performance information. About the only source of such data is insurance-ratings firm A. M. Best, and its performance rankings are limited to a few standard profiles of insurance buyers. For instance, which insurers delivered the top performance to men who were age 35 in 1975 and who purchased $50,000 whole-life policies they surrendered 20 years later, in 1995? The answer according to Best: Guardian, State Farm, and Northwestern Mutual. While a high ranking on such a measure is obviously desirable, there is no assurance that a company treated other buyers as generously—or that it will perform as well in the future.

For variable life, which incorporates mutual fund–like investing, you obviously want to know about the past performance of a policy's investment funds, or subaccounts. You can obtain plenty of information on performance and also policy expenses from Morningstar, a Chicago firm well known for its mutual fund research. A single issue of the *Morningstar Variable Annuity/Life Performance Report* costs $45 (800-876-5005).

As a general rule, shop for insurers first and agents (if you use them) second. You may be aligned with an insurer for life; a particular agent might leave the insurance business a few years from now. But that does not mean you should do business with an agent who seems unknowledgeable or overly pushy or who otherwise gives you a bad feeling. Consider talking to another agent from the same company or from another company that seems to have an equally good track record.

Some agents have taken academic courses and met other requirements to earn the Chartered Life Underwriter (CLU) or Chartered Financial Consultant (ChFC) designations from the American College in Bryn Mawr, Pennsylvania. You can find people in your area by calling the American Society of CLU and ChFC (800-392-6900).

FEE-ONLY ADVISERS

If you want assistance with your insurance purchase but do not want to rely on a commission-paid agent, a third route is to hire a fee-only adviser. That is someone who is paid solely by you and who does not accept sales commissions. A fee-only adviser might charge you an hourly fee for consulting work and then assist you in buying a policy from a low-load company. Or the adviser might say you should not buy some additional coverage an agent is proposing. Seeking a second opinion is particularly wise if you are being urged to buy insurance for a reason other than basic income replacement, such as to pay federal estate taxes at an affluent individual's death.

For the names of fee-only financial planners, you can contact the National Association of Personal Financial Advisors, Buffalo Grove, Illinois (800-366-2732). Not all fee-only planners have cash-value insurance expertise, however.

There are a small number of fee-only advisers who mainly or exclusively handle insurance matters. Three such nationally known advisers are Glenn S. Daily in New York (212-249-9882); Peter C. Katt, Mattawan, Michigan (616-372-3497); and Elliot S. Lipson in Atlanta (770-396-4441).

You could also call Wholesale Insurance Network (800-808-5810). Its parent, a financial subsidiary of General Electric, helps life insurers distribute low-load policies through fee-only advisers and agents. Specify that you want the names of fee-only advisers in your area.

ILLUSTRATIONS: JUST THAT AND NOTHING MORE

When you buy cash-value life insurance, it is easy to be misled by seemingly precise illustrations of how a policy will perform many years in the future. Some questionable companies inflate their illustrations with unrealistic assumptions; some high-quality companies look lackluster on paper because they play it conservative. Probably the only certainty is that a policy will not perform exactly as shown.

Still, you should carefully examine the illustrations you receive to get a sense of how a policy might work. A good agent will carefully lead you through any illustrations he or she provides and answer any questions.

Make sure the illustration includes numbers showing what the death benefit and cash value will be in future years in a worst-case scenario. Those are the "guaranteed" values that assume the lowest possible interest rate and highest possible charges for that policy. There are usually dramatic differences between those guaranteed figures and the projected, or "current," numbers, which show how a policy will perform in the future if and only if a host of assumptions prove true. It is useful also to see numbers for a worse- but not worst-case scenario, such as one in which policy interest rates average one or two percentage points below the current level.

APPENDIX D

GUIDE TO
RETIREMENT
PLANNING

$

HOW MUCH SHOULD YOU
SAVE FOR RETIREMENT?

aving for retirement is tough. Figuring out how much you need to save is not much easier.

Many factors affect the amount of money you will need to retire comfortably, and many of the important numbers are things you can only guess at today. For example, how many years will your retirement last? How much will you collect from Social Security or a company pension? What returns will you earn on your investment portfolio in your working years and in a retirement that may last 20 or more years?

A QUICK CALCULATION

Luckily, you do not need definitive answers to all those questions in order to come up with a reasonable savings target. Determining a number that makes sense does not have to be an ordeal—or take an inordinate amount of time. The retirement-savings worksheet on the following pages, prepared by mutual fund company T. Rowe

Price Associates of Baltimore, is a simple tool that can help many people estimate how much of their salaries they ought to set aside each year for retirement. Spending a few minutes with the worksheet may reassure you about your current savings habits—or give you needed impetus to save more.

The worksheet makes most sense for people in their 20s, 30s, and 40s, who are still many years from retirement. For them, the goal is to come up with a rational savings target and then take the needed action to set money aside and invest it appropriately. If you are closer to retirement, though, use the worksheet only as a starting point in figuring whether you are saving enough to comfortably retire when you would like. You will also need to examine your financial resources and your plans for retirement in greater detail. (In the next section, you can find some tips on taking a closer look as retirement approaches.)

RETIREMENT-SAVINGS WORKSHEET

Completing this worksheet can help you estimate what percentage of your salary you ought to be setting aside for retirement. The answer you get will be based on the assumption you want savings and investments to replace 50% of your preretirement salary during a retirement that will last 30 years; after that, your funds will be entirely depleted.

The worksheet asks for the pretax rate of return you expect on investments *before* you retire and *after* you retire. Although you are asked about a before–retirement return in three separate places (lines 5, 8, and 14), you typically should use the same return in each case.

The example is for a person who wants to retire in 20 years. It assumes a 9% annual investment return during the person's working years and a 7% return in retirement.

	YOU	EXAMPLE
1. Current salary.	$_____	$50,000
2. Factor from Table 1 (on page 566) corresponding to the rate of return you expect on investments *after* you retire and the number of years until you retire. (For example, if you expect to earn 7% a year on your investments after you retire in 20 years, the correct factor is 15.86.)	×_____	× ___15.86
3. Total assets needed in retirement to generate 50% of current salary. (Multiply line 1 by line 2.)	=_____	= ___793,000
4. Current value of taxable investments.	_____	20,000

5. Factor from Table 2 (on page 566) corresponding to the rate of return you expect on taxable investments *before* you retire and the number of years until you retire. (For example, if you expect to earn 9% a year before you retire in 20 years, the correct factor is 3.51.) ×_____ × __3.51__

6. Projected value of taxable investments at retirement, assuming a 28% tax rate. (Multiply line 4 by line 5.) =_____ = __70,200__

7. Current value of tax-deferred investments. _____ __100,000__

8. Factor from Table 3 (on page 567) corresponding to the rate of return you expect to earn on your tax-deferred investments *before* you retire and the number of years until you retire. (For example, if you expect to earn 9% a year before you retire in 20 years, the correct factor is 5.60.) ×_____ × __5.60__

9. Projected value of tax-deferred investments at retirement. (Multiply line 7 by line 8.) =_____ = __560,000__

10. Projected value of your current taxable and tax-deferred investments at retirement. (Add line 6 and line 9.) _____ __630,200__

11. Additional amount needed. (Line 3 minus line 10.) If the result is less than zero, congratulations, you are well on your way. Keep up the good savings. _____ __162,800__

12. Current salary from line 1. ÷_____ ÷ __50,000__

13. Line 11 divided by line 12. =_____ = __3.25__

14. Factor from Table 4 (on page 567) corresponding to the rate of return you expect *before* you retire and the number of years until you retire. (For example, if you expect to earn 9% a year before you retire in 20 years, the correct factor is 1.57.) ×_____ × __1.57__

15. Percentage of salary you should be saving each year to fund your retirement goal. (Line 13 multiplied by line 14.) =_____% = __5.10%__

Source: T. Rowe Price Associates, Inc.

TABLE 1: FACTORS FOR TOTAL CAPITAL NEEDED AT RETIREMENT

Pretax Investment Returns (%)	YEARS UNTIL RETIREMENT					
	10	15	20	25	30	35
4	17.30	20.16	23.48	27.35	31.87	37.12
5	15.06	17.55	20.44	23.81	27.74	32.31
6	13.22	15.40	17.94	20.89	24.34	28.35
7	11.69	13.61	15.86	18.47	21.52	25.07
8	10.41	12.12	14.12	16.45	19.17	22.33
9	9.33	10.87	12.67	14.76	17.19	20.02
10	8.43	9.81	11.43	13.32	15.52	18.07

SOURCE: T. Rowe Price Associates, Inc.

TABLE 2: FACTORS FOR FUTURE VALUE OF TAXABLE SAVINGS

Pretax Investment Returns (%)	YEARS UNTIL RETIREMENT					
	10	15	20	25	30	35
4	1.33	1.53	1.76	2.03	2.34	2.70
5	1.42	1.70	2.03	2.42	2.89	3.45
6	1.53	1.89	2.33	2.88	3.56	4.39
7	1.64	2.09	2.67	3.42	4.37	5.59
8	1.75	2.32	3.07	4.06	5.37	7.10
9	1.87	2.56	3.51	4.81	6.58	9.00
10	2.00	2.84	4.02	5.69	8.05	11.40

SOURCE: T. Rowe Price Associates, Inc.

TABLE 3: FACTORS FOR FUTURE VALUE OF TAX-DEFERRED SAVINGS

PRETAX INVESTMENT RETURNS (%)	YEARS UNTIL RETIREMENT					
	10	15	20	25	30	35
4	1.48	1.80	2.19	2.67	3.24	3.95
5	1.63	2.08	2.65	3.39	4.32	5.52
6	1.79	2.40	3.21	4.29	5.74	7.69
7	1.97	2.76	3.87	5.43	7.61	10.68
8	2.16	3.17	4.66	6.85	10.06	14.79
9	2.37	3.64	5.60	8.62	13.27	20.41
10	2.59	4.18	6.73	10.83	17.45	28.10

SOURCE: T. Rowe Price Associates, Inc.

TABLE 4: FACTORS FOR ADDITIONAL SAVINGS REQUIRED

PRETAX INVESTMENT RETURNS (%)	YEARS UNTIL RETIREMENT					
	10	15	20	25	30	35
4	7.30	4.09	2.57	1.73	1.21	0.87
5	6.99	3.81	2.34	1.53	1.04	0.73
6	6.68	3.56	2.12	1.35	0.89	0.61
7	6.39	3.31	1.92	1.19	0.76	0.50
8	6.11	3.08	1.74	1.04	0.65	0.41
9	5.84	2.86	1.57	0.91	0.55	0.34
10	5.58	2.66	1.41	0.79	0.46	0.27

SOURCE: T. Rowe Price Associates, Inc.

UNDERSTAND THE ASSUMPTIONS

As a rule of thumb, financial advisers figure that most retirees need 70% to 90% of their preretirement incomes to maintain their standard of living. Some will need more. Thankfully, most retirees will not have to generate all that money from their investment portfolios. They will receive part of their retirement income from Social Security and possibly something from a pension plan or part-time work.

For simplicity, the worksheet assumes you want to accumulate enough assets before retirement to rely on your portfolio to replace 50% of your preretirement salary over a 30-year retirement. It looks at money you are accumulating in ordinary taxable accounts as well as in tax-favored vehicles, such as Individual Retirement Accounts and company 401(k) plans.

There are some other key assumptions: Your salary will increase each year between now and retirement by an average inflation rate of 3.1% (the average over the past seven decades). The income you receive in retirement will go up each year by that same percentage. At the end of 30 years, your savings will be exhausted.

While the worksheet requires you to do a little math, you need to plug in only a handful of key numbers. Four are quite simple: your current salary, the number of years until you are likely to retire, your current assets in taxable accounts, and (separately) your current assets in tax-deferred accounts. Only slightly trickier is the task of estimating the annual returns you will earn on your investments—before any tax—both in your working and retirement years.

The example assumes a 9% investment return in your working years and a 7% return in retirement, reflecting the likelihood that your investment strategy will become somewhat more conservative after you retire. Over the past seven decades, an investor would have earned a 9% average return with a portfolio invested 55% in stocks and 45% in bonds. Over the same period, an investor would have earned 7% in a portfolio with a 70% weighting of bonds. You can use the same assumptions, or make your own, taking into account your own investing habits and risk tolerance. But in all cases, use pretax returns.

TAKING A CLOSER LOOK AS RETIREMENT APPROACHES

When you are decades away from retirement, there is no need to spend hours estimating what you might spend on housing, travel, and other activities once you leave the workforce. But the specifics of how much money you will need—and where it will come from—merit a close examination if you are within ten years of leaving work.

With retirement so close, people naturally think much more about how they want to live once they begin that new stage of their lives. The next step is to translate your lifestyle goals into hard numbers for your likely retirement spending and to get a good idea about how much income you can expect from Social Security, pension plans, and other sources. Then weigh your spending estimate against your likely income, either on your own or with the help of a financial adviser, such as a fee-only financial planner.

REEXAMINING EXPENSES

You do not have to start from scratch. Rather, begin by considering what it costs you to live today. Chapter 1 explains how to make a quick calculation of how much you spent on living expenses and everything else last year. Basically, just add up your total income and subtract the amounts you paid in taxes and set aside in savings. The rest you obviously spent somewhere.

Worksheet 1.3 on page 25 can help make those calculations easier. The more detailed Worksheet 1.4 on page 26 will help you piece together your spending by major categories. If you have not completed those two worksheets, take some time to do them now. Then, prepare another version of Worksheet 1.4 to reflect your likely expenses in the early years of retirement, when your spending patterns are likely to be quite different from what they are now.

Once you leave work, you can cross off such things as commuting costs, union dues, and dress-for-success suits. If you are like many people, you will have paid off the mortgage on your home. You might trim your housing costs dramatically by relocating—say, selling a large home that is expensive to keep up and buying a low-maintenance condo.

But other expenses could shoot up. If you plan to travel a lot, for instance, your spending on airline tickets, hotels, and restaurant meals could easily become a significant part of your budget. Also pay close attention to the medical benefits you are likely to receive from your employer or your spouse's employer. Your medical costs could go up sharply, particularly if you are retiring before age 65, when Medicare kicks in. (See Chapter 4 for further information on health coverage on the job and from Uncle Sam, and check the tips for evaluating an early-retirement offer in the next section of this Guide to Retirement Planning.)

INVESTIGATE SOURCES OF INCOME

Next, focus on the other side of the equation: the retirement income you will receive from various sources. Contact the Social Security Administration (800-772-1213) for an estimate of your Social Security benefits. (Ask for Form SSA-7004-SM, Request for Earnings and Benefit Estimate Statement.) Also check with your current employer—and possibly former ones, as well—about benefits under traditional pension plans, which deliver set payments based on a retiree's age, years of service, and pay.

If you are thinking of working part-time in retirement, start exploring your options and consider how much of your income you would actually get to keep after various taxes and costs. If your income exceeds certain levels while you are collecting Social Security, for instance, your benefit will be reduced.

Now consider how much income you might reasonably draw out of your personal investment accounts and tax-sheltered savings plans. Say your money is invested half in stocks and half in bonds. Over the past seven decades, such a portfolio returned an average 8% a year, while inflation averaged about 3%. Those numbers suggest that you could pull out about 5% of your assets each year and still have your nest egg grow apace with inflation.

There is a risk, though, in relying too heavily on the historical averages. If you are caught in a period of lower-than-average investment returns and higher-than-average inflation, pulling out a seemingly safe 5% a year could totally deplete your savings in only 20 years, a recent study warned. To be safe, people who are invested half in stocks and half in bonds should probably withdraw no more than 4% of their assets initially, and then increase that dollar amount in line with inflation. For a different asset mix, you might similarly consider historical returns after inflation and then pick a slightly more conservative figure.

WEIGHING DOLLARS AND TIME

If you have built up considerable wealth, you may be able to afford retirement whenever you feel ready. Most people, though, need to weigh carefully their expected income against expenses. To make the numbers work, you may need to trim back your projected spending or consider ways to increase your income.

Another key variable in the retirement-finance equation is time. Many people in their 50s or early 60s want to retire as early as possible. But that may not be a prudent move financially. Retirement planning involves balancing two distinct segments of your life: the working years, in which you build up assets, and the retirement years, in which you rely heavily on those assets to pay your bills. The point at which you shift from one segment to the other is crucial.

Spending a few more years on the job can boost your retirement finances in several ways: You can qualify for larger pension and Social Security payments. You can sock away thousands more dollars in a 401(k) account or other tax-sheltered plan. You can collect a few more years of investment earnings on your portfolio before you head into retirement. And you reduce the number of years in which you will be drawing money out of your portfolio to pay living expenses.

Try out various "what if" scenarios, maybe with the help of a retirement-planning software package. You might also want to hire a professional adviser, such as a fee-only financial planner, for a few hours' consultation. But first refer to Chapter 1 for information on finding a financial planner you can trust.

EVALUATING AN EARLY-RETIREMENT OFFER

By some estimates, one in four medium-size to large-size companies has offered early-retirement incentives in recent years to employees aged 50 to 64. So the chances are pretty good that some day you, too, will get such an offer. You will have many things to consider.

RETIREMENT PLANS

Early-retirement proposals often include juiced-up pension benefits. This reflects the fact that employees earn the bulk of their pension benefit in the final few years of work. Consider a hypothetical 55-year-old manager earning $70,000 after 25 years at one company. Under a typical pension formula, this person could retire now and collect $13,900 a year. If, however, the manager stayed on the job just two more years, with annual salary increases of 5%, the yearly check under a typical pension could be 40% larger: $19,400. Waiting five years would more than double the manager's annual pension benefit to $30,500.

When companies offer early-retirement incentives, the cost of retiring early is often reduced but not eliminated. For instance, companies typically credit employees with added years of service and age when figuring their sweetened retirement benefits. But companies do not typically factor in possible salary increases the employee might have earned between now and a later retirement date. For that reason, the best candidates for early retirement are those who have substantial savings outside of their company plans.

SEVERANCE PAY

When employers do not offer an enhanced pension, they frequently offer severance pay instead. It is rare to see both. A good severance package would offer you two to three weeks' salary for every year you have been at the company. So someone who has been at the company for 25 years might get an amount equal to one-and-a-half year's salary.

You can receive severance pay as essentially a continuance of your salary. Or you might get it in a lump sum. Your employer may decide for you or may give you a choice of how to receive the payments. Beware, however, that the tax rules can be tricky, so it may pay to ask a tax expert for advice.

HEALTH INSURANCE

One of the biggest anxieties for people contemplating early retirement is whether they will be able to afford the cost of health care until they are eligible for Medicare at age 65. The concern is justified: Without employer-assisted coverage, even a healthy couple in their early 60s might have to spend more than $5,000 a year for health insurance.

Unfortunately, scores of companies have reduced the medical benefits they offer departing workers, in some cases eliminating these benefits entirely. Some companies use health care coverage as bait to persuade employees to accept an early-retirement offer quickly: They might stipulate that only those who retire before a strict deadline—say, within two months of the first announcement of the early-retirement program—will get medical coverage.

Sometimes employers agree to pay some or all of the premiums it costs early retirees for continuing health care coverage under the federal COBRA rules. COBRA requires that departing employees be allowed to purchase coverage under their former employers' health plans for 18 months by paying the premiums the employers pay plus a 2% surcharge. A landmark health-insurance law enacted in 1996 will make individual coverage more available for some people who leave their jobs. (You can find details in Chapter 4.)

If your employer does not offer any health care assistance, it is crucial that you get an accurate estimate of how much it would cost you to provide coverage for yourself and any dependents.

A SOCIAL SECURITY "BRIDGE"

Some employers help bolster your monthly income in early retirement by making so-called bridge payments until you can begin tapping your Social Security benefits, at age 62. These payments are in addition to your pension and may be paid out of the pension plan or may come from a separate company fund. Employers usually pay only about half of what your monthly Social Security checks will be.

Finally, you need to sit down and figure out exactly what your package is worth, what other income sources—such as Social Security—you will have to live on, and whether you can survive to a ripe old age on the total. Do not forget to factor in one of the biggest enemies early retirees have: inflation. The information in the previous section of this Guide to Retirement Planning can help.

You probably cannot afford to retire early if you do not have significant savings outside of your company's retirement accounts.

Large employers often hire consultants to help employees wade through their decisions during an early-retirement offer period. If your employer does not provide such help, it would be wise to hire a financial planner for a session to evaluate whether early retirement is feasible or a pipe dream.

TAPPING RETIREMENT ASSETS

It is not uncommon these days for retirees to have a couple of pensions, a 401(k) plan with their most recent employer, maybe a 401(k) from a previous job that was rolled over into a tax-deferred Individual Retirement Account, a couple of other IRAs, and assorted taxable savings and investment accounts. Then, there is Social Security. What a mess.

Deciding how to handle all that money can seem like an overwhelming burden, since it is probably the most money you have ever handled at once. But with some planning, it is possible to arrange for a healthy stream of income and continued savings for later years.

GET AN OVERVIEW

The first step is to get an overview of all your retirement assets and determine whether some sources should be tapped before others. Coordinating withdrawals from various plans is important in order to stretch your retirement dollars to the utmost while avoiding Internal Revenue Service penalties for a variety of potential missteps. Decisions you make when you first start retirement withdrawals can erase other options in the future.

Six months before you retire, contact the employee-benefit office at your current job and at any previous jobs where you still have retirement money to assess your options. You may also find it worthwhile to hire a professional financial adviser. (Refer to the information on financial planners in Chapter 1 to help you find one you trust.)

It is usually wise to start tapping the annual earnings and the accumulated value of taxable investments and bank accounts before dipping into tax-advantaged retirement plans, such as 401(k)s and IRAs. That is because money in those plans can continue growing tax-deferred for your later retirement years. This assumes, of course, that you have been wise enough—or lucky enough—to accumulate sufficient assets to have a choice of which ones to draw on first.

A WARNING FOR THE WEALTHY

Those with million-dollar nest eggs should keep in mind that starting in the year 2000, annual income from tax-deferred retirement plans above a certain inflation-indexed ceiling ($155,000 in 1996) may be hit with a 15% tax penalty. For married couples, each spouse can receive the ceiling amount before facing a penalty.

DECISIONS, DECISIONS, DECISIONS

Here is what you should be thinking about when deciding which retirement asset to tap first.

SOCIAL SECURITY

Social Security is a flexible option. You can start collecting benefits as early as age 62—or qualify for larger checks by delaying receipt to age 65 or even age 70. In deciding when to begin collecting Social Security, you should consider potential taxation of your benefits and the fact that those under age 70 will lose some of their Social Security if they work and their earned income exceeds certain levels.

It never makes sense to delay collecting Social Security past age 70. Delaying to a later age does not get you a bigger check. All you will do is cheat yourself out of some payments. (For more information on Social Security, refer to Chapter 4.)

TRADITIONAL PENSIONS

Traditional pensions—those that pay a guaranteed benefit based on a retiree's age, years of service, and pay—frequently begin paying out when you retire, whether you want the money then or not. Typically, you receive the money as a monthly check, but more and more pensions are giving people the option of taking the proceeds as a lump sum.

If you choose the lump-sum option, you can roll over the money into an IRA, where it will stay tax-deferred until you withdraw it. If you do not roll over the money, the lump sum will become fully taxable. But until the year 2000, you can reduce the tax bite substantially by employing five-year forward averaging. Essentially, such averaging means the money is taxed as if the recipient had received it over five years, usually keeping the tax rate on the lump sum below a person's normal tax bracket. (People born before 1936 also have the option to use ten-year forward averaging, which is usually even more favorable.) You cannot forward average in the same year you roll over other money—such as that from your 401(k)—into an IRA.

Many retirees still receive their pension-plan benefits as annuities. With an annuity, you get a monthly check for the rest of your life. This is known as a "single-life" annuity. Or you can elect to receive the payments based on your own life expectancy and your spouse's as well, in what is known as a "joint-and-survivor" annuity.

THE RULE FOR MARRIED COUPLES

With joint-and-survivor annuities, you can arrange that after you die, your spouse receives either the full monthly amount you had been getting or some portion of it, commonly 50% or 75%. Generally, the larger the survivor benefit, the lower the retiree's check will be. By law, if a married retiree wants a single-life annuity, rather than one that would continue for a surviving spouse, he or she must obtain written consent from the spouse.

Your choice often is irrevocable, so you should look closely at how much income you need, both immediately and long term, before deciding. Say a 65-year-old man retires after 30 years with a pension of $50,000 a year. He could get $4,167 a month if he took payments over his lifetime alone. If that retiree wanted to ensure that his 60-year-old spouse continued receiving monthly checks after he died, he could choose a "joint-and-50%" annuity. It would pay him only $3,705 a month, but after his death, his wife would receive $1,853 a month for the rest of her life. If the couple figured she would need more than that after he died, he could choose a "joint-and-100%" annuity that would pay both of them $3,335 for life.

A joint-and-survivor annuity would not make sense if, for example, a retiree's spouse is terminally ill. If the spouse does not survive the retiree, no survivor benefit would be paid. And, in most cases, you cannot go back and select the higher, single-life payments. Couples might also pick the larger payouts from a single-life annuity if both spouses expect to receive a full pension that will adequately provide for each of them for life.

A WORD OF CAUTION

Insurance agents often try to persuade retirees to forsake the joint-and-survivor option and maximize their retirement checks by selecting single-life annuities. To "protect" the spouse, they suggest a life insurance policy. This strategy is usually called "pension max." But most retirees would be much better off with the joint annuity, especially if it is indexed for inflation (as military and some government pensions are). What is more, the cost of life insurance is so high at retirement age that a couple might not be able to afford enough coverage really to provide income protection for the spouse.

401(K) AND PROFIT-SHARING PLANS

People who have worked for employers with 401(k) retirement-savings plans and profit-sharing retirement plans usually have similar options for how to withdraw their money at retirement. Most employees choose to roll over a lump sum into an IRA, where the money can continue to grow tax-deferred. Those who do not want to withdraw the proceeds in a lump sum can elect to take the money over 5, 10, or even 15 years.

If you choose to have the money paid to you in installments, each installment will be taxable as you receive it. But if you do not need an installment to live on, you may want to roll it over into an IRA and continue tax deferral on the distribution. Caution: None of the payouts will qualify for a rollover if you stretch them out over ten or more years.

You could also use the lump-sum proceeds of your 401(k) to buy an annuity from a life insurance company. You could choose survivor benefits or a guaranteed number of payments. Check with several insurers before buying, because the payments they offer vary widely.

403(B) PLANS

The money in these plans, which are commonly available to teachers and employees of nonprofit organizations, can be rolled over into an IRA when you leave your employer. Or it could be withdrawn— all at once in a lump sum, or in installments over a number of years that you select, generally 5, 10, or 15 years. Withdrawals typically must start by the time you turn 70½.

If, as is often the case, the money in your 403(b) has been invested in a variable annuity, you may want to shift it into mutual funds when you transfer your nest egg to an IRA. You may face surrender charges on the annuity. But you should still consider this move because it is redundant to have tax-favored annuities in your tax-sheltered IRA. Moreover, because variable annuities have extra costs for the privilege of their tax advantages, you can likely boost your return by switching to ordinary mutual funds.

457 PLANS

Government employees covered by these plans do not have the flexibility to roll over the proceeds into an IRA when they retire. Once employment terminates, these retirees can take 457 proceeds in an annuity, with options that are similar to traditional pension annuity options. Or, they can take the money in a lump sum, although they will owe immediate tax on the payout unless they roll it into a new employer's 457 plan.

DEFERRED-COMPENSATION PLANS

Deferred-compensation plans for top executives are usually considered "nonqualified" plans, which means they do not qualify for special tax treatment. Typically, proceeds must be collected by employees when they retire or even earlier. The money is usually immediately taxable and is not eligible to be rolled into an IRA.

INDIVIDUAL RETIREMENT ACCOUNTS

Chances are, most corporate workers will wind up with one or more Individual Retirement Accounts. Frequently, retiring workers set up IRAs to preserve for as long as possible the tax deferral on funds they roll over from 401(k)s, profit-sharing plans, or pensions. Many people also fund IRAs over the years, stashing as much as $2,000 a year into accounts with banks, brokerage firms, or mutual fund companies. Knowing which IRAs to tap first, how much money to take out, and how it will be taxed requires considerable time and attention.

The tax rules and options vary depending on whether a retiree is tapping the account before turning age 59½, after age 70½, or sometime in between. Those in the middle typically have the most freedom. They can withdraw any amount they choose or leave the money to continue growing tax-deferred.

For withdrawals, the basic rule is that money taken out of an IRA is generally subject to federal tax at ordinary income tax rates of up to 39.6%, and probably state and local income taxes, as well. The big exception is money contributed to an IRA with after-tax dollars: If a retiree contributed money that had already been taxed—through what is known as a "nondeductible contribution"—some portion of any withdrawals will be nontaxable. If you have made both deductible and nondeductible contributions, withdrawals can be especially complicated.

Because the Internal Revenue Service requires a retiree with several IRAs to treat them collectively as one big purse, it is not possible to minimize the tax bite by withdrawing only from an account that has a high proportion of already taxed money. Instead, any time you make a withdrawal from any IRA, you have to prorate the portion of the withdrawal that is not taxable. You do this by using a ratio that divides your total nondeductible contributions by the total balance in all your accounts combined.

Assume, for instance, that a retiree wanted to withdraw $1,000 from one of two IRAs: IRA "A," composed of $50,000 of pretax contributions and $10,000 of earnings; or IRA "B," made up of $10,000 of nondeductible contributions and $5,000 of earnings. Whichever account the retiree chooses to tap for the $1,000, the portion that is nontaxable is figured by dividing the $10,000 in nondeductible contributions by the $75,000 total balance in both IRAs. So of that $1,000 withdrawal, $133 would be nontaxable and $867 taxable. Got it? That is why you have been hanging on to all of those IRA-contribution records all these years.

YOUNGER AND OLDER

People who are older or younger than the gang in the middle have other hoops to jump through in order to take from their IRAs in peace. Generally, withdrawals by people under the age of 59½ get zapped by a 10% IRS penalty for early distributions. At the other end of the IRA-age spectrum, you must withdraw a minimum percentage of all of your IRAs by April 1 of the year after you turn 70½ and each year thereafter. Fail to do that, and you face a 50% penalty tax on the amount required but not distributed.

Still, there are some ways to give yourself a bit more freedom. Consider a 57-year-old who took early retirement and transferred the $147,400 balance in his 401(k) into a tax-deferred IRA. He could begin tapping that IRA immediately, without having to pay the 10% penalty that usually applies to withdrawals by people under age 59½. How? He could take payouts calculated as if he were going to receive "substantially equal" sums each year over a combination of his and his wife's lifetimes. And the payments would not actually have to last the two lifetimes. Such periodic payments to early retirees have to continue only for five years, or until the retiree turns 59½, whichever is longer. After five years, then, the retiree in this example could stop the withdrawals, alter them, or continue them as needed.

Moreover, by fiddling with some assumptions, he could receive more or less income and still avoid the 10% penalty. In setting up the substantially equal payments, IRS rules allow you to project how much the IRA would be worth in future years, factoring in any reasonable assumption for the rate of return on your account. This retiree's financial adviser might argue that it would be reasonable to use assumptions from 5% to 9%. (The IRS does not spell out the specifics.) Using a 7% assumption, the monthly withdrawal would be $900 a month; at 5%, the monthly payment would be $800 a month; at 9%, $1,081 a month.

ROOM TO MANEUVER

Retirees over age 70½ who want to minimize IRA withdrawals also have some maneuvering room. To figure their minimum distributions, such retirees must essentially divide all their IRA balances by the number of years that IRS tables tell them they are likely to live. But to reduce the resulting payout, retirees can spread the payments over not just their own life span, but also a beneficiary's. (Even if the two people are the same age, a joint-life expectancy will work out actuarially longer than a single one.)

They can also reduce the monthly payout by using the so-called recalculation method of withdrawals. Recalculation lets retirees benefit from the actuarial oddity that dictates that the longer you live, the longer your life expectancy gets. Advisers caution couples who use recalculation that when one of them dies, the size of the payments will have to be increased beginning the following year, so that the remainder in the account will be paid out over the survivor's lifetime.

IRS Publication 590, *Individual Retirement Arrangements (IRAs)*, walks you through your IRA withdrawal options.

INDEX